Nonlinear Pricing

Nonlinear Pricing

Robert Wilson

Published in association with the
Electric Power Research Institute

New York   Oxford
OXFORD UNIVERSITY PRESS

Oxford University Press

Oxford   New York
Athens   Auckland   Bangkok   Bogota   Bombay
Buenos Aires   Calcutta   Cape Town   Dar es Salaam
Delhi   Florence   Hong Kong   Istanbul   Karachi
Kuala Lumpur   Madras   Madrid   Melbourne
Mexico City   Nairobi   Paris   Singapore
Taipei   Tokyo   Toronto

and associated companies in
Berlin   Ibadan

Library of Congress Cataloging-in-Publication Data
Wilson, Robert B.
Nonlinear Pricing / by Robert B. Wilson.
p.   cm.   "Published in association with the Electric Power Research Institute."
"Research project 2982-03"—EPRI   TR-101861
Includes bibliographical references and index.
ISBN 0-19-506885-8
ISBN 0-19-511582-1 (pbk.)
1. Electric utilities—Rates—Mathematical models.
I. Electric Power Research Institute.
II. Title.
HD9685.A2W55   1992
333.79'3231'015118—dc20   91-32603

2 4 6 8 9 7 5 3 1

Printed in the United States of America
on acid-free paper

PREFACE

This monograph stems from work with Shmuel Oren and Stephen Smith, and later Hung-po Chao. In 1979, at the Xerox Palo Alto Research Center, we began studies of the pricing of differentiated products, and in 1984, at the Electric Power Research Institute, we continued this work with studies of the pricing of capacity and usage. With Hung-po Chao at EPRI, our project continued with studies of priority service. I am grateful to these superb colleagues. Doing research with them has been interesting and challenging, and happily, also fun. Many of the ideas herein came from them, and therefore they are co-authors in spirit at least.

At EPRI my mentor on nonlinear pricing has been Philip Hanser, to whom I am indebted for continual encouragement and help, as well as for the resources to bring the project to fruition. My experience at EPRI has been informative and stimulating in other respects as well, especially in the ways it has enabled me to learn about the practical problems of pricing and service design in the electric power industry. The value of theory is its usefulness in addressing practical problems, and my contacts at EPRI have proved again that for the theorist, the problems encountered by practitioners provide a wealth of topics.

The National Science Foundation provided grants for research during summer months, for which I am grateful. My home base is the Stanford Business School, to which I am always most indebted—for wonderful colleagues and continuing institutional support. Portions of this material, taught in a course on Pricing for seven years, has been derived from ideas in my students' term papers, many of which were very insightful. I am especially grateful to Timothy McGuire for the material on which §2.1 is based. Computer programs for numerical examples were developed using versions of APL*PLUS and APL II contributed by the STSC, Inc. (now called Manugistics, Inc.).

The first draft of this monograph appeared originally as a technical report in September 1989. Several colleagues, some anonymously as referees, provided comments on the manuscript. Scott Davis of Washington University gave me line-by-line commentary; Karen Clay of Stanford and Bridger Mitchell of RAND helped me with specific aspects of telecommunications pricing. I am especially grateful to David Sibley of Bell Communications Research and the University of Texas for insightful suggestions; and to Mark Armstrong and James Mirrlees of

Oxford for finding errors in the examples in a previous version of Chapter 13. I am sure that errors remain; these are solely my responsibility. I will appreciate reports from readers who discover errors.

Those who study the complexities of multiproduct pricing in Part IV will see why publication was delayed as I endeavored to get it right—and still may have failed. In the future I will remember the maxim "don't write what you don't know." The experience deepens my appreciation for the marvelous accomplishment by James Mirrlees, who derived the basic conditions more than twenty years ago in the first work on this subject.

My wife Barbara and my daughters Jennifer and Holly encouraged me through long travails. They and I are glad it is finished.

Stanford, California   R.B.W.
October, 1992

CONTENTS

III: MULTIDIMENSIONAL TARIFFS

IV: MULTIPRODUCT TARIFFS

Nonlinear Pricing

1

INTRODUCTION

In the major regulated industries, each posted rate schedule or contract specifies a *tariff* that indicates the total charge payable by the customer for services provided. The prices (per unit) embodied in tariffs often depend on some aspect of the quantity of services or the rate at which they are purchased. The same feature is seen in many unregulated industries, usually in the form of quantity discounts, rebates, or credits toward subsequent purchases.

The way in which the quantity purchased affects the total charge takes many different forms. For example:

- Railroad tariffs specify charges based on the weight, volume, and distance of each shipment. For instance, discounts on the charge per mile per hundred-weight are offered for full-car shipments and for long-distance shipments. In other transport industries such as trucking, airlines, and parcel delivery the rates depend also on the speed of delivery or the time of the day, week, or season.
- Electricity tariffs specify energy charges based on the total kilo-Watt hours used in the billing period, as well as demand charges based on the peak power load during the year. Lower rates apply to successive blocks of kilo-Watt hours and in some cases the demand charges are also divided into blocks. Energy rates for most industrial customers are further differentiated by the time of use, as between peak and offpeak periods.
- Telephone companies offer a variety of tariffs for measured toll service and WATS lines. Each tariff provides the least-cost service for a particular range of traffic volumes. Rates are also differentiated by distance and time of use.
- Airline fares allow "frequent flier" credits toward free tickets based on accumulated mileage. The retail value of a free ticket increases sharply with the number of miles used to acquire it. Further discounts are offered for advance purchase, noncancellation, round trip, weekend stays, and duration.
- Rental rates for durable equipment and space, such as vehicles and parking lots, are lower if the duration is longer. Rates for rental cars are also differentiated by the size of the vehicle and the time of use.

● Newspaper and magazine advertising rates are based on the size and placement of the insertion, the total number of lines of advertising space purchased by the customer during the year, and in some cases the annual dollar billings.

In each of these examples, the significant feature is that the average price paid per unit delivered depends on a measure of the total size of a customer's purchase. This measure can apply to a single delivery, the total of deliveries within a billing period, accumulated deliveries over an indefinite period, or some combination. It can also depend on a variety of indirect measures of size such as the dollar value of purchases or the maximum single delivery.

Quantity discounts can be offered via smaller prices for marginal units, or via a smaller price for all units if the purchase size is sufficiently large. The size dependence can be explicit in a single tariff, or implicit in a menu of tariffs among which the customer can choose depending on the anticipated volume of purchases.

Several different terms are used to connote this practice. The generic term *nonlinear pricing* refers to any case in which the tariff is not strictly proportional to the quantity purchased. Tariffs in which the marginal prices of successive units decline in steps are called *block-declining* or *tapered* tariffs in several industries (in some instances the marginal prices increase over some range, as in the case of "lifeline" rates). The simplest example of a nonlinear tariff is a *two-part tariff*, in which the customer pays an initial fixed fee for the first unit (often justified as a subscription, access, or installation charge), plus a smaller constant price for each unit after the first. These and several other standard tariffs are sketched in Figure 1.1. A tariff that charges only a fixed fee is also called a flat-rate tariff. The tariffs in the figure pertain to a single product but in some cases a firm offers a multiproduct tariff that specifies a total charge based on the purchased quantities of two or more products. In the airline industry, for instance, frequent-flier plans offer extra mileage credit on specified routes or at specified times. In the power industry, the total charge for peak and offpeak power often depends on both the maximum power demanded and the average load factor as well as the total energy purchased.

To illustrate, Table 1.1 shows three tariffs for "wide area telecommunications service" (WATS) offered by AT&T, as reported by Mitchell and Vogelsang (1991). Each of the three tariffs specifies a monthly fixed fee plus rates for each call that depend on the distance; the table shows only the rate charged for each full minute for a distance of 1000 miles. There are two key features. First, each tariff has a block-declining structure indicated by the discounts allowed for the portions of monthly dollar billings above two threshold levels. Second, in choosing to which among the options in this menu of tariffs to subscribe, a customer perceives a more elaborate block-declining tariff obtained as the minimum among these tariffs for each combination of the number, aggregate minutes, and monthly dollar volume of calls.

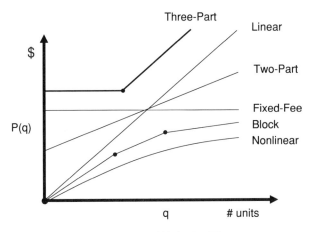

Fig. 1.1 Several kinds of tariffs.

The term nonlinear pricing is usually restricted to tariffs that are offered on the same terms to all customers in a large class. Thus, each customer pays the same marginal prices for successive units. Although the price for, say, the hundredth unit is th ۽ same for all customers, this price may differ from the prices for the tenth and the ι. ousandth units.

1.1 Motivations for nonlinear pricing

A nonlinear tariff is much like a product line: offered a menu of quantities and corresponding charges, each customer chooses a preferred quantity and pays the associated charge. Each customer's decision is essentially to select how many incremental units to buy or, when use is continual, the average rate of usage. Customers typically differ in their valuations of increments, and therefore different customers choose to buy different total quantities depending on the schedule of marginal prices charged for successive increments.

Table 1.1 AT&T WATS Tariffs Volume Discounts, Daytime Rates

Tariff	PRO WATS	High-Volume WATS	Megacom WATS
Requirement		Dedicated Line	T1 Trunk Line
Rate	$0.254/min.	$0.239/min.	$0.173/min.
Fixed Fee	$5/mo.	$63/mo.	$50/mo.
Discounts			
> $200/mo.:	8%	10%	> $7,500/mo.: 5%
> $2000/mo.:	21%	15%	> $30,000/mo.: 10%

Source: Mitchell and Vogelsang (1991), Tables 9.2 and 9.3. The "Rate" is the charge per minute at 1000 miles. More distant calls have higher rates. Each tariff imposes a minimum charge for the first 30 seconds (18 for Megacom WATS) with subsequent duration billed in increments of 6 seconds.

Similar interpretations apply to product lines of related products that differ according to one or more quality attributes. In this case an increment represents an improvement along a dimension of quality. Customers' differing valuations of quality increments lead therefore to different selections of purchases from the product line, depending on the prices the tariff assigns to successive increments. A product line of machines, for instance, is typically differentiated by attributes such as size or production rate, operating cost or personnel requirements, durability or maintenance requirements, precision or fidelity, et cetera. Many examples from service industries pertain to conditions of delivery: familiar attributes include distance, time-of-day, speed, reliability or availability, and perquisites such as comfort or convenience. For instance, for successively higher prices a customer can have a letter or parcel delivered by several classes of regular mail and two classes of express mail, the speediest of which provides guaranteed overnight delivery with computerized tracking of each parcel individually.

In all these examples the net effect of nonlinear pricing is to offer a menu of options from which customers can choose differently depending on their preferences. Agricultural, commercial, and industrial customers account for the majority of sales in the main industries that use nonlinear pricing. Most of these customers are systematic and careful to obtain the maximum net value from service; for example, it is increasingly common to employ specialized managers aided by computerized control systems for services such as communications, power, and transportation. Moreover, these customers usually have stable preferences determined by production technologies, facility configurations, and sales and distribution systems. Among residential customers, an important segment is equally careful to obtain maximum advantage from the menu of options offered; for instance, Mitchell and Vogelsang (1991) report that AT&T's "Reach Out America" options were selected by 68% of the Plan A customers in the first year and 85% in the third year.

The menu comprises the various quantities and/or qualities, to each of which the tariff assigns a charge. Whenever customers are diverse, a menu with several options is advantageous: it promotes greater allocative efficiency by enabling customers to adapt their purchases to their preferences. In the current jargon, an "unbundled" array of options allows each customer to "self-select" the best purchase. Thus the primary motive for nonlinear pricing is heterogeneity among the population of customers.

Differentiating increments by pricing them differently is advantageous whenever their price elasticities of demand differ and prices exceed marginal cost. This is explained by a standard proposition in economic theory: setting the percentage profit margin on each increment in inverse proportion to the price elasticity of its demand maximizes the aggregate dollar value of customers' benefits for any fixed revenue obtained by the firm. Heterogeneity among customers virtually assures that different increments have different price elasticities, so the secondary motive for differentiated pricing stems ultimately from some exercise of monopoly power so that prices exceed marginal cost.

Among utilities, the primary motive for pricing above marginal cost is to obtain sufficient revenue to cover periodic operating costs and to repay the cost of capital used to install capacity such as durable equipment. This motive persists in competitive industries such as (deregulated) telecommunications, gas transmission, and rail, trucking, and air transportation whenever there are economies of scale or the cost of durable capacity is recovered imperfectly by usage charges because demand is variable or stochastic. In oligopolistic industries where entry is limited by the magnitude of fixed costs in relation to profits, nonlinear pricing plays a similar role in maintaining profits sufficient to retain the maximum number of viable competing firms: this works to the ultimate advantage of customers even though it represents an exercise of monopoly power.

1.2 Practical uses for nonlinear pricing

Nonlinear pricing has several roles in practice. In some cases nonlinear pricing promotes more efficient utilization of resources. In others it is used to meet utilities' revenue requirements. And, it can also be used by firms with monopoly power to increase their profits. For example:

- Nonlinear pricing is often necessary for efficiency. This is the case when the firm's cost per unit of filling or shipping an order varies with the size of the order. Similarly, if the firm has higher inventory costs than customers do then inducing customers to make periodic large purchases promotes efficiency. In the case of electric utilities, purchasers of large quantities of power typically have higher load factors, so quantity discounts recognize lower costs of idle capacity for these customers. Quantity discounts of this sort are motivated by cost considerations.
- Nonlinear pricing can be used by a regulated monopoly to recover administrative and capital costs. In important contexts, using its monopoly power to obtain operating profits sufficient to meet its revenue requirement is the most efficient means available to a utility or other public enterprise. Efficiency in these contexts refers to avoiding allocative distortions caused by deviations from prices set equal to marginal costs. In particular, if the regulatory objective is to maximize an aggregate of customers' net benefits from the firm's operations, then a nonlinear tariff minimizes allocative distortions. In this context, nonlinear pricing is a form of "Ramsey pricing" in which different units of the same commodity are interpreted as different products, as will be explained in §5. In particular, when marginal units of larger orders have greater price elasticities of demand, it is efficient to offer quantity discounts to minimize distortions from allocative efficiency. The distributional effects are not always

favorable because customers making small purchases may pay higher prices; however, nonlinear pricing can be modified to avoid these adverse distributional effects. In sum, nonlinear pricing can be motivated by efficient use of monopoly power to meet a revenue requirement, though perhaps modified to address distributional objectives.

- Nonlinear pricing is often a useful strategy in competitive markets. For example, newspapers and magazines offer quantity discounts to attract large advertisers who have substitutes available in other media such as television. Telephone companies offer quantity discounts for long-distance calls to retain large customers who otherwise might elect to bypass local exchanges. Frequent-flier plans offered by airlines were initially competitive tactics designed to appeal to business travelers. Quantity discounts of this sort are motivated primarily by competitive pressures in submarkets segmented by customers' volume of purchases.

- Nonlinear pricing can also be used as a means of price discrimination that enables a firm with monopoly power to increase its profits. In this case, it is used mainly as a means of market segmentation in which customers are classified into volume bands. The extent to which it increases profits depends on the degree to which higher-volume customers have higher demand elasticities for incremental units. An example is a product line of machines, such as copiers or printers, that appeal to different volume bands because more expensive machines have higher rates of output and lower marginal costs. Nonlinear pricing of this sort is motivated primarily by market segmentation, but the prices are determined less by competitive pressures to survive than by profit opportunities that arise from differing elasticities of demand in various submarkets.

This list indicates that nonlinear pricing is potentially a vast subject. It is relevant to private firms as well as to public utilities, and its application can stem from considerations of cost, efficiency, or competitive pressures. In §15 we describe a host of other applications that are not recounted here, such as the design of contracts, tax schedules, and regulatory policies. In such contexts, a participant's selection from a menu of options reflects incentives depending on personal preferences and other private information. In these cases, the role of differentiated pricing of products and services to take account of diversity among customers is supplanted by the design of incentives to take account of participants' diversity due to their private information. In these as in all other cases, the primary advantage of differentiation stems from heterogeneity in the population.

The role of price discrimination

The connection between nonlinear pricing and price discrimination, as in the last item above, calls into question its purported advantages. In general, price discrimination can have adverse distributional effects and it can promote inefficient uses of monopoly power. Distributional effects are severe when different terms are offered to different customers based on observable distinctions. Allocative inefficiencies arise when prices do not minimize distortions required to meet the firm's revenue requirement. And, productive inefficiencies arise when quantities and qualities are not produced at least cost, or for a given cost greater quantities or qualities could be produced.

Historically, the principle problem is quality degradation undertaken solely to enhance product differentiation. This problem was noted by Dupuit (1844) in the earliest treatise on pricing by public utilities and it persists currently. For instance, nonrefundable advance-purchase airline fares restrict a customer's option to change an itinerary even when it would be costless for the firm—indeed, even as the plane departs with empty seats—and weekend-stay requirements that are costly for customers are enforced only because they are especially onerous for business travelers. Similarly, airlines offer different fares to different customers for identical services.[1]

A standard example of quality degradation is temporal price discrimination in which a seller, such as a publisher, holds stock in inventory and offers a declining sequence of prices designed to obtain earlier sales at higher prices to more impatient customers. Even if storage costs are nil this is inefficient because it diminishes customers' net benefits by the imputed costs of delay. Another standard example is a manufacturer who uses an inefficient product design based on limited durability or planned obsolesence. Various propositions in economic theory attempt to show that inefficient quality degradation and accompanying price discrimination will not occur or will not succeed, but the evident prevalence of such practices shows that the assumptions used are much too restrictive to be entirely realistic.[2]

Unfortunately, the adverse welfare effects of inefficient price discrimination are bypassed entirely in this book. Careful analysis of the merits of allowing inefficient uses of monopoly power to meet a firm's revenue requirement is a topic too complex and lengthy to be included here. Consequently, we consider only *efficient* uses of monopoly power in the form of Ramsey pricing. In particular, (a) we consider only cases in which the tariff offers the same terms to all customers; (b) the quality specifications of the firm's products or services are supposed to be fixed;

1. For a recent flight, the lowest fare available as a private individual was $328; if my host university made the reservation it was $288; and if my own university travel office made the reservation it was $200. For a second trip two months later in the midst of a price war, the fare was $66.

2. These propositions are referred to collectively as Swan's theorem and the Coase conjecture; cf. Swan (1972), Coase (1972), Bulow (1982), and Gul, Sonnenschein, and Wilson (1986). However, Bulow (1986) shows that Swan's theorem is false when a formulation analogous to Gul, Sonnenschein, and Wilson is used; in particular, quality degradation in the form of inefficient product durability is an optimal strategy for a monopolist manufacturer. Also, Gul (1987) shows that the Coase conjecture is false for firms in an oligopoly.

and (c) the firm's costs and production technology are fixed—and presumably operated efficiently.

1.3 Feasibility of nonlinear pricing

The implementation of nonlinear pricing requires that four preconditions are satisfied. This section elaborates these basic requirements and indicates the variety of practical situations in which nonlinear pricing is feasible.

The four preconditions can be summarized briefly as follows:[3]

- The seller has monopoly power.
- Resale markets are limited or absent.
- The seller can monitor customers' purchases.
- The seller has disaggregated demand data.

Each is discussed in turn.

Monopoly power

In severely competitive markets, prices are driven down close to the direct costs of supply. This excludes nonlinear pricing except for quantity discounts based on actual cost savings in production or delivery of large orders. Few markets are perfectly competitive, however. In *monopolistically competitive* markets, firms' products are differentiated sufficiently that each enjoys some power to set its prices above direct costs. In *oligopolistically competitive* markets, firms' products are close or perfect substitutes but the number of firms is sufficiently small to enable positive profits. These profits are limited to normal returns on irreversible investments in capacity if there is a persistent threat of entry. Nevertheless, nonlinear pricing is usually feasible in markets that are imperfectly competitive. We shall see in §12, however, that the degree of competition limits the extent of nonlinear pricing, and moreover, nonlinearities in the tariff are erased if there are many firms. Monopoly power may differ substantially among submarkets. Airlines, for instance, encounter competitive pressures that vary substantially among different routes.

A firm in a regulated industry is usually assured a monopoly regarding distribution (not necessarily production or generation) of services in its allotted district. The largest industrial customers are an exception in partially deregulated industries: in Georgia and England, for instance, electric utilities compete for customers

3. To this list, for firms in unregulated industries in the United States, might be added legal feasibility. Although the Robinson-Patman Act has not been enforced in recent years, it prohibits quantity discounts that injure competition by giving large commercial customers a competitive advantage over smaller ones competing in the same retail market for commodity products (not services). For discussions of the Robinson-Patman Act in this connection see §5.2, Scherer (1980, §21) and Varian (1989, §3.7).

with loads exceeding 900 kilo-Watts; and in the telephone industry in the United States there is strong competition for the largest commercial customers, partly from resellers who purchase bulk service from AT&T. The monopoly distribution franchise includes a service obligation along with control of investments, prices, and net revenues by the regulatory agency. The extent that monopoly power is exercised in rate design depends critically on the magnitude of the revenue requirement. A water company, for instance, may find no advantage in nonlinear pricing while an electric utility or a telephone company with substantially larger capital requirements may find it necessary.

Resale markets

A necessary condition for nonlinear pricing is that resale markets are absent, limited, or controlled by the original supplier. If resale is freely available to customers, then nonlinear pricing enables some customers to profit from arbitrage. For example, if large orders are offered at a lower average price per unit then small ones, then a customer purchasing a large order can profit from breaking a large order into several smaller lots and selling them in the resale market. Allowance of resale by bulk purchasers has been a major feature of deregulation of long-distance telephone transmission. Alternatively, if the price schedule is increasing then a customer might benefit from opening multiple accounts and purchasing a small amount from each one. The net result for the original supplier is that all sales are at the lowest average price per unit it offers.

Excluding or limiting resale is therefore essential if nonlinear pricing is to be effective. Tariffs for electric power and communications, for instance, include explicit provisions prohibiting resale whenever regulatory policies allow. If resale is feasible but expensive, nonlinearities in the tariff are restricted to levels that cannot be arbitraged by customers. If bulk resale is excluded, then to exclude multiple accounts it suffices to ensure that the price schedule is not increasing; i.e., the tariff is concave. The least restrictive requirement is that the tariff is subadditive: if the tariff charges $P(q)$ for a purchase of size q then subadditivity requires that $P(q_1 + q_2) \leq P(q_1) + P(q_2)$, which ensures that purchasing from two accounts is not cheaper than purchasing from a single account.

Resale exclusion is essentially an elaboration of the requirement of monopoly power, because it prevents competition from customers acting as secondary suppliers in resale markets. Competition from resale markets is pervasive for many durable goods even if the manufacturer of original equipment has a monopoly. Resale and rental markets for items of capital equipment offer customers a choice between purchasing new equipment, or buying or renting older equipment. Thus, each sale by the original manufacturer creates a potential competitor. Firms such as IBM and Xerox leased rather than sold their machines for this reason, until the practice was interpreted as anticompetitive under the U.S. antitrust laws. Other items are less susceptible to arbitrage: a large diamond or a large computer cannot be profitably divided into smaller ones.

On the other hand, resale and rental markets are precluded in many industries. Resale is impossible or expensive in many service industries, especially if it involves direct labor services. In capital-intensive industries, the technology may exclude resale if the seller controls essential equipment, such as switching and trunk lines in the case of communications and power, and aircraft in the case of airlines. In other industries it is excluded by regulatory provisions or business practices. For instance, resale of telephone service was prohibited until several years before deregulation of the industry, when the FCC required AT&T to allow MCI to resell long distance transmission.[4] In the electric power industry, municipal utilities have long had the privilege of reselling power to local customers, but with this exception distribution has usually been a regulated monopoly, except as noted previously for the largest industrial customers in a few partially deregulated jurisdictions. The role of restrictive business practices is especially prominent in the airline industry, partly as a residual from many years of regulation; in particular, nontransferable tickets and reservations are issued to customers by name for specific flights. Similar practices are used in various markets for leased equipment, such as rental vehicles.

Monitoring purchases

An essential ingredient of any nonlinear tariff is a system to monitor customers' purchases. Monitoring includes identifying customers, measuring their purchases, and billing. The system depends on several parameters of the tariff, such as:

● What is a customer? Customers are usually identified with transactions or billing accounts when uniform pricing is used, but when a nonlinear tariff is used the definition of a customer can have a major effect on tariff design. Extreme examples are the frequent-flier plans offered by airlines. These plans interpret the traveler as the customer, even if tickets are billed to the traveler's employer, and rebated tickets are usually restricted to the traveler's family. This definition of customers hinders employers from garnering the rebates allowed their employees. Somewhat similar is the practice among publishers of interpreting advertising agencies as customers, rather than the firms whose products are advertised. Multiple accounts may need to be excluded if the price schedule has an increasing segment, as in the case of lifeline rates for small purchases.

---

4. Reselling is sufficiently costly in telecommunications that even after the FCC directive allowing resale of switched services AT&T still has profitable WATS services that are priced nonlinearly and only the highest volume segment has encountered appreciable competition from resale. I am indebted to David Sibley for this observation.

- What are the dimensions of the tariff? Purchases can be denominated in physical units, number of transactions, or dollar amounts. Several dimensions can apply simultaneously: for example, magazines offer discounts for large single advertisements and also for total annual billings; and electric utilities offer discounts on both demand charges (for the maximum power load) and energy charges. Similarly, the billing period is a crucial parameter of the tariff.

- What are the units of purchase? Quantity discounts can apply to single orders, the rate of purchases (over a billing period, or a longer span such as year), or cumulative purchases. Any of these can be measured in physical units, number of orders, or dollar amounts. Dollar measurements are especially useful for aggregating heterogeneous items. Often the choice is affected by the source of cost economies (such as a single shipment) or by the natural time frame over which purchases tend to be stable from period to period. Telephone and electricity tariffs are usually based on monthly billing periods or annual rates of consumption, whereas airline frequent-flier plans use annual rates and also cumulative purchases measured by mileage.

- What are the quality dimensions? Nonlinear pricing depends sensitively on whether a spectrum of qualities is offered as a differentiated product line (i.e., unbundled) or instead prices are based on a single average quality. For instance, an electric utility can interrupt customers randomly or in rotation as needed in times of scarce supplies, so that all customers have the same chances of suffering an interruption, or it can offer differentiated services that provide a spectrum of service priorities. Differentiation usually entails more sophisticated monitoring: electric power differentiated by time of use requires metering and billing systems that separately record usage at different times, and differentiated services for interruptible or curtailable power require more elaborate dispatching and control systems.

- What is the method of billing? Many tariffs specify charges or rebates for single transactions or periodic billings, but others invoke elaborate procedures. The customer may be required to offer proof of purchases or to apply for discounts or rebates. Frequent-flier plans provide discounts only as rebates in kind via free tickets, quality upgrades, and accessory services such as privileged lounges. In some cases the discount is implicit, as in the case that the seller absorbs part or all of the cost of transport and delivery. A common procedure depends on a menu of contracts from which each customer chooses initially and then is billed accordingly at the end of the billing period. For example, a customer might choose between banking services at either a fixed price per check, or a monthly fee plus a lower price per check; for rental cars, between two daily rates with differing mileage charges; and for a parking space, between a monthly rate and a daily rate. Product lines of machines often take this form: the customer can choose among several increasingly expensive machines that have successively lower operating costs. If customers are uncertain what their consumptions will be, then the seller can reduce their risks by billing according to the most favorable contract the customer might have selected; e.g., several rental-car companies follow this practice and AT&T does so for some of its optional plans.

This partial list of the considerations involved in tariff design refers mainly to quantity discounts, but similar considerations apply to quality attributes. However, tariffs based on qualities impose special problems of measurement and contractual performance. For example, nonlinear pricing of service reliability, speed of delivery, or product durability cannot usually be implemented directly. Service reliability is more easily implemented by offering customers a choice of priority classes for access to scarce capacity; speed of delivery is often expressed vaguely (e.g., overnight delivery) or via queuing priorities; and product durability is better assured via maintenance or replacement warranties.

A practical aspect of tariff design is the need to make the tariff simple enough that it can be understood by customers and sales representatives. In 1980, this author found the pricing manuals used by salesmen for a copier manufacturer and a telephone company (for WATS lines) so lengthy (each were 3 inches thick) and complex as to be indecipherable, as indeed was the opinion of a salesman in each case. Among the many tariffs offered for WATS lines, a third appeared to be more expensive for each volume of the customer's usage than some combination of the others. This situation has changed dramatically with increasing deregulation of the long-distance telephone industry: AT&T now offers a simple array of WATS options that represents essentially a single four-part tariff.

Disaggregated demand data

The fundamental motivation for nonlinear pricing is heterogeneity among customers. It is because different customers value successive increments differently that a seller's optimal product design and pricing policy differentiates according to purchase size. There are some markets (such as household durables like refrigerators and cars) in which purchase size is a moot consideration since customers rarely purchase more than a single item, but in many markets quantity is an important dimension and there is great dispersion among customers' purchases.

Adapting the pricing policy to take account of the underlying heterogeneity among customers amounts essentially to designing a product line that is differentiated by quantity (or quality) of purchases. The essential demand data required for the design task are records or estimates of customers' purchases classified according to both the price paid and the quantity purchased. Alternatively, the design can be based on models that rely on other measures of heterogeneity among customers, such as sales volume or production rates for industrial customers and socio-demographic indices for residential customers.

Many firms do not routinely accumulate data that is disaggregated to this degree, and therefore do not recognize or cannot measure the advantages of nonlinear pricing. In other cases, individual customer records are maintained but the data reflect so little variation in prices that demand elasticities for various purchase sizes are difficult to estimate. A wealth of data is obtained after an initial implementation of nonlinear pricing has been tried, but considerable risks may afflict the initial trial.

It is important to recognize that nonlinear pricing need not involve fine differentiation to be advantageous. Typically it suffices to identify a few volume bands for differentiated prices in order to obtain most of the gains that a finely differentiated tariff could obtain. This is fortunate, because fine differentiation complicates the tariff and imposes costs of monitoring and billing. In practice it is often sufficient to offer a menu of several two-part tariffs.

In the next chapters we describe the basic features of nonlinear pricing and describe how a nonlinear price schedule is constructed. We emphasize the interpretation that it amounts essentially to market segmentation in terms of volume bands of customers. This interpretation provides an intuitive explanation of nonlinear pricing; in addition, it provides a systematic method of analyzing a wide variety of problems. In §2 several examples of nonlinear pricing illustrate how it is applied in practice. In the next section we introduce such applications with a few illustrations from the power industry, and then the final sections summarize the main conclusions derived in subsequent chapters.

1.4 Illustration: the electric power industry

Nonlinear pricing has an important role in many industries. The exposition therefore presents the subject in sufficient generality to be widely applicable. Also, the examples are drawn from several industries in order to illustrate the variety of contexts in which nonlinear pricing is used. Nevertheless, the text includes many topics that are familiar and important aspects of rate design in the electric power industry.

It is instructive first to recall that purchases of generating equipment put a utility in the position of a customer facing a nonlinear pricing schedule. Consider a merit order of four generators: hydro, nuclear, coal, gas. These four have increasing costs of energy ($/kWh) and decreasing capital costs per unit of power ($/kW). For a one kilo-Watt load, therefore, as the duration of the load (hrs./year) increases, the merit order typically selects these four generation sources in reverse of the order listed. In effect, the utility faces a schedule of generation costs depending on duration that is nonlinear. This schedule is not offered by any one supplier, and moreover the utility may purchase several types of generators to meet its load-duration profile, but it illustrates that choosing from a nonlinear schedule is familiar in the power industry from the customer's side of the transaction.

Nonlinear pricing of services from vendors is increasingly common in the power industry as an integral part of long-term power supply contracts allotted via auctions. Whether designed by the utility or proposed in an auction by the supplier, payment schedules are typically differentiated by power level, duration, and total energy, and also by a variety of quality attributes such as availability, ease and assurance of dispatch, and other measures of reliability. Indeed, auctions especially attract contracts with elaborate pricing rules in order to meet the utility's objectives at least cost to the supplier while ensuring sufficient incentives for compliance on both sides.

From the supplier's side, utilities in the power industry have long offered a variety of nonlinear rate schedules, especially block-declining tariffs for commercial and industrial customers. A customer incurs energy charges each month, as well as a demand charge based on the customer's peak power, that accumulate nonuniformly depending on the blocks in the rate schedule. Thus, the actual tariff combines a demand charge with an energy charge as in a two-part tariff but with significant nonuniformities due to the several blocks in the rates for usage and peak power. Wright tariffs enable an especially elaborate scheme of nonlinear pricing of both energy and maximum power level. Tariffs of both types are illustrated in §2.2 and analyzed in §11.

An alternative view of nonlinear pricing interprets the tariff as depending on an index of quality rather than quantity. This is familiar in the power industry as peakload pricing. That is, power in shoulder and peak periods has higher quality, in the sense that customers want more power at such times and some are willing to pay more. As with nonlinear pricing of quantities, the price per unit of energy varies systematically with the time of use, leading to higher prices in peak periods if capacity is scarce or generation costs are higher.

Other kinds of quality differentiation are also important. An important one in demand side management programs, as they are called in the power industry, is differentiation of rates based on the possibility of interruption or curtailment of service in times of scarce supply. This too has a cost justification because interruptible demands substitute for costly capacity to serve peak loads. Rate design based on differentiated service priorities is illustrated in §2.3 and analyzed in §10.

Of particular interest in the power industry is the burgeoning use of nonlinear pricing to retain large customers. This practice has increased in the telephone industry since deregulation in an attempt to deter large customers from electing to bypass local exchanges. But it is also an important tactic for utilities concerned about losing large customers to the form of bypass peculiar to the power industry, namely cogeneration. Quantity discounts for large purchases also have a cost justification because large customers tend to have higher load factors and therefore impose relatively lower costs for capacity to serve peakloads. An example in §5.3 illustrates the use of a nonlinear tariff by a telephone company to offer favorable rates to large customers without imposing disadvantages on small customers. The key feature is that large customers with opportunities to bypass have, in effect, greater price elasticities of demand due to their opportunities to elect bypass—and it is precisely this greater elasticity that makes nonlinear pricing effective.

Lastly, we note that nonlinear pricing is essentially an application of Ramsey pricing in which market segments are identified with volume bands. In view of the pervasive role of the principles of Ramsey pricing for rate design in the power industry, this interpretation is useful for the light it sheds on the full implications of Ramsey pricing in rate design. Although regulatory agencies usually invoke arguments based on Ramsey pricing in the limited context of uniform prices, the method has a far greater range of application.

1.5 Overview of the chapters

This book has four main parts. Part I is intended for general readers, whereas Parts II–IV are increasingly technical and they require tolerance for more mathematical symbolism. Part I includes Chapters 2 through 5. It presents the basic ideas of nonlinear pricing in elementary terms. Mathematical notation is kept to the minimum necessary for accuracy: it is used mostly for concise reference to various quantities, prices, costs, and revenues. The device that makes this elementary presentation feasible is the representation of demand data in terms of the *demand profile* defined in Chapter 3. The demand profile summarizes data in a partially aggregated form that retains information only about how the distribution of customers' purchases is affected by the prices charged. This is the usual form in which demand data is available, and it is also the most aggregated form that retains sufficient information to construct a nonlinear tariff.

Chapter 4 demonstrates how the demand profile can be used to construct a nonlinear tariff for a single product offered by a profit-maximizing monopoly firm. Chapter 5 extends this analysis to a regulated firm that maximizes the aggregate of customers' net benefits subject to the requirement that its net revenues are sufficient to recover its full costs. In addition, it shows how the tariff can be constrained to ensure that no customer is disadvantaged by nonlinear pricing, as compared to the uniform price that yields the same net revenue for the firm. General readers may also be interested in the other applications of nonlinear pricing described in elementary terms in Chapter 15, and the short history of the subject in Chapter 16.

Part II comprises Chapters 6 through 8, which rely on completely disaggregated models in which each customer's demand behavior is specified explicitly. It is intended for readers interested in the technical aspects of nonlinear pricing, and the density of mathematics is greater. Chapter 6 complements Part I's exposition in terms of the demand profile with a parallel analysis based on a disaggregated demand model in which customers or market segments are identified by a single parameter affecting their preferences or demands. This chapter describes the design of multipart tariffs, fully nonlinear tariffs, and associated access charges or fixed fees. Chapter 7 uses several examples to illustrate the consequences of income effects. Chapter 8 considers several technical aspects and indicates how the previous analyses generalize to more complex models.

Part III considers the design of tariffs for single products with one or more auxiliary quality attributes, such as the time or reliability of delivery. Chapter 9 presents two versions of nonlinear pricing for products with multiple attributes, such as the quantity and also the quality, as measured by the time, speed, or other conditions of delivery. Chapters 10 and 11 focus on applications affected by supply or capacity limitations: in the first, aggregate capacity is rationed by pricing service priorities; and in the second, a customer's capacity allotment is priced separately from actual usage.

Part IV addresses the design of tariffs for multiple products priced jointly. Chapter 12 considers first the case of separate tariffs for several products. It also shows how the analysis extends to competition among several single-product firms in a single industry. Chapters 13 and 14 develop the general theory of nonlinear tariffs for multiple products, first in terms of disaggregated demand models and then in terms of a multiproduct version of the demand profile adapted to computations.

Two supplementary chapters provide additional material of general interest. Chapter 15 outlines applications of nonlinear pricing in other contexts, such as contracting in insurance and labor markets, which are similarly affected by the feature that each participant's selection from a menu of options is affected by personal attributes or private information. Chapter 16 provides a synopsis of the literature on nonlinear pricing.

The following list of the chapters includes brief summaries of their contents. Each is accompanied by a "bottom line" statement of the main qualitative conclusion derived.

Part I: Fundamentals of nonlinear pricing

2. *Illustrations of Nonlinear Pricing:* This chapter describes the practice of nonlinear pricing by firms in several industries. Several competitive industries are included, such as publishing, airlines, and express mail, as well as regulated monopolies, such as electric power and telephone.
   Conclusion: In both regulated and competitive industries, various forms of nonlinear pricing are used to differentiate or "unbundle" quantity and quality increments.
3. *Models and Data Sources:* This chapter describes the data used to construct nonlinear tariffs. It emphasizes the representation of demand data in summary form in terms of an estimate of the demand profile.
   Conclusion: Because the advantages of nonlinear pricing stem from heterogeneity among customers, implementation relies on estimates of the price

elasticity of the distribution of customers' purchases, which can be obtained from data summarized in the demand profile.

4. *Tariff Design:* This chapter shows how the demand profile is used to construct a nonlinear tariff for a profit-maximizing monopoly firm. Construction of the schedule of marginal prices is illustrated both for demand data in tabular form, and for parameterized models estimated from demand data. Nonlinear pricing can also be interpreted as a special case of bundling in which different prices are charged for various combinations or bundles of items.

   Conclusion: For a profit-maximizing firm, the schedule of marginal prices is derived by optimizing the price charged for each increment in the purchase size. With modifications this principle applies also to access fees and multipart tariffs.

5. *Ramsey Pricing:* This chapter shows that with only slight modification, the same principles of tariff design apply to a regulated firm whose price schedule maximizes the aggregate of customers' net benefits subject to recovery of the firm's full costs. In practice, however, it is often important to modify the tariff by imposing the constraint that no customer is disadvantaged compared to an existing tariff, such as the uniform price that recovers the same revenue for the firm. Typically this is done to ensure that efficiency gains from a nonlinear tariff obtained by customers purchasing large amounts do not impose unfavorable consequences on other customers purchasing small amounts.

   Conclusion: Ramsey pricing is based on essentially the same principles of tariff design, but to ensure that no customer is disadvantaged (compared to the uniform price that meets the same revenue requirement), customers can still purchase initial increments at the revenue-equivalent uniform price.

Part II: Disaggregated demand models

6. *Single-Parameter Disaggregated Models:* This chapter reconsiders the topics in Chapter 4 in terms of parameterized models of customers' benefits or demands. Such models are used in most technical treatments of the subject. A single type parameter is used to describe the differences among customers or among market segments. Optimal tariffs are derived for versions in which the type parameter is discrete or continuous. The construction of optimal fixed fees and multipart tariffs are also derived.

   Conclusion: A model that identifies distinct market segments via a single demand parameter enables exact characterization and computation of optimal multipart and nonlinear tariffs.

7. *Income Effects:* This chapter describes the consequences for nonlinear pricing of income effects derived from customers' budget constraints. Three

different types of income effects are illustrated with numerical examples.
The computations required to calculate an optimal tariff are more complicated, but the main qualitative features are not altered.

Conclusion: Examples indicate that income effects can be severe, depending
on their form and the variance of the income elasticity of demand in the
population, but if the tariff leaves customers with large residual incomes
and the income-elasticity variance in the population is small then income
effects have little effect on tariff design.

8. *Technical Amendments:* This chapter examines several technical aspects of
nonlinear pricing. The first two sections develop conditions sufficient to
ensure that a nonlinear tariff meets all the requirements for optimal behavior by customers and by the firm. The third demonstrates that an optimal
multipart tariff, or a menu of optional two-part tariffs, closely approximates
the optimal nonlinear tariff. In particular, the profit or surplus lost by using
only n segments or options is approximately proportional to $1/n^2$. A menu
with only a few options is therefore sufficient to realize most of the potential
gain from a nonlinear tariff. The fourth shows that the main results from
previous chapters are valid also for disaggregated demand models in which
customers' are described by multiple type parameters. The fifth describes
an extension of the demand-profile formulation to encompass dependencies on the total tariff charged. The main new feature is that prices for small
purchases may be reduced in a fashion similar to lifeline rates.

Conclusion: (a) To ensure that demand projections are accurate, the assignment of customers' types to purchases must be monotone, which can
be assured by using an averaging procedure to eliminate nonmonotonicities. (b) A multipart tariff with only a few segments obtains most of the
gains from nonlinear pricing. (c) The main features of analyses based on
one-dimensional type parameters are preserved in models with many parameters. (d) If demands are sensitive to the total tariff then charges for small
purchases may be reduced to retain the optimal market penetration.

Part III: Multidimensional tariffs

9. *Multidimensional Pricing:* This chapter presents the simplest form of multiproduct nonlinear pricing in which each customer assigns, to each unit
purchased, a preferred combination of quality attributes. This form of nonlinear pricing is used when customers select delivery conditions or other
aspects of service quality. Chapter 4's method of constructing a nonlinear
tariff from the demand profile applies equally to this case, but some applications involve substitution effects requiring more elaborate calculations.

Conclusion: Nonlinear pricing can be extended straightforwardly to multiple quantity and quality dimensions if customers select arbitrary sets of

increments; however, the tariff is affected by substitution effects in customers' demands.

10. *Priority Pricing:* This chapter describes an application of multidimensional pricing to the case that customers are rationed based on supply availability. Customers select their service priorities from a menu of options priced according to a nonlinear tariff.

   Conclusion: When supply is limited by capacity constraints and demand or supply is stochastic, nonlinear prices for service priorities and quantities jointly can be designed using the principles of Ramsey pricing in a multidimensional formulation.

11. *Capacity Pricing:* This chapter extends multidimensional pricing to include charges for capacity as well as usage. The charges can take several alternative forms corresponding to either time-of-use usage charges accompanied by uniform demand charges for capacity, or nonlinear pricing of capacity increments accompanied by nonlinear pricing of the duration of usage of each capacity unit (called a Wright tariff in the power industry).

   Conclusion: When customers purchase sets of load-duration increments reflecting peakload effects, nonlinear pricing can be used to design unified tariffs for usage and capacity requirements.

Part IV: Multiproduct tariffs

12. *Multiple Products and Competitive Tariffs:* This chapter illustrates several extensions of nonlinear pricing to multiproduct contexts. In the first case considered, a single firm offers a separate tariff for each of several products. The optimal tariffs can be derived from a multiproduct version of the demand profile in which substitution effects are represented explicitly. The calculations can be done via a simple gradient procedure. In the second case, each firm in a competitive industry offers a separate tariff for its own product. One model considers pure price competition among firms whose products are imperfect substitutes; a second considers firms offering identical products but competition is affected by the firms' supply or capacity commitments. A third case mentioned briefly considers competition among multiproduct firms who adapt their pricing policies to changing demand conditions.

   Conclusion: Nonlinear pricing can be used for multiple products offered by a single firm, or by several firms in a competitive industry. Customers' opportunities to substitute one product for another have pronounced effects on tariff design. The form of implementation depends on whether multiple products are priced separately or jointly and on the competitive structure of the industry.

13. *Multiproduct Pricing:* This chapter describes the construction of a single comprehensive tariff by a multiproduct monopolist or regulated firm. The formulation relies on a model of customers' benefits or demand functions with one or more parameters that describe customers' types. When there is more than one type parameter, computations are complicated by the technical requirement that the marginal price schedules assess cumulative charges independent of a customer's pattern of accumulation. Examples indicate that a significant feature of multiproduct tariffs is an emphasis on bundling; that is, the price schedule for each product is strongly dependent on the quantities the customer purchases of other products. For instance, prices for power in peak periods can depend on the customer's offpeak load, as in the case of so-called load-factor discounts.

Conclusion: The design of a multivariate tariff for multiple products follows the same general principles as for a single product but calculations are complicated. Bundling is important: each product's prices depend on purchases of other products.

14. *Multiproduct Tariffs:* This chapter derives an approximation of the optimal multivariate tariff directly from the multiproduct demand profile. The approximation depends on ignoring customers' participation constraints. The tariff can be constructed from the "price differentials" charged for multiproduct increments. A simple gradient algorithm suffices for the calculations.

Conclusion: The multiproduct demand profile can be used directly to compute an approximately optimal multiproduct tariff, and for many problems this is the easiest approach.

Supplementary chapters

15. *Other Applications of Nonlinear Pricing:* Previous chapters emphasize applications of nonlinear tariffs to pricing in product markets. This chapter describes a few of many applications to other markets, such as insurance, contracting, and work incentives. In product pricing, nonlinear tariffs are useful because customers are diverse, whereas in other applications the role of diversity is supplanted by the privacy of participants' personal information or actions. That is, the diversity of customers' types is represented by the diversity of what a single participant might know.

Conclusion: In other contexts of product pricing, contracting, regulation, and taxation, the design of the tariff or other menu of options recognizes that each participant's selection depends on personal preferences or private information.

16. *Bibliography:* This chapter provides a brief history of the development of the theory of nonlinear pricing, and it provides references to important con-

INTRODUCTION   23

tributions. The large technical literature stems from Ramsey's formulation
of product pricing to meet a revenue requirement and Mirrlees' applications
to governmental taxation. The subsequent literature addresses a wide variety
of applications of nonlinear pricing to quantity and/or quality differentiated
products, and related applications to contracting affected by incentives and
private information.

References: All the references cited in the text or mentioned in the bibliography are collected together at the end, along with a selection of uncited
articles of related interest.

The illustrations and applications described in the text represent a substantial
selection bias in favor of the major regulated industries that use nonlinear pricing
most heavily. In particular, my own background is mostly in the electric power
industry and so it is used often as a case study.

Most of the chapters include numerical examples that indicate either the method
of calculation or the character of the results. These examples are chosen purposely
to be quite simple, since they are used only for illustrative purposes. In practice, of
course, rate design deals with more complex pricing problems. Actual applications
involve substantial tasks of data analysis, model formulation and estimation, and
complicated calculations that are treated incompletely here.

1.6   Summary

The main themes of the book can be summarized as follows.

- The illustrations and applications in the text indicate that nonlinear pricing is
  widely used, often in disguised forms. The advantages of nonlinear pricing derive ultimately from heterogeneity among customers' valuations of successive
  increments of the quantity or quality purchased. This heterogeneity in the population of customers allows product differentiation to be based on segmenting
  the market according to volume bands or quality-differentiated product lines.
  Some degree of monopoly power, reinforced by limitations on resale markets,
  is essential for nonlinear pricing to be effective. Implementation requires that
  the seller can identify customers and monitor their purchases.
- A nonlinear tariff can be constructed from ordinary demand data obtained
  from uniform pricing. The observed distribution of purchases at various prices,
  summarized in the demand profile, provides the requisite demand data. For a
  single product, elementary arithmetical calculations suffice to design the price
  schedule for a nonlinear tariff. This is done by interpreting the tariff as charging
  prices for a product line consisting of successive increments of a customer's
  purchase. Nonlinear tariffs offered by competing firms can be analyzed by the
  same methods. The calculations are comparably simple for multidimensional

pricing, but for general multiproduct pricing the calculations are complicated by the effects of substitution among products.

- Nonlinear pricing can be based on explicit consideration of each customer's predicted behavior and often this is done by using parameterized models that identify distinct market segments. At this level of detail, an optimal tariff can be characterized exactly, at least in principle. Because sufficient data to estimate such models is rarely available, however, portions of the exposition rely on a partially aggregated formulation in terms of the demand profile, which summarizes how the distribution of customers' purchases depends on the prices charged.

- Practical applications of nonlinear pricing use a multipart tariff or a menu of optional two-part tariffs. This is sufficient because a multipart tariff with a few segments realizes most of the advantages of nonlinear pricing. Multipart tariffs and optional two-part tariffs are constructed in the same way except that the optimality condition represents an average over each segment of the conditions that pertain to a fully nonlinear tariff.

- Nonlinear pricing is an efficient way for a regulated monopoly to obtain sufficient revenue to recover its full costs. However, because a nonlinear tariff benefits mostly large customers via quantity discounts, small customers can be disadvantaged compared to the uniform price that obtains the same revenue. A useful expedient to eliminate these unfavorable distributional effects is to cap the marginal prices at the revenue-equivalent uniform price.

Part I

FUNDAMENTALS OF NONLINEAR PRICING

2

ILLUSTRATIONS OF NONLINEAR PRICING

Quantity discounts have a long history in business practice. The number of deliberate applications of the principles of nonlinear pricing has, however, increased markedly in recent years. Three causes account for this growth. The elementary explanation is that an increasing number of firms offer standardized products or services in mass markets. Because these markets comprise diverse market segments, but a single tariff, price schedule, or menu of options is offered, there are advantages to tariffs that differentiate products or services according to observable aspects of customers' purchases, such as purchase size or quality selection. Moreover, the rudimentary tasks of monitoring purchases and of accounting and billing have been simplified by computerized data processing. A further explanation is that major industries such as transportation, communications, and power (electric generation and bulk gas supply) have been substantially deregulated. The competitive pressures and high capital costs in these markets require product differentiation for survival, and nonlinear pricing is an important means of differentiation. A deeper explanation, however, is the recognition that product differentiation generally and nonlinear pricing in particular are necessary ingredients of efficient product design and pricing in many industries. This explanation is developed in more detail in §5 when we study Ramsey pricing by a regulated firm with a revenue recovery requirement, and in §12 when we study imperfectly competitive markets. Here our intent is to introduce some of the practical aspects of nonlinear pricing as it is practiced in several industries.

This chapter describes several applications of nonlinear pricing. Section 1 describes the structure of rates for advertising used by two major weekly magazines in a highly competitive market. Sections 2 and 3 describe the tariffs offered in France and California by public utilities supplying electric power. These applications illustrate several practical aspects of nonlinear pricing. In both cases, the firms use elaborate tariffs that invoke nonlinear pricing on several dimensions simultaneously, some of which are dimensions of quantity and others, of quality. Second, these tariffs are motivated partly by the firm's cost considerations and partly by customers' demand behaviors—in each case, in ways peculiar to the technologies of the supplier and the customers in the industry. And third, one application is drawn from a competitive industry while the others pertain to regulated monopolies, thus illustrating a wide spectrum of possibilities for applying nonlinear pricing. Sections 4, 5, and 6 provide synopses of nonlinear pricing in the telephone, express mail, and airline markets, all of which have been substantially deregulated in recent years.

2.1 *Time* and *Newsweek*'s advertising rates

Extreme examples of nonlinear pricing are found in the rate schedules offered by newspapers and magazines for advertising insertions. In this section we describe the schedules used by *Time* and *Newsweek* magazines, two of the major news weeklies competing in the national market in the United States.[1] Because these schedules are long and complicated, we summarize the main features.

Both magazines use nonlinear pricing on several dimensions, including the size of an individual advertisement, the portion of total circulation purchased per issue, and the customer's cumulative dollar amount of advertising purchased per year. In addition, each magazine differentiates its schedule further according to quality attributes, including the color content and the audience characteristics. Each of these is described in turn.

Each magazine uses a three-column format; consequently, prices for single advertising insertions ("ads") are quoted in terms of multiples of half-columns or sixths of a page, and differentiated according to whether the number of colors (in addition to black) is 0, 1, or 4 in order of increasing quality and price. We refer to a full-page four-color ad as 1P4C, et cetera. The complexity of the resulting schedules can be reduced by dividing each price by both the size of the insertion and the price of a 1P4C ad, thus converting prices to a full-page four-color basis, which we call *normalized* prices. Dividing further by the magazine's *reach* (the size of the magazine's audience) puts the prices in terms of CPM: the cost per thousand readers reached. Although *Time*'s normalized rates are over 40% more expensive than *Newsweek*'s, its CPM-rates are only about 10% higher for 1P4C ads. *Time*'s normalized prices for each color quality decrease as the size of the ad increases, and so do the marginal prices of incremental sizes with two exceptions: for 0C and 1C ads the incremental normalized price of moving from a third-page to a half-page ad increases. (This is presumably due to the higher cost of composing a page that includes an ad taking up the top or bottom half of the page; for *Newsweek*, even the normalized prices increase at these same points.) For each size the incremental cost of 1C is positive, and the further incremental cost of 4C is also positive, but these increments decline with the size of the ad—and more so for

1. This section is based on Timothy McGuire, "Nonlinear Pricing and Unbundling by the Major Newsweeklies," Stanford Business School, December 1987. The description is based on the January 5, 1987, rate cards #71 and #58 of *Time* and *Newsweek*, respectively.

4C than for 1C. *Time*'s normalized prices for third-page and full-page ads reflect quantity discounts for full pages of 17% and 23% for 0C and 4C respectively, and *Newsweek*'s discounts are slightly less. For each size, each magazine adds a fixed percentage to the 0C price to obtain the 1C price (*Time*'s percentage is smaller), and a percentage that declines with size to obtain the 4C price.

The second category of nonlinear pricing is based on the circulation purchased. Each magazine offers advertisers various options: the national edition, various overlapping regional and "major markets" editions, and several special editions aimed at selected demographic categories such as income level or occupation. *Time* and *Newsweek* have 113 and 94 regional editions, as well as many special editions. (The magazine a subscriber receives includes the ads from all editions for which he qualifies based on geographical location and demographic characteristics.) Typically the prices for these editions have slightly higher targeted-CPMs compared to the national edition, reflecting the higher "quality" audience obtained. For 4C, *Time* charges $6390 for the first geographical edition, $3495 for the second, and zero thereafter up to 100,000 circulation, with additional circulation priced at a declining marginal rate with 15 blocks that varies from $35.46 down to $27.40 per thousand copies for more than 2.9 million copies. These rates are uniformly higher than the "professional-managerial audience" targeted-CPM of about $18 (and the "adult audience" CPM of about $4.50) for the national edition, but the special editions obtain nearly the same CPMs for such selected audiences. *Newsweek* charges a flat rate of $820 per regional edition up to the tenth and then zero, but its schedule of marginal charges per thousand copies over 196 ranges of circulation shows almost no pattern; indeed, the marginal charge is lowest at 0.4 million copies ($24) and significantly higher ($27) at 2.0 million. The irregularity of *Newsweek*'s marginal circulation charges might be due to the tabular form of the rate schedule, comprising three tables each with 196 rows and 10 columns, which tends to obscure the marginal charges that concern customers.

The third category of nonlinear pricing is based on the customer's total annual purchases of advertising, and it occurs in three parts. *Time*, for example, offers an 11-block schedule of discounts based on total annual purchases that is stated in terms of the percentage rebate that applies to the entire year's purchases: these rebates range from 0% up to 15% for purchases exceeding $8.9 million per year. Second, it offers a 4-block schedule of rebates for matching the purchases in the prior year: these range from 0% up to 4% for purchases exceeding $8.9 million. And third, further rebates of 3% or 5% are given for exceeding the prior year's spending by $0.375 or $0.750 million. Whereas the latter two types of rebates are evidently aimed to preserve market share and capture customers' annual increments in their advertising budgets, the first type is aimed at a special feature of the advertising industry. If identical or similar ads are placed in successive issues of a magazine, the reach (the number of readers who see the ad in any issue) increases but at a sharply decreasing rate; similarly, the average frequency (the number of times a specific reader sees the ad) increases at a decreasing rate. Further, frequency has a diminishing effect on the chances a reader will purchase the advertiser's product. For example, *Time*'s reach from 52 insertions over a year is only 3 times the single-issue reach, and the frequency is only 18 times as high. Thus, advertisers encounter sharply decreasing returns from multiple insertions in the same magazine. Presumably *Time*'s rebate schedules reflect this feature of customer's demands for multiple insertions. An additional possibility pertains to customers who sell multiple products: the rebates give some incentive to purchase advertising about secondary products for which the gains from advertising are less.

In sum, the rate schedules offered by these two magazines address several different dimensions of customers' decision processes. For a single insertion, the rates offer decreasing marginal prices for increments in the size of ads, as well as for quality attributes such as the number of colors. Further quantity discounts are offered for the circulation of the issue, and for the regional and demographic quality of the audience reached. Finally, rebates on annual expenditures are offered to counter the effects of diminishing marginal reach and frequency. Combining all these features into the rate schedule produces a long and elaborate tariff that is seemingly bewildering in its complexity, at least for the uninitiated. Nevertheless, in this intensely competitive industry these pricing practices have survived, and in fact are used similarly by both major news magazines.

2.2 EDF's tariffs for electric power

The public utility that produces and distributes electric power in France is *Electricité de France*, generally known as EDF. For many years its tariffs have been based on an elaborate system of nonlinear pricing. The tariffs are color-coded according to a scheme familiar to customers. We discuss the following three:

- *Tarif Bleu:* The blue tariff offers one schedule for residences and farms, and another for professional offices with power loads up to a maximum of 36 kilo-Volt-Amperes (kVA).
- *Tarif Jaune:* The yellow tariff applies to customers with loads between 36 and 250 kVA.
- *Tarif Vert:* The green tariff offers a variety of rate schedules for industrial and commercial customers with loads less than 10,000 kilo-Watts (kW) in series A, a second set of schedules for customers with loads between 10,000 and 40,000 kW in series B, et cetera.

These tariffs use nonlinear pricing in different ways that we describe briefly.[2]

---

2. The following description is based on the tariffs effective in February 1987.

The blue tariff

The blue tariff for professional offices offers three options among which each customer can select. Each option consists of a fixed charge per month plus a charge for the actual energy consumed, as measured in kilo-Watt-hours (kWh). The fixed charge, based on the power rating of the customer's appliances, is computed according to a nonlinear schedule in which customers with higher power ratings pay disproportionately *more*. Moreover, the schedule of monthly fixed charges depends on whether the customer selects the basic, "empty hours," or "critical times" option. Compared to the basic option, the monthly charge is about 25% higher for the empty-hours option, and about 50% lower for the critical-times option. The basic option has a constant energy charge (50 centimes/kWh) regardless of the circumstances in which the energy is consumed. In contrast, the empty-hours option allows a discount of nearly 50% for energy consumed at night in the designated off-peak hours (10 PM to 6 AM) and the critical-times option has a 36% lower energy charge (32 centimes/kWh) applicable to all hours, but imposes a surcharge of over 800% for energy consumed after the utility has broadcast an announcement that power is in scarce supply. The blue tariff for residences and farms offers the same options and imposes the same energy charges, but the fixed charge is less than half as much; moreover, the fixed charge is payable annually.

The blue tariff can be interpreted as a collection of three two-part tariffs, each consisting of a monthly fixed charge plus an energy charge. The basic fixed charge increases with the maximum power level at an increasing rate, although it is appreciably less for residences and farms. The likely cost basis for this schedule is that higher maximum power levels in offices are associated with lower load factors and sharper peaks that require the utility to maintain greater reserve margins of capacity to serve peak loads. Residential and agricultural customers have higher load factors, considering that the peak is in the winter and is due substantially to heating loads: another possibility is that the lower fixed charges for residences and farms reflect subsidies.

The three options offer each customer a choice of which two-part tariff to elect. The empty-hours option incurs a higher fixed charge but allows the customer substantial savings on the charges for energy consumed in night-time hours. This option reflects the cost structure of baseload generation. The critical-times option saves appreciably on both the fixed and energy charges but the surcharge that is applied when supplies are scarce essentially requires the customer to curtail demand at these critical times. Thus, customers who elect the critical-times option are accorded lowest priority for service. Because these times are substantially unpredictable and the warning time is short, the customer must be able to interrupt operations quickly and inexpensively to take advantage of this option. The lower charges reflect the fact that such customers require essentially no reserve margin and their energy can be supplied by baseload capacity or by idle peaking capacity;

indeed, as more customers elect this option the utility can alter its mix of generation technologies in favor of more baseload sources such as nuclear reactors.

The yellow tariff

The yellow tariff applicable to small industrial facilities is similar to the blue tariff but differs in several respects. First, the energy charges in all categories differ between the summer and winter seasons: energy charges are three to four times higher in winter than in summer. This difference reflects higher peak loads in winter due to the prevalent use of electric power for space heating. These peak loads are met with generators that use fossil fuel, which is substantially more expensive than the hydroelectric and nuclear sources used to meet base loads. A second feature is that the fixed charge, payable annually for each kVA of power demanded, is based on a fixed rate (rather than a nonlinear schedule).

The third and key feature, however, is that the fixed and energy charges are set nonlinearly based on the duration of each increment of the load during the year; tariffs of this form are called Wright tariffs in the United States. To understand this scheme, imagine that the customer's meter comprises many small meters: the first kVA of the customer's load is assigned to the first meter; the second kVA, to the second meter; et cetera. Whenever the customer's power load is, say, six kVAs, the first six meters are turning. At the end of the year, the first meter records the number of hours in which a first kVA was being used, the second meter records the number of hours in which at least two kVAs were being used, et cetera. The yellow tariff assigns each kVA to one of two categories, designated medium utilization and long utilization, corresponding to whether that kVA was used for less or more than a certain number of hours per year. This assignment can also be interpreted as a classification of the customer's load into peakload and baseload segments. For a kVA designated as part of the peakload segment in winter during daytime hours, the annual fixed charge is less than a third as high but the energy charge can be nearly 50% greater to reflect the lower capacity costs and higher fuel costs of the generators used to serve peak loads. The critical-times option is available only for long utilizations and only during the winter; during the summer it is identical to the empty-hours option.

The structure of the yellow tariff reflects the fundamental features of the cost structure of electricity generation. The utility can choose among several kinds of generators, such as hydroelectric, nuclear, coal, and oil or gas. Within this list, the energy cost is increasing and the capital cost is decreasing. For example, a nuclear generator has a lower energy cost and a higher capital cost than a gas turbine. For base loads, therefore, it is less expensive to use a nuclear generator, and to use a gas turbine only to meet the incremental loads that occur in periods of peak demand. To see this, it is easiest to recognize that whichever generator is used to meet infrequent peak loads will be idle most of the time, and since the gas turbine has the lowest cost of construction, its imputed cost of being idle is also the lowest. Thus, even though gas turbines are expensive to operate, they are cost-effective in meeting infrequent short bursts of demand. The yellow tariff recognizes this cost structure by imposing on peakload segments of the customer's demand, a lower fixed charge (used to recover the capital costs of constructing generators), and a higher energy charge. The net effect is a tariff that uses nonlinear pricing of load duration in the form of a piecewise-linear tariff with two segments:

- In the first segment, for durations (hours per year) short enough to be classified as part of the customer's peakload segment, the fixed charge (francs per kVA per year) is low and the energy charge (centimes per kWh) is high.
- In the second segment, for durations long enough to be classified as part of the customer's baseload segment, the fixed charge is higher and the energy charge is lower.

Thus, the key feature is that for each increment of the customer's load, the yellow tariff depends nonlinearly on the accumulated hours that the increment is demanded during the year.

The green tariff

The green tariff applicable to medium-sized industrial and commercial customers offers a wide variety of rate schedules among which each customer can select. Here we describe only a few of these schedules for series A and B.

Schedule A5 for customers with loads less than 10,000 kW offers a basic option and a critical-times option similar to the corresponding options in the yellow tariff, but with three refinements. First, an additional charge is imposed for reactive energy (centimes per kVArh). Second, the energy charge in winter is differentiated according to three periods: in addition to the nighttime and daytime periods, a third designation of peak periods within the daytime period is added. Compared to the regular daytime energy charge, the peak-period energy charge is 28% to 50% higher depending on the duration of utilization (higher for shorter utilizations, since on average there is a greater dependence on peaking generators). Third, utilization is divided into four intervals: in addition to the medium and long utilizations, short and very long utilizations are specified.[3] As in the yellow tariff, longer utilizations incur higher annual fixed charges and lower energy charges. Figure 2.1 shows how the annual charges under the green tariff Schedule A5 basic option for winter peak hours depends on the annual hours per year. The four intervals of annual utilizations are numbered 1 to 4 in the figure. The summary effects of these features is to make Schedule A5 of the green tariff a refined version of the yellow tariff in which more

---

3. Only two duration intervals are used for the critical-times option.

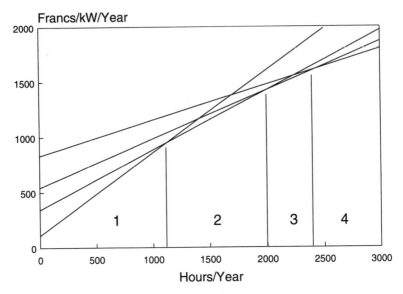

FIG. 2.1   EDF Green Tariff A5 for the basic option in winter peak hours depending on the annual utilization.

detailed account is taken of the effects of the customer's usage on the utility's costs of capacity and energy.

Schedule A8 is similar except for the addition of further distinctions that allow even lower off-peak rates in July and August (August is when nearly all of France is on vacation), and intermediate rates in Autumn and Spring; thus, it includes still further refinements. These additional refinements are also included in Schedule B for larger customers with loads between 10,000 and 40,000 kW. However, compared to Schedule A5, in Schedule B the fixed charges are lower by about 20% and the peak energy charges are lower by 7% (very long utilization) to 27% (short utilization). Taken together, therefore, we see that Schedules A5 and B constitute nonlinear pricing along the dimension of the customer's load. That is, for any prescribed length of utilization and time of use, the fixed charge and the energy charge are both lower if the customer's load exceeds 10,000 kW.

Summary

EDF's tariffs illustrate several important features of nonlinear pricing as it is applied in practice.

  1. Different tariff schedules are offered to different classes and power loads of customers. Each schedule offers a menu of options from which the customer can choose depending on its circumstances. Often these options take the form of two-part tariffs—although taken together for any one schedule,

or considered in the aggregate for several schedules, they make the total available menu substantially nonlinear. The menu offered to a small customer may include fewer refinements than one offered to a large customer because the advantages of such refinements are not worth the combined cost to the utility and the customer of implementing them.

2. Nonlinear pricing occurs along several dimensions simultaneously. EDF's tariffs, for example, use the dimensions of duration (length of utilization) and power (magnitude of load). Further incentives are offered for usage in off-peak periods, and for quick curtailment of usage at critical times of scarce supply. These dimensions reflect the underlying cost structure of the industry. In EDF's case, the key tradeoff is between capacity and energy costs, and this in turn is determined by load duration. As predicted by the theory, quantity discounts are also offered to the largest customers, although possibly these too have a basis in the cost structure if large customers tend to have more stable loads with higher load factors.

3. The tariffs serve several purposes simultaneously. One purpose is to recover the utility's costs of current operations (mostly energy costs) and amortization of costs of investments (mostly capital cost of generation and distribution equipment). In the long run, however, the tariffs also promote more efficient utilization of resources by customers. Because the tariffs reflect the long-run cost structure of power generation, they encourage customers to avoid wasteful usage. In EDF's case, for example, the tariffs encourage customers to:

- Consume power in offpeak rather than peak periods, thus reducing investments in peaking equipment and reducing energy costs. Lower energy charges in offpeak periods provide this incentive.
- Curtail demand quickly in response to supply scarcity, thus diminishing peak loads. Lower energy charges for normal hours and much higher rates at critical times provide this incentive.
- Smooth consumption over time, thus increasing average duration of utilization and thereby altering the mix of power generation in favor of cost-effective baseload sources. Lower energy charges (though higher annual demand charges) for longer utilizations provide this incentive.

In practice, few applications use nonlinear pricing in the elaborate detail and systematic conformity to costs implemented by EDF. Wright tariffs are rarely used in the United States currently although they provide incentives for consumption smoothing that are precisely consistent with the long-term cost structure of generation. Although it was popular in the early years of the industry, it fell into disuse until the recent introduction by a few utilities of so-called load-factor tariffs that are essentially Wright tariffs by another name. American regularity agencies in particular have opposed Wright tariffs, favoring instead a philosophy of "immediate causation" of short-term costs, and therefore time-of-use tariffs based on the capacity and operating costs of the marginal generator. These two kinds of tariffs are compared and studied in §11.

2.3 PG&E's curtailable service

In California, Pacific Gas and Electric Company offers a tariff for large industrial customers that has explicit options for curtailable and interruptible power service. These options provide several quality dimensions related to service priority of the sort studied in §10.

Curtailable and interruptible service are two forms of priority service that differ mainly in the extent of load reduction that a customer must accept when the utility encounters a deficiency of generating capacity. Curtailable service requires the customer to *reduce* its load: although the load reduction is partly negotiable, PG&E requires a reduction of at least 500 kW below the customer's lowest average peak-period load among the previous six summer months (summer is PG&E's peak season). Interruptible service requires the customer to eliminate its load entirely; further, the customer must accept automatic interruptions whenever the line frequency is deficient, which is often a signal that a generation shortage is imminent. Both options impose penalties if the customer fails to comply: these penalties are proportional to the excess load imposed by the customer, and they are substantially higher the second, and higher again the third time, within a year that the customer fails to comply. Both options limit load reductions to 6 hours on each occasion.

The service reliability associated with each option can be chosen by the customer from a menu of four alternatives. Each offers ordinary "firm service" as well as three alternatives that are distinguished by limits on the utility's prerogative to request a load reduction. These alternatives are shown in Table 2.1 as types A, B, and C under the firm-service tariff E20.[4] Considering only curtailable service, for example, alternative A requires the utility to provide a warning 60 minutes in advance, to limit such curtailments to 15 times per year, and to limit the cumulative duration

4. Source: Casazza, Schultz & Associates, *Electric Rate Book*, 1988. Also shown for comparison are four other options (A1, etc.) for firm service for smaller customers that reflect quantity discounts; in particular, A6 and A11 are designed to encourage offpeak usage. The price schedules shown are dated May 17, 1988, and include only those tariffs pertaining to nonresidential secondary-voltage service for the peak season (May to October). Tariff E-20 is restricted to customers with monthly maximum demand exceeding 500 kW. Demand charges are based on average maximum demand over 30-minute periods. The Peak period is 12 noon to 6 PM, and the Shoulder period is 8:30 am to 12 noon and 6 pm to 9:30 pm, both Monday to Friday; other hours are Offpeak. Prices are lower for service at primary and transmission voltages. Curtailable service requires the firm-service level to be at least 500 kW below the lowest average peak-period demands for the previous six summer billing months. Interruptible service requires that the customer agree to additional (unlimited numbers) of automatic interruptions activated by an underfrequency relay device. All curtailable and interruptible contracts specify a maximum duration of six hours in each event. Curtailable and interruptible contracts have one-year durations, and a minimum of three years. Various other restrictions apply.

Table 2.1 Pacific Gas and Electric Company Price Schedules

Type	Fixed	Demand		Energy Charge			Limits			Penalty	
	Chg. $/Mo.	Peak	Max	Peak	Shldr	Offpk	Warn	No.	Dur.	1st	2nd
		$/kW			Cents/kWh		Min.		Hrs.		$/kW
Firm Service:											
A1				10.404	10.404	10.404					
A6				24.895	12.447	6.473					
A10	50		2.85	8.658	8.658	8.658					
A11	50	8.10	2.85	12.746	10.197	5.405					
E20	100	8.10	2.85	7.633	7.269	4.264					
Curtailable Service (E20):											
A	290	4.87	2.85	7.631	7.266	4.265	60	15	50	3.11	6.23
B	290	3.04	2.85	7.626	7.261	4.264	30	30	100	4.89	9.79
C	290		2.85	7.494	7.136	4.226	10	45	200	8.45	16.90
Interruptible Service (E20):											
A	300		2.85	6.886	6.557	4.128	60	15	50	11.12	22.24
B	300		2.85	6.392	6.088	4.036	30	30	100	13.34	26.69
C	300		2.85	5.701	5.428	3.908	10	45	200	16.46	32.91

per year to 50 hours. Alternative C, in contrast, allows 10 minutes warning, 45 curtailments per year, and 200 hours cumulative duration. These specifications do not specify exact service reliabilities; instead, they are cast in terms of restrictions on easily verifiable actions of the utility. Altogether, the E20 tariff specifies seven different service conditions among which customers can choose.

The collection of tariffs shown in Table 2.1 can be interpreted as a single comprehensive tariff offering a menu of eleven options to each nonresidential customer. The charges in this super-tariff depend on three different dimensions:

- *Load size.* For example, the three firm-service tariffs A1, A10, and E20 offer successively lower marginal energy charges but successively higher fixed charges and demand charges. Also, A11 and E20 differ mainly in terms of the higher load that qualifies the customer for the lower energy charges under E20.
- *Time of use.* For example, A1 and A10 have energy charges independent of the period, whereas the other tariffs differentiate significantly among periods. A6 and A11 in particular provide substantial differences between peak and offpeak rates.
- *Service Reliability.* Alternatives A, B, and C under the E20 curtailable tariff offer successively lower demand and energy charges in all periods in exchange for acceptance of increasingly more numerous and longer curtailments with shorter warnings and higher penalties for noncompliance. The choice between curtailable and interruptible service further differentiates in terms of the magnitude of the load reduction required.

The annual demand charges represent further differentiation that conforms with the analysis of capacity pricing in §11. Nine of the options impose the same demand charge for annual maximum demand ($2.85/kW) in association with a time-of-use schedule for energy charges. The firm-service tariffs A11 and E20 impose additional demand charges ($8.10/kW) for the peak-period peakload, but offer lower energy charges, as an incentive for load reduction in peak periods: these charges reflect the fact that in peak periods the customer's load contributes directly to the system's capacity requirements (the demand charge for the annual maximum is lower because capacity is a shared resource in nonpeak periods).[5] Finally, these peak-period peakload demand charges are substantially discounted or eliminated if the customer elects curtailable or interruptible service. Curtailable or interruptible service enables the utility to avoid serving the customer in times of tight power supplies, which in turn reduces capacity requirements.

In sum, PG&E's tariff structure reflects differentiation along several dimensions of quantity and quality simultaneously. The eleven tariffs shown in the table allow customers substantial choices in terms of load size and service reliability, and within nine of these tariffs the energy charges differentiate by time of use. It is, therefore, an example of a multidimensional tariff; moreover it includes capacity charges of the sort examined in §11.

The explicit differentiation in PG&E's tariffs reflects a new development in the power industry. As recently as October 1985, for instance, all of Florida Power and Light's fixed-rate and time-of-use nonresidential tariffs (except for demands below 20 kW) imposed the same demand charge ($6.50/kW) whereas energy charges were based only on the customer's power demand, as shown in Figure 2.2. All of FPL's curtailable tariffs allowed the same reduction ($1.70/kW) in the demand charge for the curtailable portion of the customer's load, defined by "customer will curtail demand by 200 kW or more upon request of utility from time to time."[6] More recent developments at FPL and elsewhere emphasize tariff designs that are explicitly differentiated along several dimensions.

An example is the interruptible service plan proposed by Georgia Power Company.[7] This plan provides an annual credit or rebate on the customer's demand charge. For each kilo-Watt of interruptible power (in excess of the customer's firm power level), this credit is proportional to a factor that varies on two dimensions. One dimension measures the number of interruptions allowed per year; thus, it is related inversely to the service reliability. The second dimension measures the "hours use of demand" for that kilo-Watt; thus, it is roughly proportional to the customer's load factor. For example, a kW eligible for only 30 hours of interruption

5. Differentiated demand charges of this sort can also be interpreted as invoking the principles of a Wright tariff to encourage load leveling.

6. Source: Casazza, Schultz & Associates, *Electric Rate Book*, 1988. Penalties were also assessed for noncompliance with curtailment requests.

7. Proposed Rates: Interruptible Service Rider, Schedule IS-1, Georgia Power Company, 1989, page 9.8.

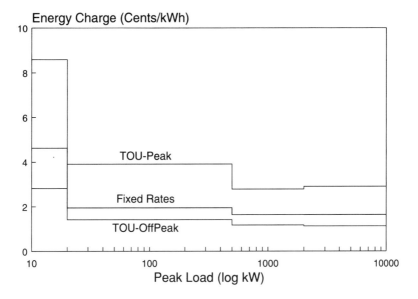

FIG. 2.2   FPL's fixed and time-of-use energy charges.

and used less than 200 hours per year earns a 23% credit on the demand charge, whereas at the other extreme a kW eligible for 240 hours of interruption and used more than 600 hours per year earns an 84% credit. The net effect is essentially a Wright tariff in which net demand charges decrease for more hours of interruption and/or more hours of usage. This is one version of the priority service tariffs addressed in §10.2.

2.4   MCI's and AT&T's telephone tariffs

The MCI Card tariff offered by the MCI Communications Corporation illustrates several of the complications involved in selecting the terms in which price schedules are quoted.[8]

An important complication in telephone tariffs is that marginal prices ($/minute) depend on the origin and destination, as well as the time of day and the service mode, according to detailed schedules filed with the U.S. Federal Communications Commission. There are many such combinations (MCI's tariff FCC #1 is over an inch thick) and therefore the major vendors of long distance service usually provide customers only with illustrations of applicable rates for a few examples. These illustrations convey the dependence of rates on the distance involved, and the differing rates for the three main time periods: day (peak), evenings, and nights and weekends (offpeak).

8. MCI Tariff FCC #1, as quoted in "MCI Card Savings," MCI Communications Corporation, February 1988.

Quantity discounts take two forms in the MCI tariffs. First, each call is charged according to a two-part tariff that in addition to the marginal charge per minute specifies a fixed charge per call ($0.55 for calls from touch-tone telephones). Second, a volume discount is offered depending on monthly billings of domestic daytime (and all international) calls: for a monthly bill between $50 and $100 this discount is 2%, and for bills over $100, it is 5%. Note that this discount applies to domestic calls only in peak periods, aggregated over different origin-destination pairs and different call durations by summing the dollar amounts of their charges. Further, the discount applies to the total dollar amount, rather than applying only to those charges exceeding a threshold. Presumably the simplicity of this tariff is designed to ensure compact presentation and easy interpretation by customers. In addition, it reflects the important feature that most customers place calls to so many destinations that more specific terms would be useless.

Other tariffs are also offered as options by the several interexchange carriers. For example, AT&T's 1990 basic tariff for interstate Measured Toll Service (MTS) uses nearly uniform prices differentiated by three times of day, eleven distance categories, and surcharges by the type of call (more for operator-assisted and person-to-person).[9] For a distance of 1000 miles, the day, evening, and night/weekend rates are $0.249, $0.1496, and $0.1300 per minute, respectively. But AT&T also offers several "Reach Out America" options. One such plan charges a monthly fee of $8.70 and provides one hour per month of free nighttime and weekend calls and lower marginal rates of $0.11 per minute thereafter, independent of distance, plus discounts on other calls depending on the time of day (10% day, 25% evening) or the destination (intrastate or international). The net effect of these two AT&T plans, the basic Measured Toll Service and the Reach Out America option, is a piecewise-linear tariff: customers obtain a quantity discount by subscribing for a Reach Out America plan.[10] For calls made only in evening or daytime hours and for a distance of 1000 miles, the Reach Out America plan is cheaper than Measured Toll Service if the number of hours per month exceeds four or six. MCI and Sprint offer similar options with slightly lower rates and smaller discounts, and Pacific Bell offers a similar Call Bonus plan for intrastate calls. In addition, in 1990 MCI offered an optional three-part tariff for daytime calls: for a monthly fee of $12 a customer receives one hour of free calls with additional usage billed at $0.20 per minute.

AT&T offers commercial customers an explicit piecewise-linear tariff for wide-area service (WATS). For daytime calls, the 1990 PRO WATS tariff provides discounts of 8% for monthly billings over $200 and 21% for billings over $2000.

---

9. AT&T's FCC tariffs #1–#12 are summarized in tables 7.5, 8.5, 9.1–9.4 in Mitchell and Vogelsang (1991).

10. Mitchell and Vogelsang (1991, p.148) report that the first year (1984–85) of the Reach Out America plan, "increased the mean minutes of night/weekend calling by 41.9%. The overall price elasticity of the group of [optional calling plan] subscribers is of the order of −2 or higher, considerably larger than AT&T estimates for all residential subscribers."

For larger customers with their own trunk lines, the Megacom WATS tariff charges $50 per month and provides discounts of 5% for billings over $7500 per month, and 10% for billings over $30,000 per month. These discounts apply to daytime rates at 1000 miles that, after the initial connection charge, are $0.173 per minute (in 6 second increments), compared to $0.249, $0.254, and $0.239 for MTS, PRO WATS, and High-Volume WATS. Multipart tariffs of this sort are addressed in §6.4.

The book by Mitchell and Vogelsang (1991) provides an excellent comprehensive description of the role of nonlinear pricing in the design of telephone tariffs, including many specific aspects not addressed here.[11]

2.5   Federal Express' mail rates

Companies offering express mail and facsimile transmission services use nonlinear pricing along several dimensions, including business volume, item size, and several dimensions of quality, such as speed and priority of delivery. In this section we describe the "discount" price schedule offered by Federal Express Corporation to high-volume customers for its Priority 1/Courier-Pak overnight delivery service, and for its Standard Air delivery service.

Table 2.2 shows the marginal prices per pound for these two services.[12] When the tariffs for these two services are graphed they show a somewhat complicated pattern. However, they show a nearly consistent pattern when graphed on a logarithmic scale, as shown in Figure 2.3. On a logarithmic scale the Courier-Pak schedule is revealed to consist essentially of the minimum of three logarithmically-linear tariffs. The first segment corresponds to the minimum charge of $9.00, the second to the interval between 1 and 50 pounds, and the third to the interval above 50 pounds. Similarly, the Standard Air schedule has two segments, the first corresponding to the minimum charge of $6 and the second to a logarithmically-linear schedule for items over 5 pounds. Note that for heavy items the difference between the two schedules consists of a fixed percentage.

2.6   Delta Airlines' frequent flier rebates

Soon after deregulation of the U.S. airline industry, "frequent flier" plans became a central part of the airlines' marketing strategies. These plans offer rebates, in

11. This area is changing rapidly. For example, on 1 August 1991 the Federal Communications Commission adopted new rules "loosening restrictions that have made it difficult for [AT&T] to offer volume discounts ... for large corporate customers"; however, restrictions remain on local carriers wanting to reduce "charges for high-volume customers such as AT&T." (*San Francisco Chronicle*, 2 August 1991, page B1.)

12. Source: "U.S. Domestic Express Rates–Sample Only," Federal Express Corporation, 1989. The per-package rates described are for Priority 1/Courier-Pak Discount Rates, providing next-day delivery, and for Standard Air Discount Rates. According to this schedule, the discount is the greater of $11.50 and 40% for Priority 1/Courier-Pak, and for Standard Air it is $10 up to 150 Lbs. or 14% for larger items. Not shown in the table is a maximum charge of $86 for 100 Lbs. with Standard Air service, which implies a zero marginal price for pounds 96–100.

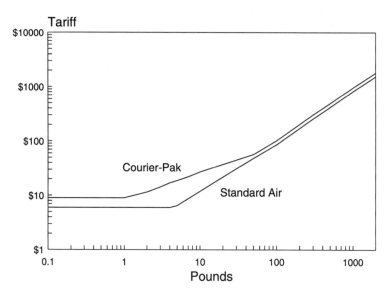

FIG. 2.3   Federal Express' discount tariffs.

the form of free tickets, depending on the number of miles accumulated by the customer. The rebates vary nonlinearly with mileage, offering rebates that increase more than proportionately with the customer's accumulated mileage. Because they impose costs on customers who might otherwise divide their travel among several airlines, frequent flier plans encourage a customer to use fewer airlines; that is, they impose switching costs. Incidentally, the rebates accrue directly to the traveler even if the fare is paid by an employer, and therefore they serve as an inducement to attract business travelers. The plans enable the airlines to monitor the frequency and length of each customer's trips; consequently, further perquisites are offered to

Table 2.2 Federal Express Discount Rates

q-th Pound	Priority 1/Courier-Pak ($/lb.)	Standard Air ($/lb.)
1	9.00	6.00
2	2.50	0.00
3–4	2.75	0.00
5	1.75	0.50
6–10	1.65	1.00
11–50	0.75	1.00
51–100	0.90	0.85
101–300	1.02	0.86
301–500	0.99	0.84
501–1,000	0.96	0.82
1,000+	0.90	0.77

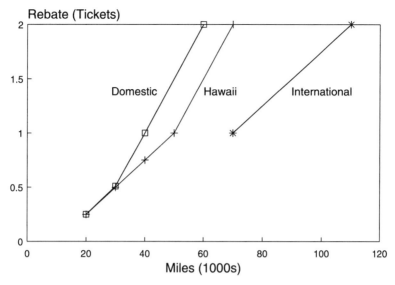

FIG. 2.4   Delta Airlines' frequent-flier rebates.

frequent business travelers who accumulate sufficient mileage within a specified period such as a year, especially on otherwise undiscounted fares.

Figure 2.4 depicts the rebates offered by Delta Airlines.[13] This figure displays only the mileage that is deducted for coach or economy class tickets; a fractional ticket, such as 0.25, indicates that the customer receives a 25% discount on the purchase of the ticket for the mileage specified. The rebate tickets allow any do-mestic U.S. origin and any destination (round trip or one way) served by the airline within one of the three regions (Domestic, Hawaii, Japan, or Europe) specified.

Except for the one kink at 30,000 miles, Delta's domestic rebate schedule is essentially a two-part tariff (with a 20,000 mile fixed fee). This aspect is explicit in other cases. For instance, United Airlines' Special Awards rebates in Winter 1991 required 8, 14, or 20 flight segments for 1, 2, or 3 domestic tickets, equivalent to a fixed fee of 2 segments and a marginal price of 6 segments for each ticket; Continental's rebates were identical except that the marginal price of a fourth ticket was 4 segments.

The airlines also offer discounts on several other dimensions. Among the most important are advance-purchase discounts, which play an important role in seg-menting the market between business travelers and others. For example, Delta's regular daytime midweek roundtrip coach fare between San Francisco and Atlanta in May 1989 was $1,104, or $884 at night, but with 3, 7, or 14 days advance pur-chase it was $940, $398, or $338. The last two fares were $40 higher on weekends, plus a further premium on popular flights both midweek and weekends. Similarly,

13. Source: "Frequent Flyer Program," Delta Airlines, Inc., 1989.

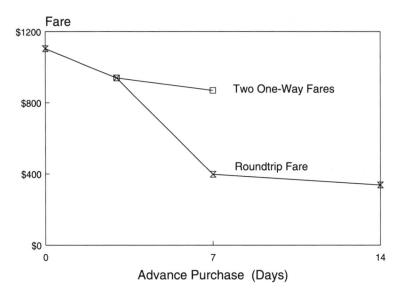

FIG. 2.5   Delta Airlines' advance purchase fares.

one-way unrestricted coach fares were $552, $470, and $435 with 0, 3, and 7 days advance purchase. These fares are displayed in Figure 2.5 for a roundtrip midweek.

A second dimension is the demand for the flight, reflecting a kind of spot pricing or peakload pricing. Delta's fares described above allowed for peak-demand premia by offering a menu of fares. The 14-day advance-purchase daytime midweek roundtrip coach fare of $338, for example, was one of three fares for otherwise identical service at $338, $358, and $398, each with a quota of seats available: each customer was assigned to the lowest-priced unfilled fare class still available.

A third dimension is the percentage of the fare that is refundable if the trip is postponed or canceled after the fare has been paid. Delta's fares described above with 0, 7, and 14 days advance purchase were 100%, 75%, and 0% refundable; consequently, some customers might choose the $398 fare, even if the purchase is made 14 days in advance, in order to obtain the higher percentage of refundability.

2.7   Summary

The illustrations in this chapter motivate the topics studied in this book. Readers familiar with pricing policies in the several industries described above may find these illustrations redundant because unraveling the intricate complexities of rate design is a constant challenge. For others, the pervasive role of nonlinear pricing may be a surprise since as a customer one is often unaware of the full menu of options involved when subscribing to power, telephone, express mail, and airline flights—as well as many other services such as rentals (equipment, vehicles, space, rooms) and banking and financial services—and products such as publications and capital equipment (computers, copiers). It is easy to focus on the option that meets one's immediate need and to take little account of the overall design. One way to appreciate the implicit role of nonlinear pricing in the design of prices for increments in performance (speed, precision, durability) for a series of items in a product line is to examine a catalogue from an equipment manufacturer or a general supplier such as Sears. Similarly, quantity discounts and time-of-use differentiated rates are specified in your monthly bills from utilities, in the fares and frequent-flier rebates offered by airlines (and more recently hotels and rental car companies), and in the implicit price schedule for viewing films in a theatre, on video, on cable television, or "free" on commercial television.

Some MBA students in my course on Pricing have been stymied initially about finding a topic for a term paper on nonlinear pricing, but when encouraged to draw on personal experience, every one has found an interesting topic. The range extends from pricing package sizes of grocery items to the terms for corporate mergers, and from contracts for original-equipment auto parts to membership fees for a flying club. My favorite is an application to pricing space, power, and launch priorities for a proposed commercial laboratory facility in earth orbit.

Space limitations prevent a longer list of illustrations than those provided here from the major regulated and recently deregulated industries. These were chosen because they fit the focus adopted in subsequent chapters. Parts I and II emphasize the advantages of nonlinear pricing as an efficient use of monopoly power to recover costs in regulated and other capital-intensive industries. Also, these illustrations display the varieties of multidimensional and multiproduct pricing addressed in Parts III and IV.

3

MODELS AND DATA SOURCES

The illustrations in §2 are drawn from several different industries but they share important features. In each case the price schedule is differentiated along one or more dimensions so that lower marginal and average prices are offered for larger quantities. These discounts stimulate demand and enhance efficiency, provided the net prices exceed marginal cost. For instance, EDF's lower marginal prices, and prices differentiated by service times and conditions, provide more accurate signals to customers about marginal costs of supply. Compared to a single price applicable to all units, profits increase; or in a regulated industry, the firm's revenue requirement can be met with greater net benefits for customers.

Some concepts that enable unified analyses of nonlinear pricing in these and other industries are developed in this chapter and the next. This chapter presents the basic tools used subsequently. We emphasize the description of customers' demand behaviors in terms of an appropriate aggregate measure of demands for successive increments in the quantity purchased, depending on the marginal prices charged. This measure, called the demand profile, provides the minimum disaggregated information about customer's demands. This is the information needed to design nonlinear tariffs for either profit maximization in unregulated industries or efficient recovery of revenue requirements in regulated industries.

Models of customers' demands can be formulated at various levels of aggregation, including levels corresponding to individuals and to more or less finely differentiated market segments. Models of individuals' demands can be based on projected benefits from enduses or on specified demand functions, and this same range of modeling options is applicable to analyses of more aggregated market segments. Empirical estimation of demand behaviors depends similarly on the choice of a level of aggregation. Reliable data on individual demands are rarely available, however. It is important as a practical matter, therefore, to adapt the analysis to the most aggregated data that still provide the requisite information for tariff design. In this and the remaining chapters of Part I the analysis is formulated in terms of this ideal level of aggregation of demand data that is appropriate for nonlinear pricing. Part II repeats this analysis at the fully disaggregated level of individual customers using explicit models of benefits or demand functions.

The advantages of nonlinear pricing stem ultimately from heterogeneity in the population of customers. For this reason, completely aggregated demand data are insufficient because they mask the relevant heterogeneity among customers. For instance, data about aggregate demand in the form of the total number of units sold at each price are insufficient because they cannot distinguish whether these quantities were bought by one or many customers; that is, they obscure the distribution of purchase sizes, which typically vary greatly among customers. Because the essential feature of nonlinear pricing is differentiation by size of purchase, on the other hand, one need not preserve information about other kinds of heterogeneity. It suffices to retain only data about the distribution of customers' purchase sizes at each price.

The *demand profile* introduced in this chapter provides data at the right level of aggregation. It does so via a convenient interpretation. Data is typically accumulated by observing customers' purchases in response to a specified price, and in this form the data specify directly the distribution of purchase sizes at each price. One can imagine a spreadsheet with each price assigned to a corresponding row and each purchase size assigned to a corresponding column. Then the data along each row records the distribution of purchase sizes observed at that price, namely the number of customers buying each successive incremental unit. The trick of interpretation is to realize that data in this format also provides down each column the demand function for this increment. That is, each column records the number of customers purchasing that increment at each of the prices indicated by the rows.

For nonlinear pricing, therefore, it suffices that demand data are disaggregated only to the extent of retaining information about customers' (aggregate) demands for successive increments in the size of purchase. It is usually practical to obtain demand data at this level of aggregation. Fortunately, data about customers' responses to uniform prices are sufficient: the firm need not have data about responses to nonlinear tariffs in order to examine the merits of nonlinear pricing. An important caveat is that the data must be sufficient to provide estimates of how demands will change as prices change. This is the binding constraint in practice whenever the firm's prior experience provides little information about demands at prices other than the current one, or other means of estimating demand elasticities.

Section 1 reviews the basic approach to modeling demand behavior that underlies both linear and nonlinear pricing. Two subsections are designated by an asterisk * indicating that they contain optional technical material. Section 2 describes the data requirements and estimation procedures for the demand models commonly used in tariff design. Section 3 mentions some of the welfare considerations affecting regulated firms. Section 4 lists several cautionary considerations that affect nonlinear pricing generally, as well as those that pertain to the restrictive assumptions invoked in this exposition. An optional Section 5 summarizes technical assumptions used in subsequent chapters.

Regarding mathematical notation

This and later chapters use notation from calculus. Various marginal measures are represented by derivatives. For instance, marginal cost is the rate at which the firm's total cost increases as the supply or output rate increases, and the marginal price is the rate at which the customer's total charge (according to the tariff) increases as the purchased quantity increases. Similarly, aggregates such as sums and averages are represented by integrals. The firm's profit contribution is the sum of the profit margins on the units sold, and customers' aggregate benefit is the sum of the differences between the buyer's valuation and the price charged.

Some readers may be deterred by this mathematical symbolism, but my experience has been that writing out the corresponding differences and summations is a greater deterrent because the formulas then appear awesomely long and complicated. Because this detracts from the main purpose of conveying the basic concepts of nonlinear pricing, a compromise has been adopted. The *notation* of the calculus is often used, but in Part I the results are not materially affected by this notation. Each marginal measure can be interpreted and evaluated as a ratio of discrete differences, and each integral can be interpreted and evaluated as a sum of discrete terms.

The reader can interpret each marginal measure as representing the increment obtained in the dependent variable if a small increment is made in the independent variable. For example, suppose $U(q, t)$ indicates the gross benefit obtained by a customer described by a parameter t (indicating the customer's "type") from a purchase of size q. Specifically, $U(q, t)$ is the customer's maximum willingness-to-pay in dollar terms for a purchase of size q. Then the marginal benefit $v(q, t)$ is defined as the (partial) derivative $\partial U(q, t)/\partial q$ as the quantity q varies, leaving the customer's type parameter t fixed. This marginal benefit is interpreted as the customer's willingness-to-pay for the q-th unit increment in the purchase size. For discrete increments, it is actually calculated as the ratio of the increment in the benefit to the increment in the purchase size. Similarly, a tariff that charges $P(q)$ for q units has a marginal price schedule $p(q)$ obtained as the derivative $dP(q)/dq$ or $P'(q)$ of the tariff. The price schedule might be offered directly by the firm, or it might be inferred from the tariff based on a calculation of the incremental charge per incremental unit in the purchase size.

Notes are added at several places in this chapter to indicate the discrete interpretations of various notations from calculus. These interpretations are important substantively because in practice nonlinear tariffs are usually implemented as multipart tariffs or block-declining price schedules with discrete price changes at discrete intervals of the quantity purchased. Multipart tariffs are addressed informally in Part I and then exact characterizations are derived in Part II.

3.1 Descriptions of demand behavior

The several levels of aggregation at which demand data can be analyzed are familiar from the process of setting uniform prices. Typically these include aggregation at the level of the entire market, segments of the market, and individual customers or types of customers. Each level of aggregation is useful for different purposes. For a profit-maximizing firm setting a uniform price, it may be sufficient to use aggregated market data to estimate the aggregate demand function—or perhaps only the price elasticity of this demand function to examine whether a price change would be profitable. However, analysis of various market segments or types of customers may reveal more information relevant to product differentiation. For regulated firms and public enterprises this finer information is necessary to assess the distribution of benefits among customers, which is a matter of special concern to regulatory agencies.

These same levels of data analysis are also useful for nonlinear pricing. Moreover, by recording and processing the data appropriately, essentially all the information required to design a nonlinear tariff can be obtained. Although we defer the description of how to construct an optimal nonlinear tariff to §4, it is possible to specify the informational requirements on the basis of general considerations that are applicable whether or not tariff design aims to optimize.

The demand function

When a uniform price is used, the major purpose of data analysis is ultimately to predict the total quantity $\bar{D}(p)$ that would be sold at each price p.[1] That is, $\bar{D}(p)$ is the demand function ordinarily used in applications of economic theory to rate design. For many purposes, moreover, it is sufficient to obtain an estimate of the price elasticity of demand, which indicates the percentage reduction in demand that would ensue in response to a one percent increase in the price. Interpreting the demand function as a differentiable function of the price, this elasticity is given by the formula

$$\bar{\eta}(p) = -\frac{p}{\bar{D}(p)} \frac{d\bar{D}}{dp}(p)$$

For a discrete price change dp, the numerator on the right is the change in total demand: $d\bar{D}(p) \equiv \bar{D}(p + dp) - \bar{D}(p)$. This formula is sometimes written in the

---

1. This notation reflects a standard convention. A bar over a demand function represents the total quantity sold in response to a uniform price, or it can be interpreted as the average demand per potential customer. Later we use $D(p, t)$ to represent the demand function for an individual customer of type t, and $N(p, q)$ to present the *number* of customers purchasing at least q units in response to the uniform price p. Thus, demand functions indicated by a symbol D are measured in terms of units of the product sold, whereas the demand profile indicated by a symbol N is measured in terms of the number or fraction of customers purchasing an incremental unit.

form

$$\bar{\eta}(p) = -\frac{d\bar{D}(p)/\bar{D}(p)}{dp/p}$$

to convey the fact that it represents the ratio of percentage changes.

Estimating a demand elasticity is never trivial. Even if actual demand $\bar{D}(p)$ in response to the price p is directly observed (and stable over time amidst many vicissitudes), an estimate of the demand elasticity requires that responses to other prices must be observed too. A firm may have tried other prices and therefore has such data, but more commonly the task of estimating responses to other prices requires the techniques of marketing research to obtain data from surveys or panel studies, or of benefit-cost studies to estimate customers' willingness-to-pay based on analyses of end uses. The output of a demand analysis, such as the demand elasticity, is simple compared to the inputs mustered to obtain a reliable estimate.[2]

The demand profile

Nonlinear pricing requires the same kind of data, but in a partially disaggregated form. Recall that a nonlinear price schedule charges a possibly different price for each increment in the customer's purchase size. The required prediction is therefore, for each increment (say the q-th unit) the demand for that increment at its marginal price $p(q)$. This demand is usually measured, not in terms of units of the product, but rather in terms of the *number* of customers purchasing this increment. That is, unlike an ordinary uniform-price demand function $\bar{D}(p)$ that measures the number of units sold at the uniform price p, we measure the number or fraction $N(p, q)$ of customers purchasing the q-th unit at the marginal price p. This measurement convention is especially useful when considering increments in the purchase size that are not units of size 1: if an increment includes δ units, then the *demand* for that increment is $N(p, q)\delta$.

Similarly, the price elasticity of demand for the q-th increment at the marginal price p is

$$\eta(p, q) \equiv -\frac{p}{N}\frac{\partial N}{\partial p}.$$

In this definition, $\partial N/\partial p$ indicates the (partial) derivative of N as the price is changed without changing the unit q to which that marginal price applies. Both N and $\partial N/\partial p$ are evaluated at (p, q). In discrete terms, this price elasticity of the demand profile is just the percentage change in demand for the q-th unit divided

2. Mitchell and Vogelsang (1991) describe AT&T's repeated underestimates during the 1980s of the numbers of customers who would elect its "Reach Out America" optional calling plans. For a thorough (though now dated) survey of the methodology and several empirical studies that estimate the price elasticity of aggregate demand for electricity, see Taylor (1975). Koenker and Sibley (1979) calibrate demand estimates for their study of nonlinear pricing of electricity against two of the elasticity estimates reported in Taylor's survey. For recent studies of demands for telecommunication services, see De Fontenay, Shugard, and Sibley (1990).

by the percentage change in its price: thus $\partial N \equiv N(p + \partial p, q) - N(p, q)$ for a price change ∂p.

The bivariate function $N(p, q)$ is called the *demand profile*. It has a central role in tariff design. One reason is that the demand profile includes more information than the demand function does. To see this, observe that the total demand in response to a uniform price p is

$$\bar{D}(p) = N(p, \delta)\delta + N(p, 2\delta)\delta + \cdots,$$

$$= \sum_{k=1}^{\infty} N(p, k\delta)\delta,$$

where δ is again the size of an increment and the index k indicates the k-th increment purchased. If quantities are finely divisible then we can interpret the increment δ as infinitesimally small even though the quantity $q = k\delta$ is not. In this case total demand is represented as the integral

$$\bar{D}(p) = \int_0^{\infty} N(p, q)\, dq .$$

This formula represents a sum over all values of the quantity q of the number $N(p, q)$ purchasing the (infinitesimally) small increment at q that is of size $dq \equiv \delta$.

These formulas express the fact that total demand is the sum of the numbers sold of first units, second units, et cetera. Thus, from the demand profile one can always reconstruct the demand function for a uniform price. Even with a nonuniform price schedule $p(q)$ the same sort of formula is true: total demand is

$$\sum_{k=1}^{\infty} N(p(k\delta), k\delta)\delta \qquad \text{or} \qquad \int_0^{\infty} N(p(q), q)\, dq .$$

The revenue is similarly

$$\sum_{k=1}^{\infty} N(p(k\delta), k\delta) \cdot p(k\delta)\delta \qquad \text{or} \qquad \int_0^{\infty} N(p(q), q)p(q)\, dq .$$

The integral on the right represents the aggregate of the charges $p(q)dq$ collected from the number $N(p(q), q)$ of customers purchasing the increment of size dq at the price $p(q)$ per unit for each quantity q.

Interpretations of the demand profile

We use two interpretations of the demand profile repeatedly. Both derive from a basic feature: nonlinear pricing can be construed as pricing a product line comprising the incremental units of the product. Thus, the first, second, ..., units of the generic product are treated as separate products priced separately. The fact that each unit's purchase requires buying its predecessors in the sequence is implicit; for example, a second unit requires prior or simultaneous purchase of a first unit.

The first interpretation of the demand profile $N(p, q)$ is that it describes the distribution of purchase sizes in response to each uniform price p. That is, if p is fixed and q is increased then a graph of $N(p, q)$ depicts the declining number of customers purchasing each successive q-th unit. This is the same as the number of customers purchasing at least q units, so for each fixed price p the demand profile $N(p, q)$ is the right-cumulative distribution function of the customers' purchase sizes. In summary:

- *For each price p the demand profile specifies the number or fraction $N(p, q)$ of customers purchasing at least q units.*

Because this number is observable, the demand profile can be measured directly from demand data. This requires, of course, that information about customers' purchase sizes is accumulated and recorded. It is in this sense that the demand profile is a disaggregated version of the demand function: the demand data is disaggregated according to size of purchase.

Figure 3.1 shows how the distribution of purchase sizes is predicted from ordinary models of customers' benefits in which each customer is described by a parameter t indicating his type. Assuming a particular benefit function $U(q, t)$ and tariff $P(q)$, the diagram plots a customer's net benefit from each purchase size $q = 0, \ldots, 4$ as a function of the type parameter t. For simplicity, this function is assumed to be linear and to increase as the type parameter increases. As q increases, a customer's gross benefit increases. But for each fixed type t there comes a point where the next increment in the gross benefit is less than the increment in the tariff, namely the marginal price for the next unit, whereupon he ceases to purchase additional increments. The diagram therefore shows for each type t the net benefit corresponding to the *optimal* purchase size, which is the largest quantity for which the marginal benefit of the last unit purchased exceeds the marginal price charged. Such a model predicts that the customers purchasing exactly q units are those with type parameters between t_{q-1} and t_q as shown in the figure. Those purchasing the q-th increment are all those purchasing at least q units, namely those described by type parameters exceeding t_{q-1}. Conversely, the firm can use the observed distribution of purchase sizes to estimate the distribution of types in the population: again, the number actually purchasing at least q units is the estimated number with type parameters exceeding t_{q-1}.

The second interpretation of the demand profile is that it describes the distribution of customers' willingness to pay. If we fix q and increase the marginal price p, then the demand profile measures the declining number of customers

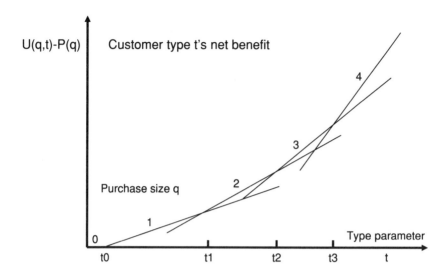

FIG. 3.1 Purchase sizes q selected by customers of different types t. Customers with larger type parameters obtain their maximum benefits from larger purchases.

willing to pay this price for the q-th increment. Thus:

● *The demand profile specifies for each q-th unit the number or fraction $N(p, q)$ of customers willing to pay the price p for that unit.*

This interpretation is useful in applications based on parameterized models of customers' behavior. For instance, suppose market segments, volume bands, or customer types are indicated by a parameter t, and a benefit-cost analysis indicates that type t obtains the dollar benefit $U(q, t)$ from purchasing q units, and therefore a marginal benefit $v(q, t) \equiv \partial U(q, t)/\partial q$ from the q-th unit. Then the demand profile $N(p, q)$ measures the estimated number of customers whose types t are such that $v(q, t) \geq p$, indicating that they are willing to pay at least p for the q-th unit.

The two interpretations of the demand profile are represented schematically in Figure 3.2. The number of customers purchasing at least q^* units at the price p^*, and the number willing to pay at least p^* for the q^*-th unit, are the same because they are both measured as the number of customers whose demand functions intersect the shaded region of price-quantity pairs $(p, q) \geq (p^*, q^*)$. Thus, $N(p^*, q^*)$ is the number of customers with types $t \geq t^*$, where t^* is the type that is indifferent along both boundaries of the shaded region. In particular, the demand function of type t^* passes through the point (p^*, q^*).

In summary, the demand profile can be interpreted as the distribution of purchase

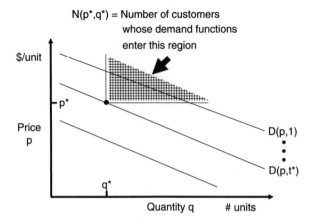

FIG. 3.2 Measurement of the demand profile from customers' demand functions. At (p^*, q^*) the demand profile measures the number of customers purchasing more than q^* at price p^*, or purchasing q^* at prices exceeding p^*.

sizes q for each uniform price p, say[3]

$$N(p, q) = \#\{t \mid D(p, t) \geq q\} \;,$$

where $D(p, t)$ is the demand function of customers of type t. Or, it can be measured as the distribution of marginal valuations for each unit q, say

$$N(p, q) = \#\{t \mid v(q, t) \geq p\} \;.$$

These two interpretations are used in different ways. The first is most useful for analysis of demand data; the second, for applications of benefit-cost models. In addition, for analyses of welfare effects, the second allows one to infer the distribution of customers' net benefits.

   The following two subsections present more technical renditions of the demand profile that can be skipped.

The implicit type model *

To simplify exposition, later chapters in Parts I and II focus on models in which the heterogeneity among customers is described by a single type parameter that varies in the population—although §8.4 demonstrates that this restriction is immaterial for most practical purposes. We can anticipate that result here by reconsidering the basic meaning of a type parameter.

   Type parameters are never observed directly; moreover, they have no fundamental units of measurement outside a particular parameterization of customers'

3. The notation # indicates the number of customers satisfying the stated condition, not the number of types per se. The two usages are equivalent if the number of customers per type is constant across types.

benefit or demand functions: any monotone transformation of a type parameter will again serve the same practical purposes. Further, their ultimate role is only to predict the customer's purchase size, which is a one-dimensional quantity. Thus, there is a fundamental sense in which one can expect that a single type parameter should suffice for practical purposes.[4]

This conjecture can be made more precise as follows. Suppose the demand profile is measured in terms of fractions of the population rather than absolute numbers of customers. We can define an implicit type parameter by the property that a customer of type t is one who purchases q if the price is p provided p, q and t are related by the equality $t = 1 - N(p, q)$. If we further assume that these types are uniformly distributed in the population, then we obtain a model that accounts exactly for the observable demand behavior.[5] Thus, the exposition in §6 concentrates initially on the case of one-dimensional type parameters because this is largely sufficient for practical analysis of single-product pricing problems.

More general versions of the demand profile *

Use of the demand profile $N(p, q)$ described above invokes several implicit assumptions. In this subsection we clarify what these assumptions are by describing the general formulation and how the demand profile is derived as a special case.

Our aim in a general formulation is to specify the demand for q-th increments induced by a tariff P. A customer of type t prefers to purchase a q-th increment if his preferred purchase includes q or more increments. This says that there exists some purchase $x \geq q$ such that the net benefit from x exceeds the net benefit from any purchase $y < q$. In mathematical notation, therefore, the demand for q-th increments is[6]

$$\mathcal{N}(P, q) \equiv \#\{t \mid (\exists\, x \geq q)(\forall\, y \not\geq q)\, U(x, t) - P(x) \geq U(y, t) - P(y)\} \ .$$

In principle, this demand depends on the entire tariff schedule P. For most of the applications we address, however, the only relevant values of x and y are $x = q$ and $y = q - \delta$, where δ is the size of an increment. That is, to know whether type t purchases the q-th increment it is sufficient to know whether the q-th increment provides an incremental benefit that exceeds its price. This defines the special form of the demand profile for increments of size δ:

$$N(p(q, \delta), q; \delta) \equiv \#\{t \mid [U(q, t) - U(q - \delta, t)]/\delta \geq p(q, \delta)\} \ ,$$

4. This applies only to tariffs for single products. With multiple products, multiple type parameters are useful for realistic description of customers' demand behaviors. Typically one wants at least as many type parameters as there are quantity and quality dimensions to a customer's bundle of purchases.

5. The demand function for each implicit type can be inferred as the solution of a differential equation derived from the definitions above.

6. Read $\exists$ as "there exists ... such that" and $\forall$ as "for all."

where $p(q, \delta) \equiv [P(q) - P(q - \delta)]/\delta$ is the marginal price per unit of the q-th increment of size δ. The basic demand profile defined previously is just the special case in which increments are arbitrarily small:

$$N(p(q), q) \equiv \lim_{\delta \to 0} N(p(q, \delta), q; \delta), \qquad \text{where} \qquad p(q) \equiv \lim_{\delta \to 0} p(q, \delta).$$

For this demand profile to be an accurate prediction of customers' demand behaviors, it is sufficient that the price schedule and customers' demand functions are nonincreasing, and that the price schedule intersects each demand function just once, from below. This assures that a customer's marginal benefit from an incremental purchase is positive for purchases less than the optimal purchase, and negative for purchases exceeding the optimal purchase; thus, buying the q-th increment is beneficial if and only if q is less than the optimal purchase. Assuring that this property is true is therefore an auxiliary requirement that must be imposed on the design of the optimal price schedule. To enforce this requirement, later chapters either impose assumptions sufficient to ensure that it holds automatically, or specify remedies that constrain the price schedule sufficiently that it becomes true.

Other versions of the demand profile are used for special purposes. For instance, suppose that the tariff imposes a minimal charge P_* that provides a minimal purchase q_*. The number of customers willing to pay this minimal charge is

$$N_*(P_*, q_*) \equiv N(P_*/q_*, q_*; q_*),$$

where in this case the relevant increment is $\delta = q_*$ and the average price per unit of the minimal purchase is P_*/q_*.

A more general *master profile* is used occasionally to take account of both the total tariff and the marginal price schedule:

$$M(P(q), p(q, \delta), q; \delta) \equiv \#\{t \mid U(q, t) \geq P(q) \ \& $$
$$[U(q, t) - U(q - \delta, t)]/\delta \geq p(q, \delta)\},$$

and $M(P, p, q) \equiv \lim_{\delta \to 0} M(P, p, q; \delta)$. For instance, the demand for a minimal purchase (as above) is

$$N_*(P_*, q_*) \equiv M(P_*, 0, q_*; q_*).$$

Or, if a two-part tariff $P(q) = P_o + pq$ is used then the demand for a q-th increment is

$$N_o(P_o, p, q) \equiv M(P_o + pq, p, q),$$

of which a special case is the basic demand profile $N(p, q) \equiv N_o(0, p, q)$ as originally defined.

Other kinds of demand profiles adapted to various special purposes can be constructed. In each case, the demand profile summarizes the demand for an increment (of some positive size δ, or the limiting case as $\delta \to 0$) based on assumptions about the relevant values of x and y in the general definition that are (or for simplicity, are assumed to be) relevant to the problem addressed. For the main topics addressed here, it suffices to consider only the basic demand profile $N(p, q)$ as originally defined: the next section describes how it is estimated from demand data.[7]

Regarding notation: to ease exposition we do not distinguish between the demand profiles $N(p, q; \delta)$ and $N(p, q)$ when the size of the increment δ is presumably small or is obvious from the context.

3.2   Estimation of the demand profile

The demand profile is comparatively easy to estimate when the firm has ample demand data obtained from a variety of prices. We first describe how this can be done using the interpretation that the demand profile represents the distribution of purchase sizes at each uniform price. When the firm has not previously used other prices than the current one, however, estimation of the demand profile or its price elasticity is usually based on a parameterized model of customers' benefits. Consequently, we also present a second procedure that relies on the interpretation that the demand profile represents the distribution of customers' marginal valuations of incremental units.

Direct measurement of the demand profile

This first approach supposes that the firm has used several uniform prices in the past. Moreover, the firm has had the foresight to record for each price the distribution of customers' purchase sizes over a standard billing period. For instance, during the 1980s most long-distance telephone rates declined steadily (in both real and nominal terms), producing thereby a wealth of data about customers' usage in response to different rate levels—as well as some novel forms of nonlinear tariffs.[8] Typically this data is disaggregated by customer class (commercial, residential), location (urban, rural), and product (regular MTS service, WATS lines). In addition, most firms are able to record a rich array of additional data that can aid demand estimation, such as line-of-business data for commercial customers and socio-demographic data for households.

Represent the several prices (or price levels, in real terms) that have been charged by the increasing sequence p_j, where j is an index that distinguishes the different

---

7. The definitions of the various demand profiles can be extended straightforwardly to encompass several products; cf. §12.1 and §14.1. In this case, $x \geq q$ in the definition of $\mathcal{N}$ means $x_i \geq q_i$ for each product i represented in the bundle $q = (q_1, \ldots, q_n)$ of quantities of the products.

8. For illustrations of the construction of telephone customers' usage distributions see Pavarini (1979), and Heyman, Lazorchak, Sibley, and Taylor (1987).

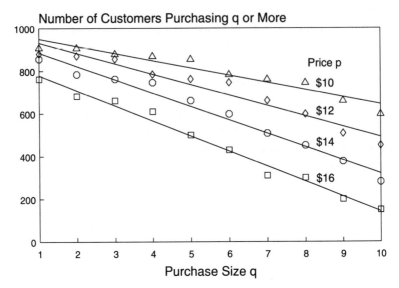

FIG. 3.3 Estimation of the demand profile from the distribution of purchase sizes. The four prices yield different distributions of purchase sizes. In the figure, estimates of these distributions are obtained by linear approximations.

prices; for example, cents per minute per mile in the case of a telephone company. Similarly, represent the possible purchase sizes by an increasing sequence q_k, where k is an index that distinguishes several volume bands of total usage per billing period; for example, minute-miles per month of long distance calls, in the case of a telephone company. Corresponding to each price p_j the data provides a measure n_{jk} of the number or fraction of *potential* customers whose purchase size was in volume band k when the price was p_j. The direct estimate of the demand profile is then

$$N(p_j, q_k) = \sum_{\ell \geq k} n_{j\ell} \,,$$

at these prices and quantities. That is, if the data in the array (n_{jk}) are represented as a spreadsheet with rows indexed by prices and columns indexed by volume bands, then the demand profile is the new array obtained by replacing each element by the sum of the elements further along the same row.

Usually, however, this estimate is insufficient because it does not cover all the possible prices and quantities that might be relevant for rate design. A variety of methods are available to obtain a smooth estimate of the demand profile. For example, a so-called spline curve can be fitted to the direct empirical estimates (Press et al. (1986), §3); or the empirical estimates can be construed as data for use in a regression equation whose parameters are then estimated by the usual statistical techniques of regression analysis. If a regression model is used, then for each price p_j an estimate is made of $N(p_j, q)$ construed as a function of the purchase size q; or the regression can be applied to a bivariate function of both the price and the quantity. A hypothetical example is shown in Figure 3.3 using a linear function at each price. For each price $p = \$10, \dots, \$16$ the data points represent the distribution of customers' purchases. The regression lines are chosen to minimize the sum of squared errors.

In subsequent examples we describe some of the functions that are commonly estimated to obtain this sort of smooth approximation of the demand profile. Even so, it is a good practice to initiate, and later to confirm, rate studies with analyses based on the direct empirical estimates; only later might one examine refinements based on smoothed estimates of the demand profile.

Another useful step is to compare the two estimates of the demand profile based on its two interpretations. The second interpretation conforms exactly to the first if the alternative direct estimate

$$N(p_j, q_k) = \sum_{h \geq j} n_{hk}$$

closely approximates the first direct estimate. Discrepancies between these two estimates might plausibly be resolved in favor of the first, however. The reason is that the second relies on the presumption that customers' behaviors maximize their net benefits, whereas the first does not invoke this assumption as strongly and is therefore relatively immune to idiosyncratic behavior by customers.

Indirect measurement of the demand profile

When the extent of price variation has been small, a firm must rely on an indirect approximation of the demand profile derived from estimation of customers' demand functions or benefit functions. Usually this is done by hypothesizing that each customer (within a relatively homogenous class, such as residential customers) is described sufficiently by a list t of type parameters. These parameters define a measure $U(q, t)$ of the customer's benefit, which is usually specified as an explicit function of the quantity q in which the parameters in the list t enter as coefficients. For instance, a very simple model supposes that the function U is quadratic of the form

$$U(q, t) = t_1 q - \tfrac{1}{2} t_2 q^2,$$

using the two type parameters $t = (t_1, t_2)$. From such a model one can derive the marginal benefit function $v(q, t)$ of type t. And by inverting the relation $p = v(q, t)$ to solve for q, this can be converted to the predicted demand function $D(p, t)$ of type t in response to the uniform price p. For the example above, this yields

$$v(q, t) = t_1 - t_2 q \quad \text{and} \quad D(p, t) = \frac{1}{t_2}[t_1 - p],$$

both of which are linear (in q or p).

Converting this model into an estimate of the demand profile requires an auxiliary datum, which is the distribution of types in the population of potential customers. This estimate is usually specified in the form of a density function $f(t)$, or in a discrete version, as the proportion of each type t in the population. An equivalent specification is a distribution function $F(t)$ indicating the number or fraction of potential customers with type parameters not exceeding t. The estimate of the demand profile is then obtained as the sum or integral[9]

$$N(p, q) = \int_{T(p,q)} f(t) \, dt , \qquad \text{or} \qquad N(p, q) = \int_{T(p,q)} dF(t) ,$$

where $T(p, q)$ is the set of types t for which $v(q, t) \geq p$ or $D(p, t) \geq q$. For example, for the quadratic model above,

$$T(p, q) = \{t \mid t_1 - t_2 q \geq p\} ,$$

which comprises all the types (t_1, t_2) on one side of the line for which $t_1 - t_2 q = p$. This line represents those customers who are indifferent about purchasing the q-th increment at the price p.

Given a model of customers' benefits specified in terms of their type parameters, the remaining empirical problem is to estimate the distribution of types in the population of potential customers. This is done in two steps. The first is to specify a form of the distribution function $F(t; \beta)$ that depends on a list β of parameters. These parameters appear as coefficients in an explicit model of the type distribution, and similarly the demand profile $N(p, q; \beta)$ depends on these coefficients. The second step is to estimate the coefficients using data about the distribution of purchase sizes in response to various prices that have been offered.

Example 3.1: To illustrate the first step, suppose the distribution function is supposed to be a bivariate Normal distribution with parameters (μ, σ, ρ) representing the means, variances, and correlation of the type parameters $t = (t_1, t_2)$ in the population. Then, for the quadratic model above, $N(p, q; \beta)$ is the probability $\bar{\Phi}(x)$ that a standard Normal random variable (one with mean 0 and variance 1) exceeds the number x defined as

$$x \equiv [p - (\mu_1 - \mu_2 q)] / \Delta(q; \sigma, \rho) ,$$

$$\text{where} \quad \Delta(q; \sigma, \rho) \equiv \sqrt{\sigma_1^2 - 2\rho\sigma_1\sigma_2 q + \sigma_2^2 q^2} ,$$

---

9. The sum or integral on the right is interpreted as adding up all the increments in $F(t)$ as t varies. This is a general way of saying that one adds up the numbers (densities or frequencies) of customers at all the types in the set $T(p, q)$.

in which σ_i^2 is the variance of t_i, and ρ is the correlation between t_1 and t_2. The distributional coefficients are therefore the five parameters $\beta \equiv (\mu_1, \mu_2, \sigma_1^2, \sigma_2^2, \rho)$ of the type distribution.

The second step is the statistical task of estimating these parameters from observed distributions of purchase sizes for various prices. From the first step, the predicted relationship among the number N of customers purchasing the q-th increment at the price p is $y = [p + \mu_2 q - \mu_1]/\Delta(q; \sigma, \rho)$ where $y \equiv \bar{\Phi}^{-1}(N)$. The data consists of observations of triplets $(y; p, q)$ and the aim is to find the estimate of the parameters in the list β that provides the best fit of the data to the predicted relationship. Any of the variety of standard procedures for statistical estimation can be used for this task. $\diamond$

As in the example, a nonlinear regression model is often used to estimate the parameters of the type distribution. In such a model the independent variables are the prices p_j and the volume bands q_k, and the dependent variable is $N(p, q; \beta)$, for which the observed data points are the numbers $(\sum_{\ell \geq k} n_{j\ell})$ of customers purchasing at least q_k at the price p_j. An ordinary least-squares estimate of β, for instance, chooses the estimate $\hat{\beta}$ that minimizes the sum of squared deviations from the predicted relationship:

$$\sum_j \sum_k \left[N(p_j, q_k; \hat{\beta}) - \sum_{\ell \geq k} n_{j\ell} \right]^2$$

Statistical software programs to calculate such estimates are widely available. Other approaches to this sort of estimation include maximum likelihood estimation and probit and logit techniques, as well as a variety of others included in standard statistical software.[10] The estimation is considerably simplified if the demand function has a single type parameter that specifies the (constant) price elasticity; in this case one needs only to estimate the parameters of the distribution of this elasticity in the population.

A familiar part of standard statistical methodology controls for so-called nuisance parameters; thus, additional independent variables are included to account for characteristics of the customer (for example, line and size of business or number of household members) and incidental characteristics of the product (season of the year or time of day, type of service contract). Including such variables can improve the forecasting accuracy of the model, although for rate design one usually wants eventually to use the model with these nuisance parameters set at their averages for the population to which the price schedule is offered to all customers on the same terms. If separate demand profiles are estimated for various market

---

10. An exposition of the use of probit models for related kinds of estimation is provided by McFadden and Train (1991). Detailed applications of these models to electricity and telephone pricing are reported by Train et al. (1987, 1989).

segments, but these segments are offered the same tariff, then for rate design one uses the sum of the segments' demand profiles. A fortunate aspect of the demand profile is that it enters linearly into the specification of the firm's costs and revenues. Consequently, it is sufficient, and indeed optimal, to use a simple unbiased estimator of the demand profile since that will in turn yield an unbiased estimate of costs and revenues.

Additional sources of information can also be gleaned from socio-demographic data (for households) and line-of-business data (for commercial customers) by using the techniques of correlation analysis and its variants. For example, correlation analysis of purchase size distributions with regional socio-demographic averages (for example, size of household, income, number of appliances) can be used to extend observations from pilot programs, survey data, or panel studies to other regions.

3.3   Welfare considerations

Many of the important applications of nonlinear pricing are in the major regulated industries, such as power, communications, and transport. In these industries it is especially important to recognize the distribution of net benefits among customers. Nonlinear pricing need not improve the welfare of all customers if it is applied indiscriminately. In particular, because the price schedule usually declines as the purchase size increases, customers making small purchases prefer the uniform price that raises the same revenue for the firm when that price is less than the nonlinear price schedule's charges for initial units. In §5 we analyze the form of nonlinear pricing that is often adopted to avoid disadvantaging small customers. Called Pareto-improving nonlinear pricing, it refers to the increasingly common practice of offering at least two price schedules: each customer can choose whether to purchase at the uniform price (small customers prefer this) or the nonlinear price schedule that offers quantity discounts (large customers prefer this). This policy assures that no customer is disadvantaged by the adoption of a nonlinear tariff. When options of this sort are offered, small customers are unaffected by nonlinear pricing but large customers (and the firm) can benefit substantially.

There are two approaches to measuring the incidence of benefits among customers. One method relies on an explicitly parameterized model of customers' types that specifies directly the net benefit each type obtains. Consequently, the firm's profit contribution and consumers' benefits can be aggregated by summing these amounts pertinent to each customer. The second, indirect method uses the demand profile to infer the number of customers purchasing each increment. This enables the firm's profit contribution and the consumers' surplus to be obtained by aggregating over increments.

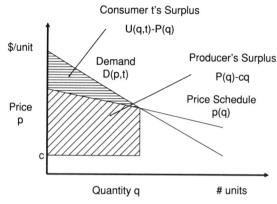

FIG. 3.4 Division of the total surplus between the producer's and consumer's surplus. The latter are measured as the areas between the price schedule and the schedules of the firm's marginal cost and the customer's demand.

Surplus measurement via parameterized models

Suppose for simplicity that the firm's total cost is simply the sum of the costs it incurs to serve individual customers. Then its profit contribution, or producer's surplus, can be represented by a formula of the form:

$$\text{Producer's Surplus} \equiv \int_a^b [P(q(t)) - C(q(t))] \, dF(t).$$

In this formula $q(t)$ is the purchase selected by type t, for which the customer pays the tariff $P(q(t))$ and the cost incurred by the firm is $C(q(t))$. We use the interval $a \le t \le b$ to represent the range of type parameters in the population.

The customer's purchase satisfies the demand condition $q = D(p(q), t)$, or equivalently $p(q) = v(q, t)$. This purchase provides type t with the net benefit $U(q(t), t) - P(q(t))$ and the aggregate obtained by all customers is

$$\text{Consumers' Surplus} \equiv \int_a^b [U(q(t), t) - P(q(t))] \, dF(t).$$

Figure 3.4 depicts the division of the total surplus between the producer's and consumer's surplus for one customer. The seller's profit on each unit is the marginal price collected, less the marginal cost, so the producer's surplus is the area between the schedules of marginal price and marginal cost. Similarly, the consumer's surplus is the difference between the customer's marginal valuation $v(q, t)$ and the marginal price $p(q)$ so the total on all units purchased is the area between the demand function $D(p, t)$ and the price schedule.

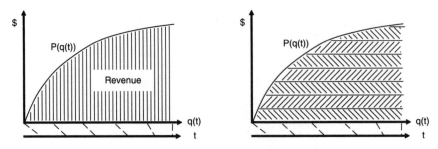

FIG. 3.5 Two versions of the firm's revenue. The representation in the right panel results from integration by parts: it accumulates the revenues obtained from successive increments in the purchase size.

Surplus measurement via the demand profile

The second approach measures the firm's profit contribution using a different accounting convention. In this version, the firm observes that a profit margin $p(q) - c(q)$ is obtained from each of the $N(p(q), q)$ customers who buy the q-th increment. Summing these amounts for all increments yields an alternative statement of the profit.

This technique is called integration by parts or in a discrete version, summation by parts. The effect of integrating by parts is represented in Figure 3.5 for the term representing the firm's revenue. The left diagram represents the revenue as the tariff $P(q(t))$ charged for the purchase $q(t)$ by type t. This is then multiplied by the number of customers of this type and then summed over all types. The dashed lines represent the translation from types to their purchases. The right diagram represents this revenue as the marginal price charged for each unit times the number of customers purchasing this unit, as represented by the corresponding horizontal slice of the area representing the revenue. The number of q-th units purchased is the number of customers purchasing at least q units: if the translation between q and t is increasing, then this is the number of customers with types exceeding that type $t(q)$ purchasing exactly q units; namely, the type for which $v(q, t(q)) = p(q)$.

A similar procedure applies to the construction of the consumers' surplus. One exploits the fact that, according to its second interpretation, the demand profile specifies the distribution of customers' marginal valuations or reservation prices for each incremental unit. For a fixed value of q, the number of customers barely willing to pay the marginal price p for the q-th unit is the number who would cease buying the q-th unit if the price were raised slightly, which is measured by the resulting decrease in $N(p, q)$. Interpreting the demand profile as the right-cumulative distribution function of reservation prices, the associated number or density of customers with the reservation price p for the q-th unit is therefore $-\partial N(p, q)/\partial p$.[11]

---

11. This is not the same as the number purchasing exactly q units, which is $|dN(p(q), q)/dq|$. This is calculated as a total derivative that measures the rate at which N declines as q increases *and p*

Consequently, the total consumers' surplus from purchases of the q-th unit at the marginal price $p(q)$ is

$$\int_{p(q)}^{\infty} [p - p(q)][-\partial N(p, q)/\partial p] \, dp \equiv \int_{p(q)}^{\infty} [p - p(q)] \, d[-N(p, q)]$$

$$= \int_{p(q)}^{\infty} N(p, q) \, dp \, .$$

The second line restates the first (using again the method of integration by parts) to express this consumers' surplus as the area under the demand profile to the right of the marginal price $p(q)$ charged for the q-th increment. In words, the first formula credits $p - p(q)$ to consumers' surplus for each of the customers willing to pay more than the price $p(q)$ charged. The second uses the alternative accounting scheme in which $1 is credited for each of the $N(p, q)$ customers willing to pay more than the higher price p. Thus, customers' net benefit from purchases of the q-th unit is the sum of the number willing to pay the next higher price $p(q) + \$1$, the number willing to pay $p(q) + \$2$, et cetera, each weighted by their contribution $dp = \$1$ per customer to the aggregate surplus.

The total consumers' surplus from purchases of all increments is therefore

$$\int_{0}^{\infty} \int_{p(q)}^{\infty} N(p, q) \, dp \, dq \, .$$

The welfare measures used in later chapters can be computed from this formula and the preceding formula for the producer's surplus.

Another aspect of welfare analysis recurs repeatedly in later chapters. At times the analysis addresses optimal pricing by a profit-maximizing monopolist, at others it considers monopolistic competition and oligopolistic competition, and it also examines the problem of efficient pricing to meet the revenue requirement of a regulated firm. Although these appear at first to be distinct problems, they are essentially similar because they are all special cases of the formulation of Ramsey pricing developed in §5.1. The theme of Ramsey pricing is to choose the tariff to maximize the total of consumers' surplus subject to meeting a revenue requirement for the firm. A special case is pricing by a profit-maximizing monopoly if the revenue requirement is so severe that this is the only scheme that will raise sufficient revenue. Further, if the revenue requirement is not so severe, Ramsey pricing suggests that the regulated firm should price *as though* it were one of several firms in an oligopolistic market, which has the effect of reducing its profits down to the level of the revenue requirement. These ideas are set forth in more detail in §5.1 and §12.3.

---

decreases due to the change in q. This is necessary to account for how the predicted number is affected by the slope of the price schedule.

Thus, the analysis of profit and efficiency motivations for rate design can be combined into a unified framework. It is a general principle that pricing must be done efficiently if it is to raise the maximum revenue. There is always a further dimension of customer satisfaction and the distribution of benefits among customers. Our main analysis of this dimension is in §5.2, where we explain the design of so-called Pareto-improving tariffs assuring that no customer is disadvantaged by nonlinear pricing as compared to a revenue-equivalent uniform price. However, in some cases it is necessary to impose further constraints on the distribution of benefits among customers, and typically these constraints incur losses in allocative efficiency.

3.4   Cautions and caveats

There are numerous amendments that are bypassed in this exposition, but it is worth mentioning some briefly.

1. Customers' benefits and demand behaviors are assumed to be exogenous; that is, their behaviors are unaffected by the introduction of nonlinear pricing. Although this may be a valid assumption in the short run, it is usually false in the long run. For example, the introduction of appreciable quantity discounts for large purchases may induce some customers to alter end-uses and their investments in appliances and production technologies. Although these adaptations typically take time, if only because of the durability of capital equipment, eventually they alter demand behavior. For this reason, measures of demand responses to quantity discounts based on existing responses to uniform prices can severely underestimate the eventual changes in demand. Rate design can anticipate these secondary responses by benefit-cost analyses of appliances and production equipment in major end uses, and consideration of adoption delays due to behavioral factors.

2. Customers' benefits are assumed to be denominated in money terms. A more general approach allows income effects, risk aversion, impatience or discounting of delayed benefits, and other behavioral parameters. These are omitted here for simplicity, because a sufficient exposition would entail vastly more technical detail and notational complexity. Also, they are rarely of prime importance for rate design in the industries that use nonlinear pricing intensively.

3. The exposition of parameterized models here and in §6 assumes that the firm knows or can estimate the distribution of types in the population. In fact, this distribution is usually variable and at any one time the firm can usually only estimate the underlying probabilistic process by which customers' types are created or evolve over time. This simplification is adopted because nonlinear pricing is usually applied to markets with large stable populations of customers, for which the population distribution (that

is, the histogram of types in the population) differs little from the long-term average distribution. Further, nonlinear pricing schedules are usually offered over relatively long time spans during which the average distribution is the primary concern.

4. Customers are assumed to obtain benefits directly from consumption of the product. In fact, many customers are other firms who are intermediaries in production or distribution. If they operate in competitive markets then their benefits are passed on to their retail customers via lower prices. But if they operate in imperfectly competitive markets allowing some monopoly power then they may be able to retain some of the gains as profits. We bypass this complicated subject until it is taken up briefly in §5. Further details are in Brown and Sibley (1986, Chapter 6).

5. The firm is assumed to be a monopoly. In fact, several amendments are necessary if the firm operates in an imperfectly competitive market. Estimates of the demand profile and customers' benefits are always conditioned on the prices prevailing for other products, especially those that are close substitutes or complements, as well as general economic conditions. This consideration is particularly important when competing firms also use nonlinear pricing, and it is severe when each firm's price schedule is a response to others' schedules. A single firm that offers several products encounters similar problems described in Part IV.

6. In all chapters where we address the problem of cost recovery by a regulated firm, we assume for expositional purposes that it is sufficient to consider only the case that the tariff is designed to maximize the total of customers' net benefits subject to a net revenue requirement for the firm. In fact, one can also consider the possibility that some types of customers are given greater weight in the measurement of aggregate welfare. We ignore this possibility here because it complicates the exposition without adding significant new insights into the application of nonlinear pricing. But all the methods described in these chapters can be extended to address such considerations if necessary.

The gist of these provisos is that nonlinear pricing is a vast subject to address in all its myriad versions. Our exposition is intended mainly to convey the basic principles rather than to include all the variations in a single comprehensive theory.

The following optional section lists some basic assumptions of a mathematical character that are used in subsequent chapters.

3.5 Standard assumptions *

No single set of assumptions provides a uniform standard for all the applications of nonlinear pricing. This section lists some basic assumptions that prevail throughout subsequent chapters and that are largely sufficient for most practical applications. Additional assumptions are imposed in later chapters addressing particular topics. The exposition generally emphasizes the formulation of nonlinear pricing problems and the main ideas involved in their analysis. The key analytical characterizations are conveyed mainly in the form of first-order necessary conditions for an optimal solution. Mathematically sophisticated readers will notice that as a result the treatment of sufficiency conditions is abbreviated, and sometimes absent altogether. My partial remedy for this deficiency is the exposition in §8.1 and 2.

The sufficiency assumptions invoked in the journal literature are often much stronger than necessary, and possibly their restrictiveness and daunting complexity have impeded applications. On the other hand, the recent work by Milgrom and Shannon (1991) provides the exact necessary and sufficient condition in terms of the property called quasi-supermodularity. I have not revised the exposition to cast the construction in terms of this condition, but it appears that in the future this will be the right framework for the development of the theory of nonlinear pricing.

The firm's cost function

Except in §15, we assume throughout that the firm's cost depends only on the distribution of purchase sizes among customers. Serving a customer i incurs a specific cost $C(q_i)$ that depends on the quantity q_i that i purchases, but not directly on the identity i of the customer, nor on any type parameters that describe the customer.[12] In particular, any two customers purchasing the same quantity impose the same costs on the firm.

The firm may incur an additional cost that depends on the aggregate quantity supplied to all customers, but for expositional simplicity we usually assume that the firm's marginal cost of aggregate supply is constant: §4.2 indicates how more general costs structures can be included. The cost function C is generally assumed to be nonnegative, increasing, and convex except possibly for a fixed cost of access or hookup. (However, many of the results apply equally to the case of decreasing marginal cost if care is taken to avoid local optima.) The marginal cost $c(q) \equiv C'(q)$ is therefore nondecreasing. We bypass the role of increasing returns to scale by assuming that for a firm in a regulated industry a revenue requirement is specified sufficiently large to recover the full costs of operations and investments in capacity.

With a few exceptions, we do not distinguish supplies by the firm and purchases by customers according to date, location, contingencies, or other conditions of delivery. Thus, cost is interpreted as an average over the billing period and an expectation over possible contingencies. The exceptions, mostly in Part III, pertain

---

12. A distinguishing feature of the applications of nonlinear pricing to principle-agent problems and related contexts is that the seller's cost depends on the customer's type.

to cases in which the conditions of delivery are interpreted as quality attributes of the product.

The simplest version of these assumptions is used frequently for examples: the firm's marginal cost is constant. Often we simplify further by assuming this marginal cost is zero.

An unfortunate deficiency of the exposition is that insufficient attention is given to the particular structure of the costs of capacity, production, and distribution in the main industries that use nonlinear pricing. Also, little account is provided about the role of general features such as economies of scale or scope. For expositions that include more detail about such aspects I recommend Mitchell and Vogelsang (1991) regarding the telecommunications industry, and Joskow and Schmalansee (1983) regarding the electric power industry.

The demand profile

We show in §4 that an optimal tariff can be constructed from the demand profile. The relevant assumptions on the demand side, therefore, impose structure on the demand profile. We describe here only the assumptions pertinent to the construction of a nonlinear tariff for a single product with a single quantity dimension: supplementary assumptions are made in Parts III and IV.

Much of the exposition assumes that the demand profile depends only on the marginal price, and not the total tariff.[13] This is a restrictive assumption—and generally false because it ignores the fact that some customers will cease purchasing as the tariff is raised; that is, it ignores the role of market penetration. Consequently, in §4.4, §6.7, and §7.4 we address explicitly the choice of the fixed access fee that accompanies the tariff, and optimize it too in a fashion that recognizes the effect on market penetration. It suffices initially to ignore fixed fees because (as shown in §6.7) when the firm incurs no setup cost from serving a customer, an optimal tariff imposes no fixed fee.

The demand profile $N(p, q)$ is nonnegative and decreasing in the quantity variable q by definition, and we generally assume further that it is also decreasing in the price variable p. This corresponds to the familiar intuition that a higher price restrains demand. We also assume that $N(p, q) = 0$ if the price p or the quantity q is sufficiently large; that is, potential demand is bounded. To apply calculus methods, the demand profile should also be twice differentiable. To ensure that the necessary condition for an optimum is also sufficient to identify a global optimum, the profit contribution (defined in various ways in different chapters) must have a single local maximum; that is, it is unimodal or quasi-concave. This is violated by some models used in practice, so one must be careful to discard inferior local optima.

---

13. This simplifies the exposition considerably. §8.5 shows that extensions to more general formulations are possible but complicated.

Simple versions of these assumptions are used for many of the examples in later chapters. For instance, the simplest model has a linear demand profile of the form $N(p, q) = 1 - ap - bq$, and by choosing the units of measurement appropriately, the coefficients a and b can be taken to be 1. An example of a demand profile that violates an assumption is $N(p, q) = 1 - p^a q^b$, because it remains positive for every q if the price is zero.

Customers' benefit and demand functions

Customers' benefit and demand functions are assumed to be very regular. As a function of the quantity q, each benefit function $U(q, t)$ is nonnegative, increasing, bounded, concave, and twice differentiable. As a function of the customer's list t of type parameters, it is assumed to be increasing in each component of t. This is partly a convention, since type parameters can often be redefined appropriately by rescaling or by some other transformation. The substantive assumption is that by some redefinition of the type parameters the benefit function can be made monotone.

The customer's marginal valuation function $v(q, t) \equiv \partial U(q, t)/\partial q$ is also assumed to be increasing in the type parameters. This is a strong assumption since it says in effect that the customers' demand functions are strictly ordered in terms of their type parameters, independently of the quantity purchased. This is a strongly sufficient assumption to ensure that the resulting demand profile predicts correctly how customers will respond to the price schedule. It is far from necessary, however, as we explain in §8.1 and §8.4.

Various benefit functions and marginal valuation functions are used in the numerical examples. The quadratic benefit function mentioned in Section 2 is a simple version with a linear marginal valuation function. The benefit function with a demand function having a constant price elasticity $1/[1 - bt]$ is $U(q, t) = aq^{bt}$, and by choice of units of measurement the coefficients a and b can be taken to be 1.

The type distribution

To obtain the requisite properties of the demand profile, the types' distribution function must also satisfy some regularity conditions. If there is a single type parameter, and the distribution function $F(t)$ has a density function $f(t) \equiv F'(t)$, then an amply sufficient condition is that F has an increasing hazard rate, meaning that the ratio $h(t) \equiv f(t)/[1 - F(t)]$ increases as t increases, or is constant. This condition is not very restrictive, since it is satisfied by nearly all the distribution functions commonly used in empirical work. These include the Normal, exponential, and uniform distributions that we use often in examples—as in §6.6. Analogous assumptions for distribution functions of multiple type parameters are cumbersome to state: §13 relies on the assumptions used in the basic work by Mirrlees (1976, 1986). The net effect of these assumptions is to avoid bunching of customers at particular purchase sizes.

In §6 we establish that only the ratio of the type elasticities of the marginal benefit function and the right-cumulative distribution function affect the construction of an optimal tariff. Consequently, §8.1 replaces the assumptions that the marginal valuation and the hazard function are increasing functions of the type parameter with the weaker assumption that the ratio of these type elasticities is decreasing.

The tariff and the price schedule

The tariff is generally required to be nonnegative and increasing. Practical considerations often require that it is also subadditive. This means that the charge for several small purchases is no less than the charge for the purchase that is the sum of the smaller amounts. This property prevents a customer (or arbitrageur) from circumventing the tariff by dividing a large purchase into several smaller ones. A strongly sufficient condition for this property is that the tariff is concave, or equivalently the marginal price schedule has no increasing segments. In §4 and §6 we show how an optimal price schedule that does not initially satisfy this condition can be altered so that it is nonincreasing as required.

A further implicit constraint is that each customer's predicted purchase is an optimal response to the tariff offered. This requires that a customer's purchase satisfies both the first and second-order necessary conditions as well as global optimality. The usual form of a customer's first-order necessary condition is that the marginal valuation of an incremental unit equals the marginal price, and the second-order condition states further that increasing the quantity purchased would decrease rather than increase the net benefit obtained. The latter requires essentially that the tariff is less concave than the customer's benefit function. Alternatively, it states that the customer's demand function intersects the price schedule from above—and only once, to ensure global optimality. Versions of this constraint imposed directly via assumptions on the benefit or demand functions are called single-crossing conditions in the technical literature. This constraint is satisfied automatically by many commonly-used parameterized models, but §8 shows how to extend the analysis to more general models.

The net effect of the assumptions placed on customers' benefit functions and on the type distribution is to ensure that the demand profile constructed from them has the required properties. In practice, empirically estimated demand profiles usually have the right properties. It is possible in principle that the demand profile could be non-monotone, but such cases are far removed from realistic predictions of customers' behavior. Nevertheless, parameterized models pose a hazard in that poorly formulated versions are capable of anomalous predictions.

3.6 Summary

This chapter introduces the basic apparatus used subsequently to describe customers' demand behaviors in response to nonlinear pricing. With ordinary uniform pricing the basic datum required for rate design is an estimate of the aggregate demand function. Nonlinear pricing requires disaggregated data that indicates demands for the different increments in the purchase size. This requirement reflects the primary feature of nonlinear pricing that it is a kind of product differentiation in which successive increments are interpreted as distinct products. Disaggregated data also preserve relevant information about the heterogeneity of customers' demand behaviors.

The cogent summary of demand data is the demand profile. It can be interpreted as specifying either how the distribution of purchase sizes varies as the price changes, or how the distribution of customers' valuations of an incremental unit varies as the quantity changes. The first interpretation is convenient for estimating the firm's profit contribution from a nonlinear tariff, and the second, the consumers' surplus.

The characterizations developed in this chapter for the single-product contexts studied in Parts I and II are generalized in Part III to study products with multiple quality attributes, and in Part IV, to multiproduct tariffs.

4

TARIFF DESIGN

A nonlinear tariff represents a special kind of product line. For each increment purchased during the billing period a customer is charged a corresponding price specified in the schedule of marginal prices. Thus, the price schedule differentiates among increments. This chapter uses the product-line interpretation to construct the optimal price schedule from customers' demands for increments.

We assume in this chapter that the firm is a profit-maximizing monopoly seller of a single product. Section 1 demonstrates that the optimal schedule of marginal prices can be constructed by choosing each increment's price to maximize that increment's profit contribution. For this purpose, the demand profile $N(p(q), q)$ is interpreted as representing the demand for q-th increments when the marginal price is $p(q)$. Section 2 adds some technical refinements. Section 3 sketches the considerations involved in the construction of a fixed access fee to accompany the schedule of marginal prices; however, no fixed fee is charged if the firm incurs no fixed cost in serving an individual customer. Section 4 reconsiders these results in terms of the bundling interpretation of product differentiation. Section 5 extends the analysis to the design of multipart tariffs with block-declining price schedules.

The exposition in this chapter uses elementary methods—except for some optional material in Section 2 indicated with an asterisk (*). It presents the main ideas in tariff design without technical details. Advanced topics receive abbreviated treatment, and in particular some aspects summarized here are not precise unless further assumptions are specified. Subsequent chapters examine these topics in more detail, but they also rely on more complicated analysis.

4.1 The price schedule of a monopolist

For a single product, a monopolist would ordinarily choose the price to maximize the profit contribution, which is the profit margin times the demand at the chosen price. The data required for this calculation are the firm's cost schedule and estimates of demand or demand elasticities at each price. Similar data are required to determine prices for a product line of differentiated quantities but the demand estimates must be disaggregated according to purchase sizes.

We assume here that the available data provide estimates of demand for each of several prices denoted by p and several purchase sizes denoted by q. These estimates can be represented as a tabular array in which the rows correspond to the different prices, the columns correspond to the different purchase sizes, and an entry in the table indicates the number or fraction $n(p, q)$ of customers who at the price p will purchase q units. This is the form in which demand data is ordinarily accumulated if appropriate care is taken to record customers' purchases: for each price p that has been offered the firm observes the distribution of purchase sizes among customers. A first trial of nonlinear pricing typically begins with data from only a few prices used in the past; in this case, estimates must be based on inferences about customers' demand elasticities, as described in §3. Care must also be taken to recognize the role of the billing period and the dimensions in which purchase sizes are measured. For example, purchase sizes must be interpreted consistently in terms of the number of units purchased within the assigned billing period; thus the rate, say units per month, is the relevant measure.

The key idea in the analysis recognizes that the tariff can be interpreted as imposing a different charge for each successive increment in the purchase size. Thus, a tariff represented as a schedule in which $P(q)$ is the total amount charged for a purchase of size q can also be represented as a schedule in which a price $p(q)$ per unit is charged for the q-th increment in the purchase size. For example, if the possible purchase sizes are the integral amounts $q = 1, 2, \ldots$ then $p(q) = P(q) - P(q-1)$ is the price charged for the q-th unit. If increments are of size δ then $p(q) = [P(q) - P(q - \delta)]/\delta$ is the price per unit charged for the q-th increment, namely the last increment to reach q units. In practice, the same price is usually charged for a range of increments, as in a block tariff, but here we allow initially that a different price is charged for each increment.

This idea is implemented by further recognizing that a customer buying the q-th increment must also buy all lesser increments. This feature is essentially a consequence of the exclusion of resale markets. The demand for each increment is the number of customers purchasing amounts that require that increment. This is the same as saying that the demand for the q-th increment is the demand for all purchase sizes at least as large as q. Using the tabular array $n(p, q)$, the demand for the q-th increment at the price p is therefore the number

$$N(p, q) = \sum_{x \geq q} n(p, x).$$

of customers purchasing q or more.

The tabular array $N(p, q)$ is the *demand profile* defined and described in §3. Each row of N is a list of partial sums from the same row of n. For the purpose of constructing optimal tariffs, the demand profile can be measured as either the number of customers or the fraction of potential customers demanding the q-th increment at the price p.[1]

It is important to realize that the demand profile differs from the aggregate demand obtained from a single uniform price p, which is

$$\bar{D}(p) = \sum_q n(p, q)q$$

$$= \sum_{q=\delta, 2\delta, \ldots} N(p, q)\delta \, ,$$

where δ is the increment in the purchase size and $p\delta$ is charged for each increment. The demand profile is a disaggregated version of the total demand function that preserves the information about customers' purchases sizes in response to each uniform price.

Similarly, when a nonincreasing price schedule $p(q)$ is offered the number of customers purchasing the q-th increment is predicted to be $N(p(q), q)$. Consequently, the aggregate demand is

$$Q = \sum_q N(p(q), q)\delta \, ,$$

which counts the sum of the numbers of customers purchasing each increment $q = \delta, 2\delta, \ldots$.

An alternative representation of the demand data that preserves even more information is the collection of demand functions $D_i(p)$, one for each customer i in the population. That is, $D_i(p)$ indicates the purchase size chosen by customer i at the uniform price p for each unit. If the data is available in this form, then the demand profile can be constructed by interpreting $N(p, q)$ as the number of customers i for whom $D_i(p) \geq q$. The shorthand notation we use for this is

$$N(p, q) = \# \{i \mid D_i(p) \geq q\} \, .$$

The demand profile is used in the following construction because it embodies the minimal information needed to find the optimal tariff. It is important to realize, however, that its use involves an implicit assumption. To ensure that $N(p(q), q)$ will in fact be the realized demand for the q-th increment requires that a customer who would purchase at least q units at the uniform price $p = p(q)$ will also purchase at least q units when offered the entire schedule of prices for increments. Typically the price schedule is nonincreasing and so is the maximum price that

1. Later examples assume that the demand profile measures fractions of the number of potential customers in the population. The units of revenue measures, such as the firm's profit or consumers' surplus, are therefore dollars per billing period per potential customer in the population.

Table 4.1 Demand Profile for Example 4.1: Optimal Tariff for Marginal Cost $c = \$1$

p	q:	1	2	3	4	5 units		$\bar{D}(p)$
				$N(p,q)$				
$2/unit		90	75	55	30	5		255
$3		80	65	45	20	0		210
$4		65	50	30	5	0		150
$5		45	30	10	0	0		85
$p(q)$:		$4	$4	$3	$3	$2/unit		$4
$P(q)$:		$4	$8	$11	$14	$16		
$R(p(q),q)$:		$195	$150	$90	$40	$5		
Total Profit :							$480	$450
'CS'(q) :		$45	$30	$40	$5	$0	$120	$85
'TS'(q) :							$600	$535

each customer is willing to pay for the q-th increment; reliance on the demand profile to summarize the demand data imposes the further requirement that the schedule of prices for increments intersects each customer's demand function at most once, and from below. In practice, this qualification is usually met without difficulty, but in Section 2 we present more details about its role in the analysis.

To complete the formulation, we assume initially that the firm's cost schedule reflects a constant cost c per unit, or $c\delta$ for an increment of size δ. In particular, the variable cost of supplying a purchase q is cq, and if $m(q)$ customers select the purchase size q then the total variable cost is $C(Q) = cQ$ where $Q = \sum_q m(q)q$ is the total quantity supplied.

The total profit contribution expected from a price schedule $p(q)$ for increments can therefore be expressed as the sum of the profit contributions from the various market segments differentiated according to the increments in the purchase size:

$$\text{Pft} \equiv \sum_q N(p(q), q) \cdot [p(q) - c]\delta .$$

In this case, to find the optimal price schedule it suffices to find the optimal price for each market segment separately. That is, the optimal price for the q-th increment is the one that maximizes that increment's profit contribution:

$$R(p(q), q) \equiv N(p(q), q) \cdot [p(q) - c] .$$

The following simple example illustrates the calculation.

Example 4.1: Suppose that the possible prices and purchase sizes are the ones shown in Table 4.1, which tabulates the demand profile. Each column corresponds to a market segment for a product line in which the purchase sizes or "volume bands" are 1, 2, 3, 4, and 5 units with $\delta = 1$. The entry in the first column and the first row, for instance, shows that at least one unit is purchased by 90 customers if the price is $2 per unit. (The number who purchase exactly one unit is 15 since 75 purchase at least two units.) At the bottom of the first column is shown the optimal price $4 charged for the first unit, assuming that the marginal cost of supply is $c = \$1$. This optimal price is found by calculating, for each price $p = \$2, \ldots, \$5$, the profit contribution. The profit contribution from the price $2, for instance, is the demand of 90 units at this price times the profit margin $2 - \$1 = \$1$, yielding the total contribution $90, which is less than the contribution of $65 \times (\$4 - \$1) = \$195$ obtained from the optimal price of $4 per unit. Similarly, the profit contribution from the third increment ($q = 3$) is $55, $90, $90, or $40 from the four possible prices, and the maximum of these is $90, obtained with either the price $3 or the next higher price $4, although we have indicated that the lower price is chosen. The entries in the table that correspond to optimal choices of the prices are italicized. The optimal prices shown in the table imply a tariff $P(q)$ that charges $4, $8, $11, $14, and $16 for the purchase sizes 1, 2, 3, 4, and 5, respectively.

When using numerical data as in the table, it is useful to check the demand profile for consistency. In addition to the requirement that the demand profile is nonincreasing along each row and down each column, there is the further require-ment that the optimal schedule of marginal prices predicts a consistent pattern of purchases. For instance, on the assumption that customers respond to lower marginal prices with larger purchases, it would be inconsistent that a decreasing marginal price schedule predicts, say, a demand for fourth units that exceeds the demand for third units. In the example, this consistency check is satisfied because the demand for each successive unit is less than the previous one. That is, the predicted demands for first, ..., fifth units are 65, 50, 45, 20, and 5, respectively, when the optimal price schedule is offered. Consistency can be violated when the units of measurement used in the tabulation exceed the actual increments chosen by customers.

Also shown in the table is the aggregate demand function $\bar{D}(p)$ that indicates the total demand if the firm charges a uniform price p for all units. Note that $\bar{D}(p) = \sum_{q=1,..,5} N(p,q)$. The optimal *uniform* price is the one that maximizes the aggregate profit contribution $\bar{D}(p) \cdot [p - c]$. For the example shown in the table, the optimal uniform price is $4, which yields a profit contribution of $450 from sales of 150 units. In contrast, the optimal tariff yields a higher profit contribution of $480 from sales of 185 units, corresponding to an average price of $3.60 per unit. Also shown in the table are minimal estimates of consumers' and total surplus, denoted CS and TS, based on the demand profile's indication of the numbers of customers willing to pay higher prices than those charged; for example, 45 customers are willing to pay a dollar more than the $4 charged for the first unit. ◇

The advantage of nonlinear pricing can be seen in the table. Offering price breaks for large purchase sizes stimulates demand that would otherwise be choked off by the higher uniform price. This particular tariff has the further advantage that it increases the firm's profit without disadvantaging any customer, since the optimal price schedule charges no more for each unit than does the optimal uniform price. In §5 we show that this feature can be generalized: whenever the uniform price exceeds marginal cost there exists a nonuniform price schedule that raises the same net revenue for the firm, increases the net benefits for some customers, and does not reduce the net benefit of any customer.

The gains from nonlinear pricing evident in this example stem from heterogeneity among customers. Segmenting the market into volume bands enables the seller to offer lower prices for the larger purchase sizes selected by some customers. The discounts are equally available to all customers, but only those customers demanding larger purchases take advantage of the opportunity.

The demand profile summarizes the heterogeneity among customers at the coarsest level of aggregation that still allows analysis of nonlinear tariffs. As described in §3, for each specified price it indicates the distribution of purchase sizes demanded by customers; and for each specified increment it indicates the distribution of customers' reservation prices. In applications it is often useful to represent this information in terms of the price elasticities of demands for different units. For instance, a price p° yields a higher profit contribution than another price p if

$$N(p^\circ, q)[p^\circ - c] > N(p, q)[p - c].$$

This can be stated equivalently when $dN \equiv N(p^\circ, q) - N(p, q) > 0$, and therefore $dp \equiv p^\circ - p < 0$, by the condition that

$$\frac{p^\circ - c}{p^\circ} > \left[\frac{dN/N}{-dp/p}\right]^{-1} ;$$

or the reverse inequality if the signs of dN and dp are reversed. The optimal price $p(q)$ therefore provides a percentage profit margin that is approximately equal to the reciprocal of the price elasticity $\eta(p, q) = [dN/N]/[-dp/p]$ of the demand profile for the q-th unit:

$$\frac{p(q) - c}{p(q)} \approx \frac{1}{\eta(p(q), q)}.$$

The price elasticity measures the percentage increase in demand per percentage decrease in the price. Thus, this condition says that the percentage profit margin times the rate at which demand decreases per unit decline in the percentage margin should be 1, indicating that the profit from existing customers that is lost by decreasing the price is compensated by the profit on new demand it brings from other customers.

Characterizations of this kind are exact if we interpret the price p as a continuous variable and the demand profile is differentiable. The price that maximizes the profit contribution $N(p, q)[p - c]$ in this case satisfies the necessary condition

$$N(p(q), q) + \frac{\partial N}{\partial p}(p(q), q) \cdot [p(q) - c] = 0 .$$

This condition states that the firm's marginal profit from a small change in the price charged for the q-th unit is nil. In particular, a \$1 increase in the price obtains an additional revenue of \$1 from each of the N customers who purchase this unit, but it also loses the profit margin $p(q) - c$ from each of the $|\partial N / \partial p|$ customers who respond to this price increase by refraining from purchasing this unit. The price elasticity of the demand profile in this case is

$$\eta(p, q) \equiv -\frac{p}{N(p, q)} \frac{\partial N}{\partial p}(p, q) ,$$

so the necessary condition can be stated equivalently as

$$\frac{p(q) - c}{p(q)} = \frac{1}{\eta(p(q), q)} .$$

That is, for the optimal marginal price $p(q)$, the percentage profit margin on q-th units is precisely the reciprocal of the price elasticity of the demand profile. This "inverse elasticity rule" is common to all monopoly pricing situations but here it is applied separately to each market for incremental units.

Typically the demand profile's induced price-elasticity increases as q increases, so the optimal price schedule $p(q)$ is decreasing and the optimal tariff $P(q)$ is a concave function of the purchase size.[2] This can be seen in extreme form for the last unit q^* purchased by any customer: $N(p(q^*), q^*) = 0$ for this value of q, but $\partial N / \partial p < 0$, so $p(q^*) = c$. That is, the last unit is sold at marginal cost.[3] In some cases, however, the price schedule computed in this way can have increasing segments or folds; we mention in Section 2 the amendments required when this happens.

2. This is quite different than saying that the price elasticity of customers' demands increases. For the parameterized models studied in §6, the price-elasticity of the demand profile is the product of the type-elasticity of the type distribution and the ratio of the price and type elasticities of the demand functions of customers purchasing exactly the amount q. Even if each customer's demand function has a constant price-elasticity, the price-elasticity of the demand profile varies with the ratio of the type-elasticities of the type-distribution and customers' demand functions, and indeed must eventually decline to zero for customers with the highest types. Higher price-elasticities of demand for customers purchasing large amounts tends to increase the price-elasticity of the demand profile, but it is far from necessary.

3. This can be misleading in contexts where the price drops slowly until a steep decline at the end. Also, this property depends on there being a last unit of finite magnitude that is sold. Although this is the realistic case in practice, we later exhibit examples in which $q^* = \infty$ and the price remains above marginal cost for all units $q < \infty$; see the "bad examples" in Section 2 and Example 8.1. A convenient test of whether a model is well formulated is to check whether it implies exhaustion of demand at some finite quantity.

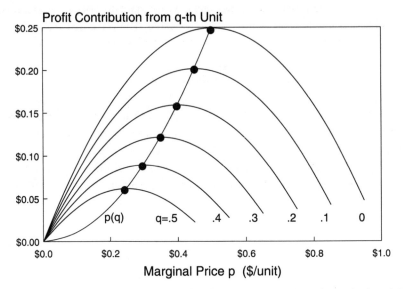

FIG. 4.1 Maximization of the profit contribution from the q-th unit via optimal selection of the marginal price $p(q)$. Assumes $N(p, q) = 1 - p - q$ and $c = 0$.

An alternative statement of the optimality condition requires that the price schedule satisfies $\frac{d}{dq}R = \frac{\partial}{\partial q}R$ all along the locus $(p(q), q)$ of the price schedule. That is, as q increases the decline in the profit contribution R from the q-th unit can be attributed entirely to shifts in demand and marginal cost, indicating that there is no further possibility for profit improvement from alteration of the price schedule. This condition can be applied to test the optimality of a price schedule using ordinary accounting data.

Examples

Example 4.2: Figure 4.1 depicts the maximization of the profit contribution for an example in which the demand profile is $N(p, q) = 1 - p - q$ and the marginal cost is $c = 0$. For each of several values of the q-th unit, the profit contribution is maximized at the marginal price $p(q)$ shown in the figure.[4] The feature that the optimal marginal price is larger for smaller values of q is typical, but as mentioned above it is not universal.   ◇

Example 4.3: A more elaborate example is derived from an explicit model of customers' demand functions of the kind studied in §6. Each potential customer is described by two parameters t and s such that his net benefit is $U(q, x; t, s) - P(q) - p^*x$ if he spends $P(q)$ to purchase q units of the firm's product and spends

4. This curve is a step function if a multipart tariff is used; that is, a single marginal price applies over each of several intervals of q.

p^*x on a composite x representing all other commodities. The benefit function U is quadratic of the form

$$U(q, x; t, s) = qt + xs - \frac{1}{2}[q^2 + 2aqx + x^2],$$

where the parameter a measures the degree to which the firm's product is a sub-stitute for other commodities. The customer's demand for the firm's product is therefore

$$D(p, p^*; t, s) = ([t - p] - a[s - p^*])/[1 - a^2],$$

assuming that no nonnegativity restriction is imposed on the composite aggregate x. Consequently, the customer of type (t, s) purchases at least q units if $t - as \geq q[1 - a^2] + p - ap^*$. Suppose that among customers in the population, t and s have a bivariate Normal distribution with means 1, standard deviations 1, and correlation r. Then the demand profile, measured as a fraction of the population, is the probability that a standard Normal random variable ξ with mean 0 and standard deviation 1 exceeds the value

$$z(p, q) \equiv (q[1 - a^2] + [p - 1] - a[p^* - 1])/\sqrt{1 - 2ra + a^2}.$$

That is, $N(p, q) = \Pr\{\xi \geq z(p, q)\}$. For this model of customers' demand behav-iors, Figure 4.2 shows the firm's optimal marginal price schedule $p(q)$ for several values of the parameters. Generally, increasing p^* raises the price schedule and increasing r lowers it. The main effect of increasing the substitution parameter a is to lower the price schedule if $p^* < 1$ and to raise it if $p^* > 1$. Observe that the last-listed price schedule has an increasing segment around $q = 4$: this is due to price competition with other commodities. As mentioned, this anomaly is addressed in Section 2.   ◇

4.2 Extensions and qualifications

There are several extensions and qualifications to be considered in using the con-struction of the optimal tariff described in previous sections.

Variable marginal cost

The analysis in Section 1 assumes a constant marginal cost but this is not necessary. If marginal cost varies with the quantity supplied to the customer then the proper marginal cost to use in the calculation of the marginal price for the q-th unit is the marginal cost $c(q)$ of producing and delivering this unit. Alternatively, if the firm's total cost varies with the aggregate of the quantities supplied to all customers, then the marginal cost to be used is the marginal cost anticipated for the last unit of the aggregate supply to be produced. More generally, it may be that the firm's

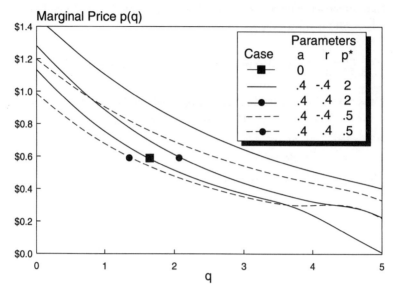

FIG. 4.2   The marginal price schedule for several values of the parameters in Example 4.3.

total cost $\mathcal{C}(\mathcal{Q})$ of supplying a list $\mathcal{Q} = (q_1, \ldots, q_n)$ of quantities q_i to customers $i = 1, \ldots, n$ is a function of both the aggregate supply $Q = \sum_i q_i$ and the individual quantities:

$$\mathcal{C}(\mathcal{Q}) = C_1(Q) + \sum_i C_2(q_i).$$

In this case the relevant marginal cost for an individual purchase q is

$$c(q) = C_1'(Q) + C_2'(q),$$

where $C_1'(Q)$ is the marginal cost of the aggregate supply.[5] To apply this construction, one must proceed iteratively until the anticipated marginal cost of the aggregate used to construct the tariff agrees with the marginal cost predicted from the aggregate of the purchases induced by the tariff design.

   If marginal cost varies over time due to changing demand and supply conditions, then its average is the relevant measure. If there are capacity limitations then a further premium is added to reflect the rationing of scarce supplies: the premium

---

5. This is true even when each individual's purchase has an imperceptible effect on the aggregate, as in models where demand is described by a smooth distribution function over purchase sizes and Q represents the average purchase.

measures the benefits foregone by other customers who might have been served instead.[6]

An alternative formulation supposes that the firm has a fixed supply or capacity Q available and therefore aggregate demand is restricted by the feasibility condition

$$\int_0^\infty N(p(q), q)\, dq \leq Q.$$

In this case the marginal cost c is augmented by a nonnegative Lagrange multiplier γ chosen sufficiently large to keep aggregate demand within the limit of aggregate supply.

Example 4.4: Suppose the demand profile is $N(p, q) = 1 - pq^a$ where $0 < a \leq 1$. Then the optimal price schedule is $p(q) = \frac{1}{2}[c + \gamma + q^{-a}]$ when the Lagrange multiplier is γ, and the resulting demand for the q-th unit is $N(p(q), q) = \frac{1}{2}[1 - (c+\gamma)q^a]$. Consequently, the optimal multiplier that keeps demand within a supply limit Q is

$$\gamma = \max\left\{0, \left(\frac{1}{2}\frac{a}{[1+a]Q}\right)^{1/a} - c\right\}.$$

Note that the multiplier is zero if the marginal cost is already large enough to restrain demand sufficiently. ◇

This reflects the general principle that supply constraints are enforced by inflating marginal cost to include an imputed price of scarce capacity.

Direct derivation of the necessary condition *

As a technical aside for readers interested in mathematical aspects, we note that the necessary condition for the optimal price schedule can be derived directly by maximizing the total profit contribution from the tariff $P(q)$. Assuming total costs are simply the sum of the costs incurred for each customer, the profit contribution is the producer's surplus

$$PS \equiv \int_0^\infty [P(q) - C(q)] \cdot \nu(q)\, dq,$$

where the density of customers purchasing the quantity q is $\nu(q) \equiv -dN/dq$ evaluated at $(p(q), q)$. This density takes account of the density $-\partial N/\partial q$ of customers purchasing q at the uniform price $p = p(q)$, and *also* the shift in demand due to the slope $p'(q)$ of the marginal price schedule. In this form the problem involves the

---

6. Average marginal cost is relevant here because we are considering only a single product. If service is differentiated between peak and offpeak periods then marginal costs are assigned separately to each product, as in later chapters on multiple products.

calculus of variations and the relevant optimality condition is the Euler condition, which here takes the form:

$$\frac{d}{dq}\left\{N + \frac{\partial N}{\partial p} \cdot [p(q) - c(q)]\right\} = 0.$$

This condition appears weaker than the one derived previously, but the transversality conditions from the calculus of variations require also that the quantity in curly brackets is zero at the largest quantity q^* purchased, and therefore it is zero for all $q \leq q^*$. This is the form of the necessary condition for an optimal price schedule derived directly in Section 1.

A similar conclusion is derived by first reformulating the profit contribution using integration by parts:

$$PS \equiv \int_0^\infty [P(q) - C(q)] \cdot \nu(q) \, dq = \int_0^\infty N(p(q), q) \cdot [p(q) - c(q)] \, dq \,,$$

apart from any fixed fee and fixed cost. Using the reformulated version on the far right, the optimal marginal price $p(q)$ for the q-th unit is selected pointwise to maximize the profit contribution from all purchases of that unit. This justifies the construction in Section 1.

Sufficiency of the necessary condition

The preceding analyses characterize the price schedule in terms of the first-order necessary condition for an optimum. In general, this condition can have multiple solutions. Extraneous solutions, such as local minima, can be excluded by imposing also the second-order necessary condition. A useful form of this condition is that the price elasticity $\eta(p(q), q)$ of the demand profile is an increasing function of the price at the solution selected. More generally, the first-order necessary condition provides a unique solution for the optimal price schedule if the price elasticity of the demand profile is everywhere an increasing function of the price. This property is often satisfied in practice because it reflects the realistic fact that at higher prices customers have more opportunities to substitute competing products and services: the greater sensitivity to price is represented by higher price elasticities at higher prices.

Decreasing price schedules and the ironing procedure

Many applications require that the tariff is a concave function of the purchase size in order to preclude arbitrage by customers. This is equivalent to the requirement that the price schedule is nonincreasing—allowing quantity discounts but never imposing quantity premia. This requirement may affect the optimal price schedule if the marginal cost is a strongly increasing function of the purchase size, or the demand profile becomes insensitive to the price p as the quantity q increases. In particular, the price schedule is increasing at q if $\partial^2 N/\partial q \partial p$ is too large at $(p(q), q)$. Many models used in practice assure that the price schedule is decreasing because the price elasticity of the demand profile increases at a rate that is larger for larger values of q. In other cases, however, the schedule of marginal prices can increase over some intervals of the purchase size, or even have folds or gaps. In such cases, the price schedule can be modified according to the following procedure.

Suppose that the solution of the necessary condition for optimality,

$$N(p(q), q) + \frac{\partial N}{\partial p}(p(q), q) \cdot [p(q) - c(q)] = 0 \,,$$

results in a price schedule $p(q)$ that is increasing over some interval $a < q < b$. Two such situations are depicted in Figure 4.3. In the left panel the price schedule is well defined but not monotone, whereas in the right panel the optimality condition allows multiple solutions at some values of q where the price schedule folds backward.[7] In such situations, the optimal constrained price schedule must be constant, say $p(q) = p$, over a wider interval $A \leq q \leq B$ such that $A \leq a < b \leq B$, $p(A) = p$, and $p(B) = p$. Over this interval, the optimality condition must be satisfied *on average*; that is,

$$\int_A^B \left\{ N(p, q) + \frac{\partial N}{\partial p}(p, q) \cdot [p - c(q)] \right\} dq = 0 \,.$$

Observe that these conditions provide three equations to determine the three values A, B, and p that need to be specified. If the initial price schedule is increasing over several intervals then it may be necessary to repeat this procedure several times in order ultimately to obtain a nonincreasing price schedule. That is, first one applies the procedure separately to each shortest segment where the schedule is increasing; if the new schedule still has increasing segments, then the process is repeated; and so on until no increasing segment remains. Flattening the price schedule this way is called "ironing."

Difficulties of a related kind are depicted in Figure 4.4. In the left panel the price schedule has a segment that declines more steeply than customers' demand schedules and therefore intersects their demand schedules from above; the right panel illustrates that this can also occur where the price schedule folds downward. In both cases the price schedule has a gap because customers will not select purchase sizes wherever the price schedule declines so steeply. In §8 we describe a variant of the ironing procedure that can be used determine the endpoints of the gap.

---

7. There can be further complications if the necessary condition allows solutions in different connected components; cf. §8.1.

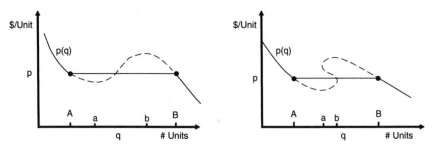

Fig. 4.3   Construction of a nonincreasing price schedule via the ironing procedure. The horizontal segment is selected so that the optimality condition is satisfied on average.

A specific example of a price schedule with an increasing segment is shown in Figure 4.5, which displays the "optimal" price schedule for Example 4.3 in the case that the parameters are $a = 0.6$, $r = 0.6$, and $p^* = 0.5$. In this case the products are close substitutes, the customers' valuations of the products are highly correlated, and the competing product has a relatively low price. The horizontal dashed line shows the optimal flattened segment of the price schedule obtained by applying the ironing procedure. This segment occurs at a price slightly less than the price p^* of the competing commodity, as one expects.

An example of a price schedule with a steeply declining segment is presented in §12.1, Figure 12.3.

Predictive power of the demand profile

The exposition above assumes that the demand profile is an adequate predictor of customers' purchase behavior in response to a nonlinear price schedule. As we have noted, when arbitrage by customers is possible, an increasing segment of the price schedule may need to be eliminated to preserve the predictive power of the demand profile. More generally, whenever the price schedule intersects a customer's demand function at more than one point, or intersects at some point from above rather than below, then the predictive power of the demand profile fails and a more complicated analysis is required. To exclude these problematic

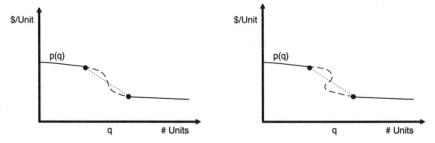

Fig. 4.4   A gap in the price schedule where it declines more steeply than customers' demand functions.

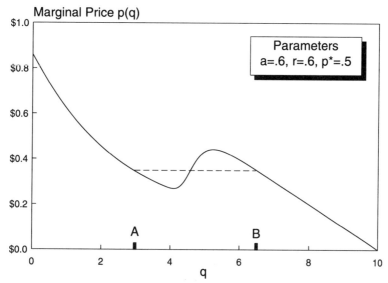

FIG. 4.5   An instance of Example 4.3 in which the ironing procedure is applied to ensure that the price schedule is nonincreasing.

cases, theoretical analyses of nonlinear pricing use assumptions sufficient to assure that the optimal price schedule intersects each customer's demand function once, from below. These same assumptions also justify the use of the demand profile to summarize customers' demand behavior. The full analysis of more general formulations is deferred to §6 and §8, where we present a formulation capable of handling cases with more complex features.

One must also check that a specified demand profile is realistic. The following are typical "bad" examples.

1. If the demand profile is $N(p, q) = 1 - kp^a q^b$ and the marginal cost is zero, then a mechanical application of the optimality condition indicates that the optimal marginal price schedule is $p(q) = \beta/q^{b/a}$, where $\beta^a = 1/k[1+a]$. The predicted result, however, is that the same fraction $1 - k\beta^a$ of the customers purchase *every* increment.

2. A demand profile with some similar properties is $N(p, q) = 1 - p/[1-q]$, provided $p + q < 1$. If marginal cost is zero, then the optimal price schedule is $p(q) = \frac{1}{2} \max \{0, 1 - q\}$. However, the predicted outcome is again that the same fraction $1/2$ of the customers buy all increments $q \leq 1$; thus, the actual purchase size is 1 for all of these customers, and each pays the total charge $P(1) = 1/4$. This is another instance of bunching of customers at a single purchase size, but in this case the purchase is finite. If the marginal cost c is positive then there is no bunching and the price schedule is

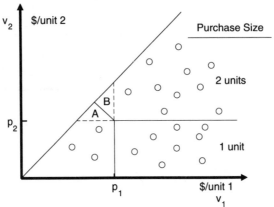

FIG. 4.6   Bundling analysis of nonlinear pricing. Note: o indicates valuations of one type of customer.

$$p(q) = \tfrac{1}{2} \max \{ c, 1 + c - q \}.$$

These examples indicate that it is a good practice to check that the overall implications of a demand profile specification are realistic. Sufficient conditions to preclude such pathologies are presented in §8.

4.3   The bundling interpretation

An alternative view construes nonlinear pricing as an instance of *bundling*. Products are said to be bundled if the charge for a purchase of several products in combination is less than the sum of the charges for the components. Bundling applies to products that are diverse (such as the options on a new automobile), but if the "products" are units of the same generic commodity then the effect is the same as nonlinear pricing. That is, for a bundle of two units a customer is charged less than twice the charge for a single unit.

The bundling approach is especially useful in understanding why nonlinear pricing can be applied in situations beyond the strictures of parameterized models. Figure 4.6 depicts the two-dimensional space of customers' valuations (v_1, v_2) for a first unit and a second unit, along with a scattering of points representing the distribution of these valuations in the population. For a pair of marginal prices (p_1, p_2) for first and second units, the solid lines in the figure separate the space into three regions identifying the customers who purchase 0, 1, or 2 units. Calculation of approximately optimal prices follows the methodology in Section 1; that is, the demand profile is calculated from the distribution of points in the figure. The important observation is that the points can be scattered arbitrarily; also, random fluctuations in their locations are immaterial as along as the overall distribution is stable. In contrast, a parameterized model in which differences among customers are described by m type parameters implies that the points lie on an m-dimensional locus.

The figure also indicates why the calculation is only approximate. The demand profile approach can make two errors: customers whose valuations lie in the triangle A are believed to purchase a second unit but not a first, and in fact they buy neither; and customers whose valuations lie in the triangle B are similar but they buy both units. These errors are usually small and not serious if the size δ of a unit is small relative to customers' purchases, for then the triangles A and B are also small.[8] Later chapters assume that units are infinitesimal and that the tariff increases smoothly as the purchase size increases. The motivation for this assumption is that analysis based on marginal calculations is much simpler, and for practical applications the errors are usually small; in addition, the basic concepts of nonlinear pricing are revealed more clearly.

There is a further lesson to be learned from the figure. Customers in the triangles A and B are ones for whom the price schedule is above their demand functions at a quantity of one unit and below at a quantity of two units. Thus, at two units the price schedule does not intersect their demand functions from below. In §6 we require explicitly that the price schedule does intersect customers' demand functions once and from below. This requirement is satisfied automatically for many parameterized models. Generally it need not be satisfied, however, and when it is violated significantly the analysis must be based on detailed consideration of how customers select their purchase sizes. In the figure, for instance, the 45° boundary line between the two triangles A and B indicates customers' optimal choices of whether to purchase two units or none.

To make this explicit we show in Figure 4.7 how the demand profile is constructed from customers' responses to a uniform price p. The count of valuations in the region where a single unit is purchased is $n(p, 1) = 14$, and where two units are purchased, $n(p, 2) = 10$. Recall that $N(p, 1)$ is the number of customers buying one or more units at this price, and $N(p, 2)$ is the number buying at least two units; so, $N(p, 1) = 24$ and $N(p, 2) = 10$.

4.4 Fixed costs and fixed fees

In important cases the firm incurs a fixed cost for each customer served. The most common source of such a cost is capacity reserved for an individual customer. This cost is usually recovered by an auxiliary hookup or access fee, or by a minimum purchase requirement. The "demand charges" used in the electric power industry are fixed in relation to energy usage but they are based on the customer's maximum power demand. Fixed costs of installation (for example, connection equipment) and administration (for example, metering and billing) for individual customers

---

8. Nevertheless, whenever the calculation of a price schedule indicates a precipitous drop in price between successive units, it is well to modify the schedule to take account of the numbers of customers whose valuations are in the triangles A and B—as we elaborate in Section 4.

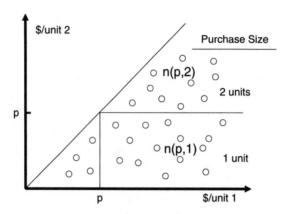

FIG. 4.7 Construction of the demand profile from the distribution of customers' valuations. Note: $n(p, 1) = 14$ and $n(p, 2) = 10$ customers.

are also significant in some applications. These costs are often recovered via a fixed fee appended to the tariff. Their role in nonlinear pricing is usually minor.

An important property of an optimal nonlinear tariff is that it imposes no fixed fee if the firm incurs no fixed cost in serving a customer. We sketch briefly why this is so. Envision the fixed fee P_o and the minimal purchase q_* as related by the condition that P_o is the amount that makes a customer purchasing q_* at the uniform price $p_* = p(q_*)$ indifferent whether to purchase at all. The minimal charge can be specified as $P(q_*) = P_o + p_* q_*$. Moreover, the fixed fee can be interpreted as

$$ P_o = \int_0^{q_*} [\hat{p}(q, q_*) - p_*] \, dq \,. $$

where $\hat{p}(q, q_*)$ is a surcharge such that the same (number of) customers purchase each unit $q \le q_*$, namely $N(\hat{p}(q, q_*), q) = N(p_*, q_*)$. The optimal choice of q_* maximizes the total profit contribution

$$ N(p_*, q_*) \cdot [P(q_*) - C(q_*)] + \int_{q_*}^{\infty} N(p(q), q) \cdot [p(q) - c(q)] \, dq \,, $$

which includes both the minimal charges collected and the marginal charges for purchases exceeding q_*. The necessary condition for an optimal choice of q_* derived from this criterion requires that

$$ P(q_*) = C(q_*) + [q_*/K(q_*)] \cdot \int_0^{q_*} \frac{\partial \hat{p}}{\partial q_*}(q, q_*) \, dq \,, $$

where $K(q) = -[q/N]\frac{d}{dq}N$ is the total elasticity of the demand for the q-th increment. If the fixed cost is nil, namely $C(0) = 0$, then the solution of this condition is $q_* = 0$, indicating that the fixed fee is also nil. Similarly, if the fixed cost is small then so too is the fixed fee.

The essential lesson is that nonlinear pricing emphasizes primarily the design of the schedule of marginal prices. If fixed costs are nil then fixed fees are not used because they would restrict the market penetration without providing benefits to other customers. This is not exactly true of multipart tariffs, which do rely on fixed fees, but only because of the limitations imposed on replacing fixed fees with marginal prices. It is important to recognize, nevertheless, that this conclusion depends on an assumption that a customer bypasses service altogether if the net benefit is negative. If customers subscribe in any case, or at least a fixed fee does not decrease market penetration, then a fixed fee is generally optimal.

If the firm incurs a fixed cost serving each customer then a positive fixed fee may be necessary to recover full costs. In this case the fixed fee may exceed the fixed cost; moreover, the tariff charged for the least purchase size generally exceeds the firm's cost. This case is presented as part of the general analysis in §6 and §8.

4.5   Multipart tariffs

Characterizing the optimal price schedule in terms of the price elasticity of the demand profile depends on the possibility of varying the marginal price for each increment of the customer's purchase. In practice, however, a different price for each increment is differentiation too fine to justify the transaction costs incurred by customers and the firm. As illustrated in §2 for *Time*, *Newsweek*, and EDF, most firms' tariffs specify prices that are constant over wide ranges. Tariffs that are piecewise-linear in this way are called multipart tariffs.

Multipart tariffs take many forms described in §1. The simplest is a two-part tariff comprising a fixed fee plus a uniform price for every unit purchased. An n-part tariff is usually presented as a fixed fee plus $n - 1$ different "block declining" marginal prices that apply in different intervals or volume bands. In the usual case that the successive marginal prices decrease, the same net effect is obtained by offering $n - 1$ two-part tariffs from which each customer can choose depending on the purchase anticipated. A set of optional two-part tariffs provides a menu with the same basic consequences for customers—although a customer uncertain about usage risks selecting a two-part tariff that will be more expensive than the corresponding n-part tariff. An important instance is the pricing of product lines of services or leased machines adapted to different rates of usage by the customer. For example, a line of small, medium, and large machines, say copiers, offered at successively higher monthly rentals and successively smaller charges per copy, constitutes a menu of three two-part tariffs or a single four-part tariff. In the case of machines, considerations of cost and design may effectively limit the tariff to a few parts. More generally, however, the profit and total surplus foregone by using an optimal n-part tariff rather than an optimal tariff with continuously varying

Table 4.2 Demand Profile for Example 4.5

$c = 1$		$\bar{N}(p, i)$		
p	q:	[0, 2]	[3, 5]	Total
$2/unit		165	90	
$3		145	65	
$4		115	35	
$5		75	10	
$p(q)$:		$4	$3/unit	
Profit:		$345	$130	$475

prices is of order $1/n^2$ for large values of n; thus, cost considerations need not be large for a tariff with only a few parts to be optimal.

The construction of a multipart tariff follows a procedure similar to the one described above. The main distinction is that the demand profile must be formulated to take account of the wider range of increments over which each marginal price applies. In addition, there is a practical proviso explained below.

Suppose that the i-th marginal price p_i is to apply to each q-th unit in the range $q_i \leq q \leq r_i$. We indicate this volume band by the notation $[q_i, r_i]$. An appropriate specification of the demand profile in terms of volume bands is

$$\bar{N}(p, [q_i, r_i]) \equiv \bar{N}(p, i) \equiv \sum_{q_i \leq q \leq r_i} N(p, q)\delta \,,$$

or if q varies continuously then

$$\bar{N}(p, i) = \int_{q_i}^{r_i} N(p, q)\, dq \,.$$

This is the number of customers purchasing increments in the range between q_i and r_i at the *uniform* price p. From each of these increments the firm obtains the profit contribution $[p-c]\delta$ if it charges the marginal price p and incurs the marginal cost c per unit. As a first approximation, the marginal price p_i to be charged for increments in this interval maximizes the profit contribution

$$\bar{N}(p_i, i) \cdot [p_i - c] \,.$$

The following example illustrates this calculation.

Example 4.5: We adapt Example 4.1 to the case that the same price p_1 must apply to the first and second units purchased, and the second price p_2 applies to all additional units. Table 4.2 shows the calculation of the price schedule, which specifies marginal prices $p_1 = \$4$ and $p_2 = \$3$, again assuming that $c = \$1$. ◇

The proviso mentioned above, and the reason that the price schedule derived for the example is only approximately optimal, can be seen as follows. In the example, if the price were $5 for the first volume band and $2 for the second then it would appear that fewer customers (75) demand increments in the first band than in the second (90). This is because the large price drop between the second and third units induces some extra customers to purchase a second unit in order to get the low price on the third; and others who would have bought a third unit at $2 will not if they must pay $5 for a second unit. Thus, the actual number who would purchase second and third units is between 75 and 90, but this number cannot be determined solely from the demand profile. The same error may occur for the price schedule calculated in Example 4.1. In general, explicit account must be taken of customers' motives to purchase a bundle of increments to obtain price breaks on the last increment(s) in the bundle, as explained in the description of bundling in Section 3.[9] For now we ignore this consideration but "optimal" will remain in quotes to acknowledge that incomplete account is taken of customers' demand behaviors at boundaries between volume bands.

An n-part tariff includes specification also of the intervals over which the marginal prices are to apply, as well as the fixed fee if any. The general construction therefore requires that the sum of the profit contributions over all the intervals, plus the sum of the fixed fees received, is maximized. We describe an approximate formulation that ignores customers' behaviors at boundaries between segments but allows simple computations. An exact formulation is presented in §6.4.

The approximate formulation

For this formulation we assume that the number of customers purchasing a q-th unit in the interval $[q_i, r_i]$ at the uniform price p_i is the same when a multipart tariff is offered. As mentioned, this ignores demand behaviors at the boundaries: for q near q_i some customers are included who should not be, and for q near r_i some customers are excluded who should not be. Also, we take $r_i = q_{i+1}$ so that there are no gaps in the price schedule. These errors are typically small if the tariff has many segments.

For this formulation, the profit contribution is

$$N_*(P(q_1), q_1) \cdot [P(q_1) - C(q_1)] + \sum_{i=1}^{n-1} \bar{N}(p_i, [q_i, q_{i+1}]) \cdot [p_i - c].$$

9. The source of this difficulty is that the demand profile is too aggregated to allow inferences about customers' behaviors at boundaries between segments of multipart tariffs. The disaggregated models studied in Part II allow exact characterizations, as in §6.4.

The first term represents one way to specify a fixed fee: the minimum purchase size is q_1 for which the customer pays $P(q_1)$ and $N_*(P, q)$ indicates the predicted number of customers willing to purchase this minimal quantity, namely the number for whom the gross benefit from q units exceeds the tariff P. One can construe $P_o = P(q_1) - p_o q_1$ as the imputed fixed fee if, as is frequently the case, this fee still requires the customer to pay for an initial purchase of q_1 units at the price p_o. If the tariff is implemented as a menu of two-part tariffs with fixed fees P_i and marginal prices p_i, then the i-th fixed fee can be calculated from the previous one via the relationships

$$P_{i-1} + p_{i-1} q_i = P(q_i) = P_i + p_i q_i ,$$

which yield the recursive formula

$$P_i = P_{i-1} + [p_{i-1} - p_i] \cdot q_i .$$

That is, the increment in the fixed fee accounts for the lower marginal prices payable for all units $q \leq q_i$. Such a menu assures that the i-th two-part tariff minimizes the amount paid for a quantity in the interval $q_i \leq q \leq q_{i+1}$.

This profit contribution is to be maximized by choosing both the prices p_i and the breakpoints q_i for each interval $i = 1, \ldots, n - 1$. One uses $q_n = \infty$ so that no upper bound is placed on the size of a purchase. Usually the prices must be constrained to be nonincreasing to avoid arbitrage by customers, as described in §1.3, and of course the breakpoints must be increasing.

Example 4.6: For this example we assume that the demand profile is $N(p, q) = 1 - p - q$. As mentioned, for the computations here we ignore customers' behaviors at the boundaries between intervals and simply use the demand profile for volume bands directly. With this proviso,

$$\bar{N}(p_i, [q_i, q_{i+1}]) = \begin{cases} [q_{i+1} - q_i][1 - p_i - \bar{q}_i] & \text{if } i < n - 1, \\ \dfrac{1}{2}[1 - p_i - q_i]^2 & \text{if } i = n - 1, \end{cases}$$

where $\bar{q}_i = \frac{1}{2}[q_i + q_{i+1}]$ is the midpoint of the volume band. Consequently, an "optimal" n-part tariff uses the marginal prices

$$p_i = \begin{cases} \dfrac{1}{2}[1 + c - \bar{q}_i] & \text{if } i < n - 1, \\ \dfrac{2}{3}c + \dfrac{1}{3}[1 - q_i] & \text{if } i = n - 1, \end{cases}$$

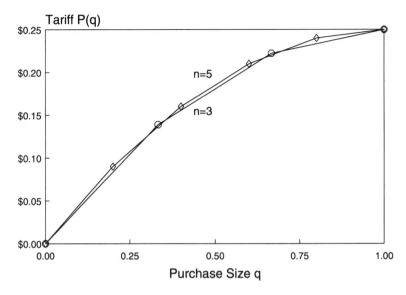

FIG. 4.8   Example 4.6: Approximate multipart tariffs for $n = 3$ and $n = 5$.

where for $i > 1$ the breakpoints between the volume bands satisfy $q_i = 1 + c - [p_{i-1} + p_i]$. Given q_1 these conditions provide a system of simultaneous equations that determine all the volume bands and the price charged for each one.

To give the flavor of these results, we suppose that the last price p_{n-1} satisfies the same formula as the others; also, we use $q_1 = [1 - c]/n$, which turns out to be correct when there is no fixed cost, fixed fee, nor minimal purchase. In this case, the breakpoints are $q_i = [1 - c]i/n$ for $i = 1, \ldots, n$ and the price for the i-th band is $p_i = \frac{1}{2}[1 + c - (1 - c)(i + .5)/n]$. If a menu of two-part tariffs is used, then the fixed fee associated with the i-th price p_i is $P_i = \frac{1}{4}[1 - c]^2 i[i + 1]/n^2$. Figure 4.8 shows the resulting multipart tariff for $n = 3$ and $n = 5$ when the marginal cost is $c = 0$. Note that the breakpoints are evenly spaced and the marginal prices decline steadily between each pair of adjacent intervals, whereas the associated fixed fees increase quadratically. In terms of sales, the same number of customers selects purchase sizes in each volume band, but the number of units sold per interval declines steadily and therefore, since the marginal prices decline too, revenues from these units decline quadratically. As the number n of intervals increases, the firm's profit increases to the maximum profit $\frac{1}{12}[1 - c]^3$ obtained from the nonlinear tariff $P(q) = \frac{1}{2}[1 + c]q - \frac{1}{4}q^2$.

Example 6.3 recomputes these results taking explicit account of customers' demand behaviors at the boundaries between intervals, and obtains an exact answer that is only slightly different if n is large. In particular, if $c = 0$ then the i-th truly optimal marginal price is $p_i^o = [n/(n - .75)]p_i$, where p_i is the value calculated in the example above; in addition, the boundaries between segments differ slightly.

This relationship is indicative of the degree to which the "optimal" price schedule approximates the truly optimal one. Generally, customers' behaviors at boundaries between segments of multipart tariffs are immaterial if there are many segments so that the marginal prices do not differ greatly between adjacent segments.   ◇

4.6 Summary

This chapter construes nonlinear pricing as a particular kind of product differentiation. The product line comprises the various incremental units, each offered at its own price, plus possibly a minimal purchase. From this perspective, the construction of an optimal price schedule reduces to the calculation of the optimal price for the minimal purchase, if any, and for each increment in the purchase size. This viewpoint is also illustrated by construing nonlinear pricing as a special case of bundling.[10]

The demand for increments is measured by the demand profile $N(p, q)$, which for each price p specifies the demand for the q-th increment. The demand profile can be estimated from data obtained from uniform prices, since for each price it represents the right-cumulative distribution function of purchase sizes among the customers in the population. Having estimated the demand profile, a firm can calculate an optimal price schedule $p(q)$ by maximizing the profit contribution from sales of q-th units. This amounts to a simple arithmetical task when the demand profile is given in tabular form, as in Table 4.1, or as in Table 4.2 in the case of a block declining price schedule. Variable marginal costs per customer and an aggregate marginal cost component can be included. Fixed costs can be recovered via a fixed fee, but the optimal fixed fee is nil if fixed costs are nil.

The analysis assumes that the price schedule is nonincreasing, but if not then it can be flattened appropriately via the ironing procedure so that the marginal contribution to consumers' and producer's surplus averages to zero over an interval of units for which the marginal price is uniform. Other technical amendments also apply; for instance, the marginal price schedule must intersect each customer's demand function once, from below, if the demand profile is to be a fully accurate predictor of customers' demand behaviors. Further, the analysis via bundling indicates that if increments are large then it is necessary to consider also how customers choose between larger and smaller purchase sizes when intermediate purchase sizes are not optimal.

The ironing procedure addresses several complications that can occur in general models of nonlinear pricing described in §8. Nonmonotonicities, folds, steep segments, and multiple components of the price schedule are rare in models used in practice, but they cannot be excluded entirely without imposing unrealistically

---

10. As shown in §13.5, multiproduct tariffs involve bundling of units of each product as well as bundling among products.

strong assumptions. Most of the exposition in subsequent chapters therefore focuses on regular cases in which these complications do not arise, but amendments to handle irregular cases are mentioned occasionally. Most amendments share the common feature that a segment of the price schedule is altered (to be flat, vertical, or a gap) over an interval (of units or types) for which the optimality condition is required only to be satisfied on average.

5

RAMSEY PRICING

Many public enterprises and regulated privately-owned utilities are allowed revenues sufficient only to recover their total costs. Besides operating and administrative costs, these include costs of capital invested in capacity. For such firms, one procedure that produces an efficient tariff design is *Ramsey pricing*. The construction in §4 of a price schedule for a profit-maximizing monopolist is an application of tariff design based on Ramsey pricing: monopoly pricing is the special case in which the firm's capital and administrative costs are so large that profit maximization is required.[1] More generally, Ramsey pricing allows the firm sufficient use of monopoly power to meet its revenue requirement.

The guiding principle of Ramsey pricing is to construct the tariff to maximize an aggregate of customers' benefits, subject to the constraint that the firm's revenues recover its total costs.[2] The most common aggregate used in applications is the simple unweighted sum of the money values of customers' net benefits, namely consumers' surplus. Additional constraints are also included in some applications. The most important requires that no customer is worse off with Ramsey pricing than the uniform price schedule that provides the same net revenue for the firm. This constraint is imposed to ensure customers' and regulators' acceptance of Ramsey pricing as an improvement over an existing uniform price schedule. Its practical effect is usually to put a cap on the prices charged for small purchases; typically it has no effect on the quantity discounts offered for large purchases.

---

1. This reflects a narrow interpretation of monopoly. Often a firm with a monopoly position in the market is also subject to the threat of entry by other firms, and to forestall entry it must keep its prices low. For analyses of pricing to deter entry, see the survey by Wilson (1992b) and for studies of the special case of contestable markets see Baumol, Panzar, and Willig (1982) and Maskin and Tirole (1988).

2. This is the main ingredient of Ramsey pricing, named after Frank P. Ramsey (1903–1930), who first proposed and analyzed an application in a 1927 article. It is sometimes called Ramsey-Boiteux pricing to recognize its further development by Marcel Boiteux (1956). It is widely used by regulatory agencies; for example, in 1983 the United States Interstate Commerce Commission adopted Ramsey pricing as the basic principle for setting railroad rates. Baumol (1987) provides a brief exposition that includes a short history of the subject. For an analysis of Ramsey pricing in relation to statutory prohibitions against undue price discrimination in public utility rates, see Henderson and Burns (1989).

Section 1 introduces the Ramsey formulation of pricing by a regulated monopoly. In this formulation, the tariff is designed to maximize consumers' surplus, namely the aggregate of customers' net benefits, subject to the firm's revenue requirement. The main concepts of nonlinear pricing carry over to this formulation except that the price elasticity of the demand profile is artificially inflated, thereby lowering the price schedule. Subsequent sections elaborate the modifications required to ensure that no customer is affected adversely by the firm's adoption of a nonlinear tariff. Section 2 introduces the concept of a Pareto-improving tariff and derives the conditions for an optimal tariff constrained by this requirement. An application to the telephone industry is described in Section 3.

5.1 The price schedule of a regulated firm

In this section we demonstrate that the net effect of Ramsey pricing is simply to reduce the percentage profit margin on each unit sold until the utility's revenue equals its total cost. The key requirement is that this reduction should be the same fraction of the monopoly percentage profit margin on every unit. This uniformity of the percentage profit margin is called the Ramsey pricing rule. The fraction of the monopoly percentage profit margin that is common to all units is called the "Ramsey number" and is usually denoted by α. For a profit-maximizing monopoly, $\alpha = 1$, and for a regulated firm with no binding revenue requirement, $\alpha = 0$. The Ramsey number is typically intermediate between these extremes.

Thus, if the construction of the optimal tariff for a profit-maximizing monopolist produces a percentage profit margin $m(q) = [p(q) - c(q)]/p(q)$ on the q-th unit, then a regulated utility would use a price schedule with the profit margin $\alpha m(q)$ for some fixed fraction α that is independent of q—were it true that customers' demands remained unchanged. In fact, however, customers respond to the lower prices offered by a regulated utility. The actual rule is therefore that the utility's price schedule should satisfy the condition that

$$\frac{p(q) - c(q)}{p(q)} = \frac{\alpha}{\eta(p(q), q)},$$

where again η is the price elasticity of the demand profile, for a value of α that recovers the utility's total costs. This Ramsey pricing rule is often expressed by the condition that the product of the percentage profit margin and the price elasticity of the demand profile should be the same (that is, equal to the Ramsey number) for every increment. Thus, an empirical test of the optimality of an existing or proposed price schedule is obtained by tabulating and comparing these products to see if there are any large differences among them.

We derive the Ramsey pricing rule by taking advantage of the dual interpretation of the demand profile. The possibility that the firm charges each customer a fixed fee or insists on a minimal purchase is omitted since the analysis parallels the treatment in §4.4; a complete exposition is included in §6.

Construction of Ramsey price schedules

Recall from §3 that the demand profile has two interpretations. For a fixed uniform price p, the demand profile $N(p, q)$ indicates the right-cumulative distribution of customers' purchase sizes. Based on this interpretation, $N(p(q), q)$ customers buy a q-th unit at the marginal price $p(q)$, and aggregate demand is

$$Q = \int_0^\infty N(p(q), q) \, dq \, .$$

From each one of the q-th units sold the firm's profit contribution is the difference $p(q) - c(q)$ between the price and the marginal cost, and the number of such units sold is $N(p(q), q)$. The firm's profit contribution from all units sold according to the price schedule $p(q)$ is therefore

$$\text{PS} \equiv \int_0^\infty N(p(q), q) \cdot [p(q) - c(q)] \, dq \, .$$

The firm's profit contribution is also called the producer's surplus to parallel the nomenclature for consumers' surplus. Assuming the firm requires a net revenue R_* to recover its total costs, we impose the constraint that $\text{PS} \geq R_*$.

According to the second interpretation, for each fixed q-th unit the demand profile $N(p, q)$ indicates the right-cumulative distribution of customers' marginal valuations of this unit. The aggregate of customers' net benefits from purchasing the q-th unit at the price $p(q)$ is therefore

$$\text{CS}(q) \equiv \int_{p(q)}^\infty [p - p(q)] \, d[1 - N(p, q)] = \int_{p(q)}^\infty N(p, q) \, dp \, .$$

In this formula the first summation or integration uses the variable p to parameterize customers' marginal valuations or reservation prices for a q-th unit and uses $1 - N(p, q)$ to represent the usual left-cumulative distribution of customers' marginal valuations. The integral on the right results from integration by parts, using the property $N(p, \infty) = 0$. The aggregate over all incremental units is therefore

$$\text{CS} = \int_0^\infty \int_{p(q)}^\infty N(p, q) \, dp \, dq \, ,$$

which is the total consumers' surplus.

The method of Ramsey pricing selects the price schedule to maximize this aggregate measure of customers' net benefits within the limit allowed by the revenue constraint. This principle can be interpreted as seeking an efficient allocation of purchases to customers subject to two provisos reflecting political considerations affecting regulatory policy. The first is dubbed the "every tub on its own bottom" constraint: the utility's full costs are recovered from its customers, rather than subsidized by other means such as general tax revenues. The second proviso is that among the many efficient allocations, the one selected maximizes consumers' surplus. The usual rationale for this selection is that each customer is affected by utilities in several industries and by an assortment of public programs, as well as taxes, subsidies, and welfare programs with substantial distributive effects. Absent a coherent scheme to coordinate all these programs to achieve distributive objectives, if each program maximizes total benefits then in aggregate the greatest potential benefit is available for redistribution via taxation and other programs with explicit welfare or distributional objectives.

For historical reasons, the optimization is usually stated equivalently as the maximization of the total surplus $TS \equiv CS + PS$ subject to the revenue constraint. A Lagrange multiplier λ is used to include the revenue constraint explicitly in this objective. It is a nonnegative number chosen large enough to meet the revenue requirement, but zero if the requirement is exceeded. Including the Lagrangian term, the problem posed is to maximize

$$\mathcal{L}_* \equiv TS + \lambda[PS - R_*], \qquad \text{or equivalently} \qquad \mathcal{L} \equiv CS + [1 + \lambda]PS,$$

where in the latter the dependence on the revenue requirement is summarized entirely by the multiplier λ. In the present context, the multiplier λ measures the reduction in total surplus caused by a unit increase in the firm's revenue requirement. This reduction is usually positive because the firm obtains a greater net revenue only by exploiting further its monopoly power, which reduces the consumers' surplus that can be achieved. In the extreme case of a profit-maximizing monopoly, only the firm's profit matters, which corresponds to $\lambda = \infty$.

Writing out the Lagrangian augmented objective function in full, we obtain:

$$\mathcal{L} \equiv \int_0^\infty \left\{ \int_{p(q)}^\infty N(p,q)\, dp + [1+\lambda] \cdot N(p(q),q) \cdot [p(q) - c(q)] \right\} dq.$$

Consequently, for each q-th unit the marginal price $p(q)$ maximizes the expression in curly brackets. This yields the necessary condition that characterizes an optimal price schedule:

$$-N(p(q),q) + [1+\lambda]\left\{ N(p(q),q) + \frac{\partial N}{\partial p}(p(q),q) \cdot [p(q) - c(q)] \right\} = 0.$$

The interpretation of this condition is straightforward: the factor in curly brackets is familiar from §4 as the firm's marginal profit contribution from the q-th increment, and the first term merely states that a \$1 price increase reduces by \$1 the consumer's surplus from each of the $N(p(q), q)$ customers who purchase that increment. The price increase also induces $|\partial N/\partial p|$ customers to refrain from purchasing the q-th increment: this affects the firm's profit contribution if $p(q) > c(q)$ but these customers' surpluses are essentially unaffected since they were indifferent whether to add this last increment to their purchases.

Using the Ramsey number $\alpha \equiv \lambda/[1 + \lambda]$, this optimality condition can be expressed equivalently as

$$\alpha N(p(q), q) + \frac{\partial N}{\partial p}(p(q), q) \cdot [p(q) - c(q)] = 0,$$

which is the standard form we use hereafter.

The optimality condition can also be expressed in terms of the percentage profit margin,

$$\frac{p(q) - c(q)}{p(q)} = \frac{\alpha}{\eta(p(q), q)},$$

where $\eta(p, q)$ is the price elasticity of the demand profile as in §4.1. This form of the optimality condition reveals that the essential effect of Ramsey pricing is to reduce the monopoly percentage profit margin, uniformly for all units, so that only the required revenue is obtained by the firm. This effect can be given several interpretations. The direct interpretation recognizes that the price for each unit includes an *ad valorum* or value-added tax to meet the firm's revenue requirement. This tax is stated as a percentage markup inversely proportional to the price elasticity of the demand for that unit. Units with lower price elasticities are taxed more because their demands are curtailed less by the tax. In particular, the tax imposes a welfare loss due to the resulting departure from the fully efficient demands that would result from marginal cost pricing, and this welfare loss (as measured in terms of consumers' surplus) is roughly proportional to the price elasticity. The resulting pricing rule uses the firm's monopoly power efficiently to meet the revenue requirement.

Two other interpretations are sometimes used. One is that regulation enforces behavior by the firm that is based on a price elasticity of the demand profile that is artificially inflated by a factor $1/\alpha$, as though price competition from other firms' products that are imperfect substitutes were more severe than it actually is. A second interpretation developed in §12 is that regulation forces the firm to behave as if it were one of $1/\alpha$ firms offering products that are perfect substitutes. Either interpretation construes the net effect of regulation as the imposition of competition when in fact there is none.

This form of the optimality condition generalizes the condition derived in §4, since $\alpha = 1$ is the case of a profit-maximizing monopoly. It also includes the case of fully efficient marginal cost pricing: when the revenue constraint is not binding, $\lambda = 0$ and $\alpha = 0$ and therefore $p(q) = c(q)$. Thus, Ramsey pricing is a generalization of both monopoly pricing and marginal-cost pricing, and between these extremes it includes a spectrum of possibilities that correspond to the various revenue requirements the firm might have. Profit margins are higher if the Ramsey number is higher, in order to recover the firm's greater fixed costs.

Ironing of the price schedule has a pronounced effect on Ramsey pricing when the firm's marginal cost is increasing and its revenue requirement is small. The extreme case where $\alpha = 0$, for instance, corresponds to completely efficient pricing, as in a perfectly competitive market: each marginal price equals the corresponding marginal cost, and therefore is increasing. The price schedule must be constrained to be subadditive (or more stringently, nonincreasing), however, if a customer can substitute several small purchases for a large one. The net result of ironing, therefore, is to charge a single uniform price equal to the marginal cost of the last unit in the largest size purchased. This may entail charging the marginal cost for a single unit, relying on each customer to make multiple unit purchases to make up a larger purchase.

Welfare aspects of Ramsey pricing

Ramsey pricing has rarely been embraced by regulatory agencies without amendments. In this subsection we mention two sources of their concern. We describe some efficiency considerations first and then introduce the distributional considerations that motivate the analysis in Section 2.

- ### Efficiency aspects of Ramsey pricing

Although some use of monopoly power may be required if a regulated firm is to recover its full costs, the kinds of monopoly power that the firm is allowed to exercise is a matter of choice; moreover, monopoly power can be abused by inefficient use.

Nonlinear tariffs derived from the principles of Ramsey pricing suppose that the firm is allowed to charge different prices for different increments. If marginal cost is constant then this is a kind of price discrimination created solely by the design of the tariff, since typically increments sold to one customer are generically the same, and the same as those sold to other customers. Indeed, it may seem puzzling that the general principles of Ramsey pricing, which are based on a criterion of efficiency, lead inexorably to nonlinear pricing and therefore to differentiated prices for increments that are physically indistinguishable in production or consumption. As mentioned above, the answer to this puzzle is that use of its monopoly power to differentiate prices is the efficient way for the firm to meet its revenue requirement. In technical terms this answer is manifest in the fact that the aggregate price elasticity (of the demand profile) is different for different increments; thus, the aggregate welfare loss incurred in meeting the revenue requirement is minimized by pricing increments differently depending on their price elasticities. This conclusion follows inevitably from the restriction that the same tariff is offered to all customers, so only the aggregate price elasticities matter, and the objective of maximizing an aggregate of customers' net benefits, such as consumers' surplus.

Apprehension about the use of price discrimination, however, has deeper roots. Quite apart from distributional aspects, concerns about price discrimination stem from the possibility that it can promote productive and allocative inefficiencies, especially through quality degradation. A typical example is an airline that uses nonlinear pricing in the form of nonrefundable discounts for advance purchases: high prices for tickets sold shortly before departure can mean that some seats go unfilled, and customers may incur costs adhering to rigid itineraries. Similarly, a publisher that decreases its price over time incurs storage costs and delays benefits for customers. It is conceivable as well that the qualities of utility services such as power and communications could be degraded artificially to facilitate price discrimination. Regulatory agencies are therefore cautious in allowing tariffs that involve price discrimination, in part to ensure that they are not sustained by quality degradation or other sources of productive or allocative inefficiencies.

The formulation of Ramsey pricing used here bypasses these considerations by assuming implicitly that the product quality and the production technology are fixed. It does not address the issue of whether productively inefficient uses of monopoly power should be allowed in order to meet the firm's revenue requirement; that is, the formulation simply assumes that quality specifications and the production and distribution systems are operated efficiently.[3]

• *Distributional effects of Ramsey pricing*

A second source of concern is that Ramsey pricing can reduce the net benefits of customers making small purchases, even though it provides compensating gains to others, when maximization of an aggregate of customers' net benefits is used as the objective. To illustrate, we present two examples that demonstrate possible consequences of unfettered use of Ramsey pricing.

Example 5.1: For this example, suppose that the demand profile is $N(p, q) = 1 - q/[1 - p]$, provided $p + q \leq 1$. Using the condition above, the optimal price schedule is found to be

$$p(q) = 1 + \frac{q}{2}\frac{1 - \alpha}{\alpha} - \sqrt{\left(\frac{q}{2}\frac{1 - \alpha}{\alpha}\right)^2 + q\frac{1 - c}{\alpha}}.$$

Figure 5.1 shows this price schedule for several values of the Ramsey number α, assuming the marginal cost is $c = 0$. Figure 5.2 shows how the resulting profit

3. For analyses of these topics see Laffont and Tirole (1992) and Spulber (1989).

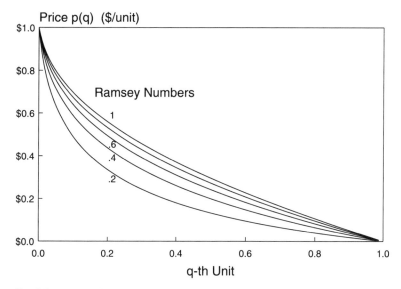

FIG. 5.1   Example 5.1: The marginal price schedule for Ramsey numbers $\alpha = 0.2(0.2)1$.

contribution increases as the Ramsey number increases. Notice that for an initial increment the price schedule charges $p(0) = 1$ for any Ramsey number that is positive. Even for a profit-maximizing monopoly, the uniform price is only half as large. Thus, the Ramsey price schedule charges more for initial units and less for the last units than a uniform price. Customers making small purchases therefore encounter tariffs that exceed the charges imposed by a uniform price.   ◇

Example 5.2: A more extreme example has the demand profile $N(p, q) = 2 + \log(1 + p)/\log(q)$, provided $q < 1$. The optimal price schedules are depicted in Figure 5.3 for the same set of Ramsey numbers as the previous example, and the marginal cost $c = 0$. The marginal price for an initial increment is $p(0) = \infty$, because the price elasticity of the demand profile is zero for an initial increment. The dependence of the profit contribution on the Ramsey number is shown in Figure 5.4.   ◇

   In both examples the prices for initial increments are essentially the monopoly prices for these increments, regardless of the Ramsey number. In the second example, moreover, the infinitely high prices are an indirect way of imposing a fixed fee.
   For customers making small purchases, the Ramsey price schedule is disadvantageous compared to the uniform price that raises the same net revenue for the firm. In the first example, for instance, a uniform price $\bar{p}$ provides the net revenue $\bar{D}(\bar{p})[\bar{p} - c]$, where the total demand is $\bar{D}(\bar{p}) = \frac{1}{2}[1 - \bar{p}]$. For each uniform price $\bar{p} < 1$ there is a Ramsey number $\alpha(\bar{p})$ such that the nonuniform Ramsey price schedule yields the same net revenue to the firm. If offered a choice between these

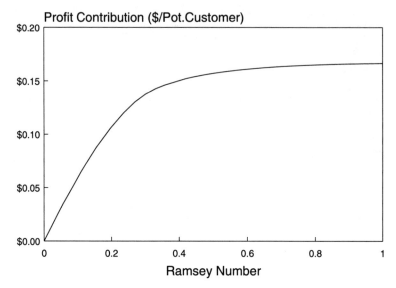

FIG. 5.2   Example 5.1: The dependence of net revenue on the Ramsey number α.

two schedules, customers making small purchases prefer the revenue-equivalent uniform price, whereas customers making large purchases prefer the Ramsey price schedule, due to its substantial quantity discounts for large purchases.

A compromise that avoids this conflict among customers puts a cap on the marginal prices allowed. Choosing the price cap to be equal to the revenue-

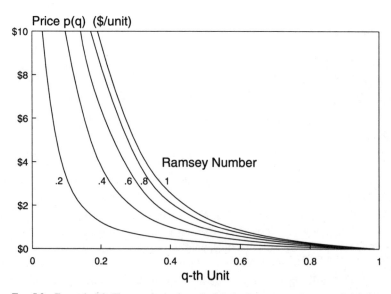

FIG. 5.3   Example 5.2: The marginal price schedule for Ramsey numbers $\alpha = 0.2(0.2)1$.

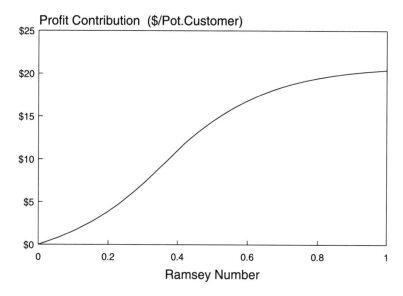

Fig. 5.4   Example 5.2: The dependence of the net revenue on the Ramsey number α.

equivalent uniform price assures that no customer is disadvantaged by the adoption
of nonlinear pricing. If this is done then the resulting schedule is

$$p^\circ(q) = \min\{\bar{p}, p(q)\} = \begin{cases} \bar{p} & \text{if } q \leq \bar{q}, \\ p(q) & \text{if } q > \bar{q}. \end{cases}$$

This compromise obtains the efficiency advantages of quantity discounts for large
customers without disadvantaging customers purchasing small amounts, but the
Ramsey number is larger. The nonuniform part $p(q)$ is computed using a larger
Ramsey number chosen so that the firm's revenue requirement is still satisfied.

Practical implementations are often based on a menu of options among which
each customer can choose. For instance, as in AT&T's tariffs described in §2.4,
one option could be the uniform price $\bar{p}$ applicable to all units, and a second
option could be the nonuniform price schedule $p(q)$ applicable to units $q > \bar{q}$ after
payment of a fixed fee $\bar{p}\bar{q}$ that provides free service for units $q \leq \bar{q}$. Customers
purchasing more than $\bar{q}$ would then prefer the second option.

In Section 2 some further comments on the distributional effects of Ramsey
pricing provide a cautionary reminder: when customers are actually intermediate
producers, the welfare consequences of a nonlinear tariff depend on the extent that
benefits from quantity discounts are passed on to retail consumers.

• *Other welfare criteria*

Ramsey pricing can also be formulated in terms of other welfare criteria than
maximization of total surplus subject to the firm's revenue requirement. The net

effect of criteria that use different welfare weights for different types of customers is to make the Ramsey number dependent on the average welfare weights of those customers' purchasing each unit. In the extreme case that customers purchasing more than some amount q_* are assigned zero welfare weights, the net effect is that $\alpha = 1$ for those units $q > q_*$. This indicates that the firm uses its full monopoly power to raise the maximum revenue from units beyond q_* so that it can provide lower prices (or as in the case of a price cap, a low uniform price), on units in the initial interval $0 < q < q_*$. Thus, the use of other welfare criteria favoring customers buying small amounts does not alter materially the conclusion that optimally the firm uses nonlinear pricing for larger amounts.

5.2 Pareto-improving tariffs

As described above, for a public utility the implementation of a nonlinear tariff is often constrained by the distributional consequences for customers. Changing from a uniform price to a multipart tariff or a fully nonlinear tariff can benefit some customers but affect others adversely. For instance, introducing a two-part tariff with a fixed fee plus a lower marginal price benefits customers with large demands but precludes others from making any purchases at all. Utilities and regulatory agencies therefore find it desirable to consider modifications that do not disadvantage any customer. Tariff amendments that have this property, and that also do not reduce the firm's revenue, are said to be Pareto-improving.[4]

Examples of Pareto-improving tariffs

There are many ways that an existing nonoptimal tariff can be modified in a Pareto-improving way, of which we describe here only a few. Initially we assume that customers' demands are independent, in the sense that the tariff offered to one customer does not affect another customer's response; this assumption is reexamined later.

• *Introduction of a two-part tariff*

When the existing tariff is linear with a uniform price for all units purchased, a Pareto-improving change can be made by introducing an appropriately designed two-part tariff as an option available to customers. It is important to realize that electing the two-part tariff must be optional, not required. The new tariff can be construed as a menu with two options: each customer can select either the existing linear tariff, say $P_1(q) = P_1 + p_1 q$ where $P_1 = 0$ and p_1 is the present uniform price, or the new two-part tariff, say $P_2(q) = P_2 + p_2 q$ where P_2 is a positive fixed fee and the marginal price is $p_2 < p_1$. It is clear that a fully informed customer

---

4. This name derives from the economist Vilfredo Pareto (1848–1923) who studied the criterion of unanimous consent for changes in economic policy.

cannot be disadvantaged by this menu, since each customer retains the option to purchase under the old tariff, and indeed those customers intending to purchase amounts substantially less than $q^* = P_2/[p_1 - p_2]$ prefer to remain with the old tariff. It remains therefore only to ensure that the firm's revenue is not reduced. A key fact is that there does exist such a choice with $P_2 > 0$ and $p_2 < p_1$ whenever p_1 exceeds the firm's marginal cost.[5] Together, the two optional tariffs provide a block-declining price schedule in which the second block offers the lower price p_2 for incremental units in excess of q^*. Because p_1 exceeds marginal cost, there is some choice of q^* beyond which the firm's revenue is increased by offering a lower marginal price p_2.

This result evidently extends also to the case that the existing pricing policy is a two-part tariff, namely $P_1 > 0$. Indeed, it can also be beneficial to introduce an option that has a lower fixed fee and a higher marginal price. In general, if the optimal tariff is concave, so that it is equivalent to a menu of optional two-part tariffs, then an existing menu of several two-part tariffs that is not fully optimal can be Pareto-improved by introducing an additional option.

- *Introduction of a quantity discount*

An alternative approach introduces a quantity discount for the largest customers to stimulate sales. Whenever the existing tariff has a marginal price (for the last unit purchased by the largest customer) exceeding marginal cost, an appropriately designed quantity discount is Pareto-improving. To see this, it is simplest to consider the addition of a quantity discount that brings entirely new sales to the firm. Suppose that under the existing tariff the maximum purchase by any customer is $\bar{q}$, where by assumption the marginal price charged for this unit exceeds the marginal cost that the firm incurs to provide it. Suppose now that the firm revises the existing tariff by offering units after the $\bar{q}$-th at some price between marginal cost and what the existing tariff charges. With this revised tariff, each customer will purchase at least as much as before, and at the same prices, except that some additional units will be purchased at lower prices exceeding the firm's marginal cost. Thus, no customer is disadvantaged and some benefit (at least the largest customer will be encouraged to purchase more), and the firm's revenues are increased.

Recall that an optimal nonlinear tariff has the property that the last unit is sold at marginal cost; thus, further quantity discounts cannot Pareto-improve an optimal tariff. The fact that a nonoptimal tariff can be improved by quantity discounts for the largest customers to increase their purchases is a familiar one for many public utilities: often they perceive opportunities to increase revenues while benefiting their industrial customers by offering favorable terms for very large purchases—

5. See Willig (1978) for a proof of this fact, which depends on the assumption of independent demands among customers.

and ultimately the increased revenue can enable lower prices or better service for all customers.

• *Introduction of an optimal nonlinear tariff segment*

Another tactic allows customers the option of purchasing units according to the price schedule for an optimal nonlinear tariff. Suppose that $P(q)$ and $p(q)$ are the current tariff and its price schedule, which may reflect uniform pricing, a two-part tariff, or any more complicated menu of options; and let $P^*(q)$ and $p^*(q)$ represent an optimal nonlinear tariff and its price schedule. Typically the current price schedule is lower for small purchases and the optimal price schedule is lower for large purchases. Thus, there is again some purchase size q^* such that the current prices are less expensive for purchases less than q^*, and the optimal prices are less expensive for incremental units in excess of q^*. In this case again no customer is disadvantaged, larger customers benefit, and the firm's revenues increase—or if not needed for cost recovery then they can be used to reduce all prices.

As in the other cases, the net effect of this Pareto-improving modification is to offer a new menu of options in which the marginal price for the q-th unit is effectively the lesser of the current price $p(q)$ and the optimal price $p^*(q)$. For this reason, some regulatory agencies (such as the United States Federal Communications Commission) explicitly require that new optional tariffs be offered without withdrawal of existing tariffs.

The modified tariff is depicted in Figure 5.5, which assumes that for each unit a customer pays the lesser of the uniform price p and the optimal monopoly price schedule $p^*(q)$. If customers are indexed by a type parameter t then, as in the figure, all types greater than a critical value t^* increase their purchases and their net benefits increase. Moreover, the firm's profit increases because the optimal price schedule $p^*(q)$ is designed to obtain the maximum profit contribution from units exceeding $q(t^*)$, which is the last unit purchased by type t^*.

Optimal constrained nonlinear pricing

A general formulation that encompasses the three versions cited above is based on explicit recognition of the requirement that the tariff design must not disadvantage any customer. This requirement adds numerous constraints to the problem of maximizing total surplus in addition to the previous constraint that the firm obtains sufficient revenue to recover its costs. In terms of the formulation in §6, if the existing tariff $P(q)$ enables a customer of type t to obtain the net benefit $U(q(t), t) - P(q(t))$, then the optimal tariff $P°(q)$ must satisfy the constraint

$$U(q°(t), t) - P°(q°(t)) \geq U(q(t), t) - P(q(t)),$$

for each type t, where $q(t)$ and $q°(t)$ are the optimal purchases of type t under the

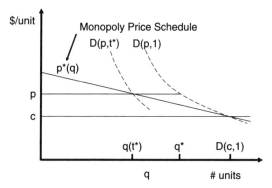

Fig. 5.5   A Pareto-improving price schedule: $p°(q) = \min\{p, p^*(q)\}$. Customer types $t > t^*$ benefit from lower marginal prices.

two tariffs. If the existing tariff is concave then these constraints imply that the marginal prices have the form

$$p°(q) = \min\{p(q), p^*(q)\} .$$

Here, $p^*(q)$ is the marginal price schedule for an unconstrained optimal nonlinear tariff that is chosen so that the required revenue is obtained by the firm. The unconstrained price schedule $p^*(q)$ provides quantity discounts for units in various intervals. In effect, for each q-th unit a customer has a choice between the old marginal price $p(q)$ and the new one $p^*(q)$. When there is a single such interval, it provides quantity discounts for all units in excess of some breakpoint q^* at which $p(q^*) = p^*(q^*)$. Thus, customers purchasing fewer than q^* units select the old tariff and are unaffected by the new tariff. Customers purchasing more than q^* units benefit from the quantity discounts provided.

A typical situation is shown in Figure 5.6, which assumes that the existing tariff charges a uniform price p. The continuity of the price schedule is a general property: discontinuities of the sort shown in Figure 5.7 do not occur in an optimal price schedule. In each case there is an interval (q_1, q_2) of purchases not selected by any customer. Such a tariff can always be improved by using a price schedule that is intermediate between the two shown, and that benefits both the customers and the firm. The reasons are essentially those already mentioned about why a uniform tariff can be improved.

The following example illustrates the analysis in the case that the existing tariff uses a uniform price.

Example 5.3: Suppose that the demand profile is $N(p, q) = 1 - p - q$, resulting from a population with types t that are uniformly distributed between zero and one, and demand functions $D(p, t) = t - p$ derived from benefit functions $U(q, t) = tq - \frac{1}{2}q^2$.

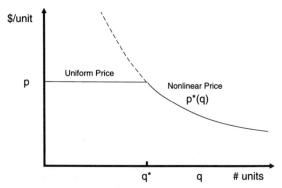

FIG. 5.6   Pareto-improving price schedule.

Assume that the firm's marginal cost is zero for simplicity. For this example, a uniform price p allows the firm to recover an amount $R(p) = \frac{1}{2}p[1-p]^2$ in revenues, resulting in a total consumers' surplus of $CS(p) = \frac{1}{6}[1-p]^3$. Hereafter, we assume that $R(p)$ is the amount of the firm's revenue requirement and we examine the consequences of meeting this revenue requirement via either unconstrained or constrained nonlinear pricing.

In the case of unconstrained nonlinear pricing, the Ramsey pricing rule implies that the optimal tariff has the property that the percentage profit margin on the q-th unit should be $\alpha/\eta(p(q), q)$, where η is the price elasticity of the demand profile. This rule implies that the optimal unconstrained nonlinear price schedule is

$$p(q) = \beta[1 - q],$$

where $\beta = \alpha/[1 + \alpha]$. The revenue realized from this price schedule is $R[\beta] = \frac{1}{3}\beta[1 - \beta]$ and the consumers' surplus is $CS[\beta] = \frac{1}{6}[1 - \beta]^2$, which by construction is the maximum attainable consumers' surplus given that the revenue constraint $R[\beta] = R(p)$ is used to determine the appropriate slope β of the marginal price schedule.

We first note that the maximum revenue obtainable from any uniform price is $2/27$, via $p = 1/3$, whereas an unconstrained nonlinear price schedule can obtain

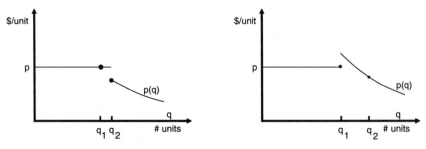

FIG. 5.7   Nonoptimal discontinuities in the price schedule.

the revenue $2/24$ by using $\beta = 1/2$, which is higher by 12.5%. Thus, for revenue requirements exceeding $2/24$ per potential customer in the population, no system of nonlinear pricing is sufficient; and for revenue requirements exceeding $2/27$ no uniform price is sufficient. In particular, there are some revenue requirements that preclude uniform pricing. In these cases, of course, $q^* = 0$ since it is infeasible to assure that no customer is disadvantaged and still raise the required revenue.

Next we note for revenue requirements obtainable by either uniform or nonlinear pricing that the distributional effects on customers are quite different. The least type served under uniform pricing is $t = p$, whereas with nonlinear pricing it is $t = \beta$. Further, for those types served the net benefit is $\frac{1}{2}[t-p]^2$ under uniform pricing but it is $\frac{1}{2}[t-\beta]^2/[1-\beta]$ under nonlinear pricing. In particular, if $0 < p < 1/3$ then the revenue constraint $R[\beta] = R(p)$ requires $\beta > p$; consequently, nonlinear pricing serves fewer customers and provides smaller net benefits to those customers with low types—although of course nonlinear pricing provides greater net benefits to high types that could more than compensate.

Now consider a nonlinear tariff that is optimal subject to the further requirement that no customers are disadvantaged as compared to uniform pricing that raises the same revenue for the firm. In this case the optimal price schedule takes the form specified above:

$$p^\circ(q) = \min \{p, p^*(q)\} \, ,$$

where now

$$p^*(q) = \gamma[1 - q], \quad \text{and} \quad \gamma = 1/3 \, ,$$

independently of which uniform price p is considered. Note that this choice of γ corresponds to the multiplier $\lambda = 1$ and the associated Ramsey number $\alpha = 1/2$ that would yield $\beta = 1/3$.[6] With this price schedule, types $t \leq 1 - 2p$ purchasing quantities less than $q^* = 1 - 3p$ are charged the uniform price p, whereas those purchasing more pay the uniform price for the first q^* units and thereafter obtain quantity discounts according to the price schedule p^* that applies to units in excess of q^*. The optimal price schedule p° assures that no customer is disadvantaged compared to uniform pricing, and those with high types obtain greater net benefits, and still the required revenue $R(p)$ is obtained for the firm.

Table 5.1 compares uniform pricing, unconstrained nonlinear pricing, and constrained nonlinear pricing in terms of the consumers' surplus that is realized for a fixed revenue requirement. Observe that unconstrained nonlinear pricing realizes the maximum consumers' surplus, but also constrained nonlinear pricing realizes more consumers' surplus than can be obtained from uniform pricing, as well as

---

6. In this example the Ramsey number α associated with the optimal price schedule p^* is independent of the uniform price p and its associated revenue $R(p)$. This feature is peculiar to a limited class of models. The fact that it does not hold generally is illustrated for the next example in Figure 5.10. My experience with examples indicates, however, that the optimal Ramsey number is often insensitive to the uniform price used as the price cap for the associated nonlinear schedule.

114   FUNDAMENTALS OF NONLINEAR PRICING

Table 5.1 Comparison of Three Pricing Policies

Revenue Requirement $R(p)$:	.0049	.0226	.0405	.0542	.0640	.0703	.0735
Uniform Pricing							
Price p:	.01	.05	.10	.15	.20	.25	.30
CS:	.1617	.1429	.1215	.1024	.0853	.0703	.0572
Constrained Nonlinear Pricing							
Breakpoint q^*:	.97	.85	.70	.55	.40	.25	.10
CS:	.1617	.1430	.1222	.1046	.0907	.0807	.0752
Unconstrained Nonlinear Pricing							
Slope β:	.0149	.0730	.1415	.2043	.2592	.3024	.3282
CS:	.1617	.1432	.1228	.1055	.0915	.0811	.0752

assuring that no customer is disadvantaged. Over much of the range of revenue requirements, constrained nonlinear pricing yields at least half as much gain in consumers' surplus as does unconstrained nonlinear pricing, and more if the revenue requirement is high. As can be seen in Figure 5.8, the differences in consumers' surplus are small compared to the effects of variations in the revenue requirement.

◇

Example 5.4: A similar pattern can be seen in Figure 5.9, which is based on Example 4.3 in the case that the substitution parameter is $a = 0.4$, the correlation

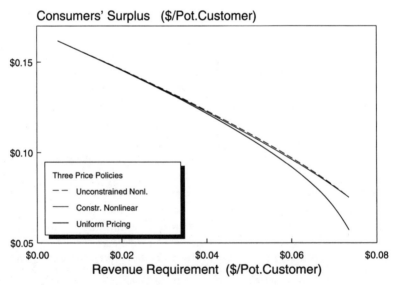

Consumers' Surplus   ($/Pot.Customer)

Three Price Policies
-- Unconstrained Nonl.
— Constr. Nonlinear
— Uniform Pricing

Revenue Requirement ($/Pot.Customer)

FIG. 5.8 Comparison of three pricing policies. Consumers' surplus is more sensitive to the revenue requirement than to constraints on the form of the price schedule.

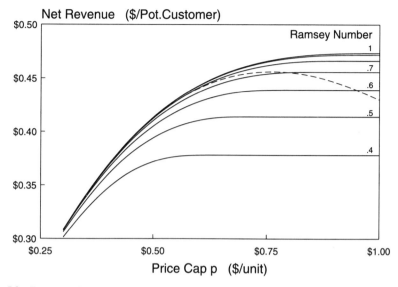

FIG. 5.9   Example 5.3: The dependence of revenue on the price cap p and the Ramsey number α. The dashed curve shows the revenue from uniform pricing.

between the type parameters is $r = 0.4$, the price of a substitute commodity is $p^* = \$0.50$, and the firm's marginal cost is $c = 0$. The figure shows the revenues from uniform pricing (the dashed curve) and constrained nonlinear pricing for several Ramsey numbers.[7] As in the previous example, revenue is relatively insensitive to the choice of the Ramsey number if the price cap p is substantially less than a monopolist's optimal uniform price. This occurs whenever a larger Ramsey number affects revenue mainly via higher prices for initial units, but these higher prices are curtailed by the price cap p. In the figure, variations around the revenue-equivalent Ramsey number produce variations in the revenue that are virtually imperceptible. There is in fact some variation but it is quite small compared to the scale of total revenue: Figure 5.10 shows the difference between the revenues from constrained nonlinear pricing and uniform pricing for several Ramsey numbers. Each circled point identifies the price cap (indicated by a mark along the abscissa) that if used with the associated Ramsey number produces the same revenue from constrained nonlinear pricing as from uniform pricing. Observe that the scale of the difference in revenues is multiplied by a factor of 10, 000 to produce perceptible variation in the vertical dimension. Figure 5.11 shows the resulting relationship between the Ramsey number and the price cap. Each point on the locus represents a Ramsey number and a price such that uniform pricing with that price yields the same revenue as constrained nonlinear pricing with that Ramsey number and price cap.

7. Revenue is measured per potential customer, defined as those 80.86% with positive demands at a zero price, by normalizing so that $N(0, 0) = 1$.

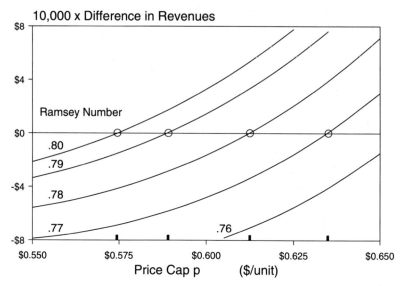

FIG. 5.10 Example 5.3: Determination of the Ramsey number that yields the same revenue as uniform pricing.

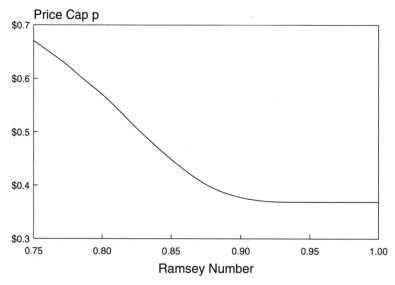

FIG. 5.11 Example 5.3: The relationship between the uniform price and the Ramsey number that yields the same revenue as constrained nonlinear pricing with that price cap.

The curve is nearly flat for small price caps because there are few customers for whom the quantity discounts offered by the declining portion of the price schedule is applicable. ◇

The chief implication of these and similar examples is that often there are appreciable gains from nonlinear pricing if the firm's revenue requirement is large; moreover, the costs of assuring that no customer is disadvantaged are relatively small. It should be remembered, however, that there are other cases in which uniform pricing is the optimal means of meeting the firm's revenue requirement: this is the case in the first example above if the types are distributed in the population according to an exponential distribution, rather than a uniform distribution as assumed. In these cases, there are no further gains from offering quantity discounts for large purchases.

In Section 3 we illustrate further with an application to the design of a Pareto-improving tariff for telephone service. In this application customers are classified into several groups based on their levels of usage under the existing tariff. The design problem is therefore posed as a constrained maximization problem of the sort usually solved by mathematical programming. That is, in addition to the usual criterion that the tariff maximizes an appropriately weighted average of consumers' surplus and the firm's net revenue, explicit constraints are added to represent the requirement that customers in each existing volume band are as well off under the new tariff as under the old one. Often this approach results in very nearly the answer derived above: if the optimal tariff is constrained to be Pareto-improving, it charges marginal prices that are the lesser of the old prices and the unconstrained optimal prices so constructed as to meet the revenue requirement. The sole exception is the price $p(q^*)$ at the margin between the old and new tariffs, since usually a customer buying a last unit at this price under the old tariff now has an incentive to buy additional units under the new tariff. The example in Section 3 has this property.

Dependent demands

The above construction of Pareto-improving tariffs depends on the assumption that customers' demands are independent. In important cases, however, customers' demands are jointly dependent in ways that preclude Pareto improvements. In fact, quantity discounts for large customers might conceivably reduce the utility's revenue.

In the extreme case that illustrates this possibility, the customers are firms in a highly competitive industry and they use the service sold by the utility as an input into their own production operations. Further, customers are heterogeneous because there are some large firms, whose monopoly on a superior low-cost technology allows positive profits, as well as some small firms (the "competitive fringe") whose marginal cost determines the price of the industry's product. To be precise, assume that both types of firms use a fixed quantity of the utility's service for each unit of output. In this case, if the utility offers an additional quantity discount advantageous only to the large firms, then the industry's market price, and therefore also the demand for the industry's product, remains unchanged, since the small firms' marginal cost remains unchanged; however, the additional cost advantage given the large firms further increases their market share. The net effect for the utility is that the increment in the large firms' purchases results in an exactly offsetting decrement in the small firms' purchases. Thus, the utility's revenues decline, because the price paid by the small firms is higher than the marginal price paid by the large firms.[8]

This is not a complete argument that no Pareto-improving tariff is possible because one must still show that there is no way to design an alternative tariff that redistributes some of the large firms' gains to the small firms and the utility so that none are disadvantaged.[9] It shows nevertheless that the simple constructions described above need not suffice.

5.3   Long-distance telephone tariffs

We describe an application of nonlinear pricing to the design of long-distance telephone rates to ensure that no class of customers is disadvantaged compared to a prevailing uniform price.[10]

In the United States since 1984, interexchange (that is, long-distance) carriers have been charged two fees ($\textit{¢}$/minute) for connections between their networks and their customers: a line charge to recover costs of the local loop that are not sensitive to traffic, and a traffic-sensitive charge for switching and trunk-line services in the local-exchange carrier's network. In 1986 these fees averaged 7.56$\textit{¢}$/min, for peak-period originating switched access for measured services. Generally they were passed on to customers as part of their uniform charge ($\textit{¢}$/min) for long-distance

---

8. As Ordover and Panzar (1980) note, this is essentially the "secondary line injury" to competing small firms that is prohibited in the United States by the Robinson-Patman Act of 1936. That is, a quantity discount for large firms can reduce the market share of small firms. In the present example the utility's revenue declines too, so such a discount might not be offered voluntarily, but the Act was intended to address cases in which a large customer has enough market power to bargain for price concessions. Such bargaining power requires, of course, that a large customer can credibly threaten to operate without the utility's service. In the case of electric power (or telecommunications), the feasibility of cogeneration (or bypass) adds credibility to such threats, but the Act also provides as a defense that the seller can meet an equally low price of a competitor. Cogeneration presumably qualifies as a competitor.

9. A complete proof, using some further assumptions, is provided by Ordover and Panzar (1980). To show that a Pareto-improving tariff is not generally possible it suffices to consider the case that the utility's current tariff uses a uniform price that maximizes its profit and, because the customers' industry is competitive, therefore also maximizes the combined profits of the utility and the customers' industry. In this case, it is evidently impossible to increase the profits of all three parties, since they are already fully maximized. In effect, if the utility's uniform price is already an optimal way of taxing the profits of the large firms, then there is no advantage from quantity discounts. It should be noted, however, that this argument is not sufficient for a fully enlightened analysis in a regulatory context, since it does not take into account the consequences for final consumers of the industry's product, who would benefit from reductions in the small firms' marginal cost.

10. This section is based on Heyman, Lazorchak, Sibley, and Taylor (1987).

Table 5.2 Distribution of Usage and Elasticities

Type	Usage Band	% of Accounts	Monthly Minutes	Elasticities	
				Current	Alternative
1	0–60	74.03	14.55	.16	.16
2	61–1000	25.47	160.21	.16	.16
3	1001–2000	0.26	1364.46	.22	.50
4	2001–7000	0.17	3547.77	.22	.50
5	7001–20000	0.05	11026.07	.31	.70
6	20000+	0.02	67425.60	.31	.98

service. For large customers these charges are appreciable and there has been a resulting incentive for such customers to install direct connections that bypass the local loop and switching. In June 1986, NYTel Company filed with the Federal Communications Commission a request for a nonlinear tariff to be billed directly to customers, partly to forestall bypass by its larger customers. The nonlinear tariff can be construed as a block-declining tariff or as the lower envelope of a set of six two-part tariffs that will be described below.

Table 5.2 shows the current distribution of NYTel's customers' average usage under the prevailing uniform charge, divided into usage bands. Also shown are the current elasticities of demand for customers in each usage band based on econometric studies, and an alternative schedule of roughly estimated elasticities based on long-run prospects for bypass: the higher elasticities for high-usage customers indicates that they are more price-sensitive due to the alternative of using bypass. In the following, we assume that demand by each usage band i has the form of the constant-elasticity demand function $q_i = t_i/p_i^{e_i}$, where p_i is the marginal price, e_i is the elasticity, and t_i indicates a type parameter associated with that class of customer. From the uniform price $p = 7.56¢$, the monthly minutes of use, and the elasticities shown in the table, the parameter t_i can be calculated. As for costs, the

Table 5.3 Predicted Consequences of NYTel's Proposed Tariff (Alternative Elasticities)

Customer Type	Proposed Tariff ($)	Change in Consumer Surplus ($)	Change in Producer's Surplus ($)
1	.0961	−0.29	0.25
2	.0713	−0.80	0.89
3	.0484	16.85	0.36
4	.0352	119.61	−50.93
5	.0302	582.87	−214.14
6	.0269	5,061.42	−1,134.39
Average		1.135	−0.007

Table 5.4 Optimized Tariff: I (Alternative Elasticities)

Type	Fixed Fee $/mon.	Usage Charge $/min.	Change in Consumers' Surplus	Change in Producer's Surplus
1	0	.0756	0	0
2	0	.0756	0	0
3	0.52	.0752	0	0.23
4	29.18	.0674	0.82	12.06
5	342.17	.0446	66.00	170.61
6	3,495.58	.0238	2,350.00	1,956.60
Average			0.50	0.50

marginal cost of service is assumed to be 1¢/minute based on a similar rate filing by New England Telephone.

Table 5.3 shows the block-declining (or "tapered") tariff proposed by NYTel and the predicted consequences based on the assumed model, as compared to the current uniform charge, based on the alternative set of elasticities. The changes in surplus are recorded in terms of $ per month per customer. Note that the proposed tariff is nearly revenue neutral but it provides substantial benefits to the larger customers. It is economically efficient in that it increases total surplus, but it is not distributionally neutral since some customer types are disadvantaged.

An alternative methodology is to impose constraints on the design of the tariff to ensure that no customer type is disadvantaged. Table 5.4 shows the result of such a calculation done with the objective of maximizing the sum of consumers' and producer's surplus. Note that these results show that it is possible with such a set of optional two-part tariffs to disadvantage no customer, and yet increase profits (that is, producer's surplus). A similar calculation for the current elasticities (rather than the alternative ones) is shown in Table 5.5: in this case the average change in profit is +10¢ per customer per month, and it is positive for every type.

These results are indicative of a developing methodology for designing rates for public utilities. The aim is to construct the rates as nonlinear tariffs so as to obtain

Table 5.5 Optimized Tariff: II (Current Elasticities)

Type	Fixed Fee $/mon.	Usage Charge $/min.	Change in Consumers' Surplus
1	0	.0756	0
2	0	.0756	0
3	0	.0756	0
4	0.49	.0754	0
5	73.27	.0690	1.04
6	2,989.17	.0313	381.00
Average			.077

the greatest gains in efficiency compatible with assuring that no major subgroup of customers is disadvantaged by the change to the new tariff. This is done mainly by adding new options to the current menu of tariffs. This constraint is useful in ensuring that the new tariff is favorably received by the cognizant regulatory agency.

5.4 Summary

A regulated firm can be construed as setting prices efficiently to meet a revenue requirement. The formulation in terms of Ramsey pricing interprets efficiency in terms of maximizing consumers' surplus, using only the minimal monopoly power required to raise the required revenue. In this case the firm proceeds in exactly the same fashion as a profit-maximizing firm except that profit margins are reduced proportionately and uniformly so that no more than the required revenue is obtained.

Applications of Ramsey pricing are often constrained by the requirement that no customer is disadvantaged by the changes proposed. In such cases, a Pareto-improving tariff can be constructed by allowing customers the option of purchasing each unit from the old price schedule or the new one. The new tariff can be of various kinds, such as a two-part tariff or the old tariff amended by inclusion of additional quantity discounts, such as a segment of an optimal price schedule. All of these can benefit some or all customers without reducing the firm's revenue, or they can be used to increase the firm's profits.

When the old tariff uses a uniform price, a nonlinear tariff that is optimally designed to meet the revenue requirement typically includes the old tariff plus quantity discounts for large purchases. In examples, the cost of assuring that no customer is disadvantaged is small compared to the effect of the revenue requirement. This feature is largely explained by the fact that the gains from nonlinear pricing are concentrated among customers making large purchases, so the costs of providing assurances to customers making small purchases are relatively small.

Nonlinear tariffs can also meet revenue requirements that cannot be attained with uniform pricing. This feature can be important in providing services that otherwise could not be offered profitably. It is especially important in industries affected by network externalities. Telecommunications provides the standard example: each customer's benefits depend on how many others subscribe to service and thereby become available to exchange calls. Starting a new service therefore requires attracting a critical mass of initial customers large enough to create mutual benefits among themselves and thereafter to attract additional subscribers. Moreover, these benefits must be sufficient to allow prices that will recover at least the hookup, access, and fixed operating costs of the system. Pricing based on, say, a fixed fee or a two-part tariff has the disadvantage that it requires a larger critical mass than does nonlinear pricing. For example, Oren, Smith, and Wilson (1982a) report on an application to the design of a special system for subscribers with impaired hearing, for which nonlinear pricing enables a critical mass that is 22% of the size required by a fixed fee, and 41% of the size required by a two-part tariff. Once the system is fully established, the optimal profit-maximizing nonlinear tariff generates more total surplus and more profits for the firm but less consumers' surplus for subscribers; the average charge per subscriber is the nearly the same for all three regimes.[11] Nevertheless, without nonlinear pricing the larger critical mass might mean that the system would never be established. Thus, to the advantages of nonlinear pricing cited in this chapter one can add that its use might be necessary to provide services that would otherwise be unprofitable or dependent on initial subsidies to reach a critical mass.

11. When there are positive externalities of this and other kinds, an optimal nonlinear tariff charges a fixed fee that is less than the firm's cost of providing access. Due to the benefits created for other subscribers, it is advantageous to attract additional customers by subsidizing access. This is a main source of the smaller critical mass, and after the system is fully established it also results in a market penetration that is larger.

Part II

DISAGGREGATED DEMAND MODELS

6

SINGLE-PARAMETER DISAGGREGATED MODELS

The basic principles of nonlinear pricing described in Part I rely on the demand profile to summarize the minimal data required to construct an optimal price schedule. This chapter presents a parallel exposition using explicit models of customers' preferences or demand behaviors. In these models, individual customers or market segments are characterized by parameters indicating their types, and their benefits or demands are estimated directly as functions of these parameters. Disaggregated models of this sort are frequently used in econometric studies to represent how customers' demands are affected by various characteristics, such as income and socio-demographic category for residential customers, or line of business and production rate for commercial customers.

The analyses in previous chapters account only for the aggregate demand for each increment in the purchase size. In this chapter the analysis is conducted at the same disaggregated level as the data in the model. Thus, the quantities selected and the prices paid by individual customers or market segments are specified explicitly. To simplify the presentation, however, the exposition is confined to the case that the differences among customers are described by a single one-dimensional type parameter with a known distribution in the population. In §8.4 we show that using a single parameter entails no substantial loss of generality when the tariff applies to a single product.

The presentation is simplified initially by assuming in Section 1 that the population of customers is finite. Section 2 adopts the other extreme hypothesis: the population of customers is so large that it can be modeled as a continuum in which each customer is described by a one-dimensional type parameter with a continuous distribution in the population. The special case of a two-part tariff is examined briefly in Section 3, followed by a detailed analysis of general multipart tariffs in Section 4. The extension to fully nonlinear tariffs is presented in Section 5, followed by several examples in Section 6. Lastly, Section 7 characterizes optimal fixed fees; in particular, optimal nonlinear tariffs omit fixed fees if the firm incurs no fixed cost in serving a customer. This is not true for optimal multipart tariffs, but the difference is insignificant if even a few options are offered.

Section 1 assumes that the firm designs the tariff to maximize its profit contribution. Later sections include Ramsey pricing in which the tariff is designed to maximize consumers' or total surplus subject to a constraint that the firm's profit contribution is sufficient to meet a revenue requirement. Only necessary conditions for an optimal tariff are considered in this chapter: sufficiency conditions are deferred to §8.

6.1 A Model with discrete types

The basic element of the formulation is a model of the heterogeneity of customers' demand behaviors. For this purpose, each customer or market segment is classified as one of several types, and the model specifies the demand behavior of each type. The possible types are indicated by an index $i = 1, \ldots, m$. We assume that the firm knows the number or fraction f_i of the customers classified into each type i, and that the demand of each type is predicted exactly.

A customer of type i is described by a utility function $U_i(q)$ indicating the gross benefit from a purchase of size q. If the customer purchases this quantity from the tariff $P(q)$ then the net benefit is $U_i(q) - P(q)$. There are no income effects so benefits are measured directly in dollar amounts, and $U_i(0) \equiv 0$.

The firm's costs generally depend on the list $Q = (q_1, \ldots, q_m)$ of all customers' purchases according to a function $C(Q)$. For example, one often assumes that $C(Q) = C(\sum_i f_i q_i)$, or $C(Q) = \sum_i f_i C(q_i)$, or some combination. We assume the latter form here for simplicity.

This formulation implies that the firm's profit contribution is

$$\text{Profit Contribution} = \sum_{i=1}^{m} f_i \cdot [P(q_i) - C(q_i)]$$

when each customer of type i purchases the quantity q_i in response to the tariff P. Providing incentives for customers to make these purchases requires that the tariff satisfies two kinds of constraints. The first kind assures that a customer prefers to make the designated purchase rather than none at all:

$$U_i(q_i) - P(q_i) \geq U_i(0) - P(0) \equiv 0.$$

This is called the participation constraint for type i. Note that it excludes charging a positive amount unless the customer makes a positive purchase. The second kind assures that a customer prefers to make the designated purchase rather than one assigned to another type:

$$U_i(q_i) - P(q_i) \geq U_i(q_j) - P(q_j), \qquad \text{for each } j \neq i.$$

These are called the incentive compatibility constraints for type i. In the following we use $P_i \equiv P(q_i)$ to denote the total charge imposed by the tariff for the purchase of size q_i.

Suppose first that all the variables P_i and q_i are restricted to a finite set of possible values. In this case the optimal tariff is found by searching among the possible combinations of these values satisfying the participation and incentive-compatibility constraints to find a combination that attains the maximum feasible value of the profit contribution. Having found such an optimal combination, the tariff is specified by assigning the total charge P_i to the purchase size q_i. For other quantities not among those assigned to any type, the usual specification is that the tariff $P(q)$ is the same as the charge for the next larger assigned purchase; this is sufficient to deter purchases in the interval $q_{i-1} < q < q_i$.

Finding an optimal combination of charges and purchase sizes as described above is a tedious task, and it is time-consuming even on a fast computer. The preferred method, therefore, is based on a specification that allows the possible purchase sizes to be any real numbers, and similarly the possible charges can be any real numbers. Hereafter, therefore, the purchase sizes are constrained only to be nonnegative real numbers ($q_i \geq 0$) and similarly for the tariff charges. In this case, of course, the model must also specify the gross benefit function $U_i(q)$ for each type in a way that is tractable for analysis. We generally assume convenient regularity conditions: U_i is increasing, concave, and differentiable. Given real domains for the purchase sizes and tariff charges, maximizing the profit contribution subject to the participation and incentive-compatibility constraints is a standard problem of nonlinear constrained optimization. For some applications, reliance on standard software to solve such problems is the best practical approach.

Characterization of an optimal tariff

Our interest here is to establish the key properties of the solution that can be derived from mathematical principles. The necessary conditions for an optimum can be expressed in terms of a Lagrange multiplier, say λ_{ij}, associated with the j-th incentive-compatibility constraint for type i. Such a multiplier is a nonnegative number that is positive only if the constraint is actually binding at the optimum. The key properties that can be derived are the following.

1. If type i is such that both P_i and q_i are positive, so that type i is an active customer, then

$$v_i(q_i) - c(q_i) = \sum_{j \neq i} \lambda_{ji} \frac{f_j}{f_i} [v_j(q_i) - v_i(q_i)],$$

where $v_i(q) = U_i'(q)$ is the i-th type's marginal benefit or willingness-to-pay for a q-th unit, and $c(q) = C'(q)$ is the firm's marginal cost.

2. If type i's net benefit is positive, so that its participation constraint is not binding, then

$$f_i = \sum_{j \neq i} [\lambda_{ij} f_i - \lambda_{ji} f_j].$$

Recall that a customer of type i is predicted ultimately to choose a purchase size q_i such that $v_i(q_i) = p(q_i)$, where $p(q_i)$ is the tariff's marginal price for the q_i-th unit. Consequently, property 1 states that the firm's profit margin $p(q_i) - c(q_i)$ on the q_i-th unit should be given by a weighted combination of the differences between the willingness to pay for this unit by other types $j \neq i$ and by type i. These weights are positive at the optimum only for those other types who are indifferent between their assigned purchases and type i's purchase q_i. Property 2 constrains what these weights can be: they must satisfy a consistency condition.

Without further assumptions, the construction of a solution that satisfies properties 1 and 2 can be difficult and usually one must rely on numerical analysis via computer programs for nonlinear constrained optimization. Here, however, we impose a further assumption of the sort used in most theoretical studies of nonlinear pricing in order to obtain a simple characterization of the optimal tariff. The purpose of this assumption is to obtain the special case that for each active type i the only binding incentive-compatibility constraint is the one for type $j = i - 1$; that is, only the next higher type is indifferent between its purchase and i's purchase. Of course this special case depends on having initially ordered the customers' types in such a fashion that this is possible. For example, one assumption that is commonly used to obtain this special case is that higher types have higher demands at every price, as we illustrate in later sections. Even with much weaker assumptions, nevertheless, this special case often obtains, simply because the optimal tariff often has the property that each type's purchase size is "envied" by at most one other type.[1]

Given such an assumption, we can exploit the fact that the multiplier λ_{ij} is positive only for $j = i - 1$. In this case, if we define $\hat{\lambda}_i = f_i \lambda_{i,i-1}$ then property 2 can be cast in the form

$$\hat{\lambda}_i - \hat{\lambda}_{i+1} = f_i, \qquad \text{and} \qquad \hat{\lambda}_{m+1} = 0,$$

from which it follows that

$$\hat{\lambda}_i = \bar{F}_i, \qquad \text{where} \quad \bar{F}_i \equiv \sum_{j \geq i} f_j.$$

1. For analyses of the general case see Champsaur and Rochet (1989), Guesnerie and Seade (1982), Matthews and Moore (1987), and Moore (1984).

Thus, $\bar{F}_i$ is the number of customers of types $i, i+1, \ldots, m$ (and $\bar{F}_{m+1} = 0$), and the weight $\hat{\lambda}_i$ must be equal to this number. Using this fact in property 1 provides the key characterization:

$$v_i(q_i) = c(q_i) + \frac{\bar{F}_{i+1}}{f_i}[v_{i+1}(q_i) - v_i(q_i)].$$

This equation determines the purchase size q_i. To induce a customer of type i to select the indicated quantity q_i, the marginal price for the q_i-th unit must be $p_i = v_i(q_i)$. And, from the incentive-compatibility condition we obtain further that the tariff is constructed recursively by the formula

$$P_i = P_{i-1} + U_i(q_i) - U_i(q_{i-1}),$$

starting from $P_{i^*} = U_{i^*}(q_{i^*})$, where i^* is the least type willing to purchase at the marginal price for its assigned quantity. If the resulting tariff is concave, then one implementation offers a menu of m two-part tariffs that associates the marginal price p_i with the fixed fee $P_i - p_i q_i$.

A useful version of the optimality condition restates it as the requirement that

$$[v_i(q_i) - c(q_i)]\bar{F}_i = [v_{i+1}(q_i) - c(q_i)]\bar{F}_{i+1}.$$

In this form it states that the firm's profit contribution from the sale of the q_i-th unit is the same whether it is sold at the marginal price $v_i(q_i)$ to those types $j \geq i$ or at the marginal price $v_{i+1}(q_i)$ to those types $j > i$. Figure 6.1 illustrates this calculation by showing for each type i the profit contribution $[v_i(q) - c(q)]\bar{F}_i$ from the q-th unit when it is assigned to type i. The purchase size q_i assigned to type i is the largest for which the profit contribution is greater than would be obtained from assigning that unit to the next higher type. Subject to this condition, the total tariff is constructed so that each type i is indifferent between its assigned purchase q_i or the purchase assigned to the next lower type. This is shown in Figure 6.2, which graphs each type i's locus of pairs (q, P) of purchase sizes and tariff payments that yield the net benefit $U_i(q_i) - P_i$ from the assignment (q_i, P_i).

This characterization is essentially equivalent to the one derived previously in §4 using the demand profile N, as can be seen by identifying $\bar{F}_{i+1}$ with the number $N(p_i, q_i)$ of customers willing to purchase the q_i-th unit at the marginal price p_i. The exposition in §4 is basically an intuitively sensible way of presenting the conclusions derived here.

Extension to a continuum of types

This analysis can be extended straightforwardly to the case that customers' types are described by a continuum of real-valued parameters t. In this case, taking the

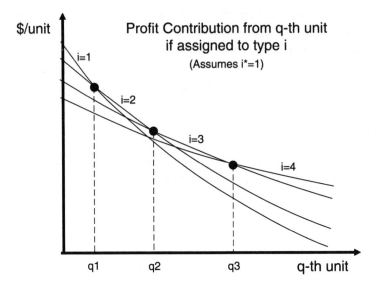

FIG. 6.1 Each type is assigned all increments for which the profit contribution exceeds that from assigning it to the next higher type.

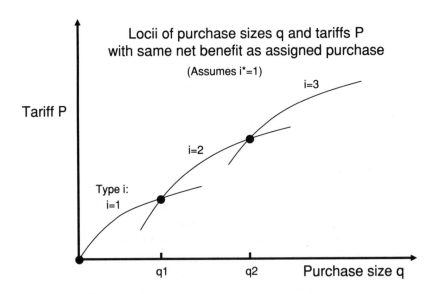

FIG. 6.2 Each type is indifferent between its assigned purchase and the purchase assigned to the next lower type.

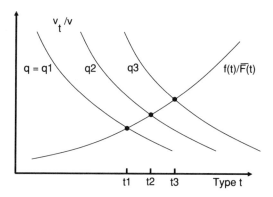

FIG. 6.3   Construction of the assignment of types to quantities purchased, for three quantities $q_1 <$ $q_2 < q_3$ and their assigned types $t_1 < t_2 < t_3$.

limit as the difference between adjacent types shrinks to zero yields the analogous characterization of each type t's purchase $q(t)$:

$$v(q(t), t) = c(q(t)) + \frac{\bar{F}(t)}{f(t)} \cdot \frac{\partial v}{\partial t}(q(t), t).$$

In this version, $f(t)$ is interpreted as the density of customers of type t, $\bar{F}(t)$ is the number of customers of types higher than t, and $v(q, t)$ is the willingness to pay for the q-th unit by type t. Given the schedule $q(t)$ of predicted purchases by the various types, the marginal price schedule is $p(q) = v(q, t(q))$, where $t(q)$ is a type purchasing q. Figure 6.3 and Figure 6.4 illustrate the calculation of the optimal price schedule for an example in which marginal cost is nil. As shown in the first figure, for many of the models used in practice the hazard rate $f(t)/\bar{F}(t)$ is increasing but $v_t(q, t)/v(q, t)$ is decreasing in t and increasing in q. The intersections shown in the first figure identify the three types t_i assigned the three quantities q_i shown, and then these are used in the second figure to identify the corresponding marginal price $\hat{p}(t) = p(q(t))$ at which each type purchases its marginal unit $q(t)$ as the type's marginal value $v(q(t), t)$ of that unit.

Alternatively, if $D(p, t)$ is the demand function of type t then one can use the property that $q = D(p, t)$ when $p = v(q, t)$ to derive:

$$\frac{\partial v(q, t)}{\partial t} = - \left[\frac{\partial D}{\partial t}(p, t) \right] \div \left[\frac{\partial D}{\partial p}(p, t) \right] \equiv -D_t/D_p.$$

Consequently, in terms of the demand function the condition that characterizes the optimal price schedule is

$$[\hat{p}(t) - c] D_p(\hat{p}(t), t) f(t) + D_t(\hat{p}(t), t) \bar{F}(t) = 0.$$

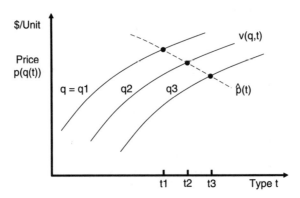

FIG. 6.4   Construction of the marginal price $\hat{p}(t) = p(q(t))$ for unit $q(t)$ assigned as the marginal unit purchased by type t. The price is the type's marginal valuation $v(q(t), t)$ for the last unit purchased.

In this version, each type t is assigned a marginal price $\hat{p}(t)$ and then the inferred purchase is $q(t) = D(\hat{p}(t), t)$, which is the quantity at which the marginal cost c is evaluated. The price schedule is inferred from the relation $p(q(t)) = \hat{p}(t)$. A somewhat more intuitive rendition of the optimality condition is:

$$[\hat{p}(t) - c] \cdot [\partial_p D(\hat{p}(t), t)] \cdot f(t)\, dt + dp \cdot [\partial_t D(\hat{p}(t), t)] \cdot \bar{F}(t) = 0 \,.$$

In this form it states that the loss from raising type t's marginal price, which reduces the profit contribution by reducing type t's demand by $\partial_p D$ for each of the $f(t)\, dt$ customers of that type, is compensated by the increment dp in the profit margin obtained from higher types. Note that type $t + dt$ is newly assigned the price $\hat{p}(t)$ previously assigned to type t, which is why the indicated change in demand for higher types is $\partial_t D$.

In subsequent sections we develop this characterization in greater detail, including the extension to Ramsey pricing when the firm must meet a revenue requirement. After specifying details of the formulation, we derive analogous characterizations of two-part and multipart tariffs. Then we reconstruct the characterization for nonlinear tariffs directly from the basic formulation.

6.2   Models with one-dimensional types

In this section we formulate a general model with a one-dimensional continuum of customers' types or market segments. This model will be used to justify the construction in Section 1 as well as the demand-profile formulation in §4.

As in the discrete case, the basic elements of the formulation include a model of each type's demand behavior and a distribution of customers' types in the population. Unlike the demand-profile formulation, this formulation requires two separate estimates obtained from demand data. However, the degrees of freedom

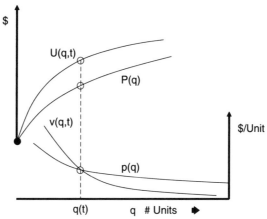

FIG. 6.5 A customer's purchase selection: the net benefit $U(q, t) - P(q)$ is maximized where the marginal benefit $v(q, t)$ intersects the price schedule $p(q)$.

in the estimation procedure remain essentially the same: the distribution of types merely counts the number of customers with each estimated demand function, and indeed could be uniform without any loss of generality.

The type index t is assumed to be a real number in an interval of possible types. The distribution function $F(t)$ indicates the number (viz., the measure or proportion) of customers having type indices not greater than t. The preferences of a customer of type t are specified by a utility function $U(q, t)$ indicating the gross benefit obtained from purchase of a quantity q. If the customer purchases this quantity at a cost $P(q)$ then the net benefit is $U(q, t) - P(q)$. Again, there are no income effects, benefits are measured directly in dollar amounts, and $U(0, t) = 0$. Figure 6.5 portrays schematically a customer of type t's selection of an optimal purchase $q(t)$: the selected quantity maximizes the net benefit available from the locus of quantities and associated charges along the tariff. In the figure, the concavity of the tariff reflects a decreasing schedule of marginal prices.

Each type can also be described by its demand function $D(p, t)$, indicating the optimal purchase in response to the uniform price p. If $v(q, t) \equiv U_q(q, t)$ is type t's marginal valuation of the q-th unit, then the demand function satisfies $v(D(p, t), t) = p$, provided this is evaluated where the price schedule intersects the demand function from below.

We use the following technical assumptions:[2]

> **A1:** The type distribution function has a corresponding density function $f(t) = F'(t)$ that is positive on an interval $a \leq t \leq b$. The number of customers having types greater than t is denoted by $\bar{F}(t) \equiv 1 - F(t)$. We generally assume that the hazard rate $f(t)/\bar{F}(t)$ is increasing.

2. An additional assumption A4 is included in §8.1 to obtain fully sufficient conditions. These assumptions can be recast in terms of the property of quasi-supermodularity as in Milgrom and Shannon (1991) to obtain necessary and sufficient conditions.

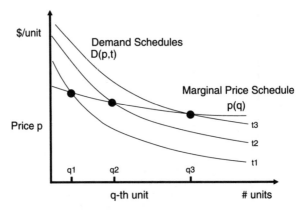

FIG. 6.6   Representative demand functions and a price schedule.

A2: The utility function is smoothly differentiable and increasing in each argument q and t, and concave in q; that is, in terms of its partial derivatives, $U_q > 0$, $U_{qq} < 0$, and $U_t > 0$ if $q > 0$. Moreover, the marginal benefit from an incremental unit increases as the customer's type increases; that is, $U_{qt} > 0$ or equivalently $v_t > 0$. This says that higher types demand more at each price.

A3: The cost function is smoothly differentiable, nondecreasing, and convex; in particular, the marginal cost $c(q)$ is nondecreasing.

The first assumption A1 says essentially that there are many customers in the population and their types are not bunched around any one type. The firm is assumed to know the distribution of types, so the population and its economic environment is implicitly assumed to be sufficiently stable that the firm can learn from experience. The second is most easily seen as specifying that each type t has a demand function $D(p, t)$ that is a decreasing function of the marginal price p for incremental units. Moreover, a customer with a larger type index has uniformly higher demand, so if $t' > t$ then $D(p, t') > D(p, t)$ at every price p. This excludes the possibility that two types' demand functions intersect. Thus, the types signify market segments that are ordered by the sizes of their purchases, independently of the price charged. Figure 6.6 depicts an example for which several demand functions are shown, as well as an indication of the price schedule $p(q)$ for the q-th unit. The restrictions imposed by the assumptions are shown in the figure; most evident is the feature that a higher type has a uniformly higher demand function.

Note that a demand locus $q = D(p, t)$ shown as a function of the price p can also be interpreted as the marginal benefit $p = v(q, t)$ when interpreted as a function of the purchase size q. According to assumption A2, v is a decreasing function of q and an increasing function of t.

Connection to the demand-profile formulation

It is useful to realize that the elements of this formulation are essentially summarized by the demand profile $N(p, q)$ used in §4. To see this, observe that an alternative type index is the customer's rank $r = F(t)$, which has a uniform distribution on the unit interval. Assumption A2 implies that r indicates the customer's rank order in terms of his purchase size for any specified price. This assumption also implies that the demand profile, constructed according to either definition

$$N(p, q) = \#\{t \mid v(q, t) \geq p\} = \#\{t \mid D(p, t) \geq q\},$$

is a decreasing function of both the price p and the purchase size q. Conversely, given the demand profile, the equation $1 - r = N(p, q)$ can be solved for either p or q as a function of the other two parameters. If we solve for q then we obtain the demand function $q = D(p, r)$ of the r-th ranked customer, and if we solve for p then we obtain the marginal utility $p = v(q, r)$ indicating the customer's willingness to pay for a q-th unit. Moreover, the customer of rank r has a utility function that can be calculated as the sum

$$U(q, r) = \int_0^q v(x, r) \, dx$$

of the marginal valuations of the units purchased. Alternatively, $\int_p^\infty D(\pi, r) \, d\pi$ represents his consumer's surplus at the uniform price p, provided there are no income effects.

The condition that identifies an optimal price schedule also has an exact analogy. To make the connection between the conditions derived in Section 1 and in §4 for the case of a profit-maximizing firm, assume again that the type index has a distribution function $F(t)$ that need not be uniform. Using the demand profile representation, we previously derived the condition

$$N(p, q) + N_p(p, q) \cdot [p - c] = 0$$

to characterize the price $p = p(q)$ on the optimal price schedule for the marginal price of the q-th unit. Alternatively, as above we can use the identity $1 - r = N(p, q)$ to solve for the rank $r(p, q)$ of the type $t(p, q)$ whose purchase is q when the marginal price is p. The demand profile is therefore

$$N(p, q) = 1 - r(p, q) = \bar{F}(t(p, q)),$$

where by definition $t(p, q)$ satisfies $p = v(q, t(p, q))$. This implies that

$$N_p(p, q) = -f(t(p, q))t_p(p, q) = -f(t(p, q))/v_t(q, t(p, q)).$$

Substituting these relationships into the optimality condition in terms of the demand profile yields the alternative condition

$$\bar{F}(t) - [f(t)/v_t(q,t)][v(q,t) - c] = 0,$$

which is the same as the condition derived in Section 1 to characterize the optimal assignment of the purchase size $q(t)$ to type t. This first-order necessary condition for a local optimum has a unique solution for the global optimum if the left side is a decreasing function of q (when searching for the optimal assignment $q(t)$) or of t (if the problem is interpreted as searching for the optimal assignment $t(q)$ of purchases to types): these monotonicity conditions translate into the monotonicity conditions imposed as sufficiency conditions in §4 and §8.1.

Overall, this construction indicates that the specification in terms of customers' one-dimensional types is essentially equivalent to the formulation in terms of the demand profile used previously, provided customers' demand functions do not cross so that the types represent well-defined market segments.

Customers' second-order conditions

There is a further proviso, however. The customer's second-order necessary condition for a local maximum requires that $v_q(q,t) - p'(q) \leq 0$ if t purchases q. This says that the price schedule intersects the demand function from below. In terms of the demand profile this translates into a fairly complicated requirement:

$$[N_{pq}/N_q - N_{pp}/N_p] \cdot [p - c] \leq 1,$$

at $p = p(q)$. But in a model with explicit types this translates into the simpler requirement that the assignment $q(t)$ of types to purchase sizes must be nondecreasing. We defer the analysis of this requirement to §8.1.

6.3   Two-part tariffs

A special case of a nonlinear tariff is a two-part tariff, so called because it comprises a uniform price for each unit purchased, plus a fixed fee payable if any positive amount is purchased. A two-part tariff is not ordinarily the optimal form of a nonlinear tariff, but if the costs of monitoring customers' cumulative purchases are substantial then it can be advantageous.

The motive for offering a two-part tariff is often simple expediency to raise revenue by assessing an additional uniform charge against each customer. The effects can be inefficient, however, if the fixed fee excludes some customers from purchasing. That is, unlike optimal nonlinear tariffs, which in the absence of fixed costs never impose fixed fees that exclude customers, the main effect of a two-part tariff is to reduce the market penetration in exchange for higher fixed fees collected from the market remaining. A two-part tariff can be relatively efficient, as compared to using a uniform price above marginal cost to meet the same revenue requirement, because it enables the price to be set closer to marginal cost. Nevertheless, a full comparison must also take into account the reduced market penetration.

We first demonstrate the construction of an optimal two-part tariff for the case of a profit-maximizing monopolist. The firm's profit contribution is obtained from two sources: the profit margin $p - c$ on each unit sold, and the fee P collected from each customer electing to subscribe to the tariff. If t_* is the lowest type among the subscribers, so that $\bar{F}(t_*)$ is the number of subscribers, then these two sources provide in total the profit contribution or producer's surplus

$$\text{PS} = P \cdot \bar{F}(t_*) + [p - c] \cdot \int_{t_*}^{\infty} D(p, t) \, dF(t) \, .$$

That is, each type $t \geq t_*$ responds with the demand $D(p, t)$ to the uniform price p. The central issue is therefore to identify how the market penetration, represented by t_*, is affected by the tariff. In practice this is rarely predictable with accuracy; however, here we adhere to the assumption that customers' benefits from subscribing to the tariff are exactly described by the model. Thus, the net benefit obtained by a subscriber of type t is $U(q, t) - pq - P$ if he purchases q units, or in terms of the consumer's surplus, it is

$$\int_{p}^{\infty} D(\pi, t) \, d\pi - P \, .$$

The model predicts, therefore, that the marginal subscriber is that type t_* for which the consumer surplus is zero, and in particular the fee P that results in the market penetration t_* is

$$P = \int_{p}^{\infty} D(\pi, t_*) \, d\pi \, .$$

Substituting this characterization into the formula for the profit contribution then poses the firm's maximization problem as the joint determination of the optimal uniform price p and the market penetration t_*. Let

$$\bar{D}(p, t_*) = \int_{t_*}^{\infty} D(p, t) \, dF(t)$$

and $\quad \bar{\eta}(p, t_*) = -p \bar{D}_p(p, t_*) / \bar{D}(p, t_*)$

be the aggregate demand and its corresponding price elasticity when the market penetration is t_*.

We display only the condition that determines the price, deferring the condition for t_* to later. Expressed in terms of the price elasticity it is that the percentage profit margin should be

$$\frac{p-c}{p} = \frac{1}{\bar{\eta}(p, t_*)}\left[1 - \bar{F}(t_*)\frac{D(p, t_*)}{\bar{D}(p, t_*)}\right].$$

Because $\bar{D}(p, t_*)/\bar{F}(t_*)$ is just the average quantity demanded, the quantity in square brackets is one minus the ratio of the minimum to the average quantity demanded.[3] In contrast to ordinary uniform pricing that sets the percentage profit margin equal to the reciprocal of the price elasticity, in the case of a two-part tariff the profit margin is reduced to take account of the effect on the market penetration. In particular, a lower price allows a deeper market penetration and thereby enables collection of the fixed fee from a larger number of subscribers. This tradeoff between the profit margin and the number of subscribers paying the fixed fee is, of course, the essence of the firm's decision problem in designing a two-part tariff.

A similar result obtains for a regulated monopoly. The objective in this case is to maximize total surplus subject to the condition that the firm's profit contribution is sufficient to meet a revenue requirement. The previous formula for the firm's profit contribution identifies the producer's surplus PS; the corresponding formula for the consumers' surplus is

$$\text{CS} = \int_{t_*}\left[\int_p^\infty D(\pi, t)\, d\pi - P\right] dF(t),$$

which sums up the types' surplus between the demand curve and the uniform price schedule p, net of the fixed fee P. The objective for the Ramsey pricing problem is therefore to maximize $\text{CS} + [1 + \lambda]\text{PS}$, using λ as the Lagrange multiplier for the firm's revenue requirement and $\alpha = \lambda/[1 + \lambda]$ as the corresponding Ramsey number. For this formulation the condition determining the optimal profit margin is exactly analogous:

$$\frac{p-c}{p} = \frac{\alpha}{\bar{\eta}(p, t_*)}\left[1 - \bar{F}(t_*)\frac{D(p, t_*)}{\bar{D}(p, t_*)}\right].$$

As in the case of nonlinear pricing, the effect of relaxing the revenue requirement is to allow further emphasis on efficiency considerations by reducing the profit margin associated with any particular market penetration. In turn, this expands the market and enables a reduction also in the fixed fee.

---

3. In more general models studied in §8.4 this ratio can exceed unity because the average demands of marginal types $t_*(\theta)$ can exceed average demand, in which case the marginal price is less than the marginal cost; cf. Oi (1971) and Schmalansee (1981a).

An important special case is an ordinary linear tariff with no fixed fee and a uniform price p. In this case the marginal subscriber is the type t_* for whom it is marginally worthwhile to purchase at the uniform price p. Thus, $D(p, t_*) = 0$ and therefore the optimality condition for the uniform price p is

$$\frac{p - c}{p} = \frac{\alpha}{\bar{\eta}(p, t_*)},$$

where $\bar{\eta}(p, t_*)$ is the price elasticity of aggregate demand. This is the standard condition derived from the Ramsey formulation of uniform pricing. The various forms of multipart and nonlinear pricing merely disaggregate this condition in varying degrees.

The same results can also be derived from a formulation in terms of the demand profile $N(p, q)$. Relying on the supposition that customers' demand functions do not cross, we observe that the market penetration can also be characterized in terms of the minimal purchase size q_* that a customer must anticipate before being willing to pay the fixed fee. Consequently, the aggregate demand $\bar{D}$ is

$$\bar{N}(p, q_*) = \int_{q_*}^{\infty} N(p, q) \, dq.$$

Further, if $r_* = F(t_*)$ represents the rank of the marginal subscriber then $q_* = D(p, r_*)$, using the demand function derived from the demand profile as in Section 2. The fixed fee that produces this market penetration is calculated as before:

$$P = \int_{p}^{\infty} D(\pi, r_*) \, d\pi.$$

Using these relationships in the previous construction enables the calculations to be carried out using the summary data in the demand profile.

We illustrate these methods by deriving the optimal two-part tariff for an example, addressing only the case of a profit-maximizing monopolist.

Example 6.1: Suppose that the r-th ranked customer has the demand function $D(p, r) = \frac{r}{B}[A - p]$. This demand function implies that

$$P = \frac{r_*}{2B}[A - p]^2 \qquad \text{so} \qquad r_*(P) = 2BP/[A - p]^2$$

is the market penetration depending on the fixed fee. Therefore the firm's profit, expressed in terms of the fixed fee P and the uniform price p is

$$\text{Profit} = \frac{1}{2}[p - c][A - p][1 - r_*(P)^2] + P[1 - r_*(P)].$$

Table 6.1 Example 6.1: Optimal Two-Part Tariffs

c/A	p/A	$10 \times PB/A^2$	Pft/A^2
.00	.39	.407	.15
.10	.45	.330	.12
.20	.51	.261	.09
.30	.57	.200	.07
.40	.63	.147	.05
.50	.70	.102	.04
.60	.76	.065	.02
.70	.82	.037	.01
.80	.88	.016	.01
.90	.94	.004	.00
1	1	0	0

The two-part tariff that maximizes this profit is:

$$p = c + \frac{1}{2}[1 - r_*][A - c], \qquad \text{and} \qquad P = \frac{r_*}{2B}[A - p]^2,$$

where $\quad r_* = \dfrac{5}{4} - \sqrt{17/16} \approx 1 - 0.78078$.

Thus the optimal two part-tariff aims to induce about 78% of the potential customers to subscribe. Table 6.1 tabulates for each unit cost c the optimal unit price p, the fixed charge P, and the resulting profit per customer in the population. Note that a high-cost firm makes little use of the opportunity to impose a subscription fee. Characteristically, the fixed fee and the unit price vary inversely as the unit cost varies. $\qquad\qquad\qquad\qquad\qquad\qquad\qquad\qquad\qquad\qquad\qquad\qquad\qquad\quad$ ◇

The optimality condition as an average

To introduce the approach taken in the next section, it is useful to recast the optimality conditions for a two-part tariff. The optimality condition for the marginal price p can be written in the alternative form

$$\int_{t_*}^{\infty} \left[[p - c] \cdot D_p(p, t) + \alpha \frac{\bar{F}(t)}{f(t)} \cdot D_t(p, t) \right] dF(t) = 0.$$

This merely states that the optimality condition derived in Section 1 for a nonlinear tariff should be satisfied on average for a two-part tariff—where the average is with respect to the distribution of types making purchases. The optimality condition for the marginal type t_* can be cast similarly as

$$\int_{p}^{\infty} \left[[\pi - c] \cdot D_p(\pi, t_*) + \alpha \frac{\bar{F}(t_*)}{f(t_*)} \cdot D_t(\pi, t_*) \right] d\pi = 0,$$

which can again be interpreted as an average with respect to prices between p and the largest possible price. This is basically the approach taken in §4, where the optimality condition is cast in terms of the aggregate or average demand profile over the interval of quantities for which each marginal price applies. It is also a justification for the ironing procedure used to flatten the price schedule when it would otherwise have an increasing segment.

The optimality condition for the marginal type t_* has its own special uses. For instance, a flat-rate tariff consists of a fixed fee without any marginal charges for usage; thus, $p = 0$. To determine the optimal fixed fee P one uses the condition above to determine the marginal type t_* willing to subscribe, and then the fixed fee is that type's consumer surplus: $P = \int_0^\infty D(0, t_*)\, dp$. This same approach applies also to a three-part tariff in which the initial segment is constrained to be a flat fee with a zero marginal price up to a specified maximum purchase size, beyond which a uniform price applies.

In the next section we show that this construction generalizes directly to the characterization of each segment of a multipart tariff.

6.4 Multipart tariffs

Implementations of nonlinear pricing often offer a menu of options comprising several two-part tariffs among which each customer chooses. Based on the net benefits anticipated from the various options, each customer chooses one two-part tariff that becomes the basis for the charges billed by the seller. Such a menu mimics a single piecewise-linear n-part tariff comprising a fixed fee plus a block-declining price schedule with $n - 1$ segments.

The formal equivalence between a multipart tariff and a menu of optional two-part tariffs is exact if the multipart tariff is concave. That is, if each customer elects the tariff that minimizes the charge billed for his actual usage then the net effect of a menu of two-part tariffs is the concave tariff that is the lower envelope of these two-part tariffs. Concavity is violated in several popular tariff designs. An especially common form of a 3-part tariff interprets the fixed fee as providing a specified free supply, beyond which a uniform price p applies: this is equivalent to specifying the marginal prices $p_1 = 0$ and $p_2 = p$ for the first and second segments of the price schedule. Similarly, lifeline rates allow a low price for purchases within a small amount, but charge a higher price for further purchases. In practice, however, there is the further difference that customers are usually unable to predict exactly which optional two-part tariff will be best over the ensuing billing period. This deficiency is partially remedied if the firm bills ex post according to the least costly option.

In spite of these considerations we describe the construction of an optimal multipart tariff in terms of a menu of optional two-part tariffs. As it turns out, the characterization obtained is valid even if the associated multipart tariff is not concave. The optimality conditions are derived initially without imposing explicitly the constraint that the marginal prices must be decreasing. If the tariff must be concave to allow implementation as a menu of optional two-part tariffs, then this constraint can be invoked to obtain a modified concave tariff.

The construction follows the approach used for a two-part tariff. Assume that the menu comprises $n - 1$ two-part tariffs indexed by $i = 1, \ldots, n - 1$. The i-th tariff charges a fixed fee P_i and a marginal price p_i. Assume these are ordered so that $P_i < P_{i+1}$ and $p_i > p_{i+1}$. Use $i = 0$ with $P_o \equiv 0$ and $p_o \equiv \infty$ to represent the option of not purchasing from any tariff. Because the customers' demand functions are assumed to be ordered by their types, the set of types t electing the i-th tariff (if any) is an interval $t_i < t < t_{i+1}$, where $t_n = \infty$. The profit contribution for the seller and the net benefit obtained by the customer from type t's purchase from the i-th tariff are their producer's and consumer's surpluses:[4]

$$
\text{PS}_i(t) = [p_i - c] \cdot D(p_i, t) + P_i, \quad \text{and} \quad \text{CS}_i(t) = \int_{p_i}^{\infty} D(p, t)\, dp - P_i,
$$

and the corresponding aggregates are

$$
\text{PS} = \sum_{i=1}^{n-1} \int_{t_i}^{t_{i+1}} \text{PS}_i(t)\, dF(t), \quad \text{and} \quad \text{CS} = \sum_{i=1}^{n-1} \int_{t_i}^{t_{i+1}} \text{CS}_i(t)\, dF(t).
$$

As usual, the Ramsey formulation of the tariff design problem can be posed as the maximization of a weighted sum $\text{CS} + [1 + \lambda]\text{PS}$ of the consumers' and producer's surpluses, where λ is a Lagrange multiplier on the constraint representing the firm's revenue requirement and $\alpha = \lambda/[1 + \lambda]$ is the corresponding Ramsey number. The variables in the design problem are the $n - 1$ pairs $\langle P_i, p_i \rangle$ of fixed fees and marginal prices. These parameters of the tariffs determine the corresponding segmentation of the market for which the boundaries are specified by the types t_i.

The condition that type t_i is indifferent between the tariffs i and $i - 1$ can be expressed in terms of type t_i's consumer's surplus as the equality

$$
P_i - P_{i-1} = \int_{p_i}^{p_{i-1}} D(p, t_i)\, dp.
$$

That is, in considering a move from tariff $i - 1$ to tariff i, the customer must perceive that the increment in the fixed fee will be compensated by the net value

---

4. In some applications the marginal cost also depends on the tariff selected, say as c_i, or on the average purchase size among those customers electing that tariff. We omit these possibilities here.

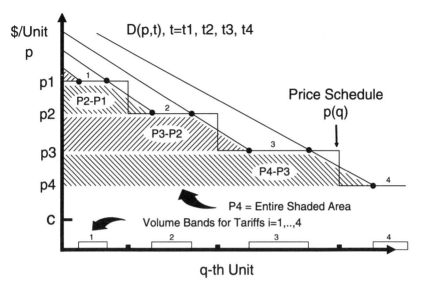

FIG. 6.7   A block-declining price schedule. Due to the increment $P_i - P_{i-1}$ in the fixed fee, type t_i is indifferent between the two-part tariffs $\langle P_{i-1}, p_{i-1} \rangle$ and $\langle P_i, p_i \rangle$.

of the greater usage engendered by the lower marginal price.[5] This equality implies that

$$P_i = P_o + \sum_{j \leq i} \int_{p_j}^{p_{j-1}} D(p, t_j)\, dp \,,$$

so the formulas for the producer's and consumers' surpluses can be expressed entirely in terms of the marginal prices p_i and the types t_i at the boundaries between adjacent market segments.

This construction is illustrated in Figure 6.7, which shows the block-declining price schedule obtained from a menu of four two-part tariffs $\langle P_i, p_i \rangle$, $i = 1, \ldots, 4$. Each increment $P_i - P_{i-1}$ in the fixed fee equals the consumer's surplus obtained by the boundary type t_i in moving from the marginal price p_{i-1} to the lower marginal price p_i for all units purchased. The fixed fee P_4 is therefore the sum of these increments, as represented by the entire shaded area. The figure also shows the segmentation of the market into disjoint volume bands associated with each of the two-part tariffs. The separation between two adjacent volume bands occurs because a customer's demand increases substantially in switching from one marginal price to the next lower one.

---

5. This equality must be phrased differently if the menu includes an initial option that offers a fixed quantity q_1 for a flat fee $P_1 > P_2$, or more generally a fixed fee plus a uniform price $p_1 < p_2$. In this case, $P_2 - P_1 = q_1 \cdot [p_1 - p_2]$ and $q_1 = D(p_2, t_2)$.

After eliminating the fixed fees from the formulation, as above, the objective function for the Ramsey pricing problem is

$$\sum_{i=1}^{n-1} \left\{ \int_{t_i}^{t_{i+1}} \left(\int_{p_i}^{\infty} D(p,t)\, dp + [1+\lambda][p_i - c] \cdot D(p_i, t) \right) dF(t) \right.$$

$$\left. + \lambda \bar{F}(t_i) \int_{p_i}^{p_{i-1}} D(p, t_i)\, dp \right\} .$$

Within the summation, the first term represents the consumer's surplus for type t; the second is the profit contribution from this type's purchases; and the third indicates that each type exceeding t_i selects some tariff $j \geq i$ and therefore pays the increment $P_i - P_{i-1}$ to the fixed fee: this increment equals type t_i's gain from reducing the marginal price from p_{i-1} to p_i, which is why he is at the boundary between these two adjacent market segments.

The variables in this version of the design problem are the $n-1$ pairs $\langle p_i, t_i \rangle$. By definition, these are constrained by the requirements that $p_i \leq p_{i-1}$ and $t_i \geq t_{i-1}$, where t_o is the least type, and t_n is the highest type. In addition, $D(p_o, t_1) = 0$ expresses the fact that type t_1 is indifferent about purchasing. Provided these relations are satisfied, the necessary condition for an optimal choice of the marginal price p_i requires that

$$\int_{t_i}^{t_{i+1}} \left\{ [p_i - c] \cdot D_p(p_i, t) + \alpha \frac{\bar{F}(t)}{f(t)} \cdot D_t(p_i, t) \right\} dF(t) = 0 .$$

This is an exact analog of the optimality condition for a fully nonlinear tariff. The only difference is that the integral represents an average over the subpopulation of customers in the market segment selecting the i-th tariff.

Note that if the market segments and the other tariffs are fixed, then satisfying this condition entails selection of both the marginal price p_i and the corresponding fixed fee P_i that leaves the two boundaries of the i-th market segment unchanged. In other cases the market segments vary to satisfy auxiliary conditions. For example, this condition can be used to determine the optimal uniform price p_1 by using the auxiliary condition $D(p_1, t_1) = 0$ to determine the marginal purchaser when the fixed fee is nil, and $t_2 = \infty$.

The necessary condition for an optimal choice of the boundary type t_i is analogous:

$$\int_{p_i}^{p_{i-1}} \left\{ [p - c] \cdot D_p(p, t_i) + \alpha \frac{\bar{F}(t_i)}{f(t_i)} \cdot D_t(p, t_i) \right\} dp = 0 .$$

This condition is again equivalent to an average, in this case over the interval of marginal prices between those charged by adjacent tariffs.

As the number $n - 1$ of two-part tariffs in the menu increases, the optimality conditions for p_i and t_i converge to the same condition, which is precisely the optimality condition for a fully nonlinear tariff corresponding to $n = \infty$. However, a nonlinear tariff is costly or impractical to implement in most applications, so nonlinear tariffs are approximated by a menu with several optional two-part tariffs, a single tariff with several linear segments, or a block-declining price schedule with several steps. Fortunately, several can mean few: a menu offering just four or five two-part tariffs usually suffices to realize most of the gains from a completely nonlinear tariff. We demonstrate this feature in the following examples; in §8.3 we describe why it is true universally.

Example 6.2: For this example, assume that type t's demand function is $D(p, t) = t[1 - p]$, the types are uniformly distributed, the firm's costs are nil, and $\alpha = 1$. In this case the optimality conditions are

$$p_i = 1 - [t_i + t_{i+1}]/2 \qquad \text{and} \qquad t_i = 1 - [p_i + p_{i-1}]/2 .$$

These are solved subject to the boundary conditions $t_n = 1$, which is the maximum type, and $p_o = 1$, which is the customers' valuation of an initial unit. The solution of these conditions indicates that the i-th boundary type and the i-th marginal price are

$$t_i = \frac{i - .5}{n - .5} \qquad \text{and} \qquad p_i = 1 - \frac{i}{n - .5} .$$

The i-th fixed fee is therefore

$$P_i = \frac{1}{3} \cdot \frac{[i - .5]i[i + .5]}{[n - .5]^3} .$$

The volume band for the i-th tariff is the interval of purchase sizes $q_i \leq q \leq Q_i$, where

$$(q_i, Q_i) = [i/(n - .5)^2] \cdot (i - .5, i + .5) ,$$

which is centered on $\bar{q}_i = [i/(n - .5)]^2$. Note that the volume bandwidths vary from $1/[n - .5]^2$ for $i = 1$ to $[n - 1]/[n - .5]^2$ for $i = n - 1$, even though the sizes of the market segments are equal. The firm's profit or producer's surplus is

$$PS(n) = \frac{1}{6} \cdot \left[1 - \frac{1}{4(n - .5)^2} \right] .$$

Thus, the profit lost from using only a few options is inversely proportional to the square of $n - .5$. This indicates that a menu with only a few options is sufficient to obtain most of the potential profit.

The equivalent piecewise-linear tariff is shown in Figure 6.8 for the case $n = 5$. The fully nonlinear tariff, corresponding to $n = \infty$, and the optimal two-part tariff,

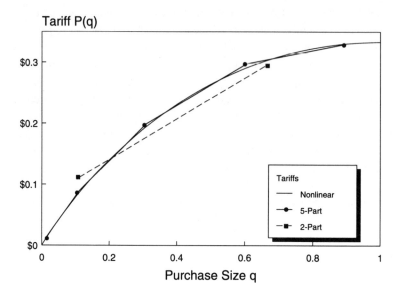

FIG. 6.8   The optimal nonlinear, 5-part, and two-part tariffs for Example 6.2.

corresponding to $n = 2$, are shown for comparison; each tariff is displayed only
for the range between the minimum and maximum purchase sizes it produces.
Evidently the 5-part tariff is virtually the same as the nonlinear tariff for practical
purposes. The two-part tariff differs significantly, and in particular it restricts both
small and large purchases substantially. The firm's profits from the 5-part and
two-part tariffs are 98.8% and 88.9% of the profits from the nonlinear tariff.   ◇

Example 6.3: We reinforce these conclusions with an example in which the role of
the Ramsey number can be included explicitly. The demand function is $D(p, t) =
t - p$ and again the types are uniformly distributed and the marginal cost is nil.
The parameters of the optimal n-part tariff in this case are

$$t_i = 1 - [n - i]/d(n), \qquad p_i = \alpha[n - i - .5]/d(n),$$

$$P_i = \alpha i/d(n) - \alpha[1 + \alpha][n - .5(i + 1)]i/d(n)^2,$$

where $d(n) = [1 + \alpha][n - .5] - .5$. The price schedule is shown in Figure 6.9
for $n = 5$ and the two cases $\alpha = 0.5$ and $\alpha = 1$. The price schedules for the
nonlinear tariffs corresponding to $n = \infty$ are also shown. In each case the sloping
portion represents the demand function for the type t_i that is indifferent between
purchasing from the two adjacent segments. The firm's profit and the consumers'

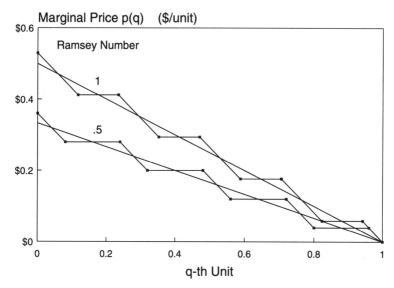

FIG. 6.9   Example 6.3: The price schedules for the 5-part tariff using the Ramsey numbers $\alpha = 0.5$ and 1.0.

surplus are:

$$PS(n) = \frac{\alpha}{3[1+\alpha]^2} \left\{ 1 - \frac{1}{4d(n)^3}[(1+\alpha^3)(n-.5)-.5] \right\},$$

$$CS(n) = \frac{1}{6[1+\alpha]} \left\{ 1 - \frac{\alpha}{4d(n)^3}[d(n)(2+\alpha)-\alpha] \right\}.$$

For each of these, the loss from using only $n-1$ options in the menu is again of order $1/n^2$. If $n=2$ then compared to a nonlinear tariff the shortfalls in producer's surplus are 5.5% or 4% for $\alpha = 0.5$ or 1, and the shortfalls in consumers' surplus are 10% or 4%. But if $n=5$ then for all values of α both producer's and consumers' surplus are within 1% of the corresponding amounts from a nonlinear tariff.   ◇

Example 6.4: For this example we use the model from Example 4.3 with the following specification of the parameters: the substitution parameter is $a = 0.4$, the correlation between the type parameters is $r = 0.4$, the price of the substitute commodity is $p^* = \$0.5$, the Ramsey number is $\alpha = 1$, and the marginal cost is $c = 0$. Figure 6.10 shows the optimal nonlinear price schedule as well as the three n-part price schedules with $n = 4$, 6, and 11. Each slanted segment of one of the n-part schedules represents the demand function of the customer of type t_i who is indifferent between the $(i-1)$-th and i-th two-part tariff in the menu with $n-1$ options. The degree to which these n-part schedules approximate the nonlinear schedule is not fully apparent visually; in fact, all three obtain profits that are within

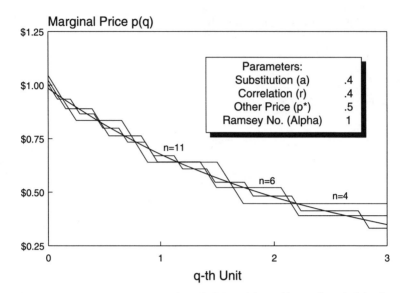

FIG. **6.10** Example 6.4: The nonlinear price schedule and the multipart price schedules for $n =$ 4, 6, 11. The multipart schedules approximate the nonlinear schedule and yield nearly the same profits.

a fraction of a percent of the profit from the nonlinear schedule. This is revealed more clearly in Table 6.2. The top panel displays the data for the 6-part schedule, using $m_i \equiv \bar{F}(t_i) - \bar{F}(t_{i+1})$ to indicate the fraction of potential customers who elect the i-th two-part tariff, and $\bar{q}_i$ to indicate the average purchase size selected by these customers. The "Averages" row shows the average fraction of customers in each volume band, and then the average among all customers served of the fixed fees, the marginal prices, and the purchase size. The bottom panel shows for each of the three n-part tariffs the market penetration (fraction of potential customers served), the profits obtained from fixed fees and marginal charges, and the total quantity sold. The fixed fees represent about a quarter of the profit, regardless of how many options are offered, and the market penetration is approximately half of the potential market of 0.8086 consisting of those customers with positive demands at a zero price. For these three n-part tariffs the total profits from fixed fees and marginal charges are $0.3610, $0.3615, and $0.3618 respectively, which differ by at most 0.2%. Thus, the potential profit is nearly realized by offering a menu with only three two-part tariffs, provided they are designed optimally.
◇

In §8.3 we demonstrate with considerable generality that compared to a fully nonlinear tariff, the loss from using an n-part tariff is approximately proportional to $1/n^2$.

Table 6.2 Example 6.4: Three Multipart Tariffs

n	i	t_i	$\bar{F}(t_i)$	m_i	P_i	p_i	q_i	Q_i	$\bar{q}_i$
6	1	.243	.404	.080	.011	.889	.159	.392	.274
	2	.456	.324	.088	.070	.763	.542	.828	.682
	3	.719	.236	.092	.179	.642	.973	1.349	1.151
	4	1.063	.144	.087	.350	.521	1.492	2.059	1.744
	5	1.583	.057	.057	.629	.391	2.215	∞	2.680
		Averages:		.081	.222	.673			1.217
		Totals:							
4				.395	.086	.275			.491
6				.404	.090	.272			.492
11				.412	.092	.270			.492

A demand-profile formulation

Multipart tariffs can also be constructed from the demand profile if it is interpreted as reflecting the demand behavior of a population of customers indexed by a single type parameter. For this we interpret the price schedule as in Figure 6.9 so that $p(q) = p_i$ in the interval $q_i \leq q \leq r_i$ between the limits $q_i \equiv D(p_i, t_i)$ and $r_i \equiv D(p_i, t_{i+1})$ of the i-th volume band, and $p(q)$ is the demand price of the boundary type t_i in the interval $r_{i-1} < q < q_i$.

Represent the demand function $D(p, t_i)$ of type t_i as the function $q(p; p_i, q_i)$ for which $N(p, q(p; p_i, q_i)) = N(p_i, q_i)$. Note that $q(p_i; p_i, q_i) = q_i$ and $q(p_{i-1}; p_i, q_i) = r_{i-1}$. Also, the increment in the fixed fee,

$$P_i - P_{i-1} = \int_{p_i}^{p_{i-1}} q(p; p_i, q_i) \, dp \,,$$

matches type t_i's gain in moving from the marginal price p_{i-1} to p_i.

Consumers' surplus is formulated as in §5. The firm's profit contribution can be formulated as the producer's surplus

$$PS = \sum_{i=1}^{n-1} \left\{ N(p_i, q_i) \cdot \int_{p_i}^{p_{i-1}} q(p; p_i, q_i) \, dp + [p_i - c] \cdot \int_{q_i}^{r_i} q \, dN(p_i, q) \right\},$$

expressed in terms of the demand profile. For each two-part tariff i in the summation, the first term represents the increment $P_i - P_{i-1}$ in the fixed fee collected from the number $N(p_i, q_i) \equiv \bar{F}(t_i)$ of customers among those types opting for tariffs $j \geq i$ and the second term represents the profit margin $p_i - c$ collected from those customers purchasing amounts in the i-th volume band, for which the integral states the average purchase size.

The previously derived condition for the optimal choice of the i-th marginal price p_i translates directly into the condition

$$\int_{q_i}^{r_i} \{\alpha N(p_i, q) + N_p(p_i, q) \cdot [p_i - c]\} \, dq = 0,$$

expressed in terms of the demand profile. Again, and as in §4.5, this condition specifies that the optimality condition for a nonlinear tariff is satisfied on average over the volume band associated with the i-th price. Similarly, the condition for the optimal choice of the boundary type t_i translates as

$$\int_{p_i}^{p_{i-1}} \{\alpha N(p, q_i) + N_p(p, q(p; p_i, q_i)) \cdot [p - c]\} \, dp = 0,$$

expressed in terms of the demand profile.

6.5   Nonlinear tariffs

As in the formulation for n-part tariffs, we interpret the nonlinear tariff design problem as the assignment of a price $p(t)$ to each type t. In these terms, the firm's profit from a nonlinear tariff can be written as the producer's surplus:[6]

$$\text{PS} = \int_0^\infty [p(t) - c] \cdot D(p(t), t) \, dF(t) - \int_0^\infty \bar{F}(t) \cdot D(p(t), t) \, dp(t),$$

This formula is obtained from the formula for the profit from an n-part tariff by taking the limit as $n \to \infty$, using the convention that $p(t)$ is the limit of the price p_i for which t is the limit of the market segment boundary t_i. As for an n-part tariff, $p(t)$ is the uniform price paid by type t for its purchase $D(p(t), t)$ and every type $t' \geq t$ pays the increment $D(p(t), t) \,|dp(t)|$ in the fixed fee to obtain the decrement $dp(t)$ in the marginal price.

This formula can be combined with the consumer's surplus $W(p, t) \equiv \int_p^\infty D(p, t) \, dp$ for type t from an optimal purchase in response to the uniform price p. In total, the objective function for the Ramsey pricing problem is:

$$\int_0^\infty \{[W(p(t), t) + [1 + \lambda][p(t) - c] \cdot D(p(t), t)] f(t)$$
$$-\lambda \bar{F}(t) \cdot D(p(t), t) p'(t)\} \, dt,$$

---

6. This formula can be derived from the definition $\int_0^\infty [P(q(t)) - c \cdot q(t)] \, dF(t)$ using integration by parts and a change of variables. A more complicated version is obtained when the marginal cost is not constant.

where λ is the Lagrange multiplier on the firm's revenue constraint. Selection of the price assignment $p(t)$ maximizing this objective requires that the Euler necessary condition is satisfied:

$$[p(t) - c] \cdot D_p(p(t), t)f(t) + \alpha \bar{F}(t) \cdot D_t(p(t), t) = 0,$$

where $\alpha = \lambda/[1 + \lambda]$. This is precisely the limit, as $n \to \infty$, of the optimality conditions for an n-part tariff.

A direct derivation

To derive this result directly, we simplify by assuming that the marginal cost c is constant and that the marginal price schedule is nonincreasing. The quantity variable is eliminated by representing the customer's preferences in terms of the so-called dual or indirect or utility function

$$W(p, t) = \max_q \{U(q, t) - pq\},$$

that indicates the customer's attainable net benefit from the uniform price p. This is just the consumer's surplus under the demand function as described previously. The optimal quantity selection is specified by the demand function $D(p, t)$, assuming as previously that the utility function is strictly concave in q, so that the demand function is decreasing with respect to the price. In this case the derivative of the indirect utility function with respect to the price is just $W_p(p, t) = -D(p, t)$. Consequently, after finding the price assignment $p(t)$ we can infer that type t purchases the quantity $q(t) \equiv D(p(t), t)$. As in previous sections, if higher types have higher demands at every price then this quantity assignment must be nondecreasing to assure that the customers' second-order necessary conditions for an optimum are satisfied; for instance, it is amply sufficient that the price assignment is nonincreasing, which we assume hereafter.

The tariff is now construed as a one-dimensional locus of pairs $\langle P, p \rangle$ indicating a fixed fee P and a marginal price p. This locus can be interpreted directly as a tariff by using the quantity q to parameterize the locus: if $\langle P(q), p(q) \rangle$ is the q-th pair along the locus then the charge for a purchase of size q is

$$\mathcal{P}(q) = P(q) + p(q)q.$$

Alternatively, assuming that the resulting charge $\mathcal{P}(q)$ is a concave function of the quantity q, the tariff can be interpreted as a menu of optional two-part tariffs, in which case

$$\mathcal{P}(q) = \min_{\langle P, p \rangle} \{P + pq\}$$

is the minimal charge payable for a purchase of size q, and this is obtained by selecting the two-part tariff $\langle P(q), p(q) \rangle$.

Using this formulation, the Ramsey pricing problem can be cast as the construction of an assignment of each type t to a pair $\langle P(t), p(t) \rangle$ comprising a fixed fee $P(t) \equiv P(q(t))$ and a marginal price $p(t) \equiv p(q(t))$. The consumer's surplus for type t is therefore $W(p(t), t) - P(t)$ net of the fixed fee, and the firm's profit contribution is $P(t) + [p(t) - c] \cdot D(p(t), t)$. This assignment is tightly constrained, however, by the customer's freedom to self-select his preferred pair among the entire menu of options offered. As in the derivation of multipart tariffs, this constraint can be expressed by the statement that a customer is unwilling to pay a higher fixed fee unless the lower marginal price it brings provides sufficient benefits. We write this as

$$P'(t) + D(p(t), t)p'(t) = 0,$$

indicating that for type t the slightly lower marginal price obtained by imitating a slightly higher type is exactly compensated by the slightly higher fixed fee required. Alternatively, the constraint can be stated as the requirement that the fixed fee is the accumulation of the increments paid by lower types, namely

$$P(t) = \int_0^t D(p(s), s)[-p'(s)] \, ds,$$

using $P(0) = 0$ to express the fact that a customer also has the option to forgo purchasing altogether. Using this relationship to integrate by parts, the firm's total profit contribution from fixed fees can be written as

$$\int_0^\infty P(t) \, dF(t) = \int_0^\infty \bar{F}(t) D(p(t), t)[-p'(t)] \, dt.$$

On the right side, the integrand states that all types exceeding t elect to pay the increment $P'(t)$ in the fixed fee in order to obtain marginal prices less than $p(t)$.

Combining these results, the objective function for the Ramsey pricing problem is, as before,

$$\int_0^\infty \{ [W(p(t), t) + [1 + \lambda] \cdot [p(t) - c] \cdot D(p(t), t)] f(t)$$
$$- \lambda \bar{F}(t) \cdot D(p(t), t) \cdot p'(t) \} \, dt.$$

This objective is to be maximized by choosing the assignment $p(t)$ from types to marginal prices. Where the optimal price assignment is nonnegative and nonincreasing, it is characterized by the Euler condition from the calculus of variations:

$$p(t) - c = \alpha \left[\frac{\bar{F}(t)}{f(t)} \right] \left[\frac{D_t(p(t), t)}{-D_p(p(t), t)} \right],$$

where $\alpha = \lambda/[1+\lambda]$. This version of the optimality condition is equivalent to the ones derived previously, differing only in notation. In terms of elasticities, it states as in §4 that

$$\frac{p(q) - c(q)}{p(q)} = \frac{\alpha}{\eta(p(q), q)},$$

where the imputed price elasticity of the demand profile is

$$\eta(p, q) = \eta_p \frac{\phi_t}{\eta_t},$$

expressed in terms of the absolute values of the price and type elasticities η_p and η_t of the demand function $D(p, t)$, and the elasticity ϕ_t of the type distribution $\bar{F}$. This derives from the identity $N(p, q) \equiv \bar{F}(t)$, which holds when $q = D(p, t)$, to characterize the demand $N(p, q)$ for the q-th increment at the price p. An alternative version is stated in terms of the profit margin $\pi = p - c$ and the complement $s = \bar{F}(t)$ of type t's rank: the ratio of the elasticities of demand with respect to π and s should be the Ramsey number α.

This version has the practical advantage that it uses directly the type-dependent demand function. In general, the problem posed in finding the optimal price schedule is one of solving two simultaneous nonlinear equations for the marginal price p, and the corresponding least type t that pays this price, for each purchase size q.

6.6   Some examples

We now examine several examples that illustrate the methods described above.

Example 6.5: We begin with examples illustrating that a uniform price is optimal in special cases.[7] Consider the case that a customer of type t has the demand function $D(p, t) = k[t - \log(p)]$ and the distribution of types in the population has an exponential distribution function $F(t) = 1 - e^{-t/m}$ so that the mean of the type index is m. In this case the optimal tariff charges a uniform price

$$p = c/[1 - \alpha m],$$

when $\alpha < 1/m$. This result is essentially a consequence of the fact that the induced price elasticity of the demand profile is the constant $\eta = 1/m$. Similarly, if $D(p, t) = kt^a p^{-b}$ and $\bar{F}(t) = t^{-1/\gamma}$ then $\eta = b/a\gamma$ and $p = c/[1 - \alpha/\eta]$ when $\alpha < \eta$.   ◇

Other examples of optimal uniform prices occur whenever the price schedule would be increasing over its entire domain were it not flattened by the ironing procedure described previously.

---

7. Sufficient conditions for a uniform price to be optimal are given by Salant (1989), and Wilson (1988) studies a special case adapted to labor markets and to airlines' advance-purchase airfares.

Example 6.6: An example with a linear price schedule is obtained from the demand function $D(p, t) = A - Bp/t$ in the case that the type distribution is exponential, as in the previous example. In this case, the optimal price schedule is $p(q) = c + \alpha m[A - q]/B$. Alternatively, if the demand function has either of the two forms $D(p, t) = A - Bp/t$ or $D(p, t) = tA - Bp$, and the type distribution is uniform so that $F(t) = t$, then again the price schedule is linear of the form $p(q) = [1 - \beta]c + \beta[A - q]/B$, where $\beta = \lambda/[1 + 2\lambda]$. However, the second of these demand functions combined with an exponential type distribution yields a uniform price $p = c + \alpha m A/B$.　　　　　　　　　　　◇

Example 6.7: For this example, assume that a customer of type t has the linear demand function

$$D(p, t) = \frac{t}{B}[A - p],$$

corresponding to the benefit function

$$U(q, t) = Aq - \frac{B}{2t}q^2.$$

Assume, moreover, that the customers' types are uniformly distributed in the population. Inserting this specification into the optimality condition indicates that the tariff should induce customers of type $t(q)$ to purchase q units, where $t(q)$ is the larger root of the quadratic equation

$$t^2[A - c] - [1 - \alpha]Bqt - \alpha Bq = 0.$$

The price schedule for marginal units that accomplishes this is then

$$p(q) = v(q, t(q)) = A - Bq/t(q).$$

For instance, in the special case that no weight is given to the profit contribution, namely $\lambda = 0$ and $\alpha = 0$, this produces the uniform price $p(q) = c$ equal to marginal cost, as one expects. In the other extreme case, all the weight is given to the profit contribution so $\alpha = 1$. The price schedule is then

$$p(q) = A - \sqrt{Bq[A - c]},$$

corresponding to the tariff

$$P(q) = q\left[A - \frac{2}{3}\sqrt{Bq[A - c]}\right].$$

That is, the firm offers a nominal uniform price $p = A$ but then offers a rebate of $\frac{2}{3}\sqrt{Bq[A - c]}$ on each unit the customer buys if his purchase size is q. With

Table 6.3 Example 6.7: Tangential Approximation of the Optimal Tariff ($A = 1$, $B = 1$, $c = 0.1$)

Tangent Point ($\hat{q}$)	0	.2	.4	.7
Fixed Charge ($)	0	.0283	.0800	.1852
Price($/unit)	1.000	.576	.400	.206
Interval (units)	$0 \leq q \leq .067$	$.067 \leq q \leq .294$	$.294 \leq q \leq .543$	$.543 \leq q \leq .794$

this pricing policy, the average profit contribution per customer is $[A - c]^2/6B$, which is greater by a third than the firm can obtain with the optimal uniform price $p = \frac{1}{2}[A + c]$ that ignores the heterogeneity among customers. The optimal price schedule, by the way, could also have been derived directly as in §4 by maximizing the profit contribution

$$N(p(q), q) \cdot [p(q) - c]$$

from the market for the q-th increment, using the demand profile

$$N(p, q) = 1 - Bq/[A - p],$$

which measures the fraction of the population purchasing the q-th increment at the price p.

A tariff expressed in square roots is presumably impractical. However, Table 6.3 shows a menu of four two-part tariffs obtained as tangents to the optimal monopoly tariff. This menu obtains nearly the same profit contribution for the firm even though it is not the optimal menu.   ◇

Example 6.8: For this example assume that customers are alike except that a customer of type t incurs a transport cost of $$t$ per unit purchased. In particular, the demand function of a customer of type t is linear of the form

$$D(p, t) = a - b[p + t],$$

and the fraction of customers having transport costs less than t is $F(t) = t^k$. For instance, if the firm has a plant at a central location in a region over which customers are uniformly distributed, then typically $k \approx 2$. Since the demand function decreases as t increases (rather than increases as assumed previously) we use $-F$ rather than $\bar{F}$ in the optimality condition. Using this specification in the optimality condition indicates that the price schedule should be designed to induce the customer of type

$$t(q) = \frac{k}{k + \alpha} \left[\frac{a - q}{b} - c \right]$$

to purchase q units. The price schedule for marginal units is therefore

$$p(q) = \frac{k}{k+\alpha}c + \frac{\alpha}{k+\alpha}\left[\frac{a-q}{b}\right],$$

and the tariff is

$$P(q) = q\left\{\frac{k}{k+\alpha}c + \frac{\alpha}{k+\alpha}\left[\frac{a-\frac{1}{2}q}{b}\right]\right\}.$$

As in the previous example, we see that if $\alpha = 0$ then a uniform price equal to marginal cost is used, and otherwise a higher nominal price is offered with quantity discounts.

The incidence of charges in excess of actual cost is

$$P(q(t)) - cq(t) = \frac{\alpha}{2b}\left[\frac{(a-bc)^2}{k+\alpha} - (k+\alpha)(b/k)^2 t^2\right],$$

where $q(t)$ is type t's purchase size. Thus customers' contributions to the firm's revenue requirements are derived mostly from those types with low transport costs, and they decrease quadratically as the transport cost increases. This feature is fairly general; namely, customers with advantages in using the product tend to bear the greater burden of meeting the firm's revenue requirements. It partly accounts for the acceptance of nonlinear pricing by regulatory agencies.

However, the fact that nonlinear pricing prescribes a particular pattern of incidence can result in its modification or rejection if this pattern is unacceptable. For instance, in the case of transport costs, a popular alternative is for the firm to absorb some of the costs of transport in order to increase the market penetration to distant customers. Considering only a profit-maximizing monopolist (that is, $\alpha = 1$) and $k = 2$, suppose that the firm offers a uniform price $p(t)$ that depends on the delivery cost t, which in this case is incurred entirely by the firm. For the example above, the optimal price is

$$p(t) = \frac{a}{2b} + \frac{1}{2}[c+t],$$

indicating that the firm charges the usual monopoly price and absorbs half of the transport cost. In this case the customer of type t contributes

$$[p(t) - c - t]q(t) = \frac{1}{b}\left[(a/2b) - \frac{1}{2}(c+t)\right]^2$$

to the firm's profit, which is again quadratic but the incidence is quite different than previously, as is the distribution of net benefits among customers. Figure 6.11 shows the price schedule $p(t)$ for the case $a/b = 1$ and $c = 0.1$. A significant feature

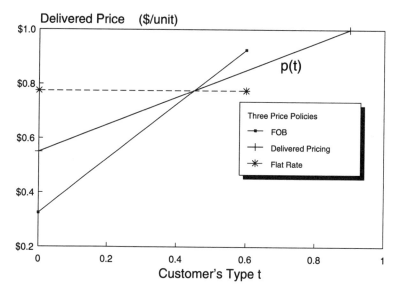

FIG. 6.11   Optimal freight absorption compared to FOB and flat-rate pricing.

is that the market penetration is much deeper with optimal freight absorption: with the optimal schedule customers as far away as $t = 0.9$ make positive purchases, where as shown in the figure, FOB pricing stops at $t = 0.6$ and a uniform delivered price also stops at $t = 0.6$ because the firm is unwilling to serve customers farther away.   ◇

Nonlinear pricing applies equally well to contexts in which customers' preferences are derived from other considerations. An important instance is a manufacturer's choice of wholesale prices to retailers who in turn select their own retail prices for resale. Franchising is similar: the franchiser shares in some of the profits of its higher-volume franchises by pricing the franchised product nonlinearly. We illustrate below with an example.

Example 6.9: Consider a manufacturer that sells its product to many retail stores. Suppose the stores are sufficiently separated spatially that their retail markets can be considered independent. In particular, each store chooses its retail price based on the manufacturer's wholesale price and the store's local demand conditions. Recognizing this, the manufacturer can obtain advantages from a nonlinear price schedule that offers quantity discounts to high-volume retailers. To represent the simplest example, suppose that stores are classified into various types indexed by a single parameter t, and that the demand function of a store of type t is $D(p, t) = t - p$, measured in, say, units per month. That is, local demand conditions are assumed to raise or lower the demand function uniformly. The optimal retail price at such a store is $p_t = \frac{1}{2}[t + c_s + p(q_t)]$, where c_s is the marginal cost at the store and $p(q_t)$ is the manufacturer's marginal price for the last unit q_t bought by the store each month. The monthly quantity sold by the store is then predicted to be $q_t = \frac{1}{2}[t - c_s - p(q_t)]$. Let c_m be the manufacturer's marginal cost, and consider now the manufacturer's pricing problem. If the types of the stores are uniformly distributed, then the manufacturer's problem can be posed as follows. Let $t(q)$ indicate the type of store that buys q units. Then a fraction $1 - t(q)$ of the stores will buy a q-th unit, and on these sales of q-th units the manufacturer obtains a profit margin $p(q) - c_m$. Assuming that the stores follow the optimal retail pricing strategy derived above, this profit margin can be alternatively formulated as $t(q) - c_s - c_m - 2q$, and similarly the gross profit on this market segment is

$$[1 - t(q)][t(q) - c_s - c_m - 2q] .$$

Choosing the corresponding type $t(q)$ optimally to maximize the gross profit, the manufacturer prefers that $t(q) = \frac{1}{2}[1 + c_s + c_m + 2q]$. The marginal price that achieves this result is

$$p(q) = t(q) - c_s - 2q = \frac{1}{2}[1 - c_s + c_m] - q .$$

The corresponding total charge for q units is therefore

$$P(q) = \frac{1}{2}q[1 - c_s + c_m] - \frac{1}{2}q^2 .$$

Consequently, the predicted quantity sold to a store of type t is

$$q_t = t - \frac{1}{2}[1 + c_s + c_m] ,$$

which is positive only if the type t is sufficiently large; that is, the manufacturer prefers to forego sales to the stores with small markets. Using this pricing policy, the manufacturer's gross profit in total (normalized by the number of retailers) is $\frac{1}{24}[1 - c_s - c_m]^3$. If both marginal costs are zero then this is $\approx .0417$; in contrast, using a single uniform price the manufacturer would charge $p = \left[8 - \sqrt{7}\right]/9 \approx .301$ and obtain the gross profit $\approx .0351$—thus, the nonlinear pricing policy yields 19% greater profits. In practice it would suffice for the manufacturer to offer only three or four price breaks to achieve most of this potential gain in profits.   ◇

6.7 Fixed costs and fixed fees

The optimal tariff includes a fixed fee whenever the firm incurs a fixed cost of serving an individual customer. The construction of this fixed fee is exactly analogous to the construction of the optimal price schedule. We show, however, that if the firm's fixed cost is nil then so too is the fixed charge when a fully nonlinear price schedule is used. Multipart tariffs typically include a positive fixed fee for the initial segment but it is small if several options are offered: it is positive only because of the limitation on the number of options.

As in previous sections, customers' types are described by a one-dimensional index t. The number or fraction of customers having types exceeding t is $\bar{F}(t)$. Type t has the benefit function $U(q, t)$ for a purchase of size q and the marginal benefit function $v(q, t) = U_q(q, t)$ for a q-th unit, both of which increase as the type index increases, and v declines as q increases. Alternatively, the benefit is the area under the demand curve $D(p, t)$. The firm's total and marginal cost functions are $C(q)$ and $c(q)$ to supply an individual customer. A fixed cost component is interpreted as $C(0)$, with the understanding that this is incurred only if the customer makes a positive purchase.

The tariff $P(q)$ and its marginal price schedule $p(q)$ are specified similarly, again with the proviso that the fixed fee $P(0)$ is paid only if the customer makes a positive purchase. In effect, demand for access is equated with demand to purchase. The tariff therefore consists of two ingredients:

- A minimum price $P_* \equiv P(q_*)$ is charged for a minimum purchase q_*. This purchase or some larger one is bought by all types exceeding a minimum type t_* making a purchase.
- A marginal price schedule $p(q)$ imposes charges for increments $q > q_*$. These increments are bought by types $t > t_*$.

Thus, the minimum quantity q_* is sold as a block for the minimum charge P_*. Alternatively, the firm can extend the price schedule to increments $q < q_*$ and charge a fixed fee $P_\circ$, so that the minimum charge is

$$P_* = P_\circ + \int_0^{q_*} p(x)\, dx\,.$$

and the total tariff is

$$P(q) = P_\circ + \int_0^q p(x)\, dx\,.$$

We use a somewhat different formulation of the Ramsey pricing problem in this section in order to address the determination of the fixed fee most simply. The firm's profit contribution or producer's surplus can be formulated in terms of the assignment $q(t)$ specifying each type's purchase:

$$\text{PS} = \int_0^\infty [P(q(t)) - C(q(t))]\, dF(t)\,.$$

Integration by parts provides an equivalent formula:

$$\text{PS} = \bar{F}(t_*) \cdot [P_* - C(q_*)] + \int_{t_*}^{\infty} \bar{F}(t(q)) \cdot [p(q(t)) - c(q(t))] \, dq(t) \, ,$$

where again $q_* = q(t_*)$ is the least purchase made, t_* is the type making this purchase, and $P_* = P(q_*)$ is the tariff charged for the purchase q_*. In this formula, the first term indicates that the measure of those types $t \geq t_*$ making positive purchases is $\bar{F}(t_*)$. From each of these types the firm's profit contribution from the minimum purchase q_* is $P_* - C(q_*)$, namely the tariff net of the firm's total cost of supplying this purchase. In effect, $F(t_*)$ is the demand for access at the price P_* when it includes an allowance q_*.

We make substitutions in this formula to take account of customers' purchase behaviors. The first is that $v(q(t), t) = p(q(t))$ for those types $t \geq t_*$, indicating that $q(t)$ is on t's demand curve at its assigned marginal price. The second indicates that the least type t_* to purchase is the one for whom the net benefit $U(q_*, t_*) - P_*$ is nil; so we substitute $U(q_*, t_*) = P_*$ in the formula. These substitutions can also be made in the formula for the consumers' surplus, so that integration by parts yields:

$$\text{CS} = \int_{t_*}^{\infty} [U(q(t), t) - P(q(t))] \, dF(t)$$
$$= \int_{t_*}^{\infty} \bar{F}(t) U_t(q(t), t) \, dt \, .$$

The Ramsey formulation of the pricing problem is again to maximize consumers' surplus subject to a revenue constraint for the firm, say $\text{CS} + [1 + \lambda]\text{PS}$ where λ is the multiplier on the firm's revenue constraint and $\alpha = \lambda/[1 + \lambda]$ is the corresponding Ramsey number. An analysis of the optimal schedule of marginal prices yields exactly the same condition as derived previously in Sections 1 and 5. It remains, therefore, to determine the minimal purchase q_*, the minimal charge P_*, or the least type t_* served. Using the formulas above, the necessary condition for an optimal choice of any one of these is:

$$U(q_*, t_*) - C(q_*) - \alpha \frac{\bar{F}(t_*)}{f(t_*)} U_t(q_*, t_*) = 0 \, .$$

This optimality condition parallels exactly the optimality condition for the purchase $q(t)$ assigned each type $t > t_*$. Using $q_* = q(t_*)$ it provides an equation that determines t_*, and thereby also $P_* = U(q(t_*), t_*)$.

An alternative construction uses the auxiliary demand profile $M(P, q) = \#\{t \mid U(q, t) \geq P\}$. The necessary condition above is essentially equivalent to selecting the minimal charge P_* to maximize the contribution

$$\int_{P_*}^{\infty} M(P, q_*) \, dP + [1 + \lambda] \cdot M(P_*, q_*) \cdot [P_* - C(q_*)],$$

to consumers' and producer's surplus from customers purchasing the minimal quantity q_*, for which the necessary condition is

$$\alpha M(P_*, q_*) + M_P(P_*, q_*) \cdot [P_* - C(q_*)] = 0.$$

This condition is applied by interpreting its solution $P_*(q_*)$ as a function of the minimal purchase q_* and then determining q_* and t_* by the requirement that

$$M(P_*(q_*), q_*) = N(p(q_*), q_*) = \bar{F}(t_*).$$

This construction suffices under the assumptions used in this chapter, but more general formulations require methods such as those in §4.4 and §8.5.

The interpretations are also analogous. For example, the percentage profit margin on the minimal purchase q_* can be interpreted as inversely proportional to the price elasticity of the demand for this initial block. Moreover, as in the analysis of multipart tariffs, this condition can be interpreted simply as an average of the corresponding condition for a nonlinear price schedule, in this case averaged over the units $q \leq q_*$ purchased by the single type t_* purchasing these units:

$$\int_0^{q_*} \left\{ v(q, t_*) - c(q) - \alpha \frac{\bar{F}(t_*)}{f(t_*)} v_t(q, t_*) \right\} dq = C(0).$$

An important corollary of this condition is that the fixed fee is nil if the fixed cost is nil. To see this, observe that the benefit from a purchase size of zero is nil independently of the customer's type; that is, $U(0, t) = 0$ and therefore $U_t(0, t) = 0$. Consequently, if $C(0) = 0$ then the condition is satisfied by the minimal purchase $q_* = 0$. In this case, t_* is merely the least type willing to make a purchase from the price schedule, namely $q(t_*) = 0$. This result evidently depends on the assumption that access is not valued apart from the opportunity to purchase; it is presumably false in the case of telephone service used only to receive calls.

When the fixed cost of service is positive, it is useful to apply the optimality condition to obtain the formulas

$$P_* = U(q_*, t_*) = C(q_*) + \alpha \frac{\bar{F}(t_*)}{f(t_*)} U_t(q_*, t_*)$$

$$= C(0) + \int_0^{q_*} [c(q) + \alpha \frac{\bar{F}(t_*)}{f(t_*)} v_t(q, t_*)] \, dq$$

$$= C(0) + p_* q_* + \int_0^{q_*} q[c'(q) + \alpha \frac{\bar{F}(t_*)}{f(t_*)} v_{tq}(q, t_*)] \, dq \, ,$$

where $p_* = p(q_*)$ and the third line is obtained from the second using integration by parts. The third line indicates that if marginal cost is constant and $v_{tq} = 0$ then the minimal charge is $P_* = C(0) + p_* q_*$, which is merely a two-part tariff with a fixed fee equal to the fixed cost and a marginal price equal to one charged on the price schedule for the q_*-th unit. Only if marginal cost or the slopes of customers' demand functions vary significantly will the minimum charge deviate much from this approximation. The following example illustrates this feature.

Example 6.10: For this example, suppose that $\alpha = 1$ and

$$U(q, t) = taq - \tfrac{1}{2} bq^2 \, , \qquad C(q) = C_o + cq \, , \qquad F(t) = t \, ,$$

where C_o is the fixed cost of serving a customer. Then the optimal price schedule is $p(q) = [a + c - bq]/2$ and type t purchases $q(t) = [a + c - 2t]/b$. Applying the optimality condition for the minimal purchase yields

$$q_* = \sqrt{2C_o/b} \, , \qquad \text{and} \qquad P_* = C_o + p_* q_* \, .$$

Thus, the minimum charge P_* consists of a fixed fee $P_o = C_o$ equal to the fixed cost, plus a uniform price $p_* \equiv p(q_*)$ for those units in the minimal purchase q_*. The firm's profit margin on the minimal purchase can therefore be interpreted as independent of the fixed cost per se. Rather, it derives entirely from the uniform price charged for the minimal purchase:

$$P(q_*) - C(q_*) = [p_* - c] \cdot q_* \, .$$

The optimal price schedule can also be interpreted as the minimum of the price schedules for a two-part tariff that charges the fixed cost plus the uniform price p_* per unit, and the nonlinear tariff that charges the schedule $p(q)$ for incremental units; that is, marginal prices above p_* are excluded.   ◇

Figure 6.12 shows the optimal price schedule constructed in this way. It also shows that the fixed fee in the amount of the fixed cost is exactly equal to the

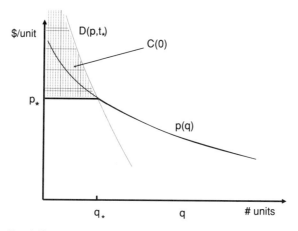

FIG. 6.12   The optimal price schedule with a fixed fee $P_o = C(0)$.

consumer's surplus for the least type t_*, calculated using the uniform price p_* for the first q_* units. From another viewpoint, the price schedule can be interpreted as the charging the maximum of $v(q, t_*)$ and $p(q)$ for each unit $q \geq 0$.

6.8   Summary

In this chapter we replace the demand profile as a summary of customers' behavior with a disaggregated formulation in which customers' benefit or demand functions are specified explicitly. The model relies on a one-dimensional parameter to identify customers' types or market segments. It is therefore limited by the maintained assumption that demand functions of different types of customers do not intersect.

We consider models in which the types are discrete and also models with a continuum of types. The latter are used to characterize the construction of multipart and nonlinear tariffs. In each case the same basic optimality condition recurs, though the form differs depending on the model used. This optimality condition is essentially the same as the one obtained from the demand-profile formulation. The optimality conditions for multipart tariffs are simply averages of the corresponding condition for a nonlinear tariff. This same interpretation applies to the determination of a fixed fee, although such a fee is positive only if the firm incurs a fixed cost in providing access to service.

7

INCOME EFFECTS

This chapter shows how income effects in customers' preferences are included in the construction of nonlinear tariffs. For simplicity, only monopoly pricing is addressed here; income effects complicate Ramsey pricing more severely so this topic is deferred to a brief treatment in §13. Income effects are included in the demand profile by allowing it to depend on the total tariff as well as the marginal price. This amendment complicates calculations because a second-order differential equation must be solved to obtain the optimal tariff. When income effects are substantial, the tariff depends on customers' incomes and on their income-elasticities of demand.

Section 1 describes how income effects alter the specification of the demand profile. Section 2 then derives the conditions that characterize an optimal tariff. Section 3 presents examples illustrating three main ways that income effects occur in formulations of parameterized models. These examples differ markedly, showing that the character of income effects is an important practical consideration. Section 4 remarks briefly on an alternative interpretation that applies when a fixed fee is charged.

7.1 Construction of the demand profile

When customers' preferences have income effects the demand profile has the general form $N(P(q), p(q), q)$, indicating that the demand for the q-th unit depends on the marginal price $p(q)$ for that unit and also on the total tariff $P(q)$. The dependence of demand for incremental units on the total tariff is usually explained by customers' budget constraints; thus, the tariff reduces the income available for other purchases. A typical model supposes that a customer t obtains the net utility $U(q, I(t) - P(q), t)$ from purchasing q units, provided $P(q) \leq I(t)$. In this specification, the customer's gross income is $I(t)$, which is divided between the tariff $P(q)$ charged for the purchase q and the residual amount $I(t) - P(q)$ used to purchase other products.[1] Assume that the firm's product is a normal good, so that the customer buys those units for which the marginal utility is positive:

$$v(q, I(t) - P(q), t) - h(q, I(t) - P(q), t)p(q) \geq 0,$$

where $v = U_q$ is the marginal utility of the q-th unit and $h = \partial U / \partial I$ is the marginal utility of income. Then the demand for q-th units is predicted by the demand profile

$$N(P, p, q) = \#\{t \mid s(q, I(t) - P, t) \geq p\},$$

where $s \equiv v/h$ is the customer's marginal rate of substitution between income and the firm's product. This demand profile measures the number of customers purchasing the q-th unit at the marginal price p and the total charge P for the purchase q.

7.2   Characterization of the optimal tariff

When the demand profile depends on the total tariff, maximization of the firm's profit contribution is more complicated because it poses a problem in the calculus of variations. The necessary conditions characterizing an optimum have two parts. The first part is the Euler condition:

$$\frac{\partial N}{\partial P} \cdot [p(q) - c(q)] - \frac{d}{dq} \left\{ N + \frac{\partial N}{\partial p} \cdot [p(q) - c(q)] \right\} = 0,$$

where N and its derivatives are evaluated at $(P(q), p(q), q)$. Because d/dq represents a total derivative, this condition involves $P(q)$, its derivative $p(q)$, and its second derivative $p'(q)$. Consequently, constructing a tariff that satisfies the Euler condition amounts to solving a second-order differential equation.[2]

The second part of the necessary conditions specifies boundary conditions that select a particular solution to the differential equation. For problems having nice regularity properties, these boundary conditions are the transversality conditions

---

1. The utility function is measured in arbitrary units. For welfare comparisons, this utility function can be converted to a monetary measure of net benefits. For example, define the function V via $U(0, I(t) + V(z), t) = z$ and then replace the utility function U by the equivalent representation

$$\hat{U}(q, I(t) - P(t), t) \equiv V(U(q, I(t) - P(q), t)).$$

$\hat{U}$ measures the income increment that obtains the same utility increment as the purchase $(q, P(q))$. This representation is used in Example 7.3 below.

2. Numerical methods for computing solutions are described in Press *et al.* (1986, §16). As will be seen below, the differential equation is ordinarily elliptic, subject to boundary conditions at the two extreme purchase sizes.

derived from the calculus of variations. If a fixed fee is excluded then the transversality conditions apply only at the maximum purchase q^* and require the following two properties:

$$N + N_p \cdot [p - c] = 0, \qquad (1)$$

$$Nc + pN_p \cdot [p - c] = 0. \qquad (2)$$

In applications without income effects these properties usually require that the maximum purchase and its tariff are determined by exhaustion of demand ($N = 0$) and equality of marginal price and marginal cost ($p = c$). With income effects, however, these conditions are often more subtle. In each example in Section 3, property (1) entails $N > 0$ at q^*, indicating that many customers select the same purchase q^*.[3] This bunching of customers at a single purchase occurs often in formulations with income effects.

If the firm incurs fixed costs and therefore charges a fixed fee then analogous transversality conditions apply at the minimum purchase q_*, which is generally positive; however, these are best addressed using the methods in §6.7 and §8.5.

Recall that §4 derives the result that condition (1) holds for all purchase sizes if there are no income effects and no fixed costs. This is because $\partial N / \partial P = 0$ if there are no income effects; therefore, the solution of the Euler condition that satisfies (1) at the maximum purchase satisfies it everywhere.

7.3 Examples

This section presents three examples illustrating the main ways that income effects interact with the diversity of types among customers. These examples are similar in that the firm's marginal cost is zero, and the customers' type parameters are distributed uniformly. Moreover, each customer's utility function has the additively separable form

$$U(q, I - P(q)) = u(q) + \frac{1}{1 - A}[I - P(q)]^{1-A},$$

in which the parameter I represents the customer's income. The parameter $A < 1$ is a measure of the magnitude of the income effect. It is the income elasticity; namely, the elasticity of the marginal rate of substitution with respect to the residual income $Y \equiv I - P(q)$, or equivalently, the ratio of the income and price elasticities of demand. If $A = 0$ then there is no income effect and the formulation is identical to the one in §6. We adopt the standardization $u(0) = 0$, and assume there is a maximum purchase q^* at which all customers' marginal benefits $v(q) \equiv u'(q)$ are

---

3. The technical reason for this feature is that $\lim_{q \to q^*} N_p \cdot [p - c] < 0$ even though marginal price and marginal cost are equal at q^*.

below the firm's marginal cost; that is, $v(q^*) \leq c \equiv 0$. As in Section 2, no fixed fee is charged, so $P(0) = 0$.

The examples differ in the way that the type parameter t affects the three components u, A, and I. In each example, the type parameter affects precisely one component; in the latter two, the type parameter is identical with the component.

Example 7.1: For this example, assume that customers differ only in their utilities for consumption of the firm's product. To be specific we use the quadratic specification

$$u(q, t) = tq - \tfrac{1}{2}q^2 ,$$

so $v(q, t) = t - q$ and $q^* = 1$. Assume that in the population the type parameter t is uniformly distributed between zero and one. All customers have the same income I and the same income elasticity A. With this specification, the demand profile is

$$N(P, p, q) = 1 - q - p/[I - P]^A ,$$

indicating the fraction of the population willing to purchase the q-th unit at the marginal price p when the charge for the purchase q is P. Using this demand profile, the Euler condition can be written as

$$p'(q) = -\frac{1}{2} \left\{ [I - P(q)]^A + A\frac{p(q)^2}{[I - P(q)]^A} \right\} .$$

Solutions of this differential equation are conveniently expressed in terms of the residual income $Y(q) = I - P(q)$ that a customer has after purchasing q. The unique solution satisfying the two transversality conditions satisfies the equation

$$\int_y^{Y(q)} [x^A(x - y)]^{-1/2} \, dx = 1 - q ,$$

where the constant y satisfies the equation

$$\int_y^I [x^A(x - y)]^{-1/2} \, dx = 1 ,$$

to ensure that $P(0) = 0$. Note that $y \equiv Y(1)$, so it is the residual income of the type $t = 1$ making the maximum purchase $q^* = 1$.

For the case $A = 0.2$, Figure 7.1 shows how the tariff varies with the size of the purchase and the customers' common income I. The effect of income on the tariff is modest: a thousandfold increase in income increases the tariff about fourfold. This is reflected in the parameters y and I: the maximum expenditure $I - y$ declines from 20% of income to only 0.1% as income increases a thousandfold. Using the

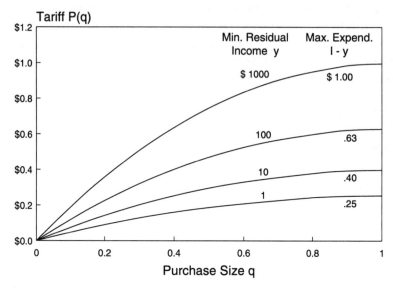

FIG. 7.1   Example 7.1: The tariff $P(q)$ for various incomes when the income elasticity is $A = 0.2$.

minimum residual income y as a surrogate for the income I, Figure 7.2 shows that the logarithm of the firm's profit per potential customer increases almost linearly with the logarithm of income, and the rate of increase is almost proportional to the income elasticity A. As one expects, the firm's profit is independent of income if there are no income effects ($A = 0$). More generally, if A is small then income has little effect on the tariff. This is one justification for omitting income effects in other chapters.   ◇

The next example, however, shows that the tariff is very sensitive to income if customers differ mainly in their income elasticities.

Example 7.2: This example assumes that customers' types are identical with their income elasticities. Thus, the utility function is

$$U(q, I - P(q), t) = u(q) + \frac{1}{1 - t}[I - P(q)]^{1-t},$$

and to be specific we assume that $u(q) = q - \frac{1}{2}q^2$, so $v(q) = 1 - q$ and $q^* = 1$. The demand profile is therefore

$$N(P, p, q) = 1 - \frac{\log(p/v(q))}{\log(I - P(q))},$$

and the Euler condition can be written as

$$p'(q) = p(q)\frac{v'(q)}{v(q)} + \frac{p(q)^2}{[I - P(q)]\log_e(I - P(q))},$$

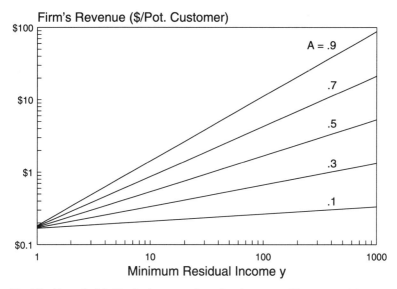

FIG. 7.2   Example 7.1: The firm's revenue for various incomes and income elasticities.

where $e = 2.7183...$ is the base of the natural logarithms. As in the previous example, solutions of this differential equation are conveniently expressed in terms of the residual income $Y(q)$. The unique solution satisfying the transversality conditions satisfies the equation

$$Y(q)[1 - \log_e Y(q)] - I[1 - \log_e I] = K[q - \tfrac{1}{2}q^2],$$

where the constant K is determined by the condition that

$$K = \frac{1}{e}Y(1)\log_e Y(1).$$

As shown in Figure 7.3, for each purchase size the tariff as a fraction of income is almost constant. For incomes \$10, \$100, and \$1,000, the tariffs at the maximum purchase are $P(1) = \$1.504$, \$15.288, and \$153.71 respectively.   ◇

Another example in which the magnitude of customers' incomes affects the tariff is the following.

Example 7.3: Suppose that a customer's type is the same as his income, namely $I(t) = t$, but customers' preferences are otherwise identical. Thus, the utility function has the form,

$$U(q, t - P) = u(q) + \frac{1}{1 - A}[t - P]^{1 - A}.$$

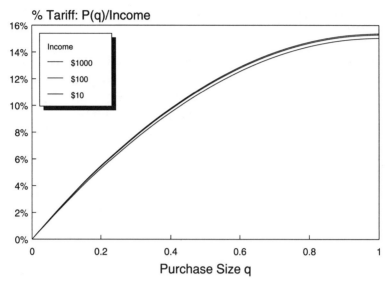

FIG. 7.3 Example 7.2: As a fraction of income, the tariff is nearly constant.

Assuming incomes are uniformly distributed between zero and B, the demand profile is

$$N(P, p, q) = \#\left\{t \mid P \le t \;\&\; v(q)[t - P]^A \ge p\right\}$$
$$= 1 - b \cdot [P + (p/v(q))^a], \qquad \text{where} \quad a = 1/A, \quad b = 1/B.$$

Using this demand profile, the Euler condition can be written as $p'(q)/p(q) = v'(q)/v(q)$. This implies that the price schedule has the form $p(q) = kv(q)$; therefore, the tariff has the form $P(q) = K + ku(q)$. Because there is no fixed fee, $K = 0$. Using only this information about the form of the tariff, the firm's revenue can be computed as

$$\int_0^{q^*} N(P(q), p(q), q)p(q)\, dq = [B - k^a][ku(q^*)/B] - \tfrac{1}{2}B[ku(q^*)/B]^2.$$

The transversality conditions select q^* and k to maximize this revenue.

One can show that the maximum purchase is independent of k. Consequently, the transversality condition (2) is satisfied at q^* where $v(q^*) = 0$, because $c = 0$ and $p(q^*) = kv(q^*) = 0$. Condition (1) can be written as

$$\{1 - b[ku(q^*) + k^a]\} - bak^a = 0,$$

because $p(q^*)/v(q^*) = k$ even though the numerator and denominator are both zero. The optimal choice of k is therefore the unique value between 0 and $B/u(q^*)$

that satisfies this equation. This is precisely the value that maximizes the firm's revenue as expressed above.

Thus, a monopolist firm charges the multiple k of the customers' gross utility $u(q)$ from the product. This tariff can be converted into monetary terms as follows. Define

$$\alpha \equiv A/[1+A], \qquad k^* \equiv ku(q^*)/B, \qquad u^* \equiv u(q^*)/B^{1-A},$$

$$t_* \equiv \alpha[1-k^*], \qquad t^* \equiv t_* + k^*.$$

Those customers with incomes below Bt_* purchase zero, and those above purchase positive amounts; in particular, all those with incomes above Bt^* purchase exactly q^* units. Among those customers purchasing, one with income less than Bt^* spends the excess over Bt_* on his purchase. Knowing t_* one can derive $k^* = 1 - t_*/\alpha$ and $t^* = 1 - t_*[\alpha^{-1} - 1]$, all of which are dimensionless fractions. Moreover, the tariff is

$$P(q) = [k^*B][u(q)/u(q^*)],$$

which expresses the tariff as the product of a fraction of the maximum income and the relative magnitude of the gross utility derived from the purchase q.

It suffices, therefore, to characterize the fraction t_* of the potential customers who forego purchasing. This fraction is determined by a rearrangement of the equation specified previously to determine k; namely, t_* is the fraction that solves the equation

$$t_*^{-A} - \frac{1}{\alpha}t_*^{1-A} = u^*.$$

The solid curves in Figure 7.4 show t_* for several values of the income elasticity A and a range of values of the standardized potential gain u^*; the dashed curves represent the corresponding values of t^*. The curves for $A = 0$, for which $t_* = 0$ and $t^* = k^* = \min\{1, u^*\}$, are not shown. Figure 7.5 shows the parameter $k^* \equiv t^* - t_*$ appearing in the formula for the tariff. For small values of u^*, k^* declines slowly as A increases, and $k^* = 1 - 1/[1 + \frac{1}{2}u^*]$ at $A = 1$.

The firm's revenue per potential customer, calculated as a fraction of the maximum income, is

$$\text{Revenue}/B = k^*\left[\frac{1}{2} + (\frac{1}{2\alpha} - 1)t_*\right],$$

which is shown in Figure 7.6. The curve for $A = 0$ is obtained as the limit

$$\lim_{A \to 0} \text{Revenue}/B = \begin{cases} u^* - \frac{1}{2}(u^*)^2 & \text{if } u^* < 1, \\ 1/2 & \text{if } u^* \geq 1. \end{cases}$$

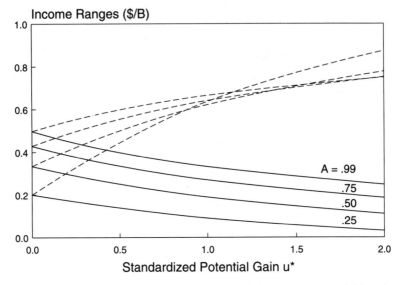

FIG. 7.4 Example 7.3: The income parameters as functions of u^*. Note: $— t_*$; $---t^*$; $k^* = t^* - t_*$.

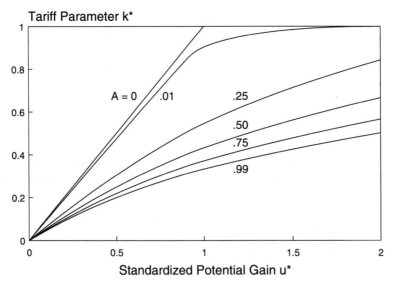

FIG. 7.5 Example 7.3: The tariff parameter k^*.

Thus, the revenue depends significantly on B and u^* even if the income elasticity is very small. At the other extreme,

$$\lim_{A \to 1} \text{Revenue}/B = \frac{1}{2} \left[1 - \frac{1}{1 + \frac{1}{2}u^*} \right],$$

which in the figure is indistinguishable from the curve for $A = 0.99$.

For a customer with relative income $\hat{t} \equiv t/B$, the opportunity to buy the product is equivalent to an increment $B\hat{U}(\hat{t})$ to his income that is given by the formula,

$$\hat{U}(\hat{t}) = \begin{cases} 0 & \text{if } \hat{t} \leq t_*, \\ \left\{ [1 - A][\hat{t} - t_*]u^*/k^* + t_*^{1-A} \right\}^{\frac{1}{1-A}} - \hat{t} & \text{if } t_* < \hat{t} < t^*, \\ \left\{ [1 - A]u^* + [\hat{t} - k^*]^{1-A} \right\}^{\frac{1}{1-A}} - \hat{t} & \text{if } \hat{t} \geq t^*. \end{cases}$$

Figure 7.7 graphs this consumer's surplus $\hat{U}(\hat{t})$ for the case $u^* = 1$ and several values of A; only those relative incomes between t_* and t^* are shown. Also shown as a dashed curve is the case $u^* = 0.5$ and $A = 0.5$ for comparison. For small income elasticities, consumer's surplus is negligible if $u^* < 1$ since the tariff extracts nearly the entire benefit; in particular,

$$\lim_{A \to 0} \hat{U}(\hat{t}) = \hat{t} \cdot \max \{0, u^* - 1\}.$$

This reflects only the fact that if there are no income effects then the diversity of customers' incomes is irrelevant and so the monopoly tariff charges the entire benefit.   ◇

7.4 Fixed fees

The demand profile also depends on the total tariff if a fixed fee is charged. To clarify the difference between income effects and fixed fees, we describe briefly the effects of fixed fees.

If a positive fixed fee is charged then the analysis in §6.7 can also be based on the alternative master profile

$$N(P, p, q) = \#\{t \mid U(q, t) \geq P \,\&\, v(q, t) \geq p\}.$$

As in the case of income effects, the master profile measures the number of customers willing to pay both the marginal price p for the q-th unit and the total charge P for the purchase q. Indeed, this is the proper interpretation of the demand profile if it is derived from data obtained using two-part tariffs. Note, however, that customers' preferences do not include income effects per se. Indeed, if a customer's benefits from the minimum purchase q_* are sufficiently large to pay the fixed fee

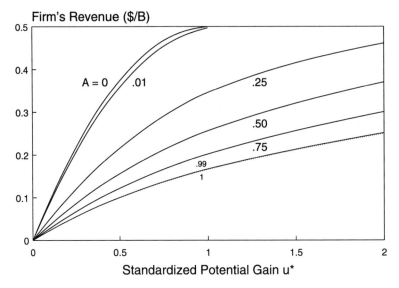

FIG. 7.6 Example 7.3: The firm's revenue for various income elasticities.

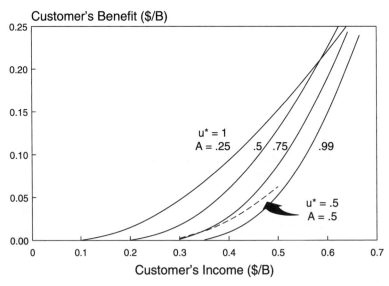

FIG. 7.7 Example 7.3: Dollar value of a customer's benefit, depending on relative income $\hat{t}$, for $u^* = 1$. Note: $---$ is the case $u^* = 0.5$, $A = 0.5$.

then for larger purchases demand behavior is determined only by marginal considerations. Consequently, the Euler condition and the transversality conditions (1)
and (2) at the maximum purchase q^* imply that the price schedule $p(q)$ is determined directly by solving the usual optimality condition $N + N_p \cdot [p - c] = 0$ in
the range $q_* \leq q \leq q^*$, for which $N_P = 0$. For smaller purchases $q < q_* \equiv q(t_*)$,
however, the constraint $P(q) = U(q, t_*)$ is binding for the least type t_* making
a positive purchase; thus, $P(q_*) = U(q_*, t_*)$. The transversality conditions that
determine q_* and $P(q_*)$ essentially replicate the determination of q_* and t_* in the
analysis of fixed fees in §6.7, so they are not repeated here. Alternatively, if the
tariff is extended to $q = 0$ then $P(q) = U(q, t_*)$ for $q \leq q_*$. Recall that the main
conclusion is that the firm charges a fixed fee equal to its fixed cost, and for those
units $q < q_*$ it charges the uniform price $p_* = p(q_*)$; thus, t_* is determined by the
condition

$$U(q_*, t_*) = C(0) + p(q(t_*))q(t_*),$$

and $q(t_*) = 0$ if $C(0) = 0$.

7.5   Summary

The examples in Section 3 illustrate that income effects can influence the design
of nonlinear tariffs in various ways. Although income effects are represented suc-
cinctly by the dependence of the demand profile on the tariff, these examples
indicate that the origins of this dependence can be diverse, and the optimal tariffs
reflect this diversity.

   These examples are presented for the case of a profit-maximizing monopoly,
but they pertain also to Ramsey pricing by a regulated utility since the effect of a
revenue constraint is mainly to reduce profit margins proportionately, as in §4.

   The model in Example 7.1 is the basic motivation for ignoring income effects
in other chapters. The optimal tariff is insensitive to income effects whenever
customers' marginal rates of substitution are insensitive to the tariff. The two important cases are that customers' income elasticities are small and/or their residual
incomes are large in relation to their expenditures on the firm's product. This is the
usual motivation for ignoring income effects when constructing tariffs for services
offered to residential customers. Commercial customers are usually supposed on
theoretical grounds to have no significant income effects because they are not
subject to budget constraints.

   Examples 7.2 and 7.3 represent two alternative extreme possibilities in which
customers differ primarily in their income elasticities or their incomes. Example 7.2 exhibits acute sensitivity to income. It indicates that income effects could
be dominant if customers' heterogeneity were due mainly to differing income elasticities. Although there seems to be little empirical evidence on this issue, some
authors argue that income elasticities are uniform; cf. Roberts (1979, Section IV),
who calls this Pigou's Law. Example 7.3 is an intermediate case providing insight

into the role of income differences among residential customers. The primary conclusion is that income effects influence the magnitude of the firm's profit margin,
but do not alter the basic form of the tariff. In the example, for instance, the profit
margin is proportional to k^*, B, and $u(q)/u(q^*)$. Of these, the latter two represent
the range of incomes and the relative magnitude of the customer's benefit. The
parameter k^* increases with u^* and decreases with A. The dependence of the tariff
on the range of customers' incomes represents a significant amendment to the
conclusions derived in §4.

8

TECHNICAL AMENDMENTS

The purpose of this chapter is to clarify some technical aspects of the models studied in previous chapters. The presentation invokes more mathematics than used previously, but we do not undertake a fully rigorous analysis. Our aim is mainly to describe how some complications that can arise in general formulations can be resolved. Three technical sections address supplementary topics.

Section 1 introduces the variety of complicating features that can arise in models that do not satisfy regularity assumptions of the sort introduced in §6.2. In Section 2 we describe two other derivations of the optimality conditions for a nonlinear tariff. These complement the derivation of the optimal price assignment in §6.5 by posing the problem in terms of the optimal quantity and type assignments. We indicate how these assignments can be modified by a variant of the ironing procedure to ensure that the requisite monotonicity conditions are satisfied; in addition, we provide assumptions sufficient to ensure that monotonicity is satisfied automatically by the solution to the usual form of the optimality condition.

Section 3 returns to the topic of multipart tariffs and establishes the general property that a multipart tariff with only a few segments achieves most of the advantages of a fully nonlinear tariff. Section 4 demonstrates that the optimality condition is essentially unchanged when customers' type parameters are multidimensional. Finally, in Section 5 we show how the analysis in §4 is modified when the magnitude of the total tariff affects the demand profile: the main consequence is that lower prices akin to lifeline rates are offered for small purchases.

8.1 Technical considerations

We first review the various ways that a tariff constructed directly from the optimality conditions in §4 or §6 can be unsatisfactory. There are two basic deficiencies that can occur. One is that the price schedule can be inconsistent with some customers' demand behaviors. This occurs if the price schedule intersects a customer's demand schedule from above, in which case the predicted purchase is at a local minimum of the customer's net benefit, rather than a maximum as intended. The

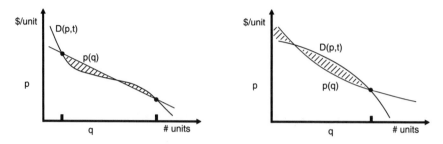

FIG. 8.1 Two examples with multiple locally optimal purchase sizes.

second deficiency is that the firm's optimality condition can have multiple solutions, and in particular some solutions can represent local minima. These two
difficulties turn out to be closely related and we present assumptions sufficient to
preclude both.

Multiple Solutions

To begin, we observe that the cautions mentioned in the discussion of bundling
in §4.3 apply here on a larger scale. Figure 8.1 shows two examples of problems
that can arise if the optimal price schedule does not intersect a customer's demand
function just once from below. In the left diagram the two circled points represent
purchases that might be optimal. The left point is optimal unless the customer's
net gains from moving to the right point exceed the losses incurred for the first few
units, as shown by the two shaded areas. The right diagram also has two possible
selections, either the one point shown or the null purchase $q = 0$.

Each diagram in the figure also shows one uncircled intersection of the demand
function and the price schedule that is not optimal for the customer because it
represents a local minimum of his net benefit, rather than a local maximum. This
occurs where the demand function intersects the price schedule from below.

These examples indicate that the design of an optimal price schedule should
avoid creating local minima and multiple local maxima in the purchase selection
problems presented to customers. Actually, we have essentially excluded multiple
local maxima by adopting assumption A2 in §6.2. To see this, observe that if a
customer of type t has a global maximum at quantity q and also had another local
maximum at a different quantity $\bar{q}$ preferred by another type $\bar{t}$ then the equality
$v(\bar{q}, t) = v(\bar{q}, \bar{t})$ would be true—but this is excluded by the assumption that the
marginal valuation function v is a strictly increasing function of the customer's
type. That is, by excluding intersections of the types' demand functions we have
already excluded nonoptimal local maxima except at quantities that are not chosen
by any customer. Our main task, therefore, is to ensure that the price schedule is
not based on the erroneous assumption that a customer selects a local minimum.

As mentioned, this amounts to ensuring that the price schedule intersects each type's demand function only from below.

To address this task we impose a further condition that excludes selection of a local minimum. This condition can be derived from consideration of a customer's second-order necessary condition for a maximum. For a customer of type t to select a purchase of size q requires both the first-order condition $v(q, t) - p(q) = 0$ and the second-order condition $v_q(q, t) - p'(q) \leq 0$. Suppose first that there is a well-defined function $t(q)$ specifying the type purchasing q and that this function is differentiable. Then the marginal price schedule is $p(q) = v(q, t(q))$ and therefore $p' = v_q + v_t t'$ at $(q, t(q))$. Thus, the second-order condition requires that $v_t t' \geq 0$, or equivalently, because v_t has been assumed in A2 to be positive, that $t'(q) \geq 0$. In sum, for purchase sizes in a range where locally the type is a smooth function of the purchase, this function must be nondecreasing. More generally, even where there is a discrete jump in the type as the purchase size increases, this jump cannot be downward. Similarly, in regions where the assignment $q(t)$ of types to purchases sizes is locally a well-defined function, the customers' second-order conditions require that this assignment is nondecreasing.

The effect of these conditions in a general context can be seen in Figure 8.2. The figure displays schematically the locus of all pairs (q, t) satisfying the firm's optimality condition

$$[v(q, t) - c(q)]f(t) - \alpha \bar{F}(t)v_t(q, t) = 0$$

for a hypothetical example in which it is supposed that multiple solutions are possible for q as a function of t and for t as a function of q.[1] Among the four connected components of the locus, one is selected as the relevant solution, although in principle the firm's preferred solution could move among several components. Along this component we have used an ironing procedure analogous to the one in §4.2: the horizontal solid line indicates a segment where the assignment $q(t)$ is constrained to be nondecreasing, and similarly the vertical dashed line indicates a segment where the inverse assignment $t(q)$ is constrained to be nondecreasing. In each case, the line is located so that the firm's necessary condition for optimality is satisfied on average over the relevant interval. Along the horizontal solid line, all types are assigned the same purchase size; in contrast, the vertical dashed line indicates a discrete jump in the purchase size as the type increases.

In the latter case, for instance, the ironing procedure is specified as follows. Suppose there is a range $\bar{a} \leq q \leq \bar{b}$ of purchases sizes for which $t(q)$ is decreasing: then over a wider range $a^* < q < b^*$ the type-assignment must be constant, say $t(q) = t^*$. Over this range the price schedule is the same as the demand schedule of

---

1. The feature in this example that the locus comprises a finite number of connected components, each of which is a smooth manifold, is a consequence of an implicit assumption that zero is a so-called regular value of the left side of the firm's optimality condition.

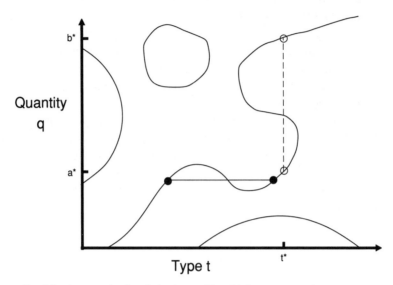

FIG. 8.2 An example of a solution locus with multiple non-monotonic components.

type t^*, say $p(q) = v(q, t^*)$. The optimality condition must be satisfied on average over this range:

$$\int_{a^*}^{b^*} \left\{ [v(q, t^*) - c(q)]f(t^*) - \alpha \bar{F}(t^*)v_t(q, t^*) \right\} dq = 0.$$

This condition plus the two endpoint conditions, $p(a^*) = v(a^*, t^*)$ and $p(b^*) = v(b^*, t^*)$, suffice to determine a^*, b^*, and t^*. The net effect of this amendment is to leave type t^* indifferent as to which quantity in the range between a^* and b^* to choose. Thus, one anticipates that no customers, except possibly type t^*, will purchase in the gap between a^* and b^*—although the firm may prefer that type t^* purchases b^*.

The ironing procedure also plays an additional role in both formulations. Recall that in §4.2 the ironing procedure was devised to assure that the resulting price schedule is nonincreasing. In either formulation, this restricts the rate at which the assignment increases:

$$q'(t) \geq -v_t(q(t), t)/v_q(q(t), t), \qquad \text{or} \qquad t'(q) \leq -v_q(q, t(q))/v_t(q, t(q)).$$

Again one uses an ironing procedure in which the optimality condition is satisfied on average over an interval on which this inequality is binding as an equality.

The effect of the ironing procedure in the first case is shown in Figure 8.3. The resulting price schedule is shown in the bottom panel as the solid curve, which includes a vertical segment labeled (1) at the quantity q^* assigned to an

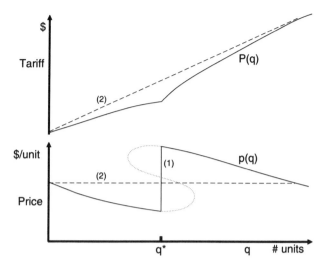

FIG. 8.3 The effect of the ironing procedure on the price schedule and the tariff when a single quantity q^* is assigned to an interval of types. The uniform price indicated by (2) results from further ironing to assure that the price schedule is nonincreasing.

interval of types. The effect on the tariff shown in the top panel is to produce a cusp at the quantity q^*. This case tends to occur when the distribution of types is bimodal: in effect, the price schedule separates into two segments, each adapted to a separate subgroup of customers. One may require further that the price schedule is nonincreasing, as shown in the horizontal segment (2) and the corresponding linear segment of the tariff that is also labelled (2). This may be necessary if a customer would otherwise purchase increments beyond q^* by dividing a large purchase $q > q^*$ into smaller purchases that are each less than q^*.

The effect of the ironing procedure in the second case is shown in Figure 8.4. For some interval of quantities, the price schedule follows the demand schedule of the type t^* selected by the ironing procedure; similarly, over this interval the tariff coincides with an indifference curve of this type. This case tends to occur when low types have relatively inelastic demands, so the price schedule falls precipitously for larger purchases: again, it can be interpreted as arising from a bimodal distribution of types or their price elasticities of demand.

Sufficient conditions for a unique solution

The complicated features of the solution locus in Figure 8.2 do not occur in models with regularity properties that exclude multiple solutions of the firm's optimality condition. Two regularity assumptions suffice: one assures that there is a unique solution for the quantity $q(t)$ assigned to type t, and the other assures that there is a unique solution for the type $t(q)$ assigned to purchase the quantity q. If both assumptions are invoked then the locus of pairs (q, t) satisfying the optimality

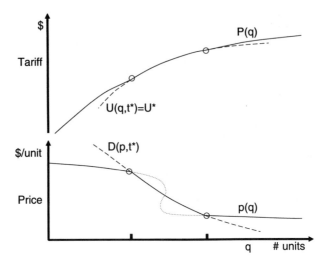

FIG. 8.4 The effect of the ironing procedure when the price schedule coincides with the demand curve of a type t^* over an interval of quantities.

condition has a single component that is nondecreasing in both variables. Either assumption assures that the solution locus has only a single component. If only one assumption is satisfied then the ironing procedure can be applied to eliminate nonmonotonicities that might occur if the other assumption is violated. Models that violate both assumptions present considerable difficulties that we do not address here.

To present these assumptions compactly it is useful to use the index $s = 1 - r = \bar{F}(t)$ as a surrogate type parameter representing the complement of the customer's rank. The marginal valuation of the q-th unit is therefore

$$\bar{v}(q, s) = v(q, \bar{F}^{-1}(s)),$$

which is a decreasing function of s. Its surrogate-type elasticity

$$\omega(q, s) \equiv -s\bar{v}_s/\bar{v}$$
$$= \left(\frac{tv_t(q, t)}{v}\right) \div \left(\frac{tf(t)}{\bar{F}(t)}\right)$$

is just the reciprocal of the price elasticity of the demand profile, and according to assumption A2 it is positive. The optimality condition can be written in these terms as

$$\frac{\bar{v}(q, s) - c(q)}{\bar{v}(q, s)} = \alpha\omega(q, s).$$

Assumptions A2 and A3 imply that the left side of this equation is a nonincreasing function of q and s. The requisite regularity assumptions therefore pertain to the monotonicity of the surrogate-type elasticity on the right side:[2]

> **A4:** The surrogate-type elasticity $w(q, s)$ is an increasing function of both (a) the quantity q and (b) the surrogate-type s.

Note from the formula for w above that the surrogate-type elasticity is the ratio of the type elasticities of the marginal valuation function v and the right-cumulative distribution function $\bar{F}$; hence, to satisfy assumption A4 it suffices that each of these elasticities is appropriately monotone.[3]

In assumption A4, part (a) assures that each type has at most one quantity on the solution locus, and similarly part (b) assures that each quantity has at most one type to whom it might be assigned. Moreover, given one part of A4, the other part assures that the corresponding assignment is nondecreasing. For the monopoly case $\alpha = 1$, Figure 8.5 illustrates how the combination of these two parts assures that the assignment of quantities to types is nondecreasing, or in this case, that the assignment of quantities to surrogate types is nonincreasing. The left and right side of the optimality condition are graphed separately for two values $s < s^*$ of the surrogate type index. Assumption A4 requires that the two curves for s lie outside the two curves for s^*; consequently, the two intersections where the optimality condition is satisfied are such that the quantity $q(s)$ assigned to s exceeds the quantity $q(s^*)$ assigned to s^*. This assures that the quantity assignment is decreasing in terms of the surrogate type s, and increasing in terms of the actual type t.

With Ramsey pricing, the net effect of reducing α is to increase the quantity obtained by each type. This is shown graphically in Figure 8.6 for an example with $c = 0$ so that the optimality condition is $w(q(s), s) = 1/\alpha$, plotted on the left vertical scale. The figure shows the determination of the quantities $q_1 > q_2 > q_3$ assigned to types $t_1 > t_2 > t_3$ or surrogate types $s_1 < s_2 < s_3$, as well as the subsequent calculation of the associated marginal prices $p_1 < p_2 < p_3$ from the customers' optimality condition, $p(s) = \bar{v}(q(s), s)$. Reducing the Ramsey number α raises the horizontal line and thereby assigns each quantity to a higher surrogate type (that is, a lower actual type), thereby reducing the marginal price paid for the last unit of that quantity shown on the right vertical scale.

2. We omit here the analogous assumption that ensures a unique determination of the fixed fee if the firm's fixed cost is positive: it requires that the elasticity $\Omega(q, s) \equiv -s\bar{U}_s/\bar{U}$ is monotone in s. We also omit more technical assumptions addressed by Guesnerie and Laffont (1984) among others; in particular, they note that the utility function U must satisfy a uniform Lipschitz condition on the boundary of the domain of types, and that the ironing procedure is feasible only if $q'(t)$ changes sign only a finite number of times.

3. Most of the distribution functions used in applied work have the property that the hazard rate $f(t)/\bar{F}(t)$ is increasing; the companion property is therefore that v_t/v is decreasing. The type elasticity of v can also be expressed as the ratio of the type and price elasticities of the demand function.

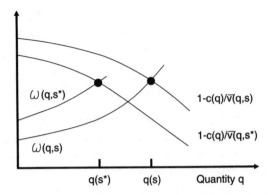

FIG. 8.5 Construction of the quantity assignment. Assumption A4 implies that if $s < s^*$ then $q(s) > q(s^*)$.

In the next section we sketch two derivations of the optimal price schedule. The first characterizes the assignment $q(t)$ of types to quantities, so it relies essentially on part (a) of A4 being satisfied locally. If part (b) is not satisfied and the assignment is not monotone, then the ironing procedure flattens the assignment so that all types in an interval obtain the same quantity. This happens when for a subinterval of types the induced price schedule would intersect their demand functions from above; consequently, the assignment, and thereby the price schedule, is modified to confine the assignment to a quantity that is a local maximum for each type. Similarly, the second derivation characterizes the assignment $t(q)$ of quantities to types, so it relies essentially on part (b) being satisfied. If part (a) is not satisfied then the ironing procedure produces an interval of quantities over which the price

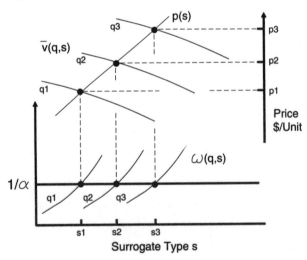

FIG. 8.6 An alternative construction of the quantity and price assignments. If $c = 0$ then each price $p_i = \bar{v}(q_i, s_i)$ where $\omega(q_i, s_i) = 1/\alpha$.

schedule coincides with one type's demand function. In both cases, in typical applications the ironing procedure tends to be needed, if at all, only for an initial interval of small types and/or quantities.

8.2   Derivations of the optimal tariff

In this section we derive the optimal price schedule for a model with a one-dimensional parameter representing customers' types. The first formulation characterizes the assignment $q(t)$ of types to quantities, and the second, the assignment $t(q)$ of quantities to types. In either case, the price schedule is subsequently derived from the customer's optimality condition: $p = v(q, t)$ if t chooses q at the marginal price p. Also, the fixed fee is set to extract all the consumer's surplus from the type purchasing the least amount.

Assumptions A1, A2, and A3 from §6.2 are imposed. In addition, either part (a) or part (b) of assumption A4 is imposed to exclude the complications described in Section 1.

The optimal quantity assignment

We first derive the optimal price schedule indirectly by constructing the optimal assignment of types to the quantities they purchase. In this formulation the tariff is represented implicitly by introducing each type's consumer's surplus as an auxiliary variable.

The consumer's surplus $W(t)$ obtained by type t is the maximum net benefit obtainable in response to the tariff offered, namely,

$$W(t) \equiv \max_{q} \{U(q, t) - P(q)\} \ .$$

Consequently, the envelope property implies that its derivative is

$$W'(t) = U_t(q(t), t) \,,$$

where $q(t)$ is an optimal purchase for type t that attains the maximum net benefit $W(t)$. We impose this equality as a constraint to ensure that the assigned quantity $q(t)$ is at least locally optimal. The amount of the tariff can be conveniently represented as $P(q(t)) = U(q(t), t) - W(t)$.

These ingredients provide the data to formulate the firm's optimization problem, as follows. The aggregate consumers' surplus is

$$CS = \int_{t_*}^{b} W(t) \, dF(t) \,,$$

where $t_* \geq a$ is the least type served. And, the producer's surplus is

$$\mathrm{PS} = \int_{t_*}^{b} [P(q(t)) - C(q(t))]\, dF(t)\,,$$

which in the Ramsey pricing formulation is constrained to be sufficiently large to meet a revenue requirement. Let λ be the Lagrange multiplier for the firm's revenue constraint, and in addition let $\mu(t)$ be a Lagrange multiplier for the constraint expressing the envelope property. Then the Lagrangian expression that is to be maximized is

$$\int_{t_*}^{b} \{ (W(t) + [1 + \lambda][U(q(t), t) - W(t) - C(q(t))]) f(t)$$
$$+ \mu(t)[W'(t) - U_t(q(t), t)] \}\, dt\,.$$

In this expression, the first term W is type t's consumer's surplus and in the second, $U - W$ is the tariff and therefore $U - W - C$ is the producer's surplus. The two functions $W(t)$ and $q(t)$ are chosen to maximize this expression, subject of course to the requirement that each is nonnegative; and λ and the function $\mu(t)$ are chosen to ensure that the corresponding constraints are satisfied.

The Euler necessary conditions for an optimum can be derived directly, but their motivation is clearer if the term involving $W'(t)$ is revised using integration by parts:

$$\int_{t_*}^{b} \mu(t) W'(t)\, dt = \mu(b) W(b) - \mu(t_*) W(t_*) - \int_{t_*}^{b} W(t) \mu'(t)\, dt\,.$$

With this revision, both $W(t)$ and $q(t)$ can be selected to maximize the resulting integrand pointwise at each type t. This yields two conditions: optimality of $W(t)$ for $t_* < t < b$ requires

$$-\lambda f(t) - \mu'(t) \leq 0\,,$$

and optimality of $q(t)$ similarly requires

$$[1 + \lambda][v(q(t), t) - c(q(t))]f(t) - \mu(t) v_t(q(t), t) \leq 0\,,$$

where as usual $v = U_q$, $v_t = U_{qt}$, and $c = C'$. In each condition, the inequality must be an equality if $W(t)$ or $q(t)$ is positive. Similarly, on the boundary where $t = b$ the optimality of $W(b)$ requires that $\mu(b) = 0$ if $W(b) > 0$; however, if there is a fixed cost then typically $W(t_*) = 0$ and $\mu(t_*) > 0$.

These two conditions can be refined further as follows. Recall that assumption A2 requires that if $q(t)$ is positive then U_t is positive, and therefore $W'(t)$ is positive and $W(t)$ is increasing. Consequently, if any type t obtains a positive quantity then

$W(t)$ is increasing and therefore positive for all sufficiently large values of t. In particular, $W(b) > 0$ and therefore $\mu(b) = 0$, so the first condition implies that $\mu(t) = \lambda \bar{F}(t)$. Inserting this formula into the second condition yields

$$[v(q, t) - c(q)]f(t) - \alpha \bar{F}(t)v_t(q, t) = 0$$

if $q = q(t) > 0$, where as usual $\alpha = \lambda/[1 + \lambda]$. Wherever this condition is satisfied, the customer's first-order necessary condition requires that the price schedule is $p(q) = v(q, t)$. The fixed fee, if any, is found by deriving the analogous transversality condition for t_*:

$$[U(q_*, t_*) - C(q_*)]f(t_*) - \alpha \bar{F}(t_*)U_t(q_*, t_*) = 0$$

if $t_* > a$, where the minimal purchase is $q_* = q(t_*)$, and then $P(q_*) = U(q_*, t_*)$ is the minimal charge and $P_o = P(q_*) - p_* q_*$ is the fixed fee, provided the uniform price $p_* = p(q_*)$ is imposed for all units $q \le q_*$. Thus, we have obtained again all the same conditions for optimality derived previously in §6.

Applications of this optimality condition are subject to several qualifications. The first is that it is not a necessary condition unless the quantity assignment also satisfies the auxiliary constraints that are not included explicitly in the formulation. As described above, one of these is that the assignment $q(t)$ must be a nondecreasing function.[4] For any interval of types where this property is violated, the ironing procedure yields an assignment that is constant on a wider interval over which the optimality condition is satisfied on average. Similarly, the ironing procedure can be applied to ensure that the induced price schedule is nondecreasing.

The second qualification is that this condition is not sufficient to identify the optimal assignment if it has multiple solutions, and even a single component can have multiple solutions for q as a function of t or t as a function of q. Either part of assumption A4 is sufficient to exclude one of these pathologies. If the other part is satisfied too, then the assignment is guaranteed to be nondecreasing.

The optimal type assignment

Next we outline an alternative derivation in which the problem is posed as the construction of an optimal assignment $t(q)$ of quantities to types. For simplicity we do not repeat the derivation of the least type served, the minimal purchase, and the minimal charge.

---

4. Because $v_t > 0$, the constraint $q'(t) \ge 0$ is equivalent to $W'' \ge U_{tt}$ in this formulation.

In this version, consumers' and producer's surplus are formulated as

$$CS = \int_{q_*}^{B} [U(q, t(q)) - P(q)] \, dF(t(q)),$$

$$PS = \int_{q_*}^{B} [P(q) - C(q)] \, dF(t(q)),$$

where $b = t(B)$. After integration by parts the demand condition $p(q) = v(q, t(q))$ can be substituted to obtain a revised objective function, expressed entirely in terms of the type $t(q)$ that makes a purchase of size q. Omitting constant terms, we obtain:[5]

$$\int_{q_*}^{B} \bar{F}(t(q)) \{U_t(q, t(q))t'(q) + [1 + \lambda][v(q, t(q)) - c(q)]\} \, dq.$$

This objective comprises two parts. The second term in brackets expresses the profit margin on q-th units in terms of the marginal valuation of the type $t(q)$ marginally willing to purchase this unit, and the factor $\bar{F}(t(q))$ measures the number of customers of all types willing to purchase a q-th unit at this price. The first term measures the incremental consumer's surplus $\frac{d}{dq}W(t(q))$ obtained from sales of the q-th unit, using the envelope property $W' = U_t$.

The necessary condition that identifies an optimal assignment for this problem is the Euler condition from the calculus of variations. This condition yields again the optimality condition derived previously:

$$[v(q, t) - c(q)]f(t) - \alpha \bar{F}(t)v_t(q, t) = 0$$

at $t = t(q)$, only now it is the type $t(q)$ assigned the quantity q that is varied to attain the optimum. Part (b) of assumption A4 assures that this condition has a unique solution $t(q)$; if part (a) is not satisfied then it may be necessary to apply the ironing procedure to construct an assignment that is nondecreasing. Having determined $t(q)$, the optimal price schedule is $p(q) = v(q, t(q))$.

Alternative welfare criteria

These derivations apply also to welfare criteria other than maximization of total surplus subject to the firm's revenue requirement. In the first formulation, for

5. The omitted constant terms are included in the formulation in §6.7 where the optimal fixed fee is derived.

instance, one can pose the objective of Ramsey pricing as the maximization of the
weighted surplus measure

$$\int_a^b \{w(t) \cdot W(t) + w_{\circ} \cdot [P(q(t)) - C(q(t))]\} \, dF(t)$$

subject to the firm's revenue requirement and the envelope property. In this version,
the net benefits of customers of type t receive the welfare weight $w(t)$ and the firm's
welfare weight is $w_{\circ}$ applied to its net revenue $P(q(t)) - C(q(t))$ from each type
t. The only differences in the resulting optimality conditions are that the Ramsey
number is now contingent on the type t,

$$\alpha(t) \equiv \int_t^b \left[1 - \frac{w(t)}{\hat{w}_{\circ}}\right] \, dF(t)/\bar{F}(t),$$

and the sufficiency condition A4(b) must be strengthened to ensure a monotone
assignment of quantities to types. The essential feature is that $\alpha(t)$ represents the
conditional expectation of one minus the relative welfare weights of customers
with types exceeding t, where $\hat{w}_{\circ} \equiv w_{\circ} + \lambda$ is interpreted as the total welfare
weight allowed the firm in view of its revenue requirement.

In important cases the imposition of welfare weights has no material effect on
the main qualitative conclusions derived previously. For example, if all weight is
given to the least type then $w(t) = 0$ and $\alpha(t) = 1$ for all higher types $t > a$. This
indicates that the firm fully exploits its monopoly power to raise the maximum
revenue from those higher types with zero welfare weights. This is done in order
to meet its revenue requirement *and* to subsidize purchases by the least type who
otherwise might be excluded from purchasing or would purchase smaller amounts
at higher prices. If the resulting price schedule is initially increasing and higher
types could exploit opportunities to buy at the low prices for initial units, then
application of the ironing procedure results in a uniform price for an initial interval of purchase sizes, followed by the monopoly nonuniform price schedule for
subsequent units, much as in §5.

Summary

We have presented altogether four derivations of the condition characterizing an
optimal price schedule for a nonlinear tariff, in addition to the analogous characterizations of multipart tariffs. The demand-profile and type-assignment formulations
assign quantities to prices and types, respectively, whereas the others assign types
to prices or quantities. This illustrates the general principle that actually three variables are relevant: $\langle p, q, t \rangle$ are related via the prediction that type t buys quantity q
at the marginal price p. The demand-profile formulation in §4 eliminates the type
variable t and construes the marginal price as a function $p(q)$ depending only on

the unit q for which it is charged. The type purchasing q at marginal price $p(q)$ is then inferred from the requirement that $q = D(p(q), t)$, where D is the type-dependent demand function. The formulation in §6 views the marginal price as a function $\hat{p}(t)$ of the type t paying that price for the marginal unit purchased; that is, $\hat{p}(t) \equiv p(q(t))$. The formulations in this chapter eliminate the price variable and consider only the assignments of types to quantities and the reverse. Each formulation has some advantage in terms of clarifying how monotonicity of the assignment can be enforced to ensure that customers' optimality conditions are satisfied. In each case a third variable is eliminated from the formulation initially and then reconstructed later.

For models that satisfy strong regularity assumptions, these several approaches to the same problem are all equivalent because no difficulties arise in ensuring that the requisite monotonicity conditions are met. If some assumptions are not met, however, then the versions differ in terms of the remedies required to enforce monotonicity. The ironing procedure enforces monotonicity by requiring that the associated optimality condition is met on average over an interval for which the assignment is constant; indeed, this is merely a variant of the optimality conditions for each segment of a multipart tariff. One must in principle check a solution to verify monotonicity from each perspective. In practice, however, it is usual that the features of the model ensure monotonicity of some kinds and therefore one focuses on the remainder. The aim is to ensure both that the predicted purchases are optimal for customers, and that the price schedule is optimal for the firm.

8.3   Approximate optimality of multipart tariffs

The striking feature of the examples of multipart tariffs in §6.4 is that doubling the number of options in the menu cuts by approximately three-quarters the surplus lost due to the limited number of options. This feature is stated in mathematical terms by saying that the loss is of order $1/n^2$. In this section we demonstrate why this property is true in considerable generality. As in §6, we use the price-assignment formulation because it is naturally adapted to the study of multipart tariffs.

Recall from §6 that the objective function of the Ramsey pricing problem is

$$S[p] \equiv \int_0^\infty \{[W(p(t), t) + [1 + \lambda] \cdot [p(t) - c] \cdot D(p(t), t)] f(t)$$
$$+ \lambda \bar{F}(t) \cdot D(p(t), t) \cdot p'(t)\} \, dt,$$

where $W(p, t)$ is type t's consumer surplus at the uniform price p and λ is the multiplier associated with the firm's revenue requirement. For this formulation, the optimality condition for a nonlinear tariff is the Euler condition $E(p(t), t) = 0$, where

$$E(p, t) \equiv [p - c] \cdot D_p(p, t) + \alpha \frac{\bar{F}(t)}{f(t)} \cdot D_t(p, t),$$

and $\alpha = \lambda/[1+\lambda]$ is the associated Ramsey number. For an n-part tariff represented as a menu of $n-1$ optional two-part tariffs with segments $i = 1, \ldots, n-1$ having marginal prices p_i designed to be selected by types in the intervals $t_i \leq t < t_{i+1}$ the analogous conditions are satisfied on average. The optimality condition for p_i is

$$\int_{t_i}^{t_{i+1}} \left\{ [p_i - c] \cdot D_p(p_i, t) + \alpha \frac{\bar{F}(t)}{f(t)} \cdot D_t(p_i, t) \right\} dF(t) = 0 \,,$$

or equivalently

$$\int_{t_i}^{t_{i+1}} E(p_i, t) \, dF(t) = 0 \,,$$

so that the Euler condition is satisfied on average for the types selecting the i-th option. Similarly, the optimality condition for t_i is

$$\int_{p_i}^{p_{i-1}} \left\{ [p - c] \cdot D_p(p, t_i) + \alpha \frac{\bar{F}(t_i)}{f(t_i)} \cdot D_t(p, t_i) \right\} dp = 0 \,,$$

or equivalently,

$$\int_{p_i}^{p_{i-1}} E(p, t_i) \, dp = 0 \,,$$

which is again an average.

Let p and p^n be the optimal nonlinear and n-part price schedules as functions of the type parameter. Our task is to show that the difference $S[p] - S[p^n]$ between the objective values they yield is of order $1/n^2$. To do this we must assume that (1) α is fixed independently of n; (2) the Euler condition has a unique solution, as in A4; and (3) E has bounded derivatives. We use

$$\delta \equiv \max_t |p(t) - p^n(t)| \,, \qquad \epsilon = \max_i |F(t_{i+1}) - F(t_i)| \,,$$

and $\qquad \bar{E} \equiv \int_0^\infty |E(p^n(t), t)| \, dF(t) \,,$

as measures of how much the two schedules differ, the size of the largest market segment for the n-part tariff, and how much on average the n-part schedule fails to satisfy the Euler condition. Also, in terms of the rank index $r \equiv F(t)$ define $E^*(p, r) \equiv E(p, F^{-1}(r))$ and $r_i \equiv F(t_i)$.

The demonstration uses the fact that the difference between the objective values is approximately $\delta \bar{E}$. Thus, it suffices to show that $\bar{E}$ is of order $n\delta^2$ and that δ is of order $1/n$. This is a generalization of the familiar fact that if S were an ordinary function of p then, because $S'(p) = 0$ at the optimum:

$$S(p) - S(p^n) \approx \frac{1}{2}[p - p^n]^2 \cdot |S''(p)| \approx |p - p^n| \cdot |S'(p^n)|$$

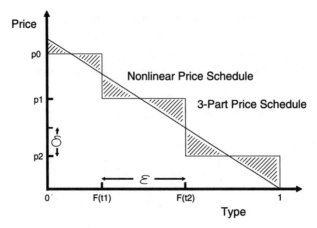

FIG. 8.7   The price assignments for optimal nonlinear and 3-part tariffs. The shaded area is approximately proportional to the difference in objective values obtained.

when $p^n \to p$ as $n \to \infty$. Here $E(p^n(t), t)$ or its average $\bar{E}$ plays the role of $S'(p^n)$. To illustrate the construction in the present, more complicated case, Figure 8.7 depicts an example of the price schedules $p(t)$ and $p^3(t)$ for a nonlinear tariff and a 3-part tariff, and the shaded areas indicate the difference between them. Along the nonlinear price schedule the Euler condition is satisfied exactly, but generally it is not satisfied along the 3-part tariff. One can visualize $\bar{E}$ as approximately proportional to the shaded area, which comprises $2n$ triangular portions. Our aim is to show that each shaded portion is approximately proportional to $\frac{1}{2}\delta\epsilon$ and that both δ and ϵ are of order $1/n$. This will prove that overall $\delta\bar{E}$ has the same order as $\delta[2n][\frac{1}{2}\delta\epsilon] \approx 1/n^2$.

To evaluate $\bar{E}$ recall that the optimality conditions for the n-part tariff ensure that the Euler condition is satisfied on average over each horizontal interval $t_i < t < t_{i+1}$ for p_i and each vertical interval $p_i < p < p_{i-1}$ at t_i. This means that the portions of $\bar{E}$ attributed to adjacent shaded areas are equal in magnitude—and opposite in sign before the absolute value is taken. The key step is to show that apart from constants of proportionality the magnitude of each portion has the same order as $\delta\epsilon$. To see this, we use the optimality condition for p_i to obtain:

$$
0 = \int_{t_i}^{t_{i+1}} E(p_i, t)\, dF(t)
$$

$$
= [r_{i+1} - r_i] \left\{ E(p_i, t_i) + \frac{1}{2}[r_{i+1} - r_i] E_r^*(p_i, r_i) + \dots \right\}
$$

$$
= [r_{i+1} - r_i] \left\{ \Big(E(p(t_i), t_i) + [p(t_i) - p_i] E_p(p(t_i), t_i) + \dots \Big) \right.
$$

$$
\left. + \frac{1}{2}[r_{i+1} - r_i] E_r^*(p_i, r_i) + \dots \right\}.
$$

Here, the integral in the first line is interpreted as a function of r_{i+1}, the second line is an expansion as a Taylor's series around the value r_i, and the third equality uses a Taylor's series expansion of $E(p, t_i)$ around $p = p(t_i)$. Cancelling the factor $r_{i+1} - r_i$ yields the conclusion that the differences $p(t_i) - p_i$ and $r_{i+1} - r_i$ are approximately proportional to each other. A similar analysis of the optimality condition for t_i establishes that also the differences $p(t_i) - p_i$ and $r_i - r_{i-1}$ are approximately related by a proportionality factor. The net result, therefore, is that all these differences are related approximately by proportionality factors, and thereby they all have the same order. In particular, δ and ϵ have the same order. Further, if one similarly calculates a Taylor's series expansion for each portion of $\bar{E}$ then one finds that each has the order of $\delta\epsilon$, or equivalently, the order of δ^2, as we intended to show.

This argument that δ and ϵ have the same order can also be interpreted at a more intuitive level as follows. If δ were much larger than ϵ, for instance, then somewhere along the price schedule $p^n(t)$ there would be a precipitous decline that would not be accompanied by a comparably large market segment. The corresponding adjacent portions of $\bar{E}$ could not be equal, therefore, contradicting the optimality of the n-part tariff. Essentially, this expresses the fact that, apart from proportionality factors, δ/ϵ must approximate the average rate of decline of the nonlinear tariff's price schedule over each market segment.

Lastly, to complete the demonstration we observe that ϵ must also be of order $1/n$ so that the sizes of the market segments add up to the total; or equivalently, δ must be of order $1/n$ so that the successive price differences add up to the difference between the maximum and minimum price offered. Combining these conclusions yields the indicated result that the difference in objective values is of order $1/n^2$.

This result accounts for the reliance on just a few price breaks in the illustrations described in §2. A multipart tariff comprising only a few linear segments, or a menu with a few optional two-part tariffs, usually suffices to realize most of the profit and consumers' surplus that a nonlinear tariff would provide. For instance, if the potential surplus provided by a single two-part tariff is, say, 80% then typically a menu of three two-part tariffs yields more than 95%. This is ample for most practical purposes.

A corollary, incidentally, is that if the number of options is large then the optimal market segments are roughly equal in size, since they are all of order $1/n$ apart from proportionality factors. This is not necessarily true for the widths of the corresponding volume bands, however. In Example 6.2 their orders vary from $1/n^2$ for the lowest and smallest ($i = 1$) to $1/n$ for the highest and largest ($i = n - 1$). This feature that the bandwidths for higher volume segments are much larger is common in practice. The price schedules offered by Federal Express provide illustrations.

8.4   Multiple dimensions of customers' types

In this section we show how the construction of the optimal price schedule can be extended to multidimensional descriptors of customers' types. This extension is important for practical applications because usually no one of the various dimensions on which customers can be sorted is entirely sufficient to predict demand behavior. Also, in many instances the firm has only socio-demographic data that are imperfectly correlated with customers' demand behavior. To relate the exposition to §4, the formulation is cast in terms of the demand profile.

Suppose there are m type descriptors indexed by $j = 1, \ldots, m$. Thus, each customer is described by a list $t = (t_1, \ldots, t_m)$. The population can be described by a multidimensional distribution function F with the property that $F(\hat{t})$ is the number or fraction of customers described by lists t such that $t_j \leq \hat{t}_j$ on every dimension j. Assume that a customer described by the list t has the gross benefit function $U(q, t)$, the marginal willingness to pay $v(q, t)$ for the q-th unit, and the demand function $D(p, t)$. Recall that $U_q(q, t) = v(q, t)$ and $v(D(p, t), t) = p$.

To adapt this formulation to a one-dimensional type specification, we can separate the population of types into one-dimensional families. Thus, let θ indicate any (possibly multidimensional) parameter indexing families of types such that the following properties are satisfied:

- No type is in two families and each type is in some family.
- The types in each family all lie on a single one-dimensional curve.
- The types are ordered so that in each family higher types purchase more at each price.

In the following we use $G(\theta)$ to indicate the distribution function of the auxiliary parameter θ indexing the families. The domain of G is denoted by Θ. We use $F(t \mid \theta)$ to indicate the conditional distribution function of the type t given that it lies in the family θ, and then $\bar{F}(t \mid \theta) = 1 - F(t \mid \theta)$ is the fraction of types in family θ purchasing more than t does.

Let $t(p, q \mid \theta)$ indicate the type in family θ that purchases q units at the marginal price p. That is, this is the unique value of t in family θ that satisfies the condition that $v(q, t) = p$. The net result of the assumptions made is that this is a well defined function. For convenience in the exposition, we assume further that it is differentiable. Note that within family θ the conditional demand profile

$$N(p, q \mid \theta) = \bar{F}(t(p, q \mid \theta) \mid \theta),$$

specifies the fraction of customers in that family demanding the q-th unit at the price p. Consequently, the aggregate demand profile is

$$N(p, q) = \int_{\Theta} N(p, q \mid \theta) \, dG(\theta) \, .$$

With this preparation, we can proceed almost exactly as in the case of one-dimensional types. A convenient way to write the contribution to family θ's consumers' surplus from a price schedule $p(q)$ uses integration by parts to obtain

$$CS(\theta) = \int_0^{\infty} N(p(q), q \mid \theta)[\delta U(p(q), q \mid \theta)] \, dq \, ,$$

where we define

$$\delta U(p(q), q \mid \theta) = \sum_k \frac{\partial U}{\partial t_k} \left[\frac{\partial t_k(p(q), q \mid \theta)}{\partial p} p'(q) + \frac{\partial t_k(p(q), q \mid \theta)}{\partial q} \right] \, .$$

Similarly, the firm's profit contribution from this family is the producer's surplus

$$PS(\theta) = \int_0^{\infty} N(p(q), q \mid \theta) \cdot [p(q) - c(q)] \, dq \, ,$$

apart from any fixed fee and fixed cost component. Using λ as a Lagrange multiplier on the firm's revenue constraint, therefore, the expression to be maximized is

$$\int_{\Theta} [CS(\theta) + [1 + \lambda] PS(\theta)] \, dG(\theta) \, ,$$

where Θ is the domain of the auxiliary parameter θ indexing the families.

Repeating the derivation from §4, we find now that the Euler condition that characterizes an optimal price schedule is

$$\frac{p(q) - c(q)}{p(q)} = \alpha \frac{- \int_{\Theta} N(p(q), q \mid \theta) \, dG(\theta)}{p(q) \int_{\Theta} [\partial N(p(q), q \mid \theta) / \partial p] \, dG(\theta)}$$

$$= \frac{\alpha}{\eta(p(q), q)} \, ,$$

where $\alpha = \lambda / [1 + \lambda]$ is the Ramsey number and $\eta(p, q) \equiv -p N_p(p, q) / N(p(q), q)$ is the price elasticity of the *aggregate* demand profile averaged over the families of types. This condition is the exact analog of the one-dimensional case, and it shows that previous constructions did not depend on the customers' types being one-dimensional.

The gist of this derivation is simply to indicate that there is no necessary requirement that customers' types are one-dimensional. The fundamental Ramsey rule for an optimal price schedule depends only on the demand profile, and this is essentially independent of the dimensionality of the type description of the customers.

Although we have not addressed multipart tariffs and fixed fees here, the preceding analysis extends to these cases as well. Recall from §6.4, that the optimality conditions for each segment of a multipart tariff require that the optimality condition for a nonlinear tariff is satisfied on average for that segment. The extension to multidimensional types is entirely analogous: again the optimality condition for a nonlinear tariff must be satisfied on average, but now the average is calculated also over the families of types indexed by θ. For instance, in the demand-profile formulation of multipart tariffs the first of the two optimality conditions is rewritten as

$$\int_{\Theta} \left[\int_{q_i(\theta)}^{r_i(\theta)} \{ \alpha N(p_i, q \mid \theta) + N_p(p_i, q \mid \theta) \cdot [p_i - c] \} \, dq \right] dG(\theta) = 0 \,,$$

where the limits $q_i(\theta)$ and $r_i(\theta)$ of the volume band for the i-th two-part tariff are now contingent on the family θ.[6] Fixed fees are analyzed as in §4.4; however, because the minimal purchase depends on the family the optimality conditions are best stated in terms of the fixed fee rather than the minimal charge.

One caution must be added: this construction depends on the possibility of arranging customers' types into some collection of one-dimensional families such that within each family demand varies monotonely. This is a fairly weak requirement, but it is not vacuous and in some instances it is impossible to meet. The following examples show that it is possible to address situations in which each customer's demand function is intersected by many others. In particular, the first example allows demands of the sort motivating the analysis of lifeline rates in Section 5, yet the analysis in terms of multidimensional types shows that the optimal price schedule does not include an initial lifeline segment.

Example 8.1: Suppose that each customer is described by a type $t = (a, b)$ indicating that the willingness-to-pay for the q-th increment is $v(q; a, b) = a - bq$. That is, those customers willing to pay a price p for the q-th increment are those with types (a, b) for which $a - bq \geq p$. Assume that the values of a and b are independently distributed in the population, and each is uniformly distributed between zero and one. Then the fraction of the population purchasing the q-th increment at the price p is

$$N(p, q) = \frac{1}{2q} \cdot \begin{cases} (1 - p)^2 - (1 - p - q)^2 & \text{if } p + q \leq 1 \,, \\ (1 - p)^2 & \text{if } p + q \geq 1 \,. \end{cases}$$

---

6. However, one must also recognize that for some families it may be that none of their members may be indifferent between tariffs $i - 1$ and i, as happens if none or all of the members of a family elect a tariff $j \geq i$; this can be interpreted as a restriction on the domain Θ in calculating the average.

The optimal price schedule is therefore

$$p(q) = \begin{cases} A - Bq & \text{if } q \leq q^*, \\ p^* & \text{if } q \geq q^*, \end{cases}$$

where

$$A = \frac{c + \alpha}{1 + \alpha}, \qquad B = \frac{\alpha}{1 + \alpha}\frac{1}{2}, \qquad q^* = \frac{1 - c}{1 + \alpha/2}, \qquad p^* = \frac{c + \alpha/2}{1 + \alpha/2}.$$

For instance, if the marginal cost is $c = 0$ and the Ramsey number is $\alpha = 1$, then the price schedule is

$$p(q) = \begin{cases} \dfrac{1}{2} - \dfrac{1}{4}q & \text{if } q \leq \frac{2}{3}, \\ \dfrac{1}{3} & \text{if } q \geq \frac{2}{3}. \end{cases}$$

Note that the price schedule is piecewise linear. The optimal tariff therefore has an initial segment that is quadratic, and a second segment that is linear like a two-part tariff.

A peculiarity of this example is that the marginal price schedule does not decline to the marginal cost. Further, the maximum and total quantities sold by the firm are infinite. This is due to the fact that customers with parameters $a > p^*$ and $b = 0$ have infinite demands at the price p^*. To make this example regular it suffices to suppose that the domain of the type parameter b is an interval $\epsilon \leq b \leq 1 + \epsilon$. If this is done then the second segment of the price schedule declines to marginal cost as usual. The optimal price schedule in this case is

$$p(q) = \begin{cases} A - Bq & \text{if } q \leq q^*, \\ A^* - B^*q & \text{if } q \geq q^*, \end{cases}$$

where now the parameters are

$$A = \frac{c + \alpha}{1 + \alpha},$$

$$B = \frac{\alpha}{1 + \alpha}\left[\frac{1}{2} + \epsilon\right],$$

$$A^* = p^*,$$

$$B^* = \frac{\alpha}{2 + \alpha}\epsilon,$$

$$q^* = \frac{1 - c}{1 + \alpha/2 + \epsilon},$$

provided $p(q) \geq c$ or equivalently $q \leq \bar{q} \equiv [1 - c]/\epsilon$, where $\bar{q}$ is the maximum purchase.   ◊

Example 8.2: For this example suppose that each customer is described by a demand function $D(p; a, b) = a - bp$. The pairs (a, b) are distributed in the population according to a bivariate Normal distribution. Assume that the marginal distributions of a and b have means and variances (A, s_a^2) and (B, s_b^2) respectively, and the joint distribution has a correlation coefficient r. The aggregate demand profile $N(p, q)$ is then the probability that $a - bp$ exceeds q. Thus, $N(p, q) = \Phi(T(p, q))$, where Φ is the standard Normal distribution function with zero mean and unit variance,

$$T(p, q) \equiv \frac{A - Bp - q}{s(p)}, \quad \text{and} \quad s(p)^2 \equiv s_a^2 - 2prs_as_b + p^2s_b^2.$$

To be accurate this sort of model requires that the distribution of type parameters is concentrated around realistic (positive) values of a and b, and that the variances (especially s_b) are not too large. The model is evidently inaccurate to the extent it assigns positive probability to negative values of a or b; however, if these probabilities are small then they have little effect on the selection of the optimal price schedule.

For the case $\alpha = 1$, $c = 0$, $A = 1$, $B = 1$, $s_a = 0.5$, and $s_b = 0.25$, Figure 8.8 shows the optimal price schedule for several values of the correlation r. Note that a higher correlation lowers prices uniformly; however, the resulting revenue is affected only slightly. For the correlation $r = 0.8$, Figure 8.9 shows for several values of q how the revenue from the q-th unit varies with the marginal price charged; also shown is the marginal price schedule $p(q)$ that obtains the maximal revenue.   ◊

The method illustrated in these examples is quite general. Suppose that an econometric model of demand describes each customer by a list $t = (t_1, \ldots, t_m)$ indicating his type, where the components t_j are various socio-demographic measures such as income, number in household, et cetera. Or for customers that are firms this list might specify attributes that identify the customer's output rate, technology or costs of production, and competitive environment, such as demand and factor elasticities. The model predicts that a customer of type t has a willingness-to-pay for the q-th increment that is given by the estimated function $v(q, t)$; or inversely, a demand function $D(p, t)$. Consequently, the predicted number of customers who will buy the q-th increment at the price p is the number of customers predicted to have types t for which $v(q, t) \geq p$ or $D(p, t) \geq q$. This number is then the value of $N(p, q)$ to be used in computing the optimal price $p(q)$ for the q-th increment. Models of this sort can be constructed using data on customers'

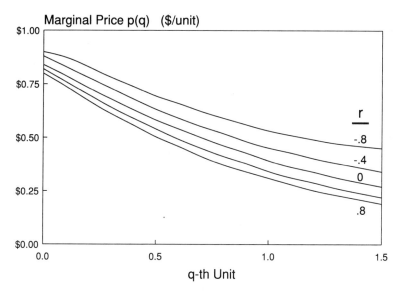

FIG. 8.8   Example 8.2: The optimal marginal price schedule $p(q)$ for correlations $r = -0.8(0.4)0.8$.

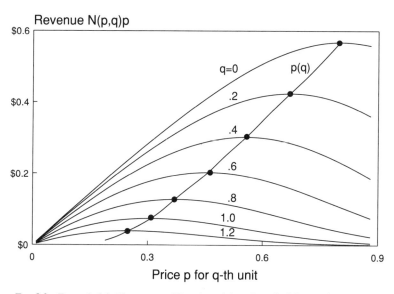

FIG. 8.9   Example 8.2: The revenue $N(p, q)p$ and the price schedule $p(q)$ for $r = 0.8$.

attributes that are correlated with their purchase sizes, and further refined from observations of customers' responses to tariffs that are offered.

As in the examples above, a typical formulation in terms of demand functions supposes a particular functional form whose estimated coefficients are represented as functions of the customer's type parameters. For instance, for the polynomial form $D(p,t) = \sum_{k=0}^{K} a_k(t)p^k$, if disaggregated demand data is available then one first estimates the coefficients $(a_k(t))_{k=0,..,K}$; then, based on the estimated distribution of the type parameters in the population, the value of the demand profile $N(p,q)$ at (p,q) is calculated as the proportion of the population for whom $D(p,t) \geq q$. Alternatively, if only aggregate data is available then the demand profile is estimated directly. Subsequent observation of customers' responses to trial offerings of nonuniform price schedules allows refined estimates, but it is also important to allow for the fact that customers require time to modify their investments in related appliances and production technologies to take full advantage of quantity discounts that are offered.[7]

8.5   A general demand-profile formulation

We conclude this chapter with a general formulation that enables a unified derivation of the conditions characterizing the price schedule and fixed fee for an optimal tariff. It also has the advantage of revealing a justification for lifeline rates and similar provisions that provide inexpensive service to customers with small demands. This formulation uses a more general form of the demand profile, but we show when and how it simplifies to the form used previously.

The master profile $N(P,p,q)$ measures the number of customers willing to pay P for the purchase q, and also willing to pay p for the q-th unit. If customers are indexed by a parameter t affecting the benefit function $U(q,t)$ and the marginal benefit function $v(q,t)$, then

$$N(P,p,q) \equiv \#\{t \mid U(q,t) \geq P \ \& \ v(q,t) \geq p\} \ .$$

This more general form of the demand profile supposes that a customer purchases the q-th unit only if the net benefit $U(q,t) - P(q)$ is positive *and* the marginal net benefit $v(q,t) - p(q)$ is positive. This excludes a non-beneficial purchase of the q-th unit made in order to qualify for compensating benefits from subsequent units; however, for most models and practical applications it captures the essential features. The master profile can be estimated from demand data that records the distribution of purchase sizes associated with each pair $\langle P,p \rangle$ specifying both a total and marginal charge. For instance, if a two-part tariff is offered in which a fixed

---

7. An estimation procedure for applications to pricing of priority-differentiated services (cf. §10) is provided by Smith (1989). An example of refined estimates based on observation of customers' responses is presented in Train and Toyama (1989) for a case in which a new time-of-use tariff was offered for electric power used for agricultural pumping.

fee P_o and a uniform marginal price p are offered, and $N_o(P_o, p, q)$ is the number of customers purchasing at least q units, then $N(P, p, q) = N_o(P - pq, p, q)$.

Using the master profile, the firm's profit contribution or producer's surplus can be written as

$$ PS \equiv N(P_*, 0, q_*) \cdot [P_* - C(q_*)] + \int_{q_*}^{q^*} N(P(q), p(q), q) \cdot [p(q) - c(q)] \, dq \, , $$

where purchases in the range $q_* \leq q \leq q^*$ are offered and $P_* == P(q_*)$ is the tariff charged for the minimal purchase q_*. This specifies that $N(P_*, 0, q_*)$ customers pay the minimal charge P_*, entitling each to q_* units, and $N(P(q^*), p(q^*), q^*)$ customers purchase the maximum allowed quantity q^*. For each unit in the interval $q_* < q \leq q^*$, the profit contribution $p(q) - c(q)$ is obtained from each of $N(P(q), p(q), q)$ customers.

The analogous formula for the consumers' surplus is obtained by interpreting the master profile as specifying the distribution of customers' reservation prices. For those customers purchasing the minimal quantity q_* the consumers' surplus is

$$ \int_{\infty}^{P_*} [U - P_*] \, dN(U, 0, q_*) = \int_{P_*}^{\infty} N(P, 0, q_*) \, dP \, , $$

and similarly the consumers' surplus from the q-th unit is

$$ \mathcal{N}(P, p, q) \equiv \int_{p}^{\infty} N(P, \pi, q) \, d\pi \, . $$

In the first of these formulas, the integration on the left side is backwards because N is the right-cumulative distribution function; the right side is obtained from integration by parts. In total, the consumers' surplus is therefore

$$ CS \equiv \int_{P_*}^{\infty} N(P, 0, q_*) \, dP + \int_{q_*}^{q^*} \mathcal{N}(P(q), p(q), q) \, dq \, . $$

As mentioned above, this formula assumes that a customer purchases the q-th unit only if $U(q, t) \geq P(q)$ and $v(q, t) \geq p(q)$; thus, it requires that the price schedule intersects each type's demand function just once, from below.[8]

For Ramsey pricing, the tariff is chosen to maximize $CS + [1 + \lambda]PS$, where λ is a Lagrange multiplier chosen large enough to assure that the firm's revenue requirement is met. We divide the conditions that characterize the optimal tariff into two parts.

---

8. §6 shows how this constraint is enforced, and the amendments to the subsequent derivation that are required.

The marginal price schedule

The condition that characterizes the optimal price schedule for units in excess of the minimal purchase is the Euler condition from the calculus of variations. It states that

$$\frac{d}{dq}E(P(q), p(q), q) = [1 - \alpha]\mathcal{N}_P(P(q), p(q), q) + N_P(P(q), p(q), q) \cdot [p(q) - c(q)]$$

(1)

if $P(q) > 0$, where $\alpha = \lambda/[1 + \lambda]$ is the Ramsey number, and

$$E(P, p, q) \equiv \alpha N(P, p, q) + N_p(P, p, q) \cdot [p - c(q)].$$

This condition specifies a second-order differential equation for the tariff, whose boundary conditions are provided by the transversality conditions that determine q^*. These boundary conditions state that

$$E(P, p, q) = 0, \qquad \text{and} \qquad [1 - \alpha]\mathcal{N}(P, p, q) + N(P, p, q) \cdot [p - c(q)] = 0, \quad (2)$$

at $\langle P, p, q \rangle \equiv \langle P(q^*), p(q^*), q^* \rangle$, provided these magnitudes are finite. That is, the analogous Ramsey condition is satisfied at q^* and for this last unit the consumers' and producer's surpluses contributed to the objective are nil. These conditions merely say that there is no effective limit on the purchase size. It is allowed to be as large as any customer demands, so that demand is exhausted ($N(P, p, q) = 0$) at marginal cost ($p = c$) at q^*.

The net effect of (1) and (2) is that the tariff is computed as follows. One starts with a good guess about the value of $P^* \equiv P(q^*)$, which determines q^* from the equations $N(P^*, p(q^*), q^*) = 0$ and $p(q^*) = c(q^*)$. The path of the differential equation (1) is then followed backwards from q^* to see if it satisfies the boundary conditions at q_*; if not, then the value of P^* is adjusted until eventually a close approximation of the solution is obtained.[9] In most practical problems, however, a modification is required. Usually those customers purchasing more than some amount Q obtain positive net benefits; for $q > Q$, therefore, $\partial N/\partial P = 0$, the right side of (1) is zero, and the price schedule is determined (independently of $P(q)$) by the condition that $E(P(q), p(q), q) = 0$, or equivalently $E(0, p(q), q) = 0$. This is just the optimality condition derived previously using the ordinary demand profile $N(p, q)$, which is essentially identical to the master profile $N(0, p(q), q)$ when the total tariff is immaterial to the determination of the price schedule.

This is illustrated in Figure 8.10 analogous to Figure 4.1 which depicts for the monopoly case that the price schedule $p(q)$ maximizes the profit contribution from each unit $q > Q$. In the interval $q_* < q \leq Q$, however, the price schedule

9. Methods for computing such solutions are found in texts on numerical methods for solving elliptic partial differential equations, such as Press *et al.* (1986, Chapter 16).

diverges from simple profit maximization, as shown by the solid curve indicating lower values of the price schedule $p(q)$ for units in this initial interval. This curve follows the path of the differential equation (1) starting from the value $P(Q)$ of the tariff at Q. However, Figure 8.11 shows that, in principle, the suppression of the marginal prices for units below Q can produce a fold in the price schedule. Such a fold actually indicates that the price schedule is discontinuous, as indicated in the figure by the dashed vertical segment. This reflects the fact that no customers will purchase amounts that lie on a backward bending segment of the marginal price schedule. Note that typically there will be a cluster of customers purchasing the quantity Q, namely, all those customers whose demand functions intersect the vertical segment.

In this figure the minimal charge is represented as $P_* = P_o + p_* q_*$, which is a two-part tariff with the fixed fee P_o and the marginal price $p_* = p(q_*)$. The minimal quantity q_* is purchased by a type t_* whose consumer's surplus at the price p_* barely covers the fixed fee P_o. The discontinuity in the price schedule occurs because the prices for those units in the interval $q_* < q < Q$ must be low enough to enable some other type T to afford the fixed fee. This occurs because type T obtains too small a surplus from quantities less than Q to justify payment of the fixed fee. Thus, the price schedule is reduced over the initial interval $q_* < q < Q$ to enable type T to obtain sufficient surplus from the marginal price schedule to justify payment of the fixed fee. As noted, this can produce an upward jump in the price schedule at Q, causing a kink or cusp in the tariff there, and bunching of many customers at the purchase size Q: besides type T there will typically be others who are not constrained by the magnitude of the fixed fee but who are deterred from further purchases by the jump in the marginal price for units beyond Q. In principle, the magnitude of the tariff could affect the price schedule along several intervals of purchase sizes, but in practice it is usually only the initial interval that is affected. Note that this situation occurs only if different types' demand schedules intersect; in the figure, types t_* and T have intersecting demand curves. We exclude these features in §6 by assuming that customers' demand functions do not intersect.

The reduced prices for an initial interval of this sort are called lifeline rates. They are intended to retain customers who assign low values to service and therefore are unwilling to pay the fixed fee unless the initial segment of the price schedule provides low prices.[10] An alternative approach is to apply the ironing procedure to obtain a uniform price that applies to all units up to (and beyond) Q, as in the right panel of Figure 4.3.

---

10. Other motives for lifeline rates are also important, including the goal of universal service, and in the case of telephone service, the network externality that a customer needs a phone to receive calls valued by other subscribers. The prices of other increments, say near q_*, can be depressed below marginal cost if there are some large customers with highly elastic demands, as in the case of options to bypass.

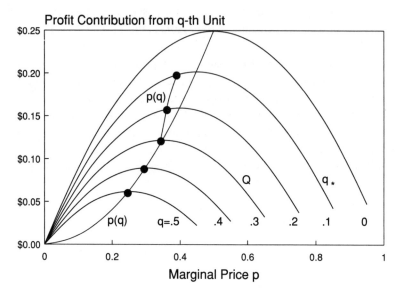

FIG. 8.10 The optimal price schedule $p(q)$ for $q > Q$ maximizes the profit contribution from that unit, but for $q < Q$ the optimal price is lower because the master profile is sensitive to the total tariff $P(q)$.

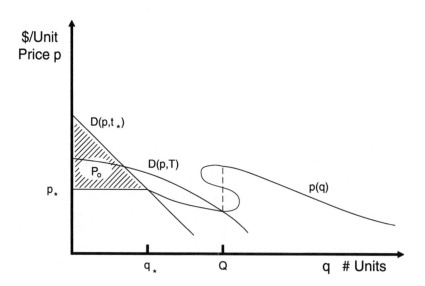

FIG. 8.11 A discontinuous price schedule can occur if marginal prices for $q < Q$ must be reduced to enable type T to afford the fixed fee P_0.

The minimal purchase and minimal charge

We now turn to the determination of the optimal minimal purchase q_* and the minimal tariff P_* that is charged for it. The transversality conditions require that

$$\alpha N(P_*, 0, q_*) + N_P(P_*, 0, q_*) \cdot [P_* - C(q_*)] =$$
$$\alpha N(P_*, p_*, q_*) + N_p(P_*, p_*, q_*) \cdot [p_* - c(q_*)] \quad (3)$$

if $P_* > 0$, and

$$N_q(P_*, 0, q_*) \cdot [P_* - C(q_*)] + p_* N_p(P_*, p_*, q_*) \cdot [p_* - c(q_*)] = [1 - \alpha][A - B] \quad (4)$$

if $q_* > 0$, where

$$A \equiv \int_{p_*}^{\infty} N(P_*, p, q_*) \, dp + p_* N(P_*, p_*, q_*), \quad \text{and} \quad B \equiv \int_{P_*}^{\infty} N_q(P, 0, q_*) \, dP.$$

To interpret these conditions we note that the right side of (4) is actually zero, because A and B are two different ways of computing the total surplus obtained from purchases of the q_*-th unit.[11]

To proceed further, it simplifies matters to assume that $N(P_*, 0, q_*) = N(P_*, p_*, q_*)$, so that customers willing to pay for the minimal purchase are also willing to pay the marginal price p_* for the q_*-th unit, as for example the type t_* in the previous figure. This assumes no customers paying the minimal charge would purchase less than q_* at the uniform price p_* if no fixed fee were imposed. In this case, (3) and (4) combined imply that

$$p_* = -\frac{N_q(P_*, 0, q_*)}{N_P(P_*, 0, q_*)} \equiv \left(\frac{\partial P_*}{\partial q_*}\right)_{N=N_*}$$

That is, as indicated on the far right, the initial marginal price p_* should also be the rate of change (with respect to q_*) in the tariff P_* required to maintain the same number $N_* \equiv N(P_*, 0, q_*)$ of customers subscribing for service. Finally, in the special case that $Q = q_*$ so that there is no lifeline segment of the tariff, the right side of (3) is zero since in this case this is just the condition $E(P_*, p_*, q_*) = 0$ for optimization of the price schedule at q_*. Consequently, we obtain the usual elasticity condition in two symmetric forms:

$$\frac{p_* - c(q_*)}{p_*} = \frac{\alpha}{[-p_* N_p/N]}, \quad \text{and} \quad \frac{P_* - C(q_*)}{P_*} = \frac{\alpha}{[-P_* N_P/N]},$$

11. This is a constraint on the master profile that should be observed when estimating it from demand data. Although it is supposed to be true in theory, it is possible and perhaps likely that it would be contradicted by the data.

one for the optimal marginal price and an analogous one for the optimal minimal charge. The former uses the marginal-price elasticity of the master profile to determine the marginal price, and the latter uses the total-price elasticity of the master profile to determine the minimal charge P_*.

The way in which these conditions are applied to determine the minimal purchase and the minimal charge is depicted in Figure 8.12 for the case that customers of type t_* purchase the minimal quantity q_*. In this case the locus along which $N = N_*$ is merely the one along which the feature that type t_* purchases q_* is preserved. The price schedule $p(q)$ is determined from its elasticity condition and the corresponding tariff schedule $P_*(q_*)$ is determined from its elasticity condition (as above) as a function of the minimal quantity q_* that it provides. The optimal minimal purchase q_* is identified as that quantity such that some type t_* satisfies both the condition that $U(q_*, t_*) = P_*(q)$ and simultaneously $v(q_*, t_*) = p(q_*)$. Thus, to find P_* and q_* one moves backward along the marginal price schedule for successively smaller values of q_* until these two conditions are satisfied simultaneously.[12]

As shown in the figure, the minimal purchase is positive if and only if the firm's fixed cost $C(0)$ is positive, and in this case also $P_* > C(0)$. However, Example 6.10 shows that in some cases $P_* = C(0) + p_* q_*$; that is, the fixed fee is merely the firm's fixed cost provided the uniform price p_* is charged for units $q < q_*$.

This figure illustrates that the optimal tariff is much easier to characterize and to compute when customers' demand schedules do not cross. In such cases the ordinary demand profile suffices to determine the price schedule and the master profile enables a relatively easy determination of the minimal purchase and the minimal charge or the fixed fee. Because of these simplifications, we use such a model for expositional purposes in other chapters. Although the general case requires solution of the complicated equations (1)–(4) to determine a fully optimal tariff, for most purposes it suffices to work with simpler models that enable easy computations and that are likely to reveal the main features of practical importance.

8.6 Summary

This chapter provides further analysis and justification for the parameterized models used in §6. Section 1 illustrates the technical complications that account for the daunting complexity of the large literature on nonlinear pricing formulated in terms of models with explicit type parameters. We also indicate the cautions

12. In the general case this poses a difficult computational problem because $P(Q)$ must be selected accurately to ensure that both conditions can be satisfied at the same value of q_*. Folds in the curve representing $p(q)$ can be handled by the ironing procedure, but folds or multiple components in the curve representing $P_*(q_*)$ apparently require one to select among the local maxima for the correct solution.

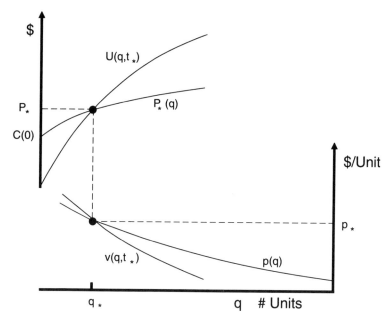

FIG. 8.12   Determination of the minimal purchase and minimal tariff from the condition that type t_* is indifferent about paying the tariff *and* about paying the marginal price.

required when applying the practical approaches described in §4 and §6. These are especially important when the demand profile is derived from an econometric model of demand behaviors that is disaggregated according to customers' types or market segments.

Sections 1 and 2 describe the difficulties that can ensue if the price schedule obtained from the basic optimality condition does not inherit sufficient monotonicity properties from the model used. Monotonicity of the quantity assignment is necessary to assure that the price schedule intersects each customer's demand schedule from below, as required for a maximum of the customer's net benefit; additional monotonicity properties suffice to identify a unique locally optimal solution to the firm's problem that is also globally optimal. Both of these requirements can be guaranteed by an assumption such as A4 that, via its two parts, assures uniqueness of the solution for the firm and monotonicity of the assignment of quantities to customers. We have also emphasized, however, that in the absence of such an assumption the difficulties can be overcome by a correct selection of the firm's solution and use of the ironing procedure to ensure monotonicity.

Sections 3 and 4 justify two other aspects. First, an optimal multipart tariff with a few segments differs only slightly from an optimal nonlinear tariff; in particular, the results obtained are approximately optimal to an accuracy that varies inversely with the square of the number of segments. Second, when customers have multidimensional types the characterizations of nonlinear and multipart tariffs remain essentially the same, differing only by a procedure that averages over families of one-dimensional types.

Finally, Section 5 shows that the demand-profile approach extends to cases in which the magnitude of the total tariff restricts market penetration. In this case the optimal price schedule derived from the master profile may involve lower prices for small purchases.

Part III

MULTIDIMENSIONAL TARIFFS

9

MULTIDIMENSIONAL PRICING

Previous chapters study the design of a tariff for a single product when each customer chooses only the number of units to purchase. This and subsequent chapters show how the methods used for a single product are applied to more elaborate problems of tariff design. This chapter begins with the simplest case in which a single product is supplied with several quality attributes chosen by the customer. The illustrations in §2 demonstrate that some firms differentiate their products in terms of quality dimensions that affect customers' valuations of usage. In addition, firms often differentiate conditions of delivery, such as the time or place of use and the reliability or speed of delivery. These options allow a customer to assign some combination of quality attributes to each unit and pay a corresponding price for the combination selected. A key aspect is that the options are flexible, in the sense that a customer can select different quality attributes for different units of the same generic product.

Section 1 specifies the basic data of the formulation in terms of the demand profile for increments of quantity and qualities. Section 2 derives the conditions characterizing an optimal tariff and shows how they apply to parameterized models of customers' preferences. Section 3 provides examples of the computational method. Calculations are more complicated when customers have superior information about the relative values of service qualities that affects their selections. Section 4 presents a model with these features: it is adapted to telecommunications and delivery services in which each customer assigns each item a delivery delay.

This chapter assumes throughout that the firm's costs and customers' benefits are additively separable across different quality attributes. The separability assumption enables a simple presentation of some of the basic ideas of multidimensional and multiproduct pricing. A detailed example is presented in §10 where the method is applied to the design of nonlinear tariffs for priority service. This chapter is also preliminary to §11, which augments the analysis to include pricing of capacity to serve peakloads.

9.1   A multidimensional formulation

The chief feature of multidimensional pricing is the presumption that a customer can assign each unit a different combination of quality attributes. Customers' freedom to select quality attributes for each unit distinguishes a multidimensional product from multiple products of the sort studied in §13. In the latter case, the firm offers several products, each with a fixed configuration of quality attributes. The two cases can be similar if an ample variety of products is offered, but if the variety is limited then pricing of multiple products is more complicated due to the restrictions on customers' choices of quality attributes. This chapter begins with the simpler formulation of multidimensional nonlinear pricing in which, in effect, an unlimited variety of quality configurations is offered.

A typical example of a multidimensional product is express mail delivery, as in the illustration in §2.5 of Federal Express' tariffs. The generic product offered by the firm is delivery. However, the customer is not constrained to send all items via any single mode: he chooses the speed of delivery for each item mailed. The tariff assesses charges depending on the sizes and numbers of items mailed within each category of delivery speed. Analogously, in the context of electric power a customer selects the time or other service attribute such as service priority or reliability for each of several blocks of energy demand; and, airline customers select the flight and service quality for each trip.

There are several ways to describe a customer's purchases. The next paragraphs outline two variations that differ in the accounting conventions used to summarize a customer's purchases over a billing period. The *assignment form* describes a customer's purchases according to the usual intuitive accounting of purchases of multiple products. But for the design of multidimensional tariffs the more convenient representation of a customer's purchases is the *profile form*, which keeps accounts of the increments of the various qualities selected by the customer. For motivation, examples refer to the familiar context of ordinary postal letter service that is differentiated into regular, airmail, and express delivery.

Although these delivery modes are usually interpreted as ordinal quality levels, we adopt notation indicating cardinal quality levels. This presumes that faster speeds of delivery are quantified according to some index inversely related to the average number of days required for delivery. It will be evident that ordinal qualities pose no special difficulties in the analysis. The formulation does rely, however, on the assumption that all customers prefer a higher quality to a lower quality if both are offered at the same price. This excludes quality dimensions, such as color or taste, that customers rank differently.

The assignment form

A particular physical item or service purchased by a customer can be represented as one unit of quantity assigned a list $(q_1, \ldots, q_m)$ of magnitudes of m quality

attributes. Over a billing period, therefore, the customer's total purchase is described by an accounting of how many items were assigned each of the possible
lists of quality magnitudes. A description in this form is called an *assignment*: it
specifies the customer's assignment of items to qualities. In the postal context, an
assignment specifies the numbers of letters delivered by the three modes: regular,
airmail, and express. This corresponds to $m = 1$ with three possible magnitudes
of the single dimension indicating speed of delivery. Alternatively, the assignment
simply records the numbers of regular, airmail, and express stamps that the customer bought. One can imagine pigeonholes corresponding to the various lists of
service qualities, and within each pigeonhole is a pile of purchase orders, one for
each letter delivered by that service mode.

An assignment can be represented as a collection of n-lists (that is, lists of
length $n = m + 1$) of the form $(q_1, \ldots, q_m, q_{m+1})$ in which q_{m+1} is the number of
items assigned the m-list $(q_1, \ldots, q_m)$ of quality magnitudes. Thus, each customer
purchases a set of n-lists, where each n-list in the set is a vector $q = (q_1, \ldots, q_n)$ of
length n whose components specify various quality or quantity magnitudes. From
this perspective, a customer's purchase set comprises several points in a space of
n quality and quantity magnitudes, each point corresponding to one of the n-lists
in the purchase set.

The assignment form is used in §13 when we study the pricing of multiple
products. Each m-list of magnitudes of quality attributes identifies one of the several products offered by the firm. The customer's purchase set then describes the
number of units of each product supplied by the firm during the billing period. In
this chapter we do not use the assignment form explicitly because an alternative
form takes better advantage of the special features of multidimensional products.
Because a customer assigns each item his preferred choice of quality attributes,
he is not constrained to accept the relatively few combinations of quality magnitudes offered by the firm—he can custom design the quality combinations as he
likes.

The profile form

To introduce the profile form of a customer's purchase set, consider again the
postal example. Suppose that airmail service is provided if the customer attaches
an airmail upgrade stamp to the letter in addition to a stamp for regular service,
and similarly a letter qualifies for express service if the customer attaches a third
stamp for an express upgrade.[1] In this case there is not a one-to-one correspondence

---

1. Interpreting quality attributes in terms of upgrades is common in several industries. Major airlines
sell booklets of certificates that allow a customer to upgrade a tourist class ticket to business or first class
on a space-available basis. (Incidentally, the fact that the certificates are sold in booklets at a discount
compared to individual upgrades is another instance of nonlinear pricing.) A mundane example is a
fishing license, which in many states requires auxiliary stamps for each of several categories of waters
and species.

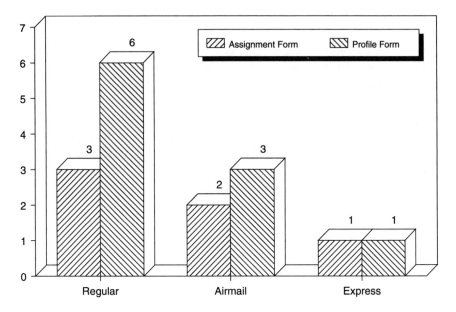

FIG. 9.1   The assignment and profile forms for the postal example.

between the numbers of items and the numbers of stamps, but basically the same information is contained in an accounting system that records only the numbers of stamps purchased. Suppose, for example, that a customer sends three, two, and one letters by regular, airmail, and express delivery in the assignment-form description. The profile-form description records that he purchases six regular stamps, three airmail upgrades, and one express upgrade, as depicted in Figure 9.1. Working backward in this list, we can deduce that the customer sends one letter by express, two by airmail, and three via regular service. Moreover, the total number of items (six letters) is recorded directly in the number of regular stamps purchased. This number is the firm's capacity requirement that is the focus of the analysis in §11 on capacity pricing: it has special importance if the firm must provide capacity in proportion to the number of letters, regardless of the speed of delivery.

In general, the profile-form description specifies for each customer and each quality increment the number of items or units assigned qualities requiring that quality increment. Thus the profile form records the customer's demand for quality increments, namely, the various possible quality upgrade stamps. Given a customer's assignment comprising several n-lists q^i indexed by i, the corresponding demand for quality increments is constructed by recording for each possible m-list $\hat{q}$ of quality magnitudes the number $D(\hat{q})$ of items in these n-lists that require the increments of qualities at $\hat{q}$. Thus,

$$D(\hat{q}) = \sum_{i \in I(\hat{q})} q_n^i, \qquad \text{where} \qquad I(\hat{q}) = \left\{ i \mid q_1^i \geq \hat{q}_1, \ldots, q_m^i \geq \hat{q}_m \right\}.$$

Note that the demand $D(\hat{q})$ for the quality increments at the m-list $\hat{q}$ includes all items assigned qualities exceeding $\hat{q}$ on all m dimensions. It is, therefore, nonincreasing along each of the quality dimensions.

In the special case that $m = 0$ there is no quality differentiation so the assignment is just the single number q_1^i of units purchased; in this case $D(\hat{q}) = q_1^i$ is just the customer's demanded number of units of quantity. This convention conforms to previous chapters: because there are no increments to quality, the demand for quality increments is identical to the demand itself.

The next step is to construct an aggregate demand profile analogous to the one used previously. Recall that when there is no quality differentiation the demand profile $N(p, q)$ at a marginal price p specifies the number of customers demanding the q-th quantity increment. Similarly, with differentiated qualities the demand profile specifies the number of customers demanding each increment of quantity *and* increments of qualities. To illustrate, suppose there are several customers indexed by t and the t-th customer's demand for quality increments is $D(\hat{q}, t)$ at the m-list $\hat{q}$ of qualities. Then for each price schedule p and an n-list $q = (\hat{q}, x)$, the demand profile

$$N(p, q) \equiv N(p, (\hat{q}, x)) = \# \left\{ t \mid D(\hat{q}, t) \geq x \right\},$$

specifies the number of customers demanding (in response to p) the x-th increment of quantity *and* each $\hat{q}_i$-th increment of qualities.[2] Note that this definition conforms to the interpretation of the postal example: given the list p of marginal prices for stamps, the demand profile $N(p, q)$ records how many customers buy an x-th unit of each stamp $\hat{q} \in \{$regular, airmail upgrade, express upgrade$\}$. By construction, the demand profile is nonincreasing in each dimension of quality; presumably it is also nonincreasing in the price dimension too, since customers respond to higher prices with lower demands.

The demand profile has direct applicability to the design of an optimal tariff. For instance, the firm's predicted revenue contribution from sale of the quality and quantity increments at q in response to a price $p(q)$ is $p(q)N(p(q), q)$, the product of the price $p(q)$ for these increments times the number of customers predicted to purchase these increments at this price. Implicit in this formulation is the requirement that a customer is eligible to purchase the quality and quantity increments at a point q if and only if he has purchased all lesser increments on all dimensions. In the

---

2. If there is no quality differentiation then $m = 0$ and $N(p, q)$ is exactly the demand profile used in previous chapters: it specifies the number of customers demanding the x-th increment of quantity.

postal example, for instance, the predicted revenue from sales of a second airmail upgrade stamp is the marginal price of a second airmail upgrade stamp times the number of customers sending at least two letters via upgraded service; namely via either airmail or express. All such customers must buy at least two airmail upgrade stamps independently of whether these stamps are used only for the airmail upgrade or combined with an express upgrade stamp. Moreover, the only customers eligible to purchase and usefully apply a second airmail upgrade stamp are those who have also purchased at least two regular stamps and a first airmail upgrade stamp.

The advantage of the profile description of customers' demands for quality increments is that it allows, via the construction of the demand profile, a symmetric description of the quality and quantity attributes of customers' purchases. It also enables a focus on the chief feature of interest for nonlinear pricing, which is how to price increments of quality and quantity jointly. For example, in the postal context it allows us to address the issue of whether quantity discounts should be offered for purchases of regular stamps or for upgrade stamps to airmail or express. Indeed, we can consider the possibility that successive units of each different upgrade stamp are priced differently. Recall that in §2.5 we describe the price schedules of Federal Express for Standard Air service (the slow mode) and Priority 1/Courier-Pak service (the faster mode) that include these features, and in particular these schedules offer quantity discounts at each level of quality.

The load-duration curve

Profile descriptions are familiar in the electric power, communications, transportation, and other industries subject to peak loads. Firms in these industries provide the nonstorable services of durable capital equipment, so capacity and potential supply are relatively stable compared to demand, which fluctuates on a short time scale. In these industries it is customary to represent a customer's purchase, say over a year, in terms of the *load-duration curve*. The load-duration curve specifies for each load level x, such as the power level measured in kilo-Watts (kW), the number $H(x)$ of hours that the customer's load exceeds x. This description is the profile form in which $m = 1$, $n = 2$, and for the m-list $\hat{q} \equiv x$ the demand for the increment is $D(\hat{q}) \equiv H(x)$. Equivalently, if the hourly intervals of the year are arranged in order so that demand declines along the ordering, then the customer's demand is described by a function $L(h)$ that specifies the power, or load, demanded in the h-th ranked hour of the year. This is the usual way that load-duration curves are measured.

In time-of-use tariffs, the hourly intervals are typically designated as peak or offpeak or intermediate designations for pricing purposes, as we have seen in the illustration in §2 of the tariffs used by EDF and Pacific Gas & Electric. This is a special case of a general tariff that specifies a charge $P(h, L(h))$, measured in $/hour, for the power $L(h)$ demanded in the h-th ranked hour of the year and then adds up these charges over the hours of the year. The perspective in this chapter interprets such tariffs in terms of the marginal price $p(h, x) = \partial P(h, x)/\partial x$, measured in \$/kWh, charged for the x-th kW of power used over the h-th ranked hour; thus, $p(h, x)$ is the marginal price $p(q)$ at $q = (h, x)$ as defined previously.

To see that a customer's load-duration curve is a demand for quality increments, one can interpret it in terms paralleling the postal example in two different ways.

- The first interpretation takes the viewpoint of a time-of-use tariff. The number of items is the number of hours that the customer demands service. The h-th regular-service stamp provides a connection for service during the h-ranked hour. An upgrade stamp of the x-th kind provides an x-th kW, and can be applied to whichever hour the customer prefers. In this interpretation, the number of items is the cumulative duration of service (in hours) and the highest level upgrade purchased indicates the customer's peak load (in kW). The customer's energy consumption is indicated by the number of upgrades of all kinds. Thus, given his load-duration curve, the customer buys enough stamps to fill in the area under the curve. In this interpretation, upgrades represent successively higher power levels.
- An alternative interpretation takes the viewpoint of a so-called Wright tariff in which upgrades represent successively longer durations. The number of items is the customer's peak load $L(0)$, which is the capacity (in kW) required to serve the customer. An upgrade stamp of the h-th kind provides an h-th hour of power from whichever unit of capacity the customer selects. Thus, the number of regular stamps indicates the peak demand (in kW), and the aggregate number of upgrade stamps again indicates the customer's energy consumption (in kWh).

A Wright tariff, for example, can recover the firm's actual cost of serving a single customer by charging the capital cost of a 1 kW peak-load generator for each regular stamp, and for an h-th hour upgrade, charging the marginal operating cost (\$/h/kW) of the type of generator that most efficiently serves a unit load of duration h. Such tariffs are often implemented in time-of-use form by imposing a demand charge equal to the capital cost of the peak-load generator for sufficient capacity to serve the customer's peak load, and then in each hour h charging for each unit of energy the operating cost of the marginal generator active in that hour. In an alternative form, an x-th kW of power over any hour is charged the marginal cost of operating the generator assigned to provide that unit. This assignment is according to the merit order in which to meet supply requirements generators are activated in order of their marginal operating costs.

The basic premise of the profile formulation is that each customer's purchase can be specified as a set comprising all the increments within its boundary. It is often convenient to represent this set by its boundary, as in the case of a load-duration

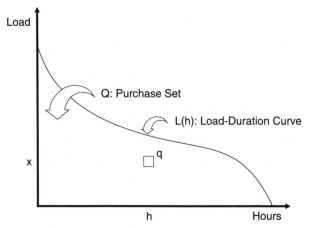

FIG. 9.2   A purchase set Q and an increment q. The purchase set is the collection of increments within the load-duration curve $L(h)$.

curve, but conceptually it is the set of increments within it that is the focus of the pricing analysis. This perspective is represented geometrically in Figure 9.2 for the case of one quality dimension ($m = 1$) and one quantity dimension ($n = 2$) as in the case of a load-duration curve in the power context. An increment at any point $q = (h, x)$ below the load-duration curve consists of unit increments along both dimensions. Consequently, it can be depicted as a small square as shown in the figure. The customer obtains the purchase set, denoted by Q, comprising the region within the load-duration curve by purchasing all the small squares it includes, paying the corresponding marginal price $p(q)$ charged for each one. Generally, if the number of dimensions is n, then an increment corresponds to a small n-dimensional cube, and again each such cube is assigned a corresponding marginal price.

   A further advantage of the formulation in terms of the demand profile is the revelation that an important duality principle applies to the design of quality and quantity differentiated tariffs. To illustrate we use again the context of electric power. We mentioned above the specification of a time-of-use tariff that charges $P(h, L(h))$ for the power $L(h)$ in each hour h. An alternative Wright tariff charges an amount $\hat{P}(H(q), q)$, measured in \$/kW, for the q-th kW of capacity if it is used for a cumulative duration $H(q)$ during the year, where $H(q)$ is the load-duration curve.[3] Time-of-use and Wright tariffs impose the same charges in total if they impose the same marginal price for each increment $q = (h, x)$. The time-of-use tariff's marginal price is $p(h, x) = \partial P(h, x)/\partial x$ and the Wright tariff's marginal price is $\hat{p}(h, x) = \partial \hat{P}(h, x)/\partial h$. If these two marginal prices are the same for every increment $q = (h, x)$, namely $p(q) = \hat{p}(q)$, then the tariffs are equivalent.[4]

3. A variant of a Wright tariff is used in load-factor pricing in which a customer receives a discount depending on the ratio of his average and peak power demands.

4. This equivalence depends on the supposition that the ordering of the hours of the years derived from the customer's load-duration curve and the firm's system load-duration curve agree; that is, the

9.2   Design of multidimensional tariffs

This section describes the basic method used to construct multidimensional tariffs when customers' benefits are additively separable. The method is similar to the procedure developed in §4 once the problem is formulated in a tractable way. Consequently, we describe the calculations briefly after presenting the rudiments of the formulation. The ingredients of the formulation differ mainly in that each customer's purchase comprises a set of multidimensional increments.

Purchase sets.

The previous section emphasized the advantages of the profile-form to describe customers' purchase sets. To complete the formulation we need also a compatible description of the firm's costs and the customers' benefits. For this purpose we represent a customer's purchase as a set Q comprising small squares or cubes representing increments of quantities and qualities jointly. A purchase set Q is represented as a subset of the positive orthant of n-dimensional Euclidean space. Such a set has an upper boundary (like the load-duration curve) and includes all small cubes (or if the small cubes are infinitesimal, all points) below this boundary. A small cube located at a point $q = (q_1, \ldots, q_n)$ has sides of lengths $dq = (dq_1, \ldots, dq_n)$ that represent increments along the n dimensions. A particular kind of purchase set is one that is rectangular, consisting of all the small cubes below a single point q: such a purchase set is denoted by $[q]$. A rectangular purchase set corresponds to a load-duration curve that is flat up to the maximum duration of service, so that the maximum and average load during service are the same. The smallest rectangular set that includes an arbitrary purchase set Q is similarly denoted by $[Q]$; in the case of a load-duration curve this represents the capacities allocated to the customer on each of the n dimensions, since it supposes that the customer's peak load is sustained for the full duration of the customer's service.

The firm's costs.

We assume here that the firm's costs are additively separable among customers, and the same for customers making the same purchase. An aggregate marginal cost could also be included but for simplicity we omit this possibility. We assume further that the firm's costs are fully defined by its cost of providing a rectangular

---

customer's load pattern is synchronized with the system load. If the customer's peak load occurs during the system's offpeak period, for example, then the two tariffs are not necessarily equivalent. Power and communications companies, as well as regulatory agencies, prefer time-of-use tariffs based on the system load-duration curve in order to take account that some customers' peak loads are not coincident with the system peak load.

purchase set. In particular, this means that if $C([q])$ is the cost of supplying the rectangular purchase set $[q]$, then

$$c(q) = \frac{\partial^n C([q])}{\partial q_1 \cdots \partial q_n}$$

is the marginal cost of supplying a small cube of increments located at q. The cost of supplying an arbitrary purchase set Q is expressed as the summation of these marginal costs of all increments within Q:

$$C(Q) = \int_Q c(q)\, dq\,.$$

In this formula, the integral is interpreted as a summation over all small cubes dq located at points q within Q. Alternatively, it can be represented as an n-fold integration over the domain Q with respect to the differential $dq = dq_1 \cdots dq_n$. Computing such summations or integrals will not be necessary, so this representation of the firm's cost is merely notational. There is, however, an important assumption embedded in this representation. The proper general form of the firm's cost includes an additional term depending on the firm's cost of supplying the capacity $[Q]$: such a term represents capacity costs incurred by the firm. This is the topic of §11 so we assume here that no such capacity costs are present.

In sum, the firm's cost of supplying each customer's purchase set is obtained simply as the sum of its costs of supplying the small cubes the set contains. In the power context, if capacity costs are zero or capacity is in excess supply, this says that the firm's cost of supplying a load-duration curve is determined by its marginal costs of supplying increments of power over increments of time. Each such pair of increments is a small square representing one kWh of energy at a particular time; it usually depends as well on the quantity dimension because, when there is a mix of generating technologies installed, successive units of power are supplied (in merit order) at increasing marginal costs, usually due to higher fuel costs as the capacities of generators with lower fuel costs are exhausted. For example, a typical merit order of power generation brings in hydro, nuclear, coal, and gas-fueled generators as the power load increases, and this ordering represents successively higher marginal operating costs ($/hour per kW of power capacity).

Similarly, in the context of express delivery services (such as Federal Express), this representation of the firm's cost supposes that it suffices to add up the marginal cost of delivering each item, depending on the mode of delivery and the weight or number of items sent via that mode by the customer.

A customer's benefits.

As with the firm's costs, we assume that a customer's benefit from a purchase set is simply the aggregate of the marginal service values it obtains from increments.

Thus, if the dollar value of the customer's benefit from a rectangular purchase set $[q]$ is $U([q])$, and the service value of a small cube located at q is

$$v(q) = \frac{\partial^n U([q])}{\partial q_1 \cdots \partial q_n},$$

then the customer's benefit from an arbitrary purchase set Q is simply

$$U(Q) = \int_Q v(q)\, dq.$$

The chief presumption in adopting this representation is that the customer's valuation of a small cube (of energy or an item delivered, etc.) may depend on local aspects, such as the time or the power level at which the energy is delivered, but not on global aspects of the purchase set such as its shape—for example, the overall load factor. In the context of electric power this presumption is restrictive, since it imposes a narrow interpretation of customers' incentives to shift demand from one hour to another; however, we adopt it here as a first approximation until the more elaborate formulations in §11 and §13 are introduced.

The optimal price schedule

Because the firm's cost and customers' benefits are additively separable, and computed simply as the sum of the marginal costs or valuations of increments, the tariff need not be more complicated.[5] It suffices, therefore, to construct a tariff that assigns a charge $P([q])$ to each rectangular purchase set $[q]$ based on marginal charges

$$p(q) = \frac{\partial^n P([q])}{\partial q_1 \cdots \partial q_n},$$

assessed for each small cube, and then to extend this tariff to each arbitrary purchase set Q via the formula

$$P(Q) = \int_Q p(q)\, dq.$$

The principal task, therefore, is to determine the rate schedule that specifies the marginal price $p(q)$ for a small cube at each point q. Indeed, excluding fixed and demand charges, this is precisely the procedure adopted by electric utilities in setting energy charges, by express mail services in setting delivery rates, and by telephone companies in setting toll charges for long-distance calls.

To present the calculation of an optimal price schedule in the simplest terms, we first proceed without elaborating the further assumptions that will be specified

---

5. This observation reflects a general principle. A fully optimal nonlinear tariff may reflect all the complexity of the cost and benefit functions, but it need not be any more complex. As long as it is fully adapted to the incentives of the participants, any further complexity is unnecessary.

later. Suppose there are many customers indexed by a type index t. If customer t has the benefit function $U(Q, t)$ for a purchase set Q, then in response to a tariff that specifies a price schedule p he prefers the purchase set

$$Q(t) = \{q \mid v(q, t) \geq p(q)\} .$$

That is, he prefers to include in his purchase set all increments having valuations exceeding the prices charged. This choice maximizes his net benefit, which is

$$U(Q(t), t) - P(Q(t)) = \int_{Q(t)} [v(q, t) - p(q)] \, dq .$$

These choices in turn determine the demand profile faced by the firm. The demand profile that results is

$$N(p(q), q) = \# \{t \mid q \in Q(t)\}$$
$$= \# \{t \mid v(q, t) \geq p(q)\} .$$

That is, the number of customers demanding the small cube of increments at q is the number of customers who include this cube in their purchase sets because its price is less than its marginal valuation. The firm's profit contribution from the price schedule p is therefore

$$\sum_t [P(Q(t)) - C(Q(t))] = \sum_t \int_{Q(t)} [p(q) - c(q)] \, dq$$
$$= \int_0^\infty N(p(q), q) \cdot [p(q) - c(q)] \, dq .$$

In the case of a monopoly profit-maximizing firm, this total contribution is maximized by choosing the price $p(q)$ for an increment at each point q to maximize its profit contribution

$$N(p(q), q) \cdot [p(q) - c(q)] .$$

This calculation can be done numerically as in §4 if the demand profile is derived in numerical form from demand data; Example 9.1 in Section 3 presents one such calculation. Alternatively, if the demand profile is approximated as a differentiable function of the price, then the optimal price necessarily satisfies the condition that

$$N(p(q), q) + N_p(p(q), q) \cdot [p(q) - c(q)] = 0 .$$

This condition is a direct analog of the condition derived in §4 in the one-dimensional case $n = 1$: the only substantive difference is that the construction of the demand profile takes account of the multiple dimensions of quality attributes.[6] Because the necessary condition has the same form as in the one-dimensional case, the same interpretations apply. For example, the firm's profit margin is inversely related to the price elasticity of the demand profile, reflecting the fact that the firm can again be interpreted as offering a product line consisting of all the possible quality and quantity increments.

One can also repeat exactly the analysis in §5.1 of a public enterprise or regulated utility whose price schedule is chosen to maximize consumers' surplus, subject to a net revenue requirement. The Ramsey price schedule in this case satisfies the analogous condition:

$$\alpha N(p(q), q) + N_p(p(q), q) \cdot [p(q) - c(q)] = 0,$$

where α is some number in the interval $0 \leq \alpha \leq 1$ that is chosen sufficiently large to meet the firm's revenue requirement. In Section 3 and again in §10 we use this condition to study several examples.

The data requirements imposed by this analysis are similar to those imposed in the case of a single quantity dimension. The demand profile $N(p, q)$ at a marginal price p for the q-th increment, interpreted as an n-dimensional cube of quality and quantity increments, is measured by observing the number of customers who include this cube of increments in their purchase sets. The data for this measurement can be obtained from observations of responses to uniform prices, or from trial implementations of nonlinear pricing schedules. In the latter case, $N(p, q)$ is the number of customers including q in their purchase sets at prices no higher than p, on the presumption that the price schedule ultimately used will be decreasing. Alternatively, because the percentage profit margin on each increment is calculated from the price elasticity of the demand profile, an econometric model can be used to obtain statistical estimates of how this elasticity varies across increments. One such model is illustrated in Example 2 in Section 3 in relation to Federal Express' rate schedule.

9.3   Examples

The examples in this section illustrate the formulation in Section 1 and the computational method in Section 2.

---

6. As in §4, the essential property required for this characterization is that the demand profile and the resulting marginal price schedule are nonincreasing. Sufficient assumptions are analogous to those in §8.1, differing mainly in the effect of multidimensionality of the domain. Assumptions A1 and A2 in Oren, Smith, and Wilson (1985) are ample; specifically, costs are increasing and convex, benefits are increasing and concave for each type and also increasing in the type parameters, and marginal benefits are increasing in the type parameters. If the price schedule is increasing over some region then it can be modified to be nonincreasing using a method like the one in §4.5. However, because the domain is multidimensional this task is difficult: for a nonincreasing price schedule, the marginal profit contribution averaged over each region must be zero.

Table 9.1 Postal Example: The Demand Profile $N(p, q)$

Price p ($)	Mode	Increment q Quantity:	1	2	3	4	Stamps	Letters
1	Reg		100	60	30	*15	205	81
	Air		50	40	25	*9	124	49
	Exp		30	25	15	*5	75	75
2	Reg		80	42	*18	7	147	66
	Air		*35	*28	*14	4	81	32
	Exp		*20	*17	*11	1	49	49
3	Reg		*55	*29	12	3	99	57
	Air		18	14	9	1	42	23
	Exp		11	6	2	0	19	19
			Optimal Schedule					
Prices ($):	Reg		3	3	2	1		
	Air		2	2	2	1		
	Exp		2	2	2	1		
Demands ($):	Reg		55	29	18	15	117	31
	Air		35	28	14	9	86	33
	Exp		20	17	11	5	53	53
Revenues ($):	Reg		165	87	36	15	303	77
	Air		70	56	28	9	163	150
	Exp		40	34	22	5	101	340
						Total:	$567	$567

Example 9.1: Calculation with Numerical Data. We begin with a simple numerical example that illustrates crudely the sort of data that might be encountered in the postal example. The raw data is shown in Table 9.1, which presents the demand profile. For each integer price $p = \$1, \ldots, \$3$ the table shows the number $N(p, q)$ of customers who buy an upgrade stamp for each possible increment q, where a typical increment q specifies an increment to one of the three delivery modes and one of four possible quantity increments $1, \ldots, 4$. If the demand profile was constructed from an assignment-form description of each customer's purchase set, then this demand profile is necessarily nonincreasing along each dimension of quality and quantity, and presumably also decreasing in the price if customers respond to higher prices with lower demands.

For purposes of illustration, assume that the only feasible prices for increments are the three prices shown in the table; also, the firm's marginal cost is zero for each combination of increments and the firm maximizes its profit contribution; that is, $c = 0$ and $\alpha = 1$. The second segment of the table shows which of the three feasible prices is optimal for each combination of a mode increment and a quantity increment, and an asterisk (*) in the first segment indicates the corresponding demand (one tie is resolved in favor of a lower price). For example, the first regular stamp could be assigned the price $1, $2, or $3, and according

to the table this would yield the profit contribution $100, $160, or $165. These
contributions are obtained as the product of the price and the corresponding tabular
entry 100, 80, or 55 in the first column (Quantity 1) and the first rows (Reg) of
the tabulation of the demand profile $N(p, q)$. Consequently, the optimal price is $3
yielding the profit contribution $165 based on a prediction from the data that 55
customers buy this first regular stamp at this price. Note that these are the prices of
stamps. The charge for, say, a second letter sent airmail is actually $2 for a second
airmail stamp *plus* the price of an additional regular stamp, which may be $3, $2,
or $1 depending on how many other regular stamps have been purchased.

The second segment of the table shows also the numbers of customers predicted
to buy each stamp and the predicted revenues. The Stamps column shows the
numbers 117, 86, 53 of letters affixed with regular, airmail, and express stamps,
obtained as the sum of the numbers in each row. The numbers of letters sent by
these modes are therefore the differences of these sums, namely 31, 33, and 53,
as shown in the Letters column. The total number of letters sent is the sum 117
indicated for regular stamps, one of which is required for each letter sent via
any delivery mode, and the total revenue is $567. Although the allocation of this
stamp revenue to letters is indeterminate, the Letters column of the table shows an
allocation $77, $150, and $340 based on the accounting rule that assigns stamps
first to express letters and last to regular letters.[7]   ◇

Example 9.2: Federal Express' Rate Schedule. Recall from §2 that the Federal
Express Company's discount rate schedules for Standard Air and Courier-Pak
delivery are piecewise-linear when graphed on logarithmic scales. Here we derive
a model of customers' behavior that imitates this feature. We focus on items
weighing more than 50 pounds, for which the two schedules are linear and parallel,
indicating that the faster Courier-Pak delivery costs a fixed percentage more than
Standard Air. Such rates reflect a tariff of the form

$$P(w \mid s) = A(s)w^b$$

for delivery of an item of weight w at speed s; consequently, the marginal charge
for the w-th pound at speed s is

$$P_w(w \mid s) = A(s)bw^{b-1},$$

and the marginal price schedule for increments has this same basic form. Our aim
is to formulate a model that prescribes a rate schedule of this form.

7. This accounting rule is not perfectly accurate since the implied demand ($1 = 29 - 28$) for a second
regular letter is less than the implied demand ($4 = 18 - 14$) for a third regular letter. Although the
demands for letters sent by various modes can be inferred from the demands for stamps, the allocation
of revenues to letters cannot be inferred uniquely if the price schedule is not uniform.

Suppose that customers' valuations $v(s, w; t)$ of an incremental w-th pound and an increment to speed s are distributed in the population of potential customers according to an exponential distribution with mean $M(s, w)$ depending on s and w. Then the demand profile is

$$N(p; s, w) = e^{-p/M(s,w)}.$$

In §12 we show that the Ramsey pricing rule with the parameter $\alpha = 1/n$ is the result of competition among n firms using a Cournot model of their competitive decisions; hence, we use this value of α to allow for the fact that Federal Express operates in a competitive market with several other private firms and the U.S. Postal Service. Assume temporarily that the firm's marginal cost is $c(s, w) = 0$. Then the formula in Section 2 implies that the optimal price for the increment (s, w) is

$$p(s, w) = M(s, w)/n.$$

Suppose we assume that the mean of the valuation distribution has the special form

$$M(s, w) = a(s)w^{b-1},$$

which is quite plausible since if $a(s)$ is increasing then the distribution of customers' valuations shifts higher as the speed increment increases, while if $0 < b < 1$ then the distribution shifts lower as the weight increment increases, as one expects. Then in terms of logarithms the price schedule has the form

$$\log p(s, w) = \log[a(s)/n] + [b - 1] \cdot \log w.$$

Thus the price schedule is log-linear as in Federal Express' rate schedule, and an increment in the quality s merely raises the logarithmic schedule by a fixed amount. The coefficient b is the common slope of the two Federal Express rate schedules for more than 50 pounds when they are graphed with logarithmic scales. Note, however, that the effect of competition, as indicated by the number n of competing firms, cannot be disentangled from the effect of quality increments. A similar conclusion also results if the firm's marginal cost has the special form $c(s, w) = \gamma(s)w^{b-1}$ for some function $\gamma(s)$ depending on the quality increment s.

◇

Example 9.3: Customers' Load-Duration Curves. Next we consider a simple example in which each customer's purchase can be described by a load-duration curve. Suppose that customers' types are indexed by a parameter t that is uniformly distributed between zero and one. Further, customer t's demand function for power in hour h is $D(p, h; t) = t - hp$, where the index of hours runs over an interval $h_* < h < 1$ and $h_* > 0$. Note that if the price p is constant then the customer's power demand decreases linearly as the hour index increases; consequently, D can also be interpreted as the customer's load-duration curve in the case that the price is constant. This model is special in that customers' peak demands coincide at h_* (that is, they have synchronous demands), and customers differ only via vertical shifts of their demand functions and load-duration curves.

The form of the demand function implies that customer t's valuation of an x-th increment of power for the h-th hour is $v(h, x; t) = [t - x]/h$, which is the marginal valuation of energy. In turn, this implies that the demand profile is

$$N(p; h, x) = \#\{t \mid t \geq x + hp\}$$
$$= \max\{0, 1 - [x + hp]\},$$

indicating the fraction of customers demanding an x-th unit of power over the h-th hour at the price p. The optimal nonlinear price schedule according to the formula in Section 2 is therefore

$$p(h, x) = \min\left\{[1 - x]/h, \frac{1}{1 + \alpha}\left(c(h, x) + \alpha[1 - x]/h\right)\right\}$$
$$= \frac{1}{1 + \alpha}\left(c(h, x) + \alpha[1 - x]/h\right),$$

where the second equality is subject to the proviso that $c(h, x) \leq [1 - x]/h$. This formula is valid also if $h_* = 0$ since the price $p(0, 1) = 1$ suffices for the last unit $x = 1$ of power demanded at the peak hour.

This schedule can be implemented via a time-of-use tariff by interpreting $p(h, x)$ as the marginal price of an x-th kWh during hour h, or via a Wright tariff, of an h-th hour of power from the x-th ranked (in the merit order) kW of capacity.   ◇

Example 9.4: Multiplicative Type Parameter. Finally, we examine the special case that a customer's type parameter affects his marginal valuations multiplicatively. In this case the marginal price for increments is a fixed fraction of the maximum among the customers' marginal valuations. Suppose that the type parameter is a single real number that is distributed in the population according to the distribution function F, and let $\bar{F}(t) = 1 - F(t)$ be the fraction of the population with type parameters exceeding t. In the multiplicative case, suppose that customer t has the benefit function

$$U(Q, t) = t\int_Q v(q)\, dq$$

for a purchase set Q, where $v(q)$ is a marginal valuation function that is the same for all customers. It will be convenient to interpret $tv(q)$ as t's marginal valuation in excess of the firm's marginal cost, so we can suppose that $c(q) = 0$. In this case the demand profile is simply $N(p, q) = \bar{F}(p/v(q))$ and therefore the optimal marginal price schedule $p(q)$ satisfies the condition

$$p(q)/v(q) = \alpha \bar{F}(p(q)/v(q))/f(p(q)/v(q)),$$

where f is the density of F. If $k(\alpha) \leq 1$ is the "right" solution of the equation $k = \alpha \bar{F}(k)/f(k)$, then the optimal price schedule is just

$$p(q) = k(\alpha)v(q).$$

The proviso that k is the right solution is unnecessary for the standard distribution functions used in applied work because their hazard rates $f(k)/\bar{F}(k)$ are increasing functions of k. This property assures that there is only one value of k that solves the required equation. Notice too that as the firm's revenue requirement decreases, α decreases and therefore also $k(\alpha)$ and $p(q)$ decrease.   ◇

9.4   An item-assignment formulation

The formulation in Section 2 assumes that a customer's total benefit from a pur-chase set is simply the aggregate of the marginal service values it obtains from increments. This assumption is inaccurate in some applications because the benefit from an item's quality assignment depends on item-specific attributes that are not observed by the firm, and therefore not priced by the tariff. Moreover, the tariff can influence the optimal assignment via its effects on the costs of substitution between higher and lower qualities. Features of this kind are especially important in telecommunications and transport in which customers select, say, the speed or delay with which each item is delivered. In such contexts an item is a message, data packet, or parcel, as in the illustration of Federal Express' express mail services; or in the context of electric power, an item is an end-use or appliance whose time of operation can be chosen by the customer.

   To address such problems, we use an assignment-form representation in a model that takes explicit account of how a customer's benefit depends on an item's attributes and the quality assigned. To simplify the analysis, we assume that a customer's type is indicated by a single parameter t and items are described anal-ogously by a single attribute denoted a; these lie in intervals T and A respectively. The analysis uses the method in §6; the demand-profile formulation is omitted.

   A customer of type t is described by two functions $\langle G, u \rangle$. The first is a distri-bution function $G(a, t)$ for the attributes of the customer's items, and we assume it has an associated density function $g(a, t)$ indicating the frequency of items with attribute a. The second is a benefit function $u(s, a, t)$ indicating the value obtained from sending a single item having the attribute a with a delivery delay s. The fea-sible set S of delays is assumed to be an interval $S = \{s \mid s \geq s_0\}$. The marginal value of delay is $v(s,a,t) \equiv \partial u(s,a,t)/\partial s$, which is presumably negative. It reduces notation therefore to assume that u is a decreasing function also of the parameters a and t, and similarly that G is a decreasing function of t. That is, the lowest type values speed more and has more items for which quick delivery is more valuable.

The firm observes only the frequency of items sent with each delay, not their attributes, so the tariff can depend only the distribution of delays selected by the customer. We consider a tariff that is additively separable across delays, but that allows quantity discounts within each class of delay. Thus, an amount $P(q(s),s)$ is charged for $q(s)$ items sent with delay s, and the marginal charge for an additional item is $p(q,s) \equiv \partial P(q,s)/\partial q$ at $q = q(s)$. Because the items' attributes have a continuous density, we interpret $q(s)$ as the density of items sent with delay s. In particular, an assignment $s(a)$ indicating the delay assigned to an item with attribute a results in a density $q(s)$ that is calculated as follows. Suppose the assignment has an inverse $a(s)$ indicating the attribute of items sent with delay s. Then $G(a(s),t)$ is the distribution of items' delays. The corresponding density of delays is therefore $q(s) = g(a(s),t)a'(s)$, or equivalently, $q(s(a)) = g(a,t)/s'(a)$.

Customers' optimal assignments

A customer of type t chooses an assignment $s(a)$ that maximizes the difference between aggregate benefits and the tariff. Two equivalent versions of this net benefit are

$$\int_A u(s(a),a,t)g(a,t)\,da - \int_S P(g(a(s),t)a'(s),s)\,ds$$
$$\equiv \int_A \{u(s(a),a,t)g(a,t) - P(g(a,t)/s'(a),s(a))s'(a)\}\,da.$$

Using the second version, the Euler condition for optimality is

$$v(s(a),a,t) = \frac{d}{ds}p(q(s),s),$$

where the right side is evaluated at $s = s(a)$ and $q(s) = g(a,t)/s'(a)$. This condition differs substantially from the one in Section 2 in that the dominant consideration for the customer is the marginal value of the item (on the left) compared to the marginal cost of delay (on the right): the latter is calculated by considering alternative reassignments of the item to smaller or larger delays, taking account of the marginal price charged for an additional item at each selected delay s. Thus, it states that no small change in the assigned delay would increase the net benefit obtained. In addition to this condition, two transversality conditions are required:

$$u(s(a), a, t) \geq p(q(s), s),$$

$$u(s(a), a, t)q(s) \geq P(q(s), s),$$

where s and $q(s)$ are as described above. The first requires that the benefit exceeds the charge for the marginal item assigned delay s, and the second requires that the total benefit exceeds the total charge. These three conditions are all intuitively obvious and they have natural extensions to discrete models.

The firm's preferred assignments

A profit-maximizing firm chooses the tariff to maximize the aggregate of the profit contributions from all customers:

$$\int_T \left\{ \int_S [P(q(s,t), s) - q(s,t)c(s)] \, ds \right\} dF(t),$$

where $F(t)$ is the distribution function of customer types in the population, and $q(s, t)$ is the density of items sent with delay s by type t. For simplicity, the cost per item $c(s)$ depends only on the delay s.[8] As in §6, we rephrase the profit contribution by integrating by parts to obtain an integral with the integrand

$$\frac{dG(a(s,t), t)}{dt} \cdot F(t) \cdot \frac{d[p(q(s,t), s) - c(s)]}{ds},$$

in which we can use the customer's optimality condition to replace the second and third factors by

$$V(s, a, t) \equiv F(t) \cdot [v(s, a, t) - c'(s)],$$

$$= F(t) \cdot \frac{d[p(q(s,t), s) - c(s)]}{ds},$$

where V is evaluated at $a = a(s, t)$. Thus, a characterization of the assignments the firm prefers is obtained by optimizing this representation of the profit contribution with respect to the assignment function $a(s, t)$. This characterization is obtained from the Euler condition, which yields:

$$\frac{G_t(a, t)}{G_a(a, t)} = \frac{V_t(s, a, t)}{V_a(s, a, t)},$$

8. In some communications and transport applications, the cost function must be constructed from a queuing model that recognizes how the distribution of items' delays affects the system design and operation. One such model is addressed in §10.3.

at $a = a(s, t)$ or $s = s(a, t)$. One can interpret $V(s, a, t)$ as the product of the number of customers selecting delays no more than s for items of type a, and the profit margin obtainable from these selections for the s-th increment. The left side of the firm's optimality condition measures $-da/dt$ for a fixed value of G and the right similarly for a fixed value of V. Thus the condition requires that the contribution from each delay increment is maximized subject to the technological constraint imposed by customers' distributions of item attributes, as represented by the left side. Again, this condition has a natural extension to discrete models.

Construction of the tariff

The last step is to construct the tariff to induce customers to select the assignments preferred by the firm. This tariff is constructed as follows. The firm's optimality condition can be interpreted as establishing a bivariate mapping from each pair $\langle a, t \rangle$ of unobserved parameters to a corresponding pair $\langle q, s \rangle$ of observed selections; that is, the firm prefers that type t assigns a density q of items with attribute a to delay s. Ordinarily this map has an inverse specifying the type $t(q, s)$ and the attribute $a(q, s)$ assigned to $\langle q, s \rangle$. Consequently, the customer's optimality condition can be written out in full as

$$\alpha(q, s)p_q(q, s) + p_s(q, s) = \beta(q, s),$$

where $\alpha = \partial q/\partial s$ and $\beta = \partial u/\partial s \equiv v$ evaluated at $\langle q, s, a(q, s), t(q, s) \rangle$. This is a partial differential equation that can be solved together with the customer's transversality conditions to obtain an optimal tariff. This task is fairly complicated, as the subsequent example shows.

The provisos mentioned along the way all pertain to requirements for monotonicity of the assignments. In particular, several steps require that the density $q(s, t)$ and the attribute $a(s, t)$ of items assigned to s by type t are monotone in the type parameter t. Typical assumptions that assure this property are that G, V, and v are monotone in the type parameter. Conditions assuring that the bivariate map mentioned above is invertible are hard to identify.

A class of examples

Because the type and attribute parameters are arbitrary indices, they can be transformed so that they are uniformly distributed, say $F(t) = t$ for $0 \leq t \leq 1$ and $G(a, t) = aN(t)$ for $0 \leq a \leq 1$, where $N(t)$ is the aggregate number of t's items. We describe a class of examples in which the benefit function is also separable, say $u(a, s, t) = [1 - a]u(s)M(t)$. Assume that $u(s)$ and the marginal cost $c(s)$ decrease with delay; moreover, $u'(s)/c'(s)$ is increasing, indicating that customers' benefits decline faster than costs do. In view of the latter, it is possible and convenient to transform the delay index so that

$$\phi s + d = u'(s)/c'(s),$$

where $d \equiv u'(0)/c'(0)$ and $\phi > 0$. Hereafter let $\phi = 1$ and let $v(s) \equiv u'(s)$. The elasticities of M and N are

$$\mu(t) \equiv -tM'(t)/M(t) \qquad \text{and} \qquad \nu(t) \equiv -tN'(t)/N(t),$$

which are assumed to satisfy

$$\mu(t) < 1, \qquad \nu(t) > 0, \qquad M(t)[1 - \mu(t)]d \leq 1.$$

Finally, define

$$L(t) \equiv \frac{N(t)/M(t)}{1 - \mu(t) + \nu(t)},$$

and assume it is decreasing, which requires $M(t) \neq N(t)$.

We first use the firm's optimality condition to derive its preferred assignment:

$$a(s,t) = 1 - M(t)^{-1}(\gamma(t) + \delta(t)/[s + d]),$$

where

$$\gamma(t) = M(t)\nu(t)\delta(t), \qquad \delta(t) = 1/[1 - \mu(t) + \nu(t)].$$

This assignment has the requisite monotonicity property that $a(s,t)$ increases as t increases. Also, this assignment implies that[9]

$$q(s,t) = L(t)/[s + d]^2,$$

which decreases with t. One then derives

$$\alpha(q,s) = -2q/[s + d], \qquad \beta(q,s) = [1 - a(s,t)]v(s)M(t),$$

evaluated at t such that $L(t) = q[s + d]^2$. Recall that $v(s) = [s + d]c'(s)$ due to the way the delay index was transformed. Consequently, the first integral of the differential equation for the price schedule yields

$$p(q,s) = \gamma(t)u(s) + \delta(t)c(s) + k(t),$$

9. Note that the firm infers a customer's type from the sufficient statistic $q[s + d]^2$; that is $t = L^{-1}(q[s + d]^2)$.

where k is an arbitrary function. Integrating again, the complete solution is

$$P(q, s) = \frac{\bar{\gamma}(t)u(s) + \bar{\delta}(t)c(s) + \bar{k}(t)}{[s + d]^2},$$

again evaluated at $t = L^{-1}(q[s + d]^2)$, where for $t_o = L^{-1}(0)$,

$$\bar{\gamma}(t) = \int_{t_o}^{t} \gamma(\tau)\, dL(\tau),$$

and analogously for $\bar{\delta}$ and $\bar{k}$. The arbitrary functon $\bar{k}$ is determined by the transversality conditions; consequently, if $\bar{s}(t)$ is the maximum delay chosen by t then

$$[1 - a(\bar{s}(t), t)]u(\bar{s}(t))M(t) = \gamma(t)u(\bar{s}(t)) + \delta(t)c(\bar{s}(t)) + k(t),$$

$$= [\bar{\gamma}(t)u(\bar{s}(t)) + \bar{\delta}(t)c(\bar{s}(t)) + \bar{k}(t)]/L(t).$$

The first of these equations determines $\bar{s}(t)$ given $k(t)$, say $\bar{s}(t, k(t))$, whereupon the second specifies an ordinary differential equation for $\bar{k}(t)$ since $\bar{k}'(t) = k(t)$. The boundary condition $P(0, s) = 0$ determines the constant of integration.[10]

Example 9.5: We illustrate with a specific example. Suppose[11]

$$N(t) = 1 - t, \qquad\qquad M(t) = 1,$$

$$u(s) = \frac{1}{2}[1 - s^2], \qquad c(s) = c[1 - s].$$

Because M is independent of t, customers' preferences are the same; however, they are still heterogeneous because their distributions of item attributes differ. These specifications yield $\mu(t) = 0$, $\nu(t) = t/[1 - t]$, and $L(t) = [1 - t]^2$. Therefore,

$$t(q, s) = 1 - [qs^2/c]^{1/2}, \qquad\qquad a(q, s) = [1 - c/s][qs^2/c]^{1/2},$$

$$\alpha(q, s) = -2q/s, \qquad\qquad \beta(q, s) = -s[1 - (1 - c/s)(qs^2/c)^{1/2}],$$

$$\gamma(t) = t, \qquad\qquad \delta(t) = 1 - t,$$

$$\bar{\gamma}(t) = [1 - t]^2 - \frac{2}{3}[1 - t]^3, \qquad\qquad \bar{\delta}(t) = \frac{2}{3}[1 - t]^3,$$

$$\bar{s}(t) = 1, \qquad\qquad \bar{k}(t) = 0.$$

---

10. In particular, if $u(s^*)$ implies $c(s^*)$ then $\bar{s}(t) = s^*$ and $\bar{k}(t) \leq 0$.

11. The transformation of the delay index replaces s by cs, but we avoid this here. A "bad" example in which the bivariate map is not invertible is obtained by making the alteration $M(t) = N(t) = 1 - t$.

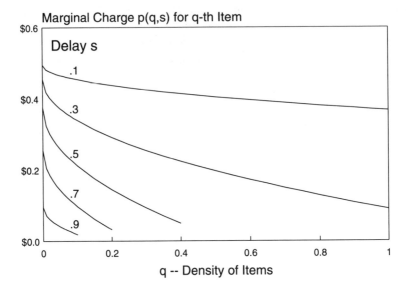

FIG. 9.3   Example 9.5: The marginal price schedule $p(q, s)$ when $c = 0.1$.

The net result is that the tariff charged for q items with delay s can be expressed as

$$P(q, s) = \hat{P}(s, L(t(q, s))) - \hat{P}(1, L(t(q, s)))/s^2 \,,$$

where
$$\hat{P}(s, \ell) = c\ell \left[\frac{2}{3} \ell^{1/2} (1/2 - c/s) - \frac{1}{2} \right] ,$$

and
$$L(t(q, s)) = qs^2/c \,.$$

As noted previously, the tariff is based essentially on an inference that it is type $t(q, s)$ who selects a density of q items to be sent with delay s. A customer of type t responds with the assignment

$$s(a, t) = c[1 - t]/[1 - t - a] , \qquad \text{or} \qquad a(s, t) = [1 - t][1 - c/s]$$

which produces a density $q(s, t) = [1 - t]^2 c/s^2$ of items assigned delay s. Type t submits items with attributes in the range $0 \le a \le [1 - t][1 - c]$ for service. Among all customers, the range of delays is $c \le s \le 1$, and the range of item densities is $0 \le q \le 1/c$. Lastly, one can add a positive fixed fee if the firm incurs a fixed cost c_o of serving each customer, but we omit details.

The marginal price schedule $p(q, s)$ and the tariff $P(q, s)$ are shown in Figure 9.3 and Figure 9.4 for a few values of the delay s, assuming $c = 0.1$. In three cases the graph is truncated at the maximum item-density q demanded by any customer. The tariff is nearly linear for speedy service but appreciable quantity discounts are offered for delayed services.   ◇

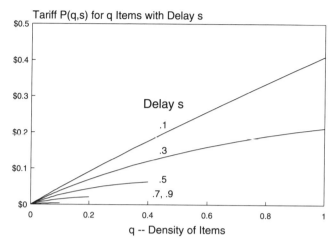

FIG. 9.4   Example 9.5: The tariff $P(q, s)$ when $c = 0.1$.

9.5   Summary

This chapter is the first of three on nonlinear tariffs depending on multiple dimensions of quality or quantity. It considers only the simplest case that customers assign multiple quality attributes to each unit of a single generic product. Moreover, the construction relies on assumptions that the firm's costs and customers' benefits are additively separable. The theme emphasized is that the methods described in previous chapters for a single product of fixed quality extend straightforwardly to this more general case. The demand profile is again formulated in terms of customers' demands for increments, but along all dimensions simultaneously. This formulation depends on the profile-form representation that records demands for upgrades, rather than the usual assignment form. The profile form corresponds to the standard representation of demands in terms of customers' load-duration curves, in which a purchase is interpreted essentially as a set of increments. A profit-maximizing nonlinear tariff has the same basic characterization: each marginal price for increments is set to maximize the profit contribution from the resulting demand for these increments. The construction of tariffs based on Ramsey pricing also remains similar.

The item-assignment formulation in Section 4 introduces the more complicated analysis required when customers have additional information, unobserved by the firm, about items' attributes that affects their selections of service qualities. Although the model is based on an interpretation of quality as service delay, the elements of the formulation and the methods used apply more generally to similar problems in which customers have superior information about the relative values of quality levels and of substitution among them.

The simplicity of the results in this chapter depend on the additive separability of costs and benefits. Later chapters eliminate this assumption but require more complex analysis.

10

PRIORITY PRICING

The formulation in previous chapters assumes that the firm can, at some cost, expand production to meet customers' demands. In practice, however, the marginal cost of increasing supply may increase steeply as the firm's capacity is exhausted, and indeed, some levels of demand may be too large to serve by any measures that can be taken in the short run. For this reason, the formulation must be interpreted as applying essentially to an environment in which demand and supply conditions are stable, and over a term long enough to adapt capacity to demand.

When demand or supply conditions are variable, an accurate formulation must recognize the important effect of short-run constraints on supply imposed by limited capacity. In important cases, these constraints significantly affect the design of the tariff. Recall from §2.3 that Pacific Gas and Electric Company's tariff includes options for curtailable and interruptible service, each of which is differentiated into three classes with different limits on the numbers and durations of events in which service is curtailed or interrupted. This tariff enables customers to obtain lower rates in exchange for greater chances of interruption. Service options of this sort differentiate delivery conditions according to the priority or reliability of delivery. Customers' voluntary selections of lower reliabilities reveal that their service valuations are relatively low. Thus, it is more efficient to interrupt them than others electing high reliability; similarly, the utility is able to meet peak loads at less than the cost of additional capacity.

Section 1 first examines the case that supplies are rationed via a system of priorities that customers select in advance of the outcome of supply and demand uncertainties. Our analysis of priority service takes advantage of the alternative interpretation that the tariff describes the firm's charges for various levels of service quality. In the present case, quality is interpreted as the reliability of service, which is closely related to a quantity interpretation. Section 2 expands the analysis to allow quantity discounts in conjunction with priority service. Nonlinear pricing of service quality and quantity jointly provides a more efficient means of meeting a revenue requirement. Finally, Section 3 studies the role of nonlinear pricing in a

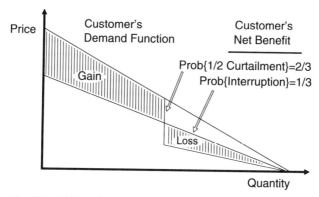

FIG. 10.1   Gains and losses from curtailment compared to interruption.

service system in which jobs require time to process and low priority jobs wait in queues while higher priority jobs are being processed.

10.1   Capacity-constrained tariffs: priority pricing

Priority service is a method used by electric utilities for rationing scarce supplies more efficiently than, say, random interruptions. The basic motive is illustrated in Figure 10.1. The top line depicts the demand function of a customer for sure service, and the one below indicates the expected portion of the service value obtained when there is a one-third chance of an interruption. The shaded areas show the customer's relative gain and loss from switching to a system in which his supply is curtailed by half as much, twice as often. A curtailment maintains a supply to serve the customer's higher-value base load; consequently, the net gain from priority service is positive. Implementations usually offer several classes of service with differing chances of interruption or curtailment. A customer can therefore assign different end-uses, circuits, or units of power to different priority classes. Figure 10.2 depicts the extreme case in which each unit with a service value above the utility's marginal cost c is assigned to a different priority class, or equivalently to a different reliability of delivery. Higher value units are assigned higher reliabilities, so again each customer's gain exceeds the loss, compared to the usual system of selecting customers randomly for complete interruption.

We begin with the simple case that the firm does not offer quantity discounts. In this case, service is differentiated on the single dimension of reliability of delivery. For simplicity, each customer is assumed to demand only one unit. This entails no loss of generality if a customer can select a different reliability for each unit demanded, but it is restrictive if each customer is constrained to assign the same reliability to multiple units. To emphasize the main ideas, the presentation is separated into two parts: the first assumes that only supply is uncertain; and the

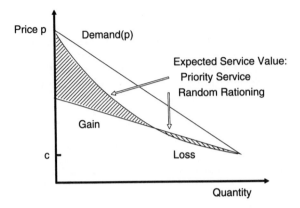

FIG. 10.2 Gains and losses from fully differentiated priority service compared to random rationing of scarce supplies.

second, demand. Priority pricing can also be used when both supply and demand are uncertain, as described later.

Supply uncertainty

In keeping with the quality interpretation, the amount q selected by a customer now represents the probability or reliability of receiving service. We show later how this probability is derived from the probability distribution of the firm's available supplies. The demand profile $N(p, q)$ retains the interpretation that it is the number of customers selecting a reliability of q or more when the marginal price for the q-th increment is p.

To take an example, suppose that each customer is identified by a value v obtained from sure service for one unit of demand. Thus, the customer obtains a net benefit $vq - P(q)$ from subscribing to priority service that charges $P(q)$ and provides service with reliability q. Note that the tariff $P(q)$ is interpreted as payable whether or not the unit is actually delivered. In many cases, $P(q) = P_o + q\hat{P}(q)$ where P_o is a fixed fee and $\hat{P}(q)$ is a charge payable only if service is delivered. Note that the customer's optimal reliability selection satisfies $v - p(q) = 0$, where $p(q) = P'(q)$ is the marginal price of reliability. In this case, the demand profile $N(p, q)$ measures the number of customers with valuations exceeding p, since this is the predicted number choosing reliabilities q or more when the marginal price of reliability at q is p. More complicated models envision that the customer also adapts his investments in appliances to the reliability selected.

We now demonstrate that the price schedule $p(q)$ for priority service is substantially determined by the supply conditions of the firm; in fact, the firm ordinarily has only a single degree of freedom remaining to specify the tariff. Suppose that the supply available to the firm is a random variable $\tilde{s}$ that has a distribution function $S(s)$, indicating the probability that $\tilde{s} \leq s$. Let $\bar{S}(s) = 1 - S(s)$ indicate the

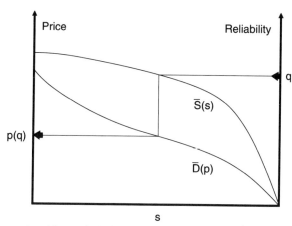

FIG. 10.3   Construction of the marginal price of reliability. The marginal price for q-th unit of reliability induces demand that can be supplied with probability q.

probability that the firm can supply at least s units. Then the schedule of marginal prices must satisfy the constraint that $\bar{S}(N(p(q), q)) = q$. That is, the reliability q or more, promised to those customers paying the price $p(q)$ charged for the q-th increment, must be feasible: the probability must be at least q that supply is sufficient to serve the number $N(p(q), q)$ of customers selecting this and higher reliabilities. From this construction we see that all the marginal prices along the schedule are determined entirely by the technology of supply: for each value of q, the marginal price $p(q)$ is found by solving the above equation.

Figure 10.3 illustrates the construction of the marginal price $p(q)$ in terms of the aggregate demand function $\bar{D}(p)$. At the price $p(q)$ the demand is $\bar{D}(p(q))$, which must equal the available supply s allocated to those customers promised reliabilities of q or more.

Another interpretation of this equation is that it requires the marginal price $p(q)$ to be sufficiently high to limit demand to the supply $s = \bar{S}^{-1}(q)$ that can be provided with reliability q. Consequently, when the supply s is known in advance, $p(q)$ is the spot price that limits demand to the supply s. Thus, apart from any fixed fee that might be charged, the tariff $P(q)$ is the expectation of the spot price customers would pay if they were to be served only when the spot price is no higher than $p(q)$ and thereby obtain the service reliability q. Since the spot price can be interpreted as the outcome of an auction of scarce supplies in each contingency, this also shows that the tariff represents the amount that one customer must pay to outbid customers obtaining lower service reliabilities. The price $p(q)$ is, therefore, the amount that compensates all those other customers selecting reliabilities less than q whose service reliabilities are degraded by serving this customer with higher priority.

The sole remaining possibility available to the firm to increase its profit is therefore to impose a fixed subscription fee. Although such a fee may limit the number of subscribers, a monopolist may find it advantageous to use this option.

Example 10.1: Suppose that the demand profile is $N(p, q) = 1 - p$, indicating that a fraction $1 - p$ of the potential customers in the population have service valuations exceeding p. Further, assume that the firm's supply, on a per customer basis, is uniformly distributed between zero and one, so that $\bar{S}(s) = 1 - s$. Then the feasibility condition requires that the marginal price for the q-th increment in reliability is $p(q) = q$. The tariff must therefore have the form $P(q) = P_o + \frac{1}{2}q^2$, where P_o is a fixed fee paid by each subscriber. Such a tariff leads a subscriber with the valuation v to select the reliability $q(v) = v$ and therefore he obtains the net benefit $\frac{1}{2}v^2 - P_o$. Only those customers for whom this net benefit is positive will subscribe; namely, those with valuations exceeding $w \equiv \sqrt{2P_o}$. Consequently, if the firm's marginal cost is zero then its profit per customer is

$$\int_w^1 P(q(v))\, dv = P_o[1 - w] + \frac{1}{6}[1 - w^3].$$

The subscription fee that maximizes this profit is $P_o = 1/8$, resulting in the market penetration $w = 1/2$, so that only half of the potential customers choose to subscribe to priority service.   ◇

This can be compared with the efficient outcome in which no subscription fee is charged and all customers obtain some chance of receiving service. Even with no subscription fee, however, the efficient tariff must increase nonlinearly with the reliability of the service selected in order to match the technology of supply. Moreover, the firm's limited supplies produce a positive profit in either case; in particular, the profit per customer is $1/6$ in the preceding example. In the case of a regulated public utility, this profit might be refunded to customers or part might be invested to expand capacity so as to shift the probability distribution of supply, thereby increasing the service reliabilities obtained by customers.[1]

Example 10.2: The preceding analysis typically understates the efficiency gains from priority service, as we illustrate by amending the previous example. Suppose that customers or end-uses are of various types indexed by t and these types are uniformly distributed. Each type can obtain a service value v at a cost $v^2/4t$, interpreted as an investment in an appliance. Thus, a customer of type t can obtain an expected net service value $u(v, q, t) = vq - v^2/4t$ if service is available with the reliability q. Assuming again that the supply distribution is $\bar{S}(s) = 1 - s$, random rationing of supplies provides $q = 1/2$, so the customer selects $v = t$ and obtains the net benefit $t/4$. Given this appliance choice, the analysis of the preceding example applies: the customer's gain from priority service, as versus random rationing, is $[t^2 - t + 1/3]/2$ if the utility's profits are refunded equally

---

1. The investment policy for efficient capacity expansion is derived by Chao and Wilson (1979) in a priority service framework.

to customers. But if the customer optimizes the choice of appliance then he will choose $v = 2tq$ and obtain the net benefit

$$u(q, t) \equiv \max_{v} \{u(v, q, t)\} = tq^2 .$$

Based on this version of customers' valuations of reliability, priority service entails a marginal charge $p(q) = 2q^2$ for the reliability q. This induces a customer of type t to choose $q = t$ and results in an expected net gain $(1/3)t^3 - (1/4)t + 1/6$ over random rationing. Each customer gains by optimizing his appliance selection and in the aggregate the average net gain per customer is 50% larger than estimated without allowing for optimization of investments in appliances. The consequences for design of the tariff are evidently substantial too.   ◇

   The analysis can be extended to the case that each customer selects a service reliability initially based on incomplete information about his valuation that will materialize subsequently. In this case, one useful implementation that avoids the difficulties of organizing a spot market works as follows. The firm offers customers a menu of service charges. After selecting a service charge based on his initial information, a customer subsequently observes his valuation and requests service if his valuation exceeds the charge he selected. In each contingency, the firm serves those customers requesting service in order of the charges they have selected (highest first) until the supply is exhausted. Thus, a customer's service reliability ultimately depends both on his and others' valuations that materialize as well as the supply available. Customers initially expecting higher valuations select higher charges and obtain higher reliabilities—but if one's valuation turns out to be too low to justify payment of the selected charge then he obtains a chance of service (at marginal cost) only if supply exceeds the realized demand for priority service. As before, the tariff is based on the expectation of the spot price that would be paid for comparable reliability.
   More general models in which both demand and supply are uncertain preserve the essential feature that the tariff is comprised of a fixed fee and, for each service reliability or priority selected by the customer, a usage charge that is the expectation of the spot prices that would otherwise be paid for comparable service quality. Special cases have features that are useful in applications. For instance, if customers' demand functions differ only via a multiplicative parameter then, when a curtailment is necessary, it is efficient to curtail the supply allowed each customer by the same proportion. Figure 10.4 amends Figure 10.3 to show how an individual customer's demand $d(p)$ that is proportional to aggregate demand $D(p)$ is curtailed proportionally when supply is scarce. This property indicates that equi-proportional rationing may be approximately optimal in many cases.[2]

2. An implementation based on this design is the Voluntary Interruptible Pricing Program (VIPP) initiated by Niagara Mohawk Power Company in 1990.

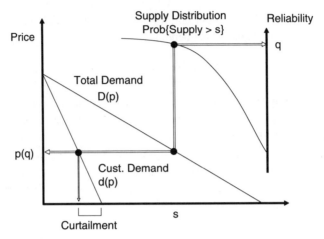

FIG. 10.4   A customer is curtailed proportionately if his demand is proportional to total demand.

Demand uncertainty

Similar features occur if there is uncertainty about demand rather than supply. We illustrate with a somewhat different formulation in which the firm implements the tariff by offering units of supply sequentially at successively lower prices, as in an auction. Suppose that the firm's supply is s and there are n potential customers, each of whom might purchase a single unit. Assume that $s < n$ so that the supply is scarce. To represent demand uncertainty, suppose that each customer's valuation might be one of the values $v_1 > v_2 > \ldots > v_m$, and the firm knows only the probability that each customer has each possible valuation. Thus, the number n_i of customers having each possible valuation v_i is uncertain for the firm, and we assume it is also uncertain for each customer—except that each customer knows his own valuation. Anticipating that the firm will offer a declining sequence of prices $p_1, p_2, \ldots, p_k$ at successive times $t = 1, 2, \ldots, k$, therefore, each customer will assess some probability q_t that he will obtain an item if he waits until time t to purchase. Assume that the customers' valuations are statistically independent, so that this assessment is the same for each customer. To estimate this probability, we can take advantage of the fact that the firm's optimal strategy is to induce customers with the valuation v_t to purchase at time t if supplies are not yet exhausted. (This is also the socially efficient strategy, since it minimizes the risk that an unserved customer has a valuation higher than one served.) If the numbers n_i were known, then the probability of obtaining an item at time t would be $q_t = 1$ in the case that enough supply remains ($s > \sum_{i=1}^{t} n_i$), or $q_t = 0$ in the case that supply was previously exhausted ($s \le \sum_{i=1}^{t-1} n_i$), or

$$q_t = \frac{s - \sum_{i=1}^{t-1} n_i}{n_t}$$

Table 10.1 Example 10.3: The Optimal Pricing Strategy

t	v_t (\$)	p_t (\$)	q_t	$p_t q_t$ (\$)
1	1.00	.6335	0.5318	.3369
2	.90	.6334	.5316	.3367
3	.80	.6311	.5271	.3326
4	.70	.6199	.4945	.3065
5	.60	.6000	.3959	.2375

in the remaining case, assuming that limited supplies are rationed randomly among those customers offering to purchase at time t. In fact the numbers n_i are uncertain, but then q_t can be calculated as the expectation of the above formulas, using the probability distribution of the customers' valuations. Given these purchase probabilities, the firm's best option (as well as the efficient procedure) is to set the prices nearly high enough to make each customer indifferent whether to purchase at the intended time or to delay another period; thus,

$$[v_t - p_t]q_t = [v_t - p_{t+1}]q_{t+1} ,$$

where $q_{k+1} \equiv 0$ since the firm makes no offers after time k. But now we see that this series of relationships fully determines all the prices:

$$p_k = v_k, \qquad p_{k-1} = v_{k-1} + [p_k - v_{k-1}]q_k/q_{k-1} ,$$

et cetera. This shows that the firm's design again reduces solely to a single choice: here it is the optimal number k of periods in which to make offers. A profit-maximizing firm that can credibly commit in advance prefers to stop early, running some risk that not all units are sold, and leaving customers with low valuations no chance of purchasing. The efficient procedure sets $k = m$ and gives every customer a chance to purchase, which is also the predicted consequence if the firm cannot commit to stop early.

Example 10.3: Suppose that supply is $s = 10$ and there are $n = 20$ customers, each of whom has an equal chance of having any one of the valuations \$0, \$0.10, ..., \$1.00. In this case, if the firm's marginal cost is $c = 0.10 per item, then its optimal cutoff time is $k = 5$ and the prices and purchase probabilities are the ones shown in Table 10.1. Note that $P(q_t) = p_t q_t$ is effectively the tariff for the reliability q_t. The price schedule p_t for delivered service is never much higher than the optimal uniform price $p = 0.60 in this example because the independence of customers' valuations precludes any substantial uncertainty about aggregate demand. But aggregate demand uncertainty increases prices substantially if customers' valuations are even slightly correlated, and then the price schedule declines steeply. ◇

An auction is one way to implement nonlinear pricing for priority service with uncertain demand. The role of time is not essential, since each customer can simply announce which of the prices p_t he is willing to pay, and then the supply can be rationed immediately to those s customers offering the highest prices. Another method is spot pricing: each customer specifies the maximum price he is willing to pay, namely his valuation, and those s customers specifying the s highest prices are served at a price equal to the highest price offered by those customers not served, or the firm's reservation price if this is higher. If customers' valuations are statistically independent, then both methods yield the same expected profit for the firm, provided it uses an optimal reservation price—which in this case is just the optimal uniform price.

10.2   Ramsey pricing of priority service

In the previous section and the accompanying examples, each unit of potential demand was considered to be a separate customer—no account was taken of the number of units purchased by each actual customer. This approach excludes pricing policies that offer quantity discounts to large customers, as would be the case with a nonlinear tariff. In this section we take an alternative approach: the principles of Ramsey pricing are applied to derive an optimal two-dimensional nonlinear tariff that assigns marginal prices to increments of both quantity and quality (service reliability) for each customer. We address only the case of supply uncertainty, and exclude demand uncertainty in the interests of simplicity. As in Section 1, the probability that the supply exceeds s is denoted by $\bar{S}(s)$.

We use a simple model of demand in which each customer is identified with a one-dimensional index t that identifies his type.[3] The number of customers with types no greater than t is specified by a distribution function $F(t)$. A customer of type t obtains the gross benefit $U(q, t)$ from q units of service provided with reliability 1. The function U is assumed to be concave and increasing in q, and increasing in t; moreover, the marginal valuation $v(q, t) \equiv \partial U(q, t)/\partial q$ of a q-th unit is also increasing in t.

The purchase of a customer of type t can be represented by a (decreasing) distribution function $Q(r, t)$ indicating the number of units assigned reliabilities greater than r, or alternatively, by a (decreasing) distribution function $R(q, t)$ indicating the reliability assigned to the q-th unit. The customer's expected gross benefit that results from this selection can be represented as

$$V[R, t] = \int_0^\infty v(q, t)R(q, t)\, dq = \int_0^\infty \int_0^{R(q,t)} v(q, t)\, dr\, dq$$

3. The method applies also to the more general case that a customer's type is multidimensional, as shown in §8.4.

$$= \int_0^1 \int_0^{Q(r,t)} v(q,t)\, dq\, dr \,.$$

Correspondingly, the price paid for this purchase can be represented as

$$P[R] = \int_0^\infty \int_0^{R(q,t)} p(q,r)\, dr\, dq$$

$$= \int_0^1 \int_0^{Q(r,t)} p(q,r)\, dq\, dr \,,$$

where we interpret $p(q,r)$ as the marginal price charged for an increment (dq, dr) of both the quantity q and the reliability r. That is, in order to purchase the set

$$\mathcal{X}(t) = \{(x,r) \mid (\exists q) \quad (x,r) \le (q, R(q,t))\} \,,$$

the customer must purchase all the increments of quantity and reliability it comprises, as in §9. The resulting imputed net revenue contribution for the firm is calculated similarly as

$$\text{NR}[R,t] = \int_0^\infty \int_0^{R(q,t)} [p(q,r) - c(q) - \gamma(r)]\, dr\, dq \,,$$

where $c(q)$ is the specified marginal cost of a q-th unit actually supplied to the customer, and $\gamma(r)$ is the imputed marginal cost of the r-th increment in reliability for a unit of service. The imputed marginal cost $\gamma(r)$ of reliability r is obtained as the Lagrange multiplier attached to the feasibility constraint that

$$\int_0^\infty Q(r,t)\, dH(t) \le \bar{S}^{-1}(r) \,,$$

which assures that demand for units with reliabilities of r or more can actually be supplied with reliability r.

Replication of the usual methodology for deriving optimal Ramsey prices identifies the relevant demand profile $N(p; q, r)$ that specifies the demand at (q, r) for an increment (dq, dr) at the marginal price p; namely, $N(p; q, r)$ is the number of customers of types t for whom $v(q, t) \ge p$. Observe that in this case the demand profile is independent of the service reliability r, say $N(p, q)$ hereafter.[4] In terms

---

4. This feature occurs because we have not included customers' appliance selections in the model.

of this demand profile, the optimal Ramsey price for this increment is the value $p(q, r)$ of p for which

$$\alpha N(p, q) + \frac{\partial N(p, q)}{\partial p} \cdot [p - c(q) - \gamma(r)] = 0 \, ,$$

where again α is the relevant Ramsey number. This characterization is exactly analogous to the usual Ramsey condition except that it reflects the two-dimensional character of the marginal price schedule. In terms of the demand profile, the feasibility condition that determines the Lagrange multiplier can be written equivalently as

$$\int_0^\infty N(p(q, r), q) \, dq \leq \bar{S}^{-1}(r) \, .$$

The following example illustrates the application of this optimality condition.

Example: Joint pricing of quantity and reliability

We assume for this example that $v(q, t) = t - q$ and that $F(t) = t$. That is, type t's demand function for sure service is $D(p, t) = t - p$ and the types are uniformly distributed between zero and one; also, the population size is normalized to be 1. Assume further that the distribution function of supply per unit of potential demand is uniformly distributed, say $S(s) = s$, so that $\bar{S}(s) = 1 - s$ is the reliability with which s units (as a fraction of potential demand) can be supplied. The marginal cost of supply is taken to be a constant: $c(q) = c$.

First we illustrate the derivation of prices for ordinary priority service in which no account is taken of customers' differing purchase sizes. In this case the number of units of potential demand that have valuations exceeding p is

$$D(p) = \int_p^1 [t - p] \, dF(t) = \tfrac{1}{2}[1 - p]^2 \, .$$

The marginal price schedule is determined by the condition that $D(p(r)) = \bar{S}^{-1}(r)$, where $p(r)$ is the marginal price charged for the r-th increment of service reliability, for any unit of demand. Consequently,

$$p(r) = 1 - \sqrt{2[1 - r]} \, ,$$

for $r \geq 1/2$. If this schedule does not raise the required revenue, then the firm must impose an additional fixed fee that curtails the market penetration.

Next we derive the optimal price schedule $p(q, r)$ when quantities and service reliabilities are priced jointly. In this case the demand profile is

$$N(p, q) = \#\{t \mid t \geq p + q\} = 1 - p - q \, ,$$

or $N(p, q) = 0$ if $p + q \geq 1$. The optimal Ramsey price is therefore

$$p(q, r) = \beta[1 - q] + [1 - \beta][c(q) + \gamma(r)]$$

on the domain where $p(q, r) + q \leq 1$, where again $\beta = \alpha/[1 + \alpha]$. Assume now that the firm's marginal cost is constant, say $c(q) = c$. Faced with this price, the customer of type t chooses

$$Q(r, t) = \max \left\{ 0, t[1 + \alpha] - [c + \gamma(r) + \alpha] \right\}.$$

That is, for each r, $Q(r, t)$ is the maximum value of q for which $v(q, t) \geq p(q, r)$, so that the marginal benefit exceeds the price charged. Using this result we can determine the imputed marginal cost of reliability from the feasibility constraint. If we let $\delta(r) = \beta + [1 - \beta][c + \gamma(r)]$ then this calculation yields

$$\delta(r) = 1 - \sqrt{2[1 - r][1 - \beta]}.$$

Therefore, as a first approximation,

$$p(q, r) = \delta(r) - \beta q$$
$$= 1 - \sqrt{2[1 - \beta][1 - r]} - \beta q.$$

To derive the price schedule exactly, however, we must take account of various implicit constraints. First, we note that the imputed marginal cost of reliability $\gamma(r)$ is necessarily nonnegative, and zero where the feasibility constraint is not binding. Thus, the constraint $\gamma(r) \geq 0$ translates to $\delta(r) \geq \beta + [1 - \beta]c$, which in turn implies that the above formula for $\delta(r)$ holds only for

$$r \geq \rho(c, \beta) \equiv 1 - \tfrac{1}{2}[1 - \beta][1 - c]^2.$$

As we shall see below, $\rho(c, \beta) = \bar{S}^{-1}(\bar{Q})$, where $\bar{Q} = \tfrac{1}{2}[1 - \beta][1 - c]^2$ is the total number of units demanded with positive reliabilities; thus, $\rho(c, \beta)$ is the minimal reliability that can be provided for each demanded unit. In general, therefore,

$$\delta(r) = \begin{cases} 1 - \sqrt{2[1 - \beta][1 - r]} & \text{if } r \geq \rho(c, \beta), \\ \beta + [1 - \beta]c & \text{if } r \leq \rho(c, \beta). \end{cases}$$

Note that if $r < \rho(c, \beta)$ then $p(q, r) = p(q)$, which is precisely the marginal price schedule if supply were certain; similarly, $\bar{Q}$ is the total demand if supply were certain.

The marginal price schedule $p(q, r)$ must also not be less than the marginal cost c; consequently,

$$p(q, r) = \begin{cases} \delta(r) - \beta q & \text{if } q \leq [\delta(r) - c]/\beta, \\ c & \text{if } q \geq [\delta(r) - c]/\beta. \end{cases}$$

As we shall verify below, however, no customer is predicted to purchase units $q > [\delta(r) - c]/\beta$, and therefore it suffices to represent the marginal price schedule simply as

$$p(q, r) = \delta(r) - \beta q$$

as stated previously, but now using the correctly stated formula for $\delta(r)$.

An alternative representation of this price schedule specifies the marginal price $p(q \mid r)$ for the q-th unit, payable only contingent on delivery of that unit, for a unit obtained with total reliability r:

$$p(q \mid r) = \frac{1}{r} \int_0^r p(q, x) \, dx$$
$$= \Delta(r) - \beta q,$$

if $r \geq \rho \equiv \rho(c, \beta)$, where

$$\Delta(r) = 1 - [1 - \beta][1 - c]\rho/r + \frac{1}{r}\frac{2}{3}\sqrt{2[1 - \beta]}\left[(1 - r)^{3/2} - (1 - \rho)^{3/2}\right].$$

These results can be contrasted with the marginal price schedule obtained for ordinary priority service. If $\alpha = 0$ and therefore $\beta = 0$, then these two price schedules agree: $p(r) = p(q, r) = 1 - \sqrt{2[1 - r]}$ for $r \geq 1/2$ and no quantity discounts are offered. But if the firm's revenue constraint is binding, then generally the joint schedule $p(q, r)$ charges more for increments of reliability for each unit (that is, $\delta(r) > p(r)$), but allows quantity discounts. The basic motivation for this result is that the firm uses the marginal price schedule partly to raise revenues, rather than relying on fixed fees as in the case of ordinary priority service, and this increases the total surplus obtained. For reliabilities $r > \rho(c, \beta)$, the marginal price schedule is independent of the firm's marginal cost c except as it affects the Ramsey number. Although the two-dimensional price schedule for this example is additively separable, this is not a general feature; in any case, the two-dimensional schedule is never the sum of the two one-dimensional schedules unless the revenue constraint is not binding ($\beta = 0$) and in this case no quantity discounts are offered.

Customers' purchasing behavior is predicted to be the following in response to the optimal marginal price schedule. First, only those types $t > 1 - [1 - \beta][1 - c]$

purchase a first unit of quantity. For each unit purchased, each customer purchases a reliability no less than $\rho(c, \beta)$: for the q-th unit the selected reliability is

$$R(q, t) = \begin{cases} 1 - \dfrac{1}{2[1 - \beta]}[1 - t + (1 - \beta)q]^2 & \text{if } q \leq \bar{Q}(t), \\ 0 & \text{if } q > \bar{Q}(t), \end{cases}$$

which is just $R(q, t) = \rho(c, \beta)$ for the last unit

$$\bar{Q}(t) = 1 - c - \frac{1 - t}{1 - \beta}$$

with positive reliability purchased by type t. For the highest type, $R(0, 1) = 1$ and $\bar{Q}(1) = 1 - c$; in particular, type $t = 1$ purchases the last unit at the marginal cost c but selects only the reliability $\rho(c, \beta)$ for this last unit. Figure 10.5 shows $R(q, t)$ for several values of the type index t, assuming that $\beta = 1/2$ as in the monopoly case.

The net revenue obtained by the firm can be calculated to be

$$\overline{\text{NR}}(c, \beta) = \frac{1}{3}\beta[1 - \beta][1 - c]^3 + \frac{1}{40}[1 - \beta]^2[1 - 4\beta][1 - c]^5$$

$$= \rho(c, \beta)\text{NR}(c, \beta) + \frac{1}{60}[1 - \rho(c, \beta)][3 + 8\beta][1 - \beta][1 - c]^3,$$

where

$$\text{NR}(c, \beta) = \frac{1}{3}\beta[1 - \beta][1 - c]^3$$

is the net revenue if supply were unconstrained. Thus the last term above represents the premia (net of marginal cost) collected for units supplied with reliabilities exceeding the minimal level $\rho(c, \beta)$.

In Tables 10.2–5 we tabulate these results for several parameter values. Table 10.2 tabulates the firm's net revenue depending on the values of the marginal cost c and the parameter β derived from the Ramsey number. Note that $0 \leq \beta \leq 1/2$ by definition, with $\beta = 1/2$ yielding the maximum possible revenue as in the case of an unregulated profit-maximizing monopoly, and $\beta = 0$ yielding the minimum possible revenue as in the case of an efficient pricing scheme without any binding revenue requirement. Table 10.3 tabulates the marginal price $p(0, r) \equiv \delta(r)$ for the first unit, depending on β, and assuming that the marginal cost is $c = 0$ where this is applicable for small reliabilities $r < \rho(c, \beta)$, as indicated by an asterisk (*). Note that $p(0, r) = p(r)$ if $\beta = 0$, since in this case the marginal price of reliability is the same as in the case of ordinary priority service.

For the monopoly case ($\beta = 1/2$), Tables 10.4 and 10.5 tabulate the marginal price schedule $p(q, r)$ and the contingent marginal price schedule $p(q \mid r)$, assuming

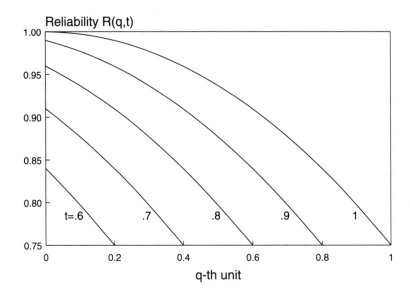

FIG. 10.5   The reliability $R(q, t)$ assigned to the q-th unit by type t when $\beta = 1/2$.

the marginal cost is $c = 0$. Note that the tabulation is only for $r \geq \rho(0, 1/2) = 3/4$ because every type $t \geq 1/2$ that purchases selects a reliability at least this high; also, prices for pairs (q, r) such that $r > 1 - \frac{1}{2}[1 - \beta]q^2$ in the lower left corner of these tables, marked with an asterisk (*), are not selected by any customer. The corresponding schedules for the efficient case ($\beta = 0$) are independent of the quantity q and are given by the first row of Table 10.3; in this case the least reliability selected is $\rho(0, 0) = 1/2$ and every type $t > 0$ purchases a positive quantity. In Table 10.5 it appears that the quantity discounts are appreciably larger than the discounts for accepting unreliable service; however, this is mainly a consequence of monopoly pricing ($\beta = 1/2$), since in the efficient case ($\beta = 0$) the quantity discounts are nil and it is solely the reliability discounts that matter. Figure 10.6 shows a graph of the contingent price $p(q \mid r)$ for three values of the reliability r

Table 10.2 Ramsey Pricing of Priority Service: The Firm's Net Revenue

β	$c = .5$	.4	.3	.2	.1	.0
0	.0008	.0019	.0042	.0082	.0148	.0250
.1	.0041	.0074	.0123	.0193	.0290	.0421
.2	.0068	.0118	.0188	.0284	.0408	.0565
.3	.0087	.0149	.0236	.0350	.0496	.0675
.4	.0098	.0169	.0265	.0392	.0551	.0746
.5	.0102	.0175	.0275	.0406	.0571	.0771

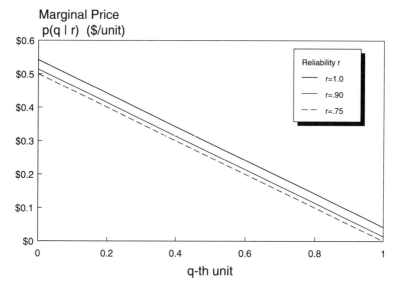

FIG. 10.6   The contingent marginal price $p(q \mid r)$ for $r = 0.75, 0.90, 1.0$.

in order to illustrate the relative magnitudes of the charges for delivered quantities as compared to the charges for reliability.

Summary

The ordinary formulation of priority service does not differentiate priority service charges according to the size of a customer's purchases. As a result, the marginal price schedule for increments of service reliability is determined entirely by demand and supply conditions. To meet a revenue constraint, therefore, the firm must ordinarily impose fixed fees that curtail market penetration.

Ramsey pricing is ordinarily applied to construct a nonlinear tariff allowing quantity discounts for customers making large purchases. Designing the tariff to maximize total surplus (subject to the firm's revenue requirement) has the advantage that it minimizes the inefficiencies caused by the firm's use of its monopoly

Table 10.3 Ramsey Pricing of Priority Service: The Schedule $p(0, r) \equiv \delta(r)$

β	$r = $ 1.0	.95	.90	.85	.80	.75	.70	.65	.60	.55	.50
0	1.000	.684	.553	.452	.368	.293	.225	.163	.106	.051	.000
.1	1.000	.700	.576	.480	.400	.329	.265	.206	.151	.100	*.100
.2	1.000	.717	.600	.510	.434	.368	.307	.252	.200	*.200	*.200
.3	1.000	.735	.626	.542	.471	.408	.352	.300	*.300	*.300	*.300
.4	1.000	.755	.654	.576	.510	.452	.400	*.400	*.400	*.400	*.400
.5	1.000	.776	.684	.613	.553	.500	*.500	*.500	*.500	*.500	*.500

Table 10.4 Ramsey Pricing of Priority Service: The Monopoly Schedule $p(q,r)$ for $c = 0, \beta = 1/2$

q	r = 1.0	.95	.90	.85	.80	.75
0	1.000	.776	.684	.613	.553	.500
.1	*.950	.726	.634	.563	.503	.450
.2	*.900	.676	.584	.513	.453	.400
.3	*.850	.626	.534	.463	.403	.350
.4	*.800	.576	.484	.413	.353	.300
.5	*.750	*.526	.434	.363	.303	.250
.6	*.700	*.476	.384	.313	.253	.200
.7	*.650	*.426	*.334	.263	.203	.150
.8	*.600	*.376	*.284	*.213	.153	.100
.9	*.550	*.326	*.234	*.163	*.103	.050
1.0	*.500	*.276	*.184	*.113	*.053	.000

power to raise sufficient revenues. In particular, higher marginal charges substitute for the fixed fee that would otherwise be necessary, and this tends to increase total surplus.

Ramsey pricing can also be applied to construct prices for quantity and reliability increments jointly. When this approach is taken to the design of priority service, it results in a nonlinear tariff in which the prices of increments in either quantity or reliability can depend on the customer's selection of both attributes. Generally, this recognition of customers' purchase sizes in the specification of priority prices enables attainment of greater efficiency, at least as measured by consumers' or total surplus. The example illustrates the way in which the optimal prices depend jointly on both dimensions of a customer's demand. In particular, the marginal charge for service reliability is higher, but this is partly compensated by quantity discounts.

Table 10.5 Example: Ramsey Pricing of Priority Service: The Monopoly Schedule $p(q \mid r)$ for $c = 0, \beta = 1/2$

q	r = 1.0	.95	.90	.85	.80	.75
0	.542	.525	.514	.506	.502	.500
.1	*.492	.475	.464	.456	.452	.450
.2	*.442	.425	.414	.406	.402	.400
.3	*.392	.375	.364	.356	.352	.350
.4	*.342	.325	.314	.306	.302	.300
.5	*.292	*.275	.264	.256	.252	.250
.6	*.242	*.225	.214	.206	.202	.200
.7	*.192	*.175	*.164	.156	.152	.150
.8	*.142	*.125	*.114	*.106	.102	.100
.9	*.092	*.075	*.064	*.056	*.052	.050
1.0	*.042	*.025	*.014	*.006	*.002	.000

10.3   Nonlinear pricing in a priority queuing system

The formulation in previous sections ignores the time required to serve a customer. Service is interpreted as a flow, so that at each instant each unit of a customer's load obtains instant service. Such a formulation is useful in contexts such as electric power and telecommunications where a customer's value of service over an interval of time can often be represented as approximately proportional to the duration of the interval. This approximation is accurate for end uses such as electric power for heating and air conditioning, or telephone service for voice conversations and data transmission.

In other contexts, however, service values are associated with specific tasks or jobs that require varying durations to complete. This can be the case for electric power if it is used to execute a task such as a manufacturing operation, for communication if tasks are transmissions of messages, for transportation if tasks are deliveries, or an airport if tasks are takeoffs and landings. A pure example is a job shop in which service values are associated with completed jobs but the durations required to complete various jobs differ substantially. Familiar examples of job shops include machine-tool operations and vehicle repair facilities, in which capacity is represented by skilled labor; and computer systems, in which capacity is represented by the speed of the central processing unit.

This section describes an application of nonlinear pricing to priority service adapted specifically to the allocation of processing in a computer system with a single processing unit. The formulation emphasizes the stochastic features of demand; supply is fixed except that jobs' service times are stochastic. Customers' demands are represented by a stationary stochastic process in which jobs arrive randomly and with differing service values, processing requirements, and delay costs. Jobs are queued for service according to priorities chosen by customers. The prices charged for processing under the various priorities affect a customer's decision about whether to submit a job for service, and the priority selected.

Our aim is to demonstrate the analysis of a basic model. We emphasize the intrinsic role of nonlinear pricing when processing times affect the efficient service priorities. The analysis is limited to maximization of total surplus; Ramsey pricing is omitted here.

Formulation

Consider a system serving many different customers, each of whom imposes service requirements that are sufficiently small relative to the capacity of the system that each one can ignore the effect of his jobs on the operating performance of the system. Each job is characterized by a triplet (v, t, c) comprising its service value v, its service time t, and the cost c per unit time of delay. Thus, if completion of the job is delayed by d in addition to the required duration t, and a price p is charged for service, then the net value obtained by the customer is $v - c[d + t] - p$. Hereafter, we use an hour as the unit of time.

When submitting a job for service, each customer's information consists only of knowing its actual service value v and which one of several possible types it is. For simplicity, the set of possible types is assumed to be finite and we use $i = 1, \ldots, n$ to index the n possible types. Jobs of type i have four characteristics:

1. Jobs of type i arise at an average rate of r_i jobs per hour.
2. The proportion of type-i jobs with service values no more than v is given by the distribution function $F_i(v)$.
3. Each type-i job requires a service time that is random and distributed according to a distribution with the average service time t_i.
4. For a type-i job the cost per hour of delay in completing service is c_i.

Assume that the distribution function F_i has a positive density on an interval of possible service values. Moreover, assume that the stochastic process of job arrivals and service times is such that the aggregate processes of arrivals of different types are independent and stationary, with Poisson distributions. Service times are likewise independent, stationary, exponentially distributed, and identically distributed within types. Finally, for simplicity assume also that the marginal cost of completing each job is zero.

If service is priced in such a way that only those type-i jobs with service values exceeding v_i are submitted, then a proportion $1 - F_i(v_i)$ of the potential demand for type-i jobs will be submitted and eventually completed. Since potential type-i jobs arise at the rate of r_i jobs per hour, they will be submitted at the average rate $s_i = r_i[1 - F_i(v_i)]$. It is convenient hereafter to use this relationship to interpret the cutoff service value v_i as a function of the submission rate s_i. Thus, service values from completed jobs of type i will accumulate at the average rate of

$$V_i(s_i) = r_i \int_{v_i}^{\infty} x \, dF_i(x)$$

dollars per hour, interpreted as a function of the submission rate s_i. Conversely, from the accumulation-rate function V_i and the submission rate s_i one can calculate the cutoff service value via $v_i = V_i'(s_i)$.

We say, therefore, that a pricing scheme is optimal if it maximizes the average rate of aggregate net value accumulation in a steady state of the system:

$$\sum_{i=1}^{n} \{V_i(s_i) - c_i L_i(s)\} \, ,$$

where $L_i(s)$ is the average number of type-i jobs in the system (either waiting in queues or being served) when $s = (s_1, \ldots, s_n)$ is the list of average submission rates for all the types. As mentioned previously, this formulation of the total surplus measure assumes that the marginal cost of service is nil.

We use two basic propositions from queuing theory:[5]

- For any fixed submission rates, average delay costs are minimized by serving jobs according to a priority order in which type i is served before type j if $c_i/t_i > c_j/t_j$.

Assume hereafter that $c_i/t_i > c_{i+1}/t_{i+1}$ so that the types are numbered in order of their priorities.

- In a steady state of the system, $L_i(s) = s_i W_i(s)$, where $W_i(s)$ is the average total delay (waiting plus service) time of type-i jobs. Moreover, $W_i(s) = q_i(s) + t_i$, where the time $q_i(s)$ spent waiting in the queue for service is (assuming as above that the types are numbered so that type i has the i-th priority service order):

$$q_i(s) = a_{i-1} a_i \sum_{j=1}^{n} s_j t_j^2 ,$$

using $a_i \equiv 1/[1 - \sum_{j=1}^{i} s_j t_j]$ and $a_0 \equiv 1$.

The first proposition establishes the optimal priority scheme. The only remaining task, therefore, is to establish how the prices are designed to ensure that customers' responses lead to the optimal submission rates. The second proposition, known as Little's Theorem, states that it is immaterial whether we count the rate that delay costs accumulate for jobs in the system at each instant, or separately count the duration until completion of each job.

The formula above for the i-th priority queuing delay $q_i(s)$ can be used to calculate the optimal submission rates: they are the ones that maximize the average rate of aggregate net value accumulation,

$$\sum_{i=1}^{n} \{V_i(s_i) - c_i s_i [q_i(s) + t_i]\} .$$

Henceforth, let s° denote the list of optimal submission rates.

An optimal nonlinear price system

We consider a pricing scheme in which each job is charged according to the priority selected by the customer and the actual time required to service the job, excluding

5. The service process is assumed to be nonpreemptive; that is, once a job's service begins it is not interrupted.

the waiting time before servicing begins. Thus, let $P_k(t)$ be the charge imposed for a k-th priority job that takes a duration t to service.

Then a customer with a type-i job having a service value v prefers to submit it if its net value is positive when it is assigned the priority that yields the least total cost of charges and delays. That is, the job is submitted if $v > v_i$, where

$$ v_i = \min_k \left(E\{P_k(t) \mid i\} + c_i[q_k(s) + t_i] \right), $$

and the expected charge $E\{P_k(t) \mid i\}$ is calculated conditional on the actual type i of the job. Optimality requires that the resulting list of submission rates is $s = s^\circ$, and this in turn requires for each type i that

$$ v_i = V_i'(s_i^\circ) $$

and the priority that achieves the minimum cost must be $k = i$.

A pricing scheme that produces optimal submission rates and priority selections has the quadratic form
$$ P_k(t) = A_k t + \tfrac{1}{2} B t^2 , $$

where if $d_k = s_k^\circ c_k q_k(s^\circ)$ is the expected delay cost from queuing for the k-th priority then $A_n = d_n a_n$ and

$$ A_k = d_k a_k + \sum_{j=k+1}^{n} d_j[a_{j-1} + a_j], $$

$$ B = \sum_{j=1}^{n} d_j / \sum_{j=1}^{n} s_j^\circ t_j^2 . $$

Although we omit the demonstration that this pricing scheme suffices, it is worth remarking that it consists of three steps:

1. The expected price for a type-i job submitted with priority i satisfies

$$ \bar{P}_i \equiv E\{P_i(t) \mid i\} = A_i t_i + B t_i^2 , $$

$$ = \sum_{j=1}^{n} s_j^\circ t_j \frac{\partial W_j(s^\circ)}{\partial s_i} , $$

as required to ensure that the induced cutoff service value v_i produces the optimal submission rates.

2. A type-i job is better submitted as priority i than $i + 1$; namely,

$$\bar{P}_i + c_i q_i < E\{P_{i+1}(t) \mid i\} + c_i q_{i+1},$$

and similarly priority i is better than $i - 1$.
3. If a type-i job is better submitted as priority i than j, and better submitted as priority j than k, then it is better submitted as priority i than k; that is, "better than" is a transitive relation.

Steps 2 and 3 can be combined to show that a type-i job is best submitted as priority i, as required. It is important to note that it is not sufficient to charge the expected price $\bar{P}_i$ for priority i—because this would fail to ensure that a type-i job is best submitted as priority i, as can be seen in Step 2.[6]

This pricing scheme shares a feature common to all priority pricing implementations that achieve the maximum total surplus, including the one in Section 1: the scheme charges the expected cost imposed on other jobs. As shown by Mendelson and Whang (1990), the linear and quadratic terms are the expected delay costs imposed on other jobs before and after this job starts its service; further, the first and second terms of A_k reflect the costs imposed on other jobs of the same and inferior priorities. From the viewpoint of nonlinear pricing, the salient feature is the role of the quadratic term. While one job is being serviced it delays all those jobs that arrive during its service period. The expected number of type-i jobs arriving during a service of duration of t is $s_i t$ and on average each of these is delayed by $t/2$; hence, the expected delay costs are proportional to t^2, which is the source of the quadratic term.[7]

A significant implication of the analysis in this section is that nonlinear pricing of service times is an intrinsic feature of an efficient implementation of priority service. When service times are short or service is continuous, pricing of service times may be inconsequential. But if service times can be long and other jobs can arrive in the interim then the delay costs imposed on other customers can be significant. Further, the expectation of these costs is fundamentally nonlinear and therefore the price schedule is also nonlinear.

10.4   Summary

This chapter has considered two examples of the methods of multidimensional pricing developed in §9. Both pertain to pricing service priorities in capacity-

---

6. However, if jobs' types were observable by the system manager, and assigned their corresponding priorities (rather than by the customer), then charging the expected price would suffice to ensure that the type-i jobs submitted would be the ones with service values exceeding the optimal cutoff service value. This is sometimes the case in, say, a machine shop where the manager can observe the work required to complete a job.

7. Actually, additional jobs are delayed as well because, for example, all priority 1 jobs that arrive before the end of the next "busy period" in which priority 1 jobs are serviced will also be delayed.

constrained systems. The first is adapted to contexts such as electric power in which demands are served immediately if at all; and the second, computer systems in which jobs are queued in order of assigned priority and time of arrival.

In a power system, if no quantity discounts are provided then the price schedule for priority service is determined entirely by demand and supply conditions. That is, the reliability of supply sufficient to serve customers paying the marginal price $p(r)$ must be r. If profits from this schedule are insufficient to meet the revenue requirement of a regulated utility, then an access or demand charge is necessary. However, higher revenue requirements can also be met with Ramsey pricing that provides quantity discounts in combination with priority service. The design of this price schedule follows the principles of multidimensional pricing outlined in §9.2. In the example studied in Section 2, the price schedule is additively separable; that is, the contingent marginal price payable on delivery for a q-th unit is the difference between a reliability charge and a quantity discount.

Prices in a priority queuing system introduce the additional aspect that the service time is observable ex post. The tariff in this case comprises a priority-dependent charge proportional to the actual or expected service time, and in addition a non-linear term dependent on the actual service time. The nonlinear contingent charge provides customers with incentives to assign their jobs efficiently. In particular, charging the expectation of the tariff for the priority selected is insufficient because it presumes the job's priority is efficient. In the example, a quadratic term suffices. This scheme is analogous to the item-assignment formulation in §9.4 except that here we exclude quantity discounts to focus on the role of charges contingent on the actual service time revealed ex post.

11

CAPACITY PRICING

More elaborate multidimensional tariffs are used when firms incur costs for capacity installed to meet customers' peak loads. Prominent examples are the telecommunications, power, and transport industries, which require substantial investments in durable capital equipment committed for long durations. Provision of capacity is important in many labor-intensive service industries too; repair shops, for instance, meet requirements on peak days by employing sufficient repairmen, but some of these are idle on offpeak days. In these industries, customers' demands vary over time, whereas capacity is comparatively stable. Moreover, the product or service is difficult or expensive to store, so inventories cannot smooth the firm's production rate.

The result of these features is that a customer's usage is not synonymous with the capacity requirement it imposes on the firm. Some capacity is idle at offpeak times. Tariffs are therefore designed to account separately for the costs of usage and capacity. A well-designed tariff provides incentives for customers to curtail loads in peak periods and thereby reduce idle capacity at other times.

Section 1 provides further background about industries affected by peak loads and Section 2 reviews two pricing policies used in these industries. A formulation in terms of multidimensional pricing is presented in Section 3 and then adapted to the construction of nonlinear tariffs for usage and capacity charges jointly.

11.1 Background

In industries subject to peak loads, portions of capacity are idle during offpeak periods. In order to economize on idle capacity, therefore, firms install various types of equipment. Base loads are met with equipment having a high cost of acquisition but a low cost of operation, whereas peak loads are met with additional equipment having a lower cost of acquisition and a higher cost of operation. The lower acquisition cost of the peaking equipment brings the advantage that its imputed cost of idleness in offpeak periods is lower. The marginal cost of operation therefore varies as demand varies: when demand is high the marginal operating cost is the higher operating cost of the peaking equipment. To take account of the differing capital and operating costs of the various equipment, tariffs recover these two cost components separately.

A variety of pricing schemes are used in these industries. One form is demand-contingent *spot pricing*, in which the price (a uniform price per unit of service) is varied continually in response to changing demand conditions to keep demand within the limits of supply, or if there is excess capacity, to track the marginal operating cost. A variant of spot pricing is *peakload pricing*, in which the firm varies the price over time according to a previously announced schedule that anticipates periods when demand is likely to be high or low; more recently this is called *real-time pricing* when the prices in various periods of the day are announced shortly before, usually the day before. Both of these are used by EDF, as described in §2.2: the critical-times option imposes higher energy charges whenever the utility announces on short notice that supplies are scarce, whereas the empty-hours option offers lower rates in night-time hours when demand is expected to be less. This form of pricing emphasizes a short-term response to demand and supply conditions, and is characterized by uniform prices that vary over time.

A second form of pricing takes a longer view and creates incentives for customers that mimic the firm's cost structure. An example is the system of capacity and usage prices commonly used by electric utilities in the United States, as well as in the basic option of EDF's blue tariff: each customer pays for capacity a "demand charge" that (for industrial customers at least) is based on the customer's annual peak load, plus for usage a price for energy that may depend on the time of use. A more elaborate scheme is the Wright tariff used occasionally in the United States and prominently in the yellow and blue tariffs offered by EDF to industrial customers. This tariff charges a periodic fixed fee for each unit of power in the peak load, and an energy charge proportional to the duration that this unit is used; both vary according to the duration that the unit is demanded during the year.

Time-of-use or realtime tariffs are adapted to the firm's short-run costs, whereas Wright tariffs are adapted to the long-run cost structure of the utility. That is, a unit of power (1 kW) supplied for a specified duration (hours/year) in the long run costs the utility the capital cost of one unit of generating capacity and an energy cost proportional to the duration and the operating cost of that type of generator. The type of generator scheduled to provide this power depends on the duration of the load expected each year of the equipment's operating lifetime. Thus, the Wright tariff provides incentives to customers that in the long run parallel the costs anticipated by the firm. In the short term, however, the energy charges imposed by a Wright tariff may differ from spot prices if the customer's pattern of usage differs from the pattern of aggregate demand.[1] A simpler variant of the Wright tariff is the *loadfactor tariff*, which allows a customer with a high load factor

---

1. There are numerous other sources of divergence: trend, cyclic, and stochastic variabilities in demand and operating costs (such as fuel); and some installed capacity units that are not part of an optimal configuration for the current demand.

(the ratio of average to peak load) a discount on energy charges to reflect the fact that the utility can serve such a customer with more baseload generating sources.

A third form uses an uncontingent uniform price for service and then rations customers via random selection, or first-come first-served selection via queues, or via designated priorities as in the case of priority service. As mentioned in §10, an efficient scheme of priority service amounts essentially to assessments of priority charges that are the expectations of the anticipated charges that would accrue for service of comparable reliability under either spot pricing or a Wright tariff.

We demonstrate in this chapter that to a substantial degree all these forms of pricing are special cases of a general scheme. There is, however, an important proviso. This chapter assumes that sufficient capacity is reserved to meet each customer's load individually. This proviso is satisfied when customers' demands are synchronized, so that their peak loads occur simultaneously and the total equipment required is simply the sum of the amounts of equipment needed to service each customer. In the case of electric power, some industrial and commercial customers have peak loads synchronous with the system peak, and in some regions a large portion of residential and commercial loads peak simultaneously because they reflect heating or air-conditioning uses that are mutually dependent on the daily and seasonal cycles of temperature and weather. In practice, however, customers' loads are substantially asynchronous and therefore equipment that is idle for one customer can be used to serve another; thus, the total capacity requirement is less than the sum of the customers' peak loads. An examination of this more complicated topic is outside the scope of the present exposition.

Our task in this chapter is therefore to describe the construction of tariffs for the case that capacity must be provided to meet each customer's peak load. Such a tariff provides incentives for customers to limit their peak loads to the extent implied by the firm's costs of providing the requisite capacity.

11.2   Cost recovery of load-duration demands

This section continues from §9.1. We elaborate further the role of purchase sets represented by load-duration curves, using the electric power industry as the prime example.

A customer's demand varies over time, but in fact time itself is usually not the relevant dimension on which to represent the variability of demand. Most utilities describe a customer's demand pattern in terms of its *load-duration* profile. Recall that the load-duration profile specifies the longest duration $H(x)$ (measured as the fraction of time over, say, a year) that the customer's load exceeds each possible power level x. Alternatively, the inverse function $L(h)$ indicates that the load exceeds $L(h)$ for a duration h; or, it specifies the smallest load $L(h)$ that is demanded for a duration no more than h. Both H and L are nonincreasing functions; the peak load is $L(0)$ and the base load is $L(1)$. The customer's average energy consumption per hour is the area under either function.

An equivalent geometric description is introduced in §9: a customer's demand is the purchase set containing the points circumscribed by the load-duration curve. Thus, a customer demands a set consisting of all the points with nonnegative coordinates that lie below a decreasing load-duration curve. A typical point, interpreted as a small square of increments, in such a set indicates a demand for a marginal unit of power for a marginal unit of duration.

To see how such a set is actually measured or metered by the utility, and how charges are imposed to recover total costs, we illustrate two idealized tariffs that correspond approximately to the time-of-use and Wright tariffs implemented in practice.

- For the time-of-use tariff, suppose that the utility charges $P(h, q)$ for q kW in hour h of the year; or equivalently, charges a corresponding marginal price $p(h, x)$ for each x-th kWh in hour h, as shown in Figure 11.1. In this case, the utility installs a meter that measures the customer's actual load $L(h)$ in each hour h. To recover its operating costs the utility collects an energy charge $\sum_h P(h, L(h))$ for the year's service. And, to recover its capital costs of capacity, the utility imposes a demand charge $P_o(q^*)$ that depends on the customer's peak load $q^* = \max_h \{L(h)\}$ during the year. Thus, a time-of-use tariff amounts to an ordinary nonlinear tariff for the demand charge plus, for each hour during the year, an additional nonlinear tariff (depending on the power level) for the energy charge.

- For the Wright tariff, a meter records for each power level x the number of hours the customer demands an x-th kW; that is, the number of hours the load is x or more. Thus, the hourly profile $L(h)$ of demand is recorded in the alternative form $H(x)$ indicating the number of hours that an x-th kW was used by the customer. The Wright tariff then collects a demand charge $\hat{p}_o(x)$ for the x-th unit (if it is used at all) plus a nonlinear tariff $\hat{P}(H(x), x)$ depending on the number of hours it is used; or equivalently a corresponding marginal price $\hat{p}(h, x)$ for the h-th hour of usage of the x-th kW, as depicted in Figure 11.2. The effective demand charge is $\hat{P}_o(q^*)$, corresponding to the marginal demand charges $\hat{p}_o(x) = \hat{P}_o'(x)$ for $x \leq q^*$. The total bill is the sum of these demand and energy charges for all the units used. Thus, a Wright tariff amounts to a demand charge based on the maximum power plus, for each unit of power, a nonlinear tariff (depending on hours of usage) for the energy charge.

The demand charges under these two tariffs are equivalent if $P_o(x) = \hat{P}_o(x)$. Under the time-of-use tariff, the energy charge for an incremental x-th kW in hour h is $p(h, x)$, whereas under the Wright tariff the energy charge for the x-th kW for an incremental h-th hour is $\hat{p}(h, x)$. These two energy charges are equivalent

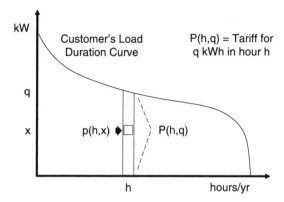

FIG. 11.1   Time-of-use tariff charges $p(h, x)$ for x-th kWh in hour h.

if p and $\hat{p}$ are the same functions when hours are measured equivalently under the two tariffs. Consequently, we next establish what this equivalent system of measurement is, and as we shall see, it depends on the utility's cost structure and the customer's load-duration curve, which together determine the utility's optimal investment in generating sources.

Suppose that the utility can produce a kW of power from any one of several generating sources indexed by $i = 1, \ldots, m$. For each unit of generating capacity the i-th source has a fixed cost F_i, measured in \$/kW, and an operating cost c_i, measured in \$/kW/hour or \$/kWh. Assume that a source with a higher index has a higher fixed cost and a lower operating cost; moreover, each source is the least cost way of producing a kW for some interval of operating duration. Thus, source $i = m$ is best for long-duration base loads and source $i = 1$ is best for short-duration peak loads. An example is shown in Figure 11.3, which supposes that

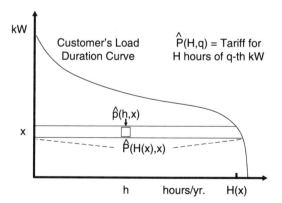

FIG. 11.2   Wright tariff charges $\hat{p}(h, x)$ for h-th hour of x-th kW.

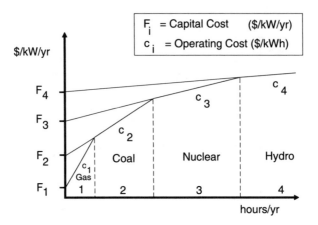

FIG. 11.3   Capital and operating costs for four types of generators.

gas, coal, nuclear, and hydro generation are cost efficient for successively longer durations.

Let H_{i-1} and H_i be the shortest and longest durations for which source i has the least cost, where $H_0 = 0$ and $H_m = 1$. In actual operation these generating sources are turned on in the merit order $i = m, m-1, \ldots$ until the current load is covered, since this is the order that minimizes operating costs. If the i-th source is the last one turned on, then the current marginal cost of energy is c_i.

To select the optimal capacity configuration to serve a customer's load, the utility uses the load-duration curve to identify the number of kWs used for durations between H_{i-1} and H_i; this is then the number of kWs of the i-th source to be installed. That is, if $L(H_{i-1}) - L(H_i)$ kWs of the i-th source are used (plus an additional $L(H_m)$ kWs of the m-th source to cover the base load), then the utility's cost of serving the customer is minimized. Thus, if we define $L_i = L(H_i)$ then the marginal cost of power is c_i whenever the current load is between L_{i-1} and L_i. An example is shown in Figure 11.4, which along the duration dimension shows the efficient generating source, and along the power dimension it shows the capacity of each type that efficiently serves the load-duration curve $L(h)$.

This construction follows exactly the design of a Wright tariff. For an x-th kW in the interval $L_i < x < L_{i-1}$, the marginal cost of capacity is the fixed cost F_i of a kW of capacity of the i-th source that is cost-effective for serving this kW, and the marginal cost of energy is the operating cost c_i. A Wright tariff with

$$\hat{p}_o(x) = F_i \,,$$

$$\hat{p}(h, x) = c_i \qquad \text{if} \quad L_i < x < L_{i-1} \,,$$

exactly recovers the utility's cost. Figure 11.5 shows how successively higher

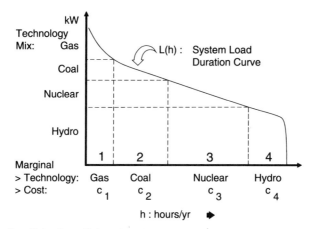

FIG. 11.4   Cost-efficient allocation of capacity among types of generators.

power increments are charged higher marginal costs per hour, corresponding to the type of generator assigned to meet that increment of capacity.

Alternatively, the Wright tariff can be implemented by charging the peaking generator's fixed cost $(\hat{p}_o(x) = F_1)$ for the capacity unit and then for usage charging c_i for hour h if this hour lies in the interval $H_{i-1} \leq h \leq H_i$ when the i-th source is the most expensive generator operating.

An equivalent time-of-use tariff is constructed as follows.[2] Each hour h in which the customer's load $L(h)$ is in the range $L_i < L(h) < L_{i-1}$ is identified with the source $i(h) = i$ that is the marginal generator in that hour. The marginal cost of energy is therefore $c_{i(h)}$, but in addition the inframarginal units of power are generated with the sources $m, m - 1, \ldots, i(h)$. The utility has two options

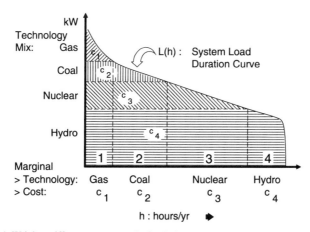

FIG. 11.5   A Wright tariff recovers costs via fixed charges per kW and marginal charges per kWh, each depending on the generator used.

2. The following construction can be derived by integrating by parts in the previous formula for the Wright tariff.

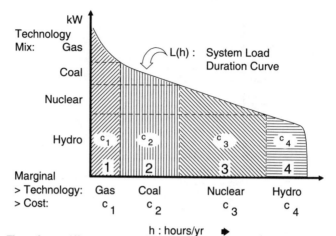

FIG. 11.6   Time-of-use tariff recovers costs via time-of-use energy charges depending on the marginal source of generation.

to recover these costs. One tariff charges $P(h, q)$ in hour h that accumulates the marginal costs of energy from the various sources used,

$$P(h, L(h)) = \sum_{j=i(h)+1}^{m} c_j[L_{j-1} - L_j] + c_{i(h)}[L(h) - L_{i(h)}],$$

plus an annual demand charge to recover the fixed costs of the capacity installed to meet the peak load. An alternative scheme collects a demand charge $q^* F_1$, based on the capital cost of a peaking generator, and then charges for all energy units a uniform price equal to the marginal cost $c_{i(h)}$ in that hour, as shown in Figure 11.6. This scheme corresponds most closely to the standard implementations of peakload pricing.[3]

These various ways of pricing to recover costs are all essentially equivalent provided short and long run considerations coincide for the firm and customers. A common feature is that they charge for units of energy according to one component of the tariff and for maximum demand according to another. In other industries as well, tariffs are often separated into usage and capacity components, even if cost recovery is not the only motive. The tariff for usage has the form studied previously in §9. The next section describes how a nonlinear tariff for the capacity charges is constructed.

11.3   Pricing load-duration demands

Recall from §9 that the capacity required to serve a purchase set Q is denoted $[Q]$. In reverse, given a capacity q the purchase set that includes all increments

3. Regulatory agencies prefer this form because usage charges can be based on actual marginal operating costs even if the configuration of generating sources is not optimal.

$x \leq q$ is denoted $[q]$; thus $q = [[q]]$. Generally this capacity is a list of the capacities required to serve the maximum demands along the several dimensions of the purchase set.

How many of these dimensions are actually relevant depends on the context. In the context of electric power there are customarily two dimensions, duration and power, but power capacity is the only one for which charges are imposed; that is, there is usually no access charge that depends on the duration of positive loads. This reflects the fact that the duration of the power load usually has no benefit in itself to customers, imposes no significant extra cost on the utility, and is not monitored. In the case of leased equipment (vehicles, PBXs, copiers, printers, computers), however, usage charges are usually combined with capacity charges reflecting the number of machines, the duration of the lease, and occasionally also the cumulative duration of actual operation. We therefore present first the case that demand charges are imposed only for a single capacity, interpreted as the maximum power load, and then the general case that demand charges are imposed on several capacities.

The presentation is simplified further by first considering only the case that usage charges are specified exogenously and it is only the design of the capacity charges that is to be optimized. Later we address a special case in which it is easy to optimize jointly the usage and capacity charges.

Demand charges for power capacity

When demand charges are imposed, a customer's purchase set Q typically limits the maximum power demand in order to avoid demand charges for capacity that the customer would use only for a short duration. Thus, the purchase set is flat along the boundary where the maximum power load is demanded. It is therefore convenient to represent the customer's choice by a capacity $(1, q) \equiv [Q]$ in which 1 indicates that the customer is hooked up for the full duration of the year with a power capacity q. Further, within this capacity the customer decides which increments $x \in [1, q]$ *not* to purchase. Thus, the customer chooses a maximum power level q and the set $R = [1, q] \setminus Q$ of increments available within the chosen capacity that are relinquished; that is, not purchased, so $Q = [1, q] \setminus R$.

Suppose that the usage charge for the increment x is $p(x)$. That is, if $x = (h, \ell)$ indicates an ℓ-th kW of power in hour h then $p(x)$ is the marginal price of the ℓ-th kW in hour h according to a time-of-use tariff, or the marginal price of the h-th hour of the ℓ-th kW according to a Wright tariff. Denoting the customer's benefit from this increment by $v(x)$, a repetition of the analysis of multidimensional tariffs in §9 indicates that the customer prefers to relinquish the increment x if $v(x) < p(x)$.

The design of the tariff for demand charges can therefore be posed in terms of the following ingredients.

- A typical customer is described by a pair $\langle U, v \rangle$ of benefit functions, depending on the customer's type t, specifying that the benefit from purchasing all of the energy $[1, q]$ available within the power capacity q is $U(q, t)$, and the marginal benefit of each increment x is $v(x, t)$. In the special case studied in §9, for instance, these are related by

$$U(q, t) = \int_{[1,q]} v(x, t) \, dx \,,$$

  due to the assumption there that customers benefit from usage but not from capacity per se.
- Similarly, the firm's costs are described by a pair $\langle C, c \rangle$ in which $C(q)$ is the cost of providing $[1, q]$ and $c(x)$ is the marginal cost of the increment x. For the firm, typically $C(q) > \int_{[1,q]} c(x) \, dx$ due to the costs of providing capacity.[4]
- Allowing equal generality in the specification of the tariff, it is described by a pair $\langle P, p \rangle$ in which $P(q)$ is the charge for the potential usage $[1, q]$ and $p(x)$ is the marginal charge for an increment x. Typically $P(q) > \int_{[1,q]} p(x) \, dx$ due to capacity charges.

Hereafter, let $p_2(q) \equiv P'(q)$ denote the marginal price of the q-th increment of power capacity; that is, the marginal price along the vertical dimension indicating power capacity. Similarly, $c_2(q) \equiv C'(q)$ is the marginal cost. Observe, however, that the actual demand charge for the q-th increment of capacity is not $p_2(q)$, which includes usage charges for all hours; rather, it is

$$\hat{p}_2(q) = p_2(q) - \int_0^1 p(h, q) \, dh \,,$$

that is ordinarily interpreted as the demand charge for a capacity increment unaccompanied by free usage.

Combining these ingredients, a customer t's net benefit from choosing the power capacity q and relinquishing the portion $R \subset [1, q]$ is

$$U(q, t) - P(q) - \int_R [v(x, t) - p(x)] \, dx \,,$$

and q and R are chosen to maximize this net benefit given the tariff offered by the firm. In particular, the choice of R, say $R(q, t)$, is fully determined as above by

$$R(q, t) = R(t) \cap [1, q] \,, \qquad \text{where} \qquad R(t) = \{ x \mid v(x, t) < p(x) \} \,.$$

---

4. Note that $c(x)$ need not be actual operating cost: it can represent the opportunity cost of selling the power to another customer or to a power pool, if customers' loads are not synchronous.

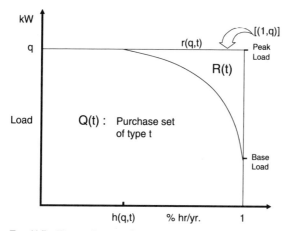

FIG. 11.7   The purchase set $Q(t)$ and the potential capacity $[1, q]$.

The firm's net revenue from this customer is

$$P(q) - C(q) - \int_R [p(x) - c(x)]\, dx\,.$$

It is useful also to define

$$r(q, t) = R(t) \cap \{x \in [1, q] \mid x_2 = q\}$$

which is the slice of $[1, q]$ that the customer relinquishes among those increments for which the power level is exactly q. Typically $r(q, t)$ is an interval $h(q, t) \leq h \leq 1$ of offpeak hours in which the customer's marginal benefits are insufficient to recoup the marginal prices of energy. These various components are depicted in Figure 11.7.

   To construct the demand profile for power capacity increments, we proceed as follows. Type t prefers to purchase the q-th increment of power capacity if the net benefit from this increment is positive:

$$v_2(q, t) - p_2(q) - \int_{r(q,t)} [v(x, t) - p(x)]\, dh \geq 0\,,$$

where $x = (h, q)$ and $v_2 = \partial U / \partial q$ is the marginal benefit from increasing the potential usage $[1, q]$. Notice that this calculation of the net benefit adjusts the incremental benefit from more capacity by subtracting out the marginal benefits from unused portions of this increment to the purchase set. Thus, the demand profile for power capacity increments is

$$N_2(p_2, q) = \#\left\{ t \mid v_2(q, t) - \int_{r(q,t)} [v(x, t) - p(x)]\, dh \geq p_2 \right\}\,.$$

This is the number of customers for whom purchasing the q-th increment of power capacity at the marginal price p_2 has a positive net benefit. The final step uses this demand profile to construct an optimal schedule of marginal prices for power capacity increments. We present the simplest case and then describe the general construction.

A single type parameter.

Suppose first that customers are described by a single type parameter, and higher types' purchase sets are larger. In this case there is a particular type $t(p_2, q)$ that is indifferent about purchasing the increment q at the marginal price p_2; this type is identified by the condition that the incremental net benefit is zero in the inequality above. This feature allows a direct calculation of the firm's profit margin on this increment that is lost if increasing the price deters type $t(p_2, q)$ from purchasing this increment of power capacity:

$$m(p_2, q) = p_2 - c_2(q) - \int_{r(q,t(p_2,q))} [p(x) - c(x)]\, dh\,.$$

The integral in this expression takes account that this marginal type relinquishes power service in those hours $h(q, t(p_2, q)) \leq h \leq 1$ represented by $r(q, t(p_2, q))$, but other types are unaffected. Thus, as in §4, the profit contribution is maximized if

$$N_2(p_2(q), q) + \frac{\partial N_2}{\partial p_2}(p_2(q), q) \cdot m(p_2(q), q) = 0\,,$$

and analogously, Ramsey pricing by a regulated monopoly requires

$$\alpha N_2(p_2(q), q) + \frac{\partial N_2}{\partial p_2}(p_2(q), q) \cdot m(p_2(q), q) = 0\,,$$

where the Ramsey number α is set to meet the firm's revenue requirement.

A single type parameter also allows a comparable characterization of the optimal usage charges in conjunction with the demand charges. As in §9, let

$$N(p, x) = \#\{t \mid v(x, t) \geq p\}$$

be the demand profile for usage increments absent any capacity constraints and suppose that each marginal price $p(x)$ for usage is chosen to satisfy the optimality condition

$$\alpha N(p(x), x) + \frac{\partial N}{\partial p}(p(x), x) \cdot [p(x) - c(x)] = 0\,,$$

using the same Ramsey number α as for the capacity charges. The marginal prices chosen in this way are optimal also when capacity charges are imposed. This is true trivially for those increments unaffected by any customer's capacity choice,

and for other increments it is immaterial what their price is since customers and
the firm care only about the sum of the demand charge for that increment together
with the usage along that increment by the marginal type who purchases it. That
is,

$$p_2 - \int_{r(q,t(p_2,q))} p(x)\,dh\,,$$

is paid for usage in hours $0 \le h \le H(p_2,q) \equiv h(q,t(p_2,q))$ by all types purchasing this increment, regardless of the usage they relinquish. Although higher types
purchase usage in additional hours as well, usage in these hours that are capacity constrained for some customers are, in effect, sold as a single block. Within
these hours, the usage prices $p(x)$ are immaterial, since varying them produces an
offsetting change in p_2 so that the price of the block remains unchanged.

Example 11.1: For this example suppose that customers' marginal valuations are
linear, and by choice of units of measurement, of the form

$$v(h,\ell,t) = t - h - \ell\,,$$

where $x = (h,\ell)$ and the type parameter t is uniformly distributed between zero
and one. If the firm's cost is $\hat{C}(h,\ell) = \ell[k+ch]$ to serve ℓ kWs for h hours, then
the cost $C(q) = q[k+c]$ of a rectangular load-duration curve $[1,q]$ is also linear,
and the marginal cost $c(h,\ell) = c$ of a single kWh is constant.
    First we derive the marginal price schedule for usage. The demand profile is

$$N(p,q) = \#\{t \mid t - h - \ell \ge p\} = 1 - [p+h+\ell]\,,$$

and therefore the optimal price is

$$p(h,\ell) = \max\{c, c + \beta[1-c-h-\ell]\}\,,$$

where $\beta = \alpha/[1+\alpha]$. At this price, type t relinquishes those hours exceeding

$$h(\ell,t) = [t-c-\ell-\beta(1-c-\ell)]/[1-\beta]$$

at each power level ℓ.
    Next we construct the demand profile for power capacity increments. Type t's
net benefit from power capacity increment q is

$$v_2(q,t) - \int_{r(q,t)} [v(h,q,t) - p(h,q)]\,dh = \int_0^{h(q,t)} [v(h,q,t) - p(h,q)]\,dh$$
$$= \frac{1-\beta}{2} h(q,t)^2\,.$$

Consequently, the demand profile is

$$N_2(p_2, q) = \#\left\{ t \mid \frac{1 - \beta}{2} h(q, t)^2 \geq p_2 \right\}$$
$$= 1 - t(p_2, q),$$

where $t(p_2, q) = \sqrt{2[1 - \beta]p_2} + c + q + \beta[1 - c - q]$

is the type that is indifferent about purchasing the q-th power capacity increment
at the marginal price p_2. Using this characterization, the hours of usage of the q-th
increment by the marginal type of customer purchasing it is

$$H(p_2, q) \equiv h(q, t(p_2, q)) = \frac{1}{1 - \beta} \sqrt{2[1 - \beta]p_2},$$

which in this instance is independent of the power level q given a fixed price p_2
for power capacity increments. The profit margin is therefore

$$m(p_2, q) = p_2 - [k + c] - \int_{H(p_2)}^{1} \beta[1 - c - h - q]\, dh.$$

Using the demand profile and the profit margin in the optimality condition $\alpha N_2 +$
$[\partial N_2/\partial p_2]m = 0$ yields the optimal marginal price:

$$p_2(q) = [1 - \beta]\left[k + c + \beta[\tfrac{1}{2} - c - q]\right].$$

The corresponding demand charge is

$$\hat{p}_2(q) = p_2(q) - \int_0^1 p(h, q)\, dh$$
$$= [1 - \beta][k - \beta c] + \beta^2[q - \tfrac{1}{2}],$$

which *increases* as the power capacity increases. The portion of hours sold as a
block is

$$H(p_2(q), q) = \sqrt{2[k + c] + 2\beta[\tfrac{1}{2} - c - q]},$$

which declines as q increases; that is, the effective peak period is shorter for larger
customers.

If there is no revenue requirement then $\alpha = \beta = 0$ and the marginal prices of
usage, capacity, and demand are $p = c$, $p_2 = k + c$, and $\hat{p}_2 = k$, each of which is

the same as the corresponding marginal cost for the firm; also the portion of hours sold as a block is constant. In contrast, a profit-maximizing monopoly uses $\alpha = 1$ and $\beta = \frac{1}{2}$, which yields the marginal prices

$$p(h, \ell) = \frac{1}{2}[1 + c - h - \ell],$$

$$p_2(q) = \frac{1}{2}[k + c] + \frac{1}{4}[\frac{1}{2} - c - q],$$

$$\hat{p}_2(q) = \frac{1}{2}k + \frac{1}{4}[q - c - \frac{1}{2}],$$

for usage, capacity, and demand. ◇

Multiple type parameters.

Generally there are multiple type parameters and customers' purchase sets are not ordered by inclusion. Matters are more complicated in this case but the same general principles remain valid. The one place in the construction that is affected is the measurement of the firm's marginal revenue. There are now possibly several different types whose purchases of a q-th increment in power capacity are deterred by raising the price, and from each of these the firm loses the direct profit margin $p_2(q) - c_2(q)$ as before; however, account must also be taken of the relinquished usage of that marginal power capacity by all types affected at the margin. Thus, the formula above for the firm's profit margin includes terms for relinquished usage by each of the types that curtail their power capacities when the marginal price p_2 is raised slightly. Each such term must be weighted by the relative number of customers of each type, since in the optimality condition the factor $\partial N_2/\partial p_2$ still records the total number of customers of all types who are deterred from purchasing the incremental power capacity.

Multiple capacities

The tariff can include charges for capacities on several dimensions, as well as fixed subscription charges. The design of such charges uses a straightforward generalization of the method for a single capacity.

As in the previous subsection, a customer is interpreted as purchasing the list $q = (q_i)_{i=1,..,n}$ of capacities providing potential usage $[q]$, and then relinquishing a portion $R \subset [q]$ for which the marginal benefit is less than the marginal price charged by the firm. For the purchase set $[q]$ a customer of type t obtains the benefit $U(q, t)$, the firm incurs the cost $C(q)$, and the tariff charges $P(q)$.

Considering the simplest case first, suppose that each of these functions is additively separable as in §9:

$$U(q,t) = U_o(t) + \sum_{i=1}^{n} U_i(q_i, t) + \int_{[q]} v(x,t)\, dx\,,$$

$$C(q) = C_o + \sum_{i=1}^{n} C_i(q_i) + \int_{[q]} c(x)\, dx\,,$$

$$P(q) = P_o + \sum_{i=1}^{n} P_i(q_i) + \int_{[q]} p(x)\, dx\,.$$

This specification excludes terms applicable to lower-dimensional faces of the boundary of the purchase set. One usually imposes the following restrictions:

- Interpret $U_o = 0$ because customers benefit only from positive purchases. If $C_o = 0$ then it suffices as usual that $P_o = 0$ so that no subscription fee is charged.
- Similarly assign $U_i = 0$ along each dimension if customers do not benefit from unused capacity. The cost $C_i(q_i)$ represents the (amortized) capital cost of the i-th capacity q_i, and $P_i(q_i)$ is the demand charge collected for this capacity.
- To conform to notation in the previous section, therefore, define

$$p_i(q) = P_i'(q) + \int_{X_i(q)} p(x)\, dx \qquad \text{where} \qquad X_i(q) = \{x \in [q] \mid x_i = q\}\,,$$

and $v_i(q,t)$ and $c_i(q)$ similarly, so that these marginal prices, benefits, and costs for a q-th unit of capacity i include usage of the entire increment.

These separability assumptions enable optimal demand for multiple capacities to be constructed in essentially the same fashion as in the previous section. We illustrate only for the case of a single type parameter. In this case the usage charges can be constructed as in §9 without considering capacity limitations, using the demand profile $N(p, x) = \#\{t \mid v(x,t) \geq p\}$. Given a specification of usage charges $p(x)$, each type t's set $R(t)$ of relinquished increments is determined. Further, for each dimension independently, a q-th increment of capacity i at the marginal price p is demanded by a number of customers given by the demand profile

$$N_i(p,q) = \#\left\{ t \mid v_i(q,t) - \int_{r_i(q,t)} [v(x,t) - p(x)]\, dx \geq p \right\},$$

where $r_i(q,t) = R(t) \cap X_i(q)$ accounts for usage relinquished from that increment. Similarly, the profit margin lost on a customer deterred from buying this increment is

$$m_i(p,q) = p - c_i(q) - \int_{r_i(q, t_i(p,q))} [p(x) - c(x)]\, dx\,,$$

where $t_i(p, q)$ is the type indifferent about buying the increment at this price. Thus, for each capacity i the optimality condition is

$$\alpha N_i(p_i(q), q) + \frac{\partial N_i}{\partial p}(p_i(q), q) \cdot m_i(p_i(q), q) = 0 \,,$$

which determines the marginal price $p_i(q)$ for the q-th increment of the i-th capacity. Lastly, if the fixed cost C_o is positive then the fixed charge P_o is optimized similarly:

$$\alpha N_o(P(q), q) + \frac{\partial N_o}{\partial P}(P(q), q) \cdot m_o(P(q), q) = 0 \,,$$

where $q = q(t_*)$ is the capacity purchased by the least type t_* making a purchase, so

$$U(q, t_*) - \int_{R(q, t_*)} [v(x, t_*) - p(x)] \, dx = P(q) \,.$$

The relevant demand profile and profit margin are

$$N_o(P, q) = \# \left\{ t \mid U(q, t) - \int_{R(q, t)} [v(x, t) - p(x)] \, dx \geq P \right\} \,,$$

$$m_o(P, q) = P - C(q) - \int_{R(q, t)} [p(x) - c(x)] \, dx \,.$$

Having determined $P(q(t_*))$, one works backward to find the imputed values of the fixed charge and then the demand charges.

Example 11.2: For this example assume that $U_o = 0$, each $U_i = 0$, and

$$U(q, t) = [A - (1 - t)^a] U(q) \,,$$

where $0 < a \leq 1$ and the types t are uniformly distributed. Then it can be shown that[5]

$$P(q) = \beta A \cdot U(q) + [1 - \beta] \cdot C(q) \,,$$

where $\beta = \alpha / [\alpha + 1/a]$. Consequently,

$$p(x) = \beta A \cdot v(x) + [1 - \beta] \cdot c(x) \,,$$

$$P_i(q_i) = [1 - \beta] \cdot C_i(q_i) \,,$$

$$P_o = [1 - \beta] \cdot C_o \,.$$

5. See Oren, Smith, and Wilson (1985, Section 4).

This is example is representative of situations in which customers differ only via a multiplicatively separable type parameter: they pay a share (here $1 - \beta$) of the fixed, capacity, and usage costs, plus an additional usage charge that is proportional to the type-independent portion of their marginal valuations of usage.   ◇

In the general case the separability assumption is not satisfied. The consequence is that the demand charges for the various dimensions of capacity cannot be determined independently. In particular, instead of the additive form $P_o + \sum_i P_i(q_i)$ for the non-usage charges, a general function of all n capacities is optimal.[6] The design problem in this case requires construction of a general multiproduct tariff $P(q)$ for the n capacities $q = (q_1, \dots, q_n)$ jointly. This is precisely the problem addressed in the next three chapters.

11.4 Summary

Capital intensive industries subject to peakloads typically price capacity and usage separately to account for separate cost components and for the noncoincidence of capacity and usage; that is, portions of capacity are idle in offpeak periods. Peak loads also encourage a mixture of production technologies in order to economize on the tradeoffs between operating costs and the capital costs of idle capacity.

These features have several consequences. Customers' purchases are described by sets as in load-duration profiles that record the extent that capacity provided for a customer is unused. Pricing includes both demand charges for capacity and usage charges; moreover due to the mix of technologies, marginal usage costs and therefore marginal prices vary over time and with the magnitude of the load. The standard pricing policies that recover both capacity and usage costs include time-of-use and Wright tariffs, among many others. All of these have the essential feature that the tariff comprises marginal charges for usage increments as well as marginal charges for capacity increments.

The accounting conventions used to compute these tariffs vary in important ways, because they conform differently to short-term and long-term costs for the firm and incentives for customers. These differences are important in practice due to demand variability and nonoptimal embedded capacity configurations. Nevertheless, the general principles of constructing the underlying tariff structure are derived from the methods of nonlinear pricing.

The method is illustrated most clearly in the separable case, which allows usage charges to be computed via multidimensional pricing as in §9. Charges for capacity increments are then constructed separately for each relevant dimension via nonlinear pricing as in §4. Fixed charges can be added if there is a significant fixed

6. In practice, firms often consider it sufficient to use an additive tariff even if the separability assumption is not satisfied. Construction of additive tariffs when separability is not satisfied follows the methodology of §12.1.

cost of serving a customer. Multiple types add two complications: usage charges cannot be determined independently of capacity charges, and calculation of the profit margin is more complicated. Both are due to the necessity of taking account of the different usage of different types affected by changes in capacity charges. The nonseparable case, possibly with multiple types, is one version of the general problem of multiproduct tariff design addressed in Part IV.

Part IV

MULTIPRODUCT TARIFFS

12

MULTIPLE PRODUCTS AND COMPETITIVE TARIFFS

Multiproduct firms and firms in competitive industries also use nonlinear pricing. The illustrations in §2 from the power and communications industries provide examples of nonlinear tariffs used by multiproduct firms in regulated industries. The illustrations from the airline and package-delivery industries provide examples of nonlinear tariffs in industries affected strongly by competitive pressures. A multiproduct firm gains by designing its tariffs to take account of substitution or complementarity among its products; there may also be such features in the production or distribution process, or economies of scope. For a firm in a competitive industry, its tariff must account for customers' opportunities to substitute other firms' products, and it must compete successfully with the tariffs offered by competitors. Competition usually lowers the price schedules, but otherwise the role of nonlinear pricing is essentially unchanged. As for a monopoly firm, there are profit advantages from differentiation of purchase sizes or quality attributes.

The construction of multiproduct tariffs is more complicated because account must be taken of substitution and complementarity among the firm's products. Similarly, in a competitive industry, each firm's construction of its tariff is complicated by substitution effects, and further, by interactions among firms. However, given fixed tariffs offered by other firms, each firm's tariff design problem is basically the same as in §4. Technical modifications of the formulation are necessary, but the basic principles and methods are unaltered.

Section 1 describes the application of nonlinear pricing to the design of separate tariffs for the products of a single multiproduct firm. The main conclusion is that the design of each tariff is modified so that their combined effects on customers' purchases are optimized. The design of a single nonseparable tariff for several products jointly is deferred to §13 because it requires more elaborate techniques.

Subsequent sections illustrate applications to standard models of competition among firms. In Section 2, the firms' products are imperfect substitutes and the firms compete entirely via prices. The formulation uses the Bertrand model of monopolistic competition: firms operate without capacity limitations and they cannot make other kinds of commitments. The construction is analogous to the one in Section 1 except that each firm is unconcerned about the effect of its tariff on the profits obtained by other firms. In Section 3, the firms' products are perfect substitutes and the firms compete via capacity or supply commitments. The formulation uses the Cournot model of oligopoly in which each firm commits to a supply or capacity level, even though they subsequently compete via prices.[1] In the Bertrand model, each firm offers a differentiated product and therefore it has some monopoly power in setting prices. In the Cournot model, the firms' products are identical but supply commitments and the limited number of firms inhibit downward spirals of severe price cutting. These two cases are called monopolistic competition and oligopoly here, but sometimes they are termed oligopoly with heterogeneous and homogeneous products. Section 4 draws a distinction between these models and ones in which each firm uses uniform pricing but adopts a nonlinear schedule of supply provided at each price.

The exposition assumes that each firm maximizes its profit contribution. As in §5, Ramsey pricing by a regulated multiproduct firm yields an analogous characterization of the optimal tariff in terms of an associated Ramsey number that reduces profit margins uniformly.

12.1   Separable multiproduct tariffs

In this section we show that the same principles of tariff design described in §4 apply also to the design of separate tariffs for several products offered by the same firm. The key feature enabling this extension is that from the multiproduct demand profile one can construct a separate demand profile for each product, which can then be applied in essentially the same fashion as for a single product provided appropriate account is taken of substitution or complementarity among products.

In general, the tariff offered by a multiproduct firm specifies the total charge $P(q)$ payable when the customer purchases the bundle $q = (q_1, \ldots, q_n)$ specifying the quantity q_i of each product i among the n products offered. The construction in §14 of multiproduct tariffs of this general multivariate form is complicated by the fact that the marginal price $p_i(q)$ charged for a unit of product i depends on the purchased quantities of other products. In practice, however, firms often offer tariffs that are additively separable of the form

$$P(q) = \sum_{i=1}^{n} P_i(q_i).$$

That is, from a customer's viewpoint the products are priced independently, even if the customer recognizes that they are substitutes or complements in consumption.

---

1. These models are named after the mathematician Joseph Bertrand (1822–1900) and the economist Antoine Cournot (1801–1877), who initiated the study of models of imperfectly competitive markets.

A typical example is an electric utility that offers separate tariffs for power in offpeak and peak periods. AT&T's Reach Out America plans described in §2.4 are similar: their main provisions provide discounts for night and weekend calls, which are substitutes for daytime calls priced separately via AT&T's MTS tariff. Another is a lessor of space or equipment such as rental cars or computers that offers separate lease-duration discounts for different items of equipment. Federal Express' separate tariffs for Courier-Pak and Standard-Air delivery described in §2.5 are analogous.

From the firm's viewpoint, it is advantageous to coordinate the design of the tariffs for its products to take account of substitution and complementarity in customers' demands, or dependencies in the firm's production or distribution costs. Our task is therefore to describe the joint construction of the n separate univariate marginal price schedules $p_i(q_i)$ for the products of a single profit-maximizing firm. As mentioned, this task consists essentially of showing how the design of each tariff is modified to optimize their joint effect on customers' purchases of bundles of the products.

The multiproduct demand profile

Recall that the single-product demand profile $N(p, q)$ indicates the number of customers purchasing at least q units at the marginal price p. A similar interpretation applies when several products are involved. For a multiproduct firm offering n products or services, a customer's purchase is a bundle described by a list $q = (q_1, \ldots, q_n)$ of quantities of the products, selected in response to a list $p = (p_1, \ldots, p_n)$ of uniform marginal prices charged for the units of the products. In this case:

- The demand profile $N(p, q)$ measures the number of customers purchasing at least q_i units of each product $i = 1, \ldots, n$ when the list of marginal prices is p.

For instance, if customers are described by type parameters t affecting their demand functions $D(p, t)$, then the demand profile is

$$N(p, q) = \#\{t \mid D(p, t) \geq q\} .$$

In this specification the inequality is required to be true for each product; that is, for each component of the multiproduct demand function: if $D(p, t) = (D_i(p, t))_{i=1,\ldots,n}$ then $D_i(p, t) \geq q_i$ for every product i. As in previous chapters, we assume that $N = 0$ if any $q_i = \infty$. The multiproduct demand profile is estimated in essentially the same fashion from demand data, although of necessity the estimation is complicated by the multiplicity of products since the demand profile is a function of $2n$ price and quantity variables.

To demonstrate our main conclusions it suffices to impose several simplifying assumptions: (A) the demand profile has an associated density function indicating the frequency distribution of purchased bundles, and this density varies smoothly with prices; (B) the number of products is just two, $n = 2$; (C) fixed costs are nil and the products' marginal costs are independent, say $c_i(q_i)$ is the marginal cost for the q_i-th unit of product i; and (D) the tariffs impose no fixed charges, $P_i(0) = 0$. This special case conveys the main ideas without introducing excessive notation and complicated mathematical analysis.

Assumption (A) is a restrictive assumption in two respects. First, it requires that with fixed uniform prices $p = (p_1, p_2)$ there exists a density function $\nu(p, q)$ for purchased bundles $q = (q_1, q_2)$ such that

$$N(p, q) = \int_{q_1}^{\infty} \int_{q_2}^{\infty} \nu(p, x) \, dx_1 dx_2 \, .$$

If the demand profile is estimated directly then this density is obtained via

$$\nu(p, q) = \frac{\partial^2 N}{\partial q_1 \partial q_2}(p, q) \, ,$$

so the main requirement is that the demand profile can be recovered entirely from this density.[2] A demand profile that violates this assumption is $N(p, q) = \max \{0, 1 - \sum_i [p_i + q_i] \}$, for which the associated density is $\nu(p, q) \equiv 0$ and therefore integration of this density does not reproduce the demand profile. The reason for this anomaly is that this demand profile implies that all purchased bundles lie on the line where $\sum_i q_i = 1 - \sum_i p_i$. Generally, (A) is violated whenever the demand profile implies that all purchased bundles lie in some subset of lower dimension. We exclude such cases here, deferring to §13.4 the analysis of parameterized models that have demand profiles of this sort.

The second restriction involved in assumption (A) is that customers' purchases are not bunched on the boundary where some $q_i = 0$; that is, where some product is not purchased. This is unrestrictive for two products like peak and offpeak power if customers typically buy some of each (perhaps because they are complements or the elasticity of substitution is constant), but it is restrictive when some customers purchase one product but not both because they are close substitutes. Assumption (A) is restrictive even when demands for the products are independent: if a customer of type $t = (t_1, t_2)$ has the benefit and demand functions

$$U(q, t) = \sum_i \left[t_i q_i - \frac{1}{2} q_i^2 \right] \qquad \text{and} \qquad D_i(p, t) = \max \{0, t_i - p_i\} \, ,$$

---

2. In technical terms, this requirement states that the distribution of purchase sizes represents a measure on the positive orthant that is absolutely continuous with respect to the Lebesgue measure.

then all types with $t_i < p_i$ purchase the same quantity $q_i = 0$ of product i. To convey the main ideas, this possibility is disallowed initially but later the construction is amended to account for bunching of purchases on the boundary.

Substitution and complementarity

The novel feature involved in the design of multiproduct tariffs is the role of substitution and complementarity. To account for these effects, the multiproduct demand profile must be amended to describe how quantity discounts offered for one product affect the demand for increments of the other product.

The measurement of the multiproduct demand profile $N(p, q)$ assumes that the same list p of marginal prices applies to all increments purchased to obtain the difference $x - q$ between q and the customer's purchased bundle x. By analogy with the demand profile, let $M(q)$ indicate the number of customers purchasing bundles exceeding q when quantity discounts are offered according to price schedules $p_i(x_i)$ for increments $x_i \geq q_i$ for each product i. In general, $M(q)$ differs from $N(p(q), q)$ by the number of customers who respond to these quantity discounts by moving their purchased bundles in or out of the set $X(q) = \{x \mid x \geq q\}$ of bundles exceeding q. This difference can be measured by the rate or flux with which customers move their purchases across the boundary of $X(q)$ as the marginal prices change. Consequently, in general one can express $M(q)$ by a formula phrased as:

$$M(q) = N(p(q), q) + \int_{q_1}^{\infty} L_1(p_1(x_1), p_2(q_2); x_1, q_2)p_1'(x_1)\, dx_1$$
$$+ \int_{q_2}^{\infty} L_2(p_1(q_1), p_2(x_2); q_1, x_2)p_2'(x_2)\, dx_2 ,$$

where each function L_i measures the flux across one segment of the boundary of $X(q)$. In particular, L_1 measures the flux in proportion to p_1' across the boundary $X^2(q)$ where $x_2 = q_2$; and similarly L_2 measures the flux in proportion to p_2' across the boundary $X^1(q)$ where $x_1 = q_1$. This formula and the construction of the auxiliary functions L_i are explained in the next paragraphs.[3]

In the above formula for $M(q)$ each function L_i indicates the "leakage" rate at which quantity discounts for product i induce customers to alter their purchases in favor of bundles outside the set $X(q)$. For instance, if products 1 and 2 are substitutes then a customer purchasing $x_1 \geq q_1$ of product 1 and exactly $x_2 = q_2$ of product 2 at the uniform marginal prices p_1 and p_2 will respond to a quantity discount on product 1 by purchasing more of product 1 and therefore less of product 2. Thus, this customer's purchase exits the set $X(q)$ when such a quantity discount is offered and he should no longer be counted when measuring the number

3. The fact that $M(q)$ has such a formula is an implication of a general mathematical proposition known as the Divergence Theorem, Stokes' Theorem, or the fundamental theorem of multivariate calculus.

of customers purchasing bundles in $X(q)$. The formula for $M(q)$ includes this effect by measuring the rate or flux at which customers' purchases move out of the set $X(q)$ in response to quantity discounts on the two products.

The leakage functions are already contained in the specification of the demand profile but this information is only implicit unless the demand profile is constructed in a way that makes it explicit. To see this, observe that the effect of changing the price p_1 for product 1 can be written as the sum of two terms

$$\frac{\partial N}{\partial p_1}(p, q) = L_1(p, q) + L_1^*(p, q),$$

in which:

- L_1 measures the flux of customers across the boundary $X^2(q)$ of $X(q)$ where x_1 varies and x_2 is fixed at $x_2 = q_2$. This is called the substitution effect since it indicates the rate at which customers enter $X(q)$ by increasing their purchases of product 2 in response to an increase in the price of product 1.
- L_1^* measures the flux of customers across the other boundary $X^1(q)$ where x_1 is fixed at $x_1 = q_1$. This is called the own-price effect since it measures the rate at which customers exit $X(q)$ by decreasing their purchases of product 1 in response to an increase in its own price.

Typically, models of customers' demand behaviors are constructed to measure these two effects separately.

If the products are substitutes and the price of product 1 is increased slightly then as depicted in Figure 12.1 the vertical component L_1 of the flux across the first boundary along the bottom edge of $X(q)$ is inward (and therefore positive) and the horizontal component L_1^* of the flux across the second boundary along the left edge is outward (and therefore negative). Thus, one measures the leakage function L_1 as the portion of $\partial N/\partial p_1$ that accounts only for the flux inward along the bottom boundary as p_1 is increased and customers respond by substituting product 2 for product 1. Similarly, L_2 is the inward flux along the left boundary as p_2 is increased and customers respond by substituting product 1 for product 2.

When the products are substitutes, the leakage rates L_i are usually positive, but they may be negative when the products are complements. However, we are mostly interested in quantity discounts corresponding to price decreases, and in the case of substitutes, so it is convenient to interpret the net effect as negative. Thus, we conventionally interpret the flux L_i as describing the rate at which, due to substitution effects, customers exit $X(q)$ across the boundary in response to concessions in the marginal price of product i by reducing their purchases of other products.

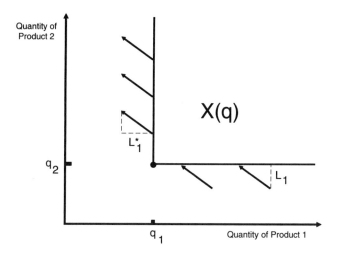

FIG. 12.1   The flux of customers' purchases in and out of $X(q)$ as the price of product 1 is increased: L_1 is the inward vertical flux along the bottom, and L_1^* is the outward horizontal flux along the left boundary.

Example 12.1: To illustrate these ideas we use an example in which each customer is described by a pair $t = (t_1, t_2)$ of type parameters and the linear demand function $D(p, t) = t - B \cdot p$. That is, t_i measures type t's maximum demand for product i, and at positive prices the demand for the i-th product is

$$D_i(p, t) = t_i - \sum_j b_{ij} p_j \, .$$

In the array B, the diagonal elements b_{ii} are positive and the off-diagonal elements b_{12} and b_{21} are negative to represent substitution effects. Assume that the type parameters are uniformly distributed in the population, so their density function is $f(t) = 1$ when $0 \le t_i \le 1$.[4] The demand profile is therefore

$$N(p, q) = \# \{ t \mid t \ge q + B \cdot p \}$$

$$= [1 - q_1 - b_{11}p_1 - b_{12}p_2][1 - q_2 - b_{21}p_1 - b_{22}p_2] \, .$$

The effect of a change in the price p_1 of product 1 therefore comprises the sum of the two leakage terms

$$L_1(p, q) = -b_{21}[1 - q_1 - b_{11}p_1 - b_{12}p_2] \, ,$$

$$L_1^*(p, q) = -b_{11}[1 - q_2 - b_{21}p_1 - b_{22}p_2] \, ,$$

---

4. One usually also assumes $b_{12} = b_{21}$ to be consistent with maximizing behavior by customers.

obtained when one differentiates the demand profile with respect to p_1. Note that the first term L_1 derives from substitution effects as indicated by the positive coefficient $-b_{21}$, which measures the rate at which an increase in the price of product 1 stimulates demand for product 2. In contrast, the second term L_1^* derives from direct curtailment of demand for product 1 as its own price is increased, as indicated by the negative coefficient $-b_{11}$. $\diamond$

Later, when we establish the conditions that characterize optimal price schedules, we assume that substitution effects are represented by the leakage functions identified from the demand profile. When the demand profile is derived directly from raw demand data, it is essential to separate price effects into direct own-price effects and substitution effects so that the leakage functions can be identified.

The next subsection can be skipped: it presents a more technical version of how substitution effects are measured for parameterized models.

An alternative construction *

When a parameterized model of customers' demand behavior is used, an alternative identification of the leakage rates is based on direct construction of the density of customers purchasing each bundle. We illustrate for the case that the numbers of type parameters and products are the same (otherwise, one follows the method in §8.4 to reduce the number of type parameters to the number of products). Let $t(p, q)$ indicate the type that at the uniform marginal prices p purchases the bundle q. A standard mathematical proposition states that the density of customers purchasing the bundle q is $\nu(p, q) = f(t(p, q))\delta(q)$, where $\delta(q) = |\partial t(p, q)/\partial q|$ is the absolute value of the determinant of the Jacobian matrix with elements $\partial t_i/\partial q_j$. Because $D(p, t(p, q)) = q$ this is just $\delta(q) = |D_t|^{-1}$. For instance, in the linear-demand example above the Jacobian matrix D_t of the demand function with respect to the type parameters is the identity matrix, and the type density is $f(t) = 1$, so $\nu(p, q) = 1 \cdot 1 = 1$.

Similarly, when the price schedules are not uniform the density of customers purchasing the bundle q is $\mu(q) = f(t(p(q), q))\bar{\delta}(q)$, where

$$\bar{\delta}(q) = |dt(p(q), q)/dq| = |I - D_p \cdot p'(q)| \cdot |D_t|^{-1} \, ,$$

where I is the identity matrix and D_p and p' are the Jacobian matrices of the demand function and the price schedule with respect to p and q respectively. In the case of two products, therefore,

$$\mu(q) = \nu(p(q), q)[1 - D_{11}p_1'(q_1) - D_{22}p_2'(q_2) + |D_p| p_1'(q_1)p_2'(q_2)] \, ,$$

where $D_{ij} \equiv \partial D_i / \partial p_j$ is evaluated at $[p(q), t(p(q), q)]$. For instance, in the previous linear-demand example

$$D_{ii} = -b_{ii} \qquad \text{and} \qquad |D_p| = |-B| = b_{11}b_{22} - b_{12}b_{21} \, .$$

On the other hand, starting from the multiproduct demand profile one derives

$$\nu(p, q) = \frac{\partial^2 N(p, q)}{\partial q_1 \partial q_2} \, ,$$

as the density of purchases at q when the prices p are uniform. Moreover, starting from the original formula for $M(q)$ one derives the density when prices are not uniform as

$$\mu(q) = \frac{d^2 N(p(q), q)}{dq_1 dq_2} - \frac{d}{dq_2} L_1 p_1'(q_1) - \frac{d}{dq_1} L_2 p_2'(q_2) \, ,$$

$$= \nu(p(q), q) + \frac{\partial L_1^*}{\partial q_2} p_1'(q_1) + \frac{\partial L_2^*}{\partial q_1} p_2'(q_2) + \Delta(p, q) p_1'(q_1) p_2'(q_2) \, ,$$

where

$$\Delta \equiv \frac{\partial L_1^*}{\partial p_2} - \frac{\partial L_2}{\partial p_1} \equiv \frac{\partial L_2^*}{\partial p_1} - \frac{\partial L_1}{\partial p_2} \, ,$$

$$\equiv \frac{\partial^2 N}{\partial p_1 \partial p_2} - \frac{\partial L_1}{\partial p_2} - \frac{\partial L_2}{\partial p_1} \equiv \frac{\partial L_1^*}{\partial p_2} + \frac{\partial L_2^*}{\partial p_1} - \frac{\partial^2 N}{\partial p_1 \partial p_2} \, .$$

Comparing this with the previous formula for μ, the own-price effects are identified

by the two differential equations

$$\frac{\partial}{\partial q_2} L_1^* = -\nu \cdot D_{11} \qquad \text{and} \qquad \frac{\partial}{\partial q_1} L_2^* = -\nu \cdot D_{22} \, ,$$

and the constraint $\Delta = |D_p|$.[5] Thus, for general parameterized models in which the separation of the total price effect into its constituent parts is not apparent, these equations identify the two components of the flux with respect to each price. We do not follow this route here since in applications it is usual to estimate own-price and substitution effects directly from demand data.

5. Alternatively, the constraints $L_i + L_i^* = \partial N / \partial p_i$ link the constants of integration. In the present case, however, the interpretation of the flux indicates that these constants are determined by the conditions that $L_1^* = 0$ at $q_2 = \infty$ and $L_2^* = 0$ at $q_1 = \infty$. In reverse, one obtains the number $M(q)$ of customers purchasing bundles in $X(q)$ via integration of μ over $X(q)$ by applying the Divergence Theorem to the formula for μ in the first line, or equivalently by applying Green's Theorem to integrate Δ in the second line.

In the linear-demand example,

$$\frac{\partial}{\partial q_2} L_1 = 0, \quad \frac{\partial}{\partial p_2} L_1 = b_{12} b_{21}, \quad \frac{\partial}{\partial q_2} L_1^* = b_{11}, \quad \frac{\partial}{\partial p_2} L_1^* = b_{11} b_{22},$$

and similarly for L_2 and L_2^*; also, $\nu = 1$ and $\partial^2 N / \partial p_1 \partial p_2 = b_{11} b_{22} + b_{12} b_{21}$. Consequently,

$$\mu(q) = 1 + b_{11} p_1'(q_1) + b_{22} p_2'(q_2) + |B| \, p_1'(q_1) p_2'(q_2),$$

which accords with the density constructed from the parameterized model with explicit type parameters.

This construction indicates that from a parameterized model one identifies the own-price effect L_1^* for product 1 via

$$L_1^*(p, q) = \int_{q_2}^{\infty} \nu(p; q_1, x_2) \cdot D_{11}(p, t(p; q_1, x_2)) \, dx_2,$$

and similarly for product 2. The substitution effect is then the residual portion of the total price effect:

$$L_1 = \frac{\partial N}{\partial p_1} - L_1^*,$$

and similarly for product 2. For instance, in the linear-demand example,

$$L_1^*(p, q) = \int_{q_2}^{q_2^*} 1 \cdot [-b_{11}] \, dx_2 = -b_{11} [q_2^* - q_2],$$

where the maximum quantity of product 2 purchased at the prices p in combination with q_1 of product 1 is $q_2^* = 1 - b_{21} p_1 - b_{22} p_2$, which is the amount purchased by a customer for whom $t_2 = 1$; therefore,

$$L_1^*(p, q) = -b_{11} [1 - q_2 - b_{21} p_1 - b_{22} p_2],$$

as derived previously.

The leakage rates have an intuitive interpretation. The own-price effect L_1^* represents the outward flux along the left boundary of $X(q)$ as p_1 changes, and the portion of this flux that occurs along a small interval $[q_2, q_2 + \epsilon]$ of quantities of product 2 is $[\partial L_1^* / \partial q_2] \epsilon$. This portion is measured by the number $\nu(p(q), q) \epsilon$ of customers purchasing bundles in this interval, multiplied by the rate D_{11} at which they reduce their purchases of product 1 as its own price is increased—and increase their purchases of product 2 at the rate D_{21}.

Note that the density ν includes all relevant information about the distribution of types in the population, whereas the coefficients D_{ij} measure the rate of customers' demand responses to a change in the price of product j independently of the distribution of types. As in the single-product case, the demand profile summarizes data about the distribution of customers' types, but the multiproduct case requires an auxiliary specification of the separation of the total price effect into its constituent own-price and substitution effects.

The optimal price schedules

We turn now to the construction of the optimal price schedules. The method is exactly analogous to the procedure in §4 except for the necessity of accounting for substitution or complementarity among the products.

To begin, observe that the q_1-th increment of product 1 is sold to all customers whose purchased bundles include at least q_1 units of product 1 and any amount of product 2. The demand for this increment at the marginal price p_1 can therefore be represented as

$$N_1(p_1, q_1; P_2) \equiv M(q_1, 0) = N(p(q), q) + \int_0^\infty L_2(p_1, p_2(x_2); q_1, x_2) p_2'(x_2)\, dx_2,$$

where $q = (q_1, 0)$ and $p(q) = (p_1, p_2(0))$. Note that we have omitted the second leakage term involving L_1 because along the bottom boundary where $q_2 = 0$ there cannot be any flux—by definition. The leakage term involving L_2 represents the demand for the q_1-th increment of product 1 that is lost due to quantity discounts offered for product 2 that induce customers to substitute product 2 for product 1. This term measures the accumulated flux of customers' purchases exiting across the left boundary of $X(q)$ as the marginal price $p_2(x_2)$ of product 2 is decreased from its initial value $p_2(0)$. A similar formula is used to define $N_2(p_2, q_2; P_1)$ as the demand for the q_2-th increment of product 2 at the marginal price p_2.

The firm's combined profit from its two products is therefore

$$\text{Pft} \equiv \int_0^\infty \int_0^\infty \sum_{i=1}^2 [P_i(q_i) - C_i(q_i)]\mu(q)\, dq_1 dq_2,$$

$$= \int_0^\infty N_1(p_1(q_1), q_1; P_2) \cdot [p_1(q_1) - c_1(q_1)]\, dq_1$$

$$+ \int_0^\infty N_2(p_2(q_2), q_2; P_1) \cdot [p_2(q_2) - c_2(q_2)]\, dq_2.$$

As usual, one obtains the second line from the first via integration by parts, using assumptions (C) and (D) to exclude fixed costs and fixed fees. The complicating feature of this formula is the fact that the profit contribution from one product is affected by the quantity discounts offered on the other product, as indicated for example by the dependence of N_1 on the tariff P_2 for product 2. As we have seen previously, however, this dependence is measured precisely by the leakage term involving L_2 in the formula for N_1 stated above. Because this term and the corresponding term in the formula for N_2 involve the rates p_1' and p_2' at which the prices change, the price schedules that maximize the firm's profit are characterized by the Euler condition from the calculus of variations.

For product 1 the necessary condition for optimality is the following:

$$N_1(p_1(q_1), q_1; P_2) + \frac{\partial N_1}{\partial p_1}(p_1(q_1), q_1; P_2) \cdot [p_1(q_1) - c_1(q_1)]$$

$$= \int_0^\infty \frac{\partial L_1}{\partial q_1}(p(q), q) \cdot [p_2(q_2) - c_2(q_2)] \, dq_2 \, .$$

The analogous condition with all subscripts reversed characterizes the optimal price schedule for product 2. There are two differences between this condition and the corresponding condition in the single-product case. First, on the left side the induced demand profile N_1 for product 1 is computed from the multiproduct demand profile and the demand lost due to quantity discounts for product 2 as measured by the leakage term involving L_2 and p_2'. Second, rather than being zero the right side accounts for the profit contribution $p_2(q_2) - c_2(q_2)$ lost on product 2 due to the quantity discount offered on product 1, which induces customers to substitute product 1 for product 2. Further, the factor $\partial L_1/\partial q_1$ measures the portion of the flux L_1 attributed to the q_1-th increment of product 1. In the linear-demand example, $\partial L_1/\partial q_1 = b_{21}$ is merely the rate at which customers substitute product 2 for product 1.

One may wonder why leakage terms do not appear in the analysis of the single-product case in §4 and §6. The reason can be seen here by collecting together the terms involving flux to obtain an alternative statement of the optimality condition for product 1's price schedule:

$$N + \frac{\partial N}{\partial p_1} \cdot [p_1 - c_1] = \int_0^\infty \left\{ \frac{\partial L_1}{\partial q_1} \cdot [p_2 - c_2] - \left[L_2 + \frac{\partial L_2}{\partial p_1} \cdot [p_1 - c_1] \right] p_2' \right\} dq_2 \, .$$

Evidently the left side is analogous to the case of a single product. Observe that the right side is zero as in the single-product case only when the profit contribution from product 2 is ignored (perhaps because $\partial L_1/\partial q_1 = 0$ when there are no substitution effects), *and* the price for product 2 is uniform ($p_2' \equiv 0$). In general, the substitution effects on the right side must be included whenever either of these features is absent. In practice, nevertheless, pricing of a single product is often based on direct empirical estimation of its demand profile N_i (rather than the multiproduct profile N) that already includes the effects of quantity discounts offered by other firms for their products.

Ramsey pricing

This analysis can be extended straightforwardly to include Ramsey pricing as in §5.1. The consumers' surplus from the separate price schedules p_1 and p_2 can be represented as

$$
CS = \int_0^\infty \int_0^\infty \left\{ \int_0^{q_1} [v_1(x_1, 0; t(q)) - p_1(x_1)] \, dx_1 \right.
$$
$$
\left. + \int_0^{q_2} [v_2(q_1, x_2; t(q)) - p_2(x_2)] \, dx_2 \right\} \mu(q) \, dq_1 dq_2 \, .
$$

The two terms within the curly brackets represent the net benefit obtained by each of the $\mu(q)$ customers of type $t(q)$ purchasing the bundle q as the accumulated difference between the customer's marginal benefit v_i and the marginal price p_i charged for the corresponding increment of product i. This accumulation is represented as the line integral from the null bundle 0 to the purchased bundle q along the path of accumulation that first purchases the increments $x_1 \leq q_1$ of product 1 and then the increments $x_2 \leq q_2$ of product 2. This formula for the consumers' surplus indicates that the first-order effect of increasing the marginal charge $p_1(x_1)$ for the x_1-th increment of product 1 by \$1 is to decrease by \$1 the consumer's surplus from each of the $N_1(p_1(x_1), x_1; P_2)$ customers who purchase bundles $q \geq (x_1, 0)$. There are no further first-order effects since the flux of customers moving their purchases in response to the price change are moving from one optimal response to another; thus (due to the envelope property) the effect on their net benefits is fully represented by the price change. An equivalent formula describes the consumers' surplus alternatively in terms of the path of accumulation that first purchases the increments of product 2.[6]

Using this formula for the consumers' surplus, and employing a Lagrange multiplier λ for the constraint representing the firm's revenue requirement, the necessary condition for an optimal choice of the marginal price $p_1(q_1)$ assigned to the q_1-th increment of product 1 is

$$
-N_1 + [1 + \lambda] \left\{ N_1 + \frac{\partial N_1}{\partial p_1} \cdot [p_1 - c_1] - \int_0^\infty \frac{\partial L_1}{\partial q_1} \cdot [p_2 - c_2] \, dq_2 \right\} = 0 \, ,
$$

where arguments of functions are omitted for notational simplicity. As described above, the first term on the left side indicates that a \$1 increase in the marginal price of the q_1-th increment of product 1 reduces by \$1 the consumer's surplus obtained by each of the N_1 customers who purchase this increment, and in the second term the factor in curly brackets is the firm's marginal profit from this price

6. As in §5.1, the consumers' surplus can also be expressed directly in terms of integrals of the demand profile.

increase. In terms of the Ramsey number $\alpha \equiv \lambda/[1+\lambda]$, therefore, the optimality condition for product 1's price schedule can be phrased as:

$$\alpha N_1 + \frac{\partial N_1}{\partial p_1} \cdot [p_1 - c_1] = \int_0^\infty \frac{\partial L_1}{\partial q_1} \cdot [p_2 - c_2]\, dq_2 \,.$$

As usual, this condition and the corresponding condition for product 2 imply that profit margins for all units of both products are scaled roughly in proportion to the Ramsey number; for instance, in the extreme case that the Ramsey number is zero and marginal costs are constant, prices are the same as marginal costs.

Inclusion of boundary purchases

Recall that assumption (A) includes the restriction that there is no bunching of customers along the boundary where the quantity of one product is zero. This restriction can be eliminated easily; indeed, the preceding formulas apply without modification if the induced demand profile N_i for each product i is assumed to include those customers bunched on the boundary where the amount purchased of the other product is zero. The essential task, therefore, is to specify how to measure the number of customers bunched on a boundary.

At a point $q = (q_1, 0)$ the customers purchasing bundles along the bottom boundary of $X(q)$ are those who prefer to purchase the q_1-th increment of product 1, but none of product 2, at the marginal prices $p(q) = (p_1, p_2(0))$. As in standard parameterized models, assume that all those on the boundary would be induced to make positive purchases of product 2 were the marginal price reduced to zero. Then the number of these customers can be measured by accumulating the own-price flux L_2^* of customers who would be newly induced to purchase some amount of product 2 as the marginal price for an initial increment is reduced from $p_2(0)$ down to zero. Thus, the number N_1° bunched on the bottom boundary of $X(q)$ is

$$N_1^\circ(p_1, q_1; p_2(0)) = - \int_0^{p_2(0)} L_2^*(p_1, p_2; q_1, 0)\, dp_2 \,,$$
$$= N(p_1, 0; q_1, 0) - N(p_1, p_2(0); q_1, 0)$$
$$+ \int_0^{p_2(0)} L_2(p; q_1, 0)\, dp_2 \,,$$

and it is this number that should be added to $N_1(p_1, q_1; P_2)$ as calculated previously to obtain the total number demanding the q_1-th increment of product 1. A convenient formula for the aggregate $\bar{N}_1$ of the customers in the interior and on the bottom boundary of $X(q)$ is

$$\bar{N}_1(p_1, q_1; P_2) = N(p_1, 0; q_1, 0) + \int_0^{p_2(0)} L_2(p; q_1, 0)\, dp_2$$

$$+ \int_0^\infty L_2(p_1, p_2(q_2); q)p_2'(q_2)\, dq_2\, .$$

When bunching on the boundary occurs, $\bar{N}_1$ is the relevant demand for the q_1-th increment at the marginal price p_1, and it plays the role previously ascribed to N_1 in the foregoing analysis that excluded bunching on the boundary.

In the linear-demand example, for instance,

$$L_2^*(p_1, p_2; q_1, 0) = -b_{22}[1 - q_1 - b_{11}p_1 - b_{12}p_2]$$

for p_2 in the range such that $t_2(p, q) \geq 0$, or equivalently $b_{21}p_1 + b_{22}p_2 \geq 0$ or $p_2 \geq p_* \equiv -b_{21}p_1/b_{22}$, and L_2^* is zero for smaller values of p_2. Thus, if $p_* < p_2(0)$ then the number on the boundary is

$$N_1^\circ(p_1, q_1; p_2(0)) = \int_{p_*}^{p_2(0)} b_{22}[1 - q_1 - b_{11}p_1 - b_{12}p]\, dp\, ,$$

$$= b_{22}\big\{[1 - q_1 - b_{11}p_1 - b_{12}p_2(0)][p_2(0) - p_*]$$

$$+ \frac{1}{2}b_{12}[p_2(0) - p_*]^2\big\}\, ,$$

and it is zero if $p_* \geq p_2(0)$. The aggregate of those customers in the interior and on the bottom boundary of $X(q)$ is therefore

$$\bar{N}_1(p_1, q_1; P_2) = N_1(p_1, q_1; P_2) + N_1^\circ(p_1, q_1; p_2(0))$$

$$= [1 - q_1 - b_{11}p_1 - b_{12}p_2(0)] + \frac{1}{2}[b_{12}/b_{22}][b_{21}p_1 + b_{22}p_2(0)]^2\, ,$$

when $p_* < p_2(0)$.

In practice each product may also attract a distinct market segment interested only in that product. This case is included by supposing that the demand profile for the segment interested only in product i is $N^i(p_i, q_i)$. Then the same sort of optimality condition applies except that, say for product 1, the role of its induced demand profile N_1 is supplanted by the combination

$$N_1(p_1, q_1; P_2) + N^1(p_1, q_1)\, ,$$

representing the demand for the q_1-th increment from both segments of the customer population. If there are many products then similar amendments apply when distinct market segments are interested in larger subsets of the products.

Computational methods

Approximately optimal price schedules can be calculated by standard methods of numerical analysis described by Press *et al.* (1986, Chapters 9 and 15). For practical applications, however, elementary methods usually suffice. We describe the simplest and illustrate with some examples.

Define the function

$$G_1(p_1, q_1) \equiv \alpha N + \frac{\partial N}{\partial p_1} \cdot [p_1 - c_1]$$
$$- \int_0^\infty \left\{ \frac{\partial L_1}{\partial q_1} \cdot [p_2 - c_2] - \left[\alpha L_2 + \frac{\partial L_2}{\partial p_1} \cdot [p_1 - c_1] \right] p_2' \right\} dq_2,$$

where on the right side the arguments of functions are omitted. This function G_1 defined for product 1 depends on the entire price schedule offered for product 2. Similarly, the analogous function G_2 defined for product 2 depends on the entire price schedule offered for product 1. The optimality conditions can be interpreted as a set of equations specifying that the two price schedules are chosen so that $G_i(p_i(q_i), q_i) = 0$ for each product i and each q_i-th unit of that product. These conditions require essentially that the gradient (with respect to the price schedules) of the objective function (profit or total surplus) is zero.

To construct an approximate solution, one solves approximate versions of these conditions at discrete values $q_i^k = k\delta$ of each quantity q_i, where δ represents the size of increments. The version is only approximate because the gradients are approximated as

$$G_1(p_1, q_1) \approx \hat{G}_1(p_1, q_1) \equiv$$
$$\alpha N + \frac{\partial N}{\partial p_1} \cdot [p_1 - c_1] - \sum_{k=1}^K \left\{ \frac{\partial L_1}{\partial q_1} \cdot [p_2 - c_2]\delta - \left[\alpha L_2 + \frac{\partial L_2}{\partial p_1} \cdot [p_1 - c_1] \right] \Delta_2^k \right\},$$

for product 1 and similarly for product 2. In this version, $\Delta_2^0 = 0$ and $\Delta_2^k = p_2(q_2^k) - p_2(q_2^{k-1})$ for $k > 1$; thus, the decline p_2' in the price schedule is assumed to occur entirely as downward jumps at the discrete quantities q_2^k. The aim is then to solve simultaneously the equations $\hat{G}_i(p_i^k, q_i^k) = 0$, where $p_i^k \equiv p_i(q_i^k)$, for each product i and each discrete quantity q_i^k of that product. Let $Q = (q_i^k)$ and $P = (p_i^k)$ be the arrays of these discrete quantities and prices and summarize these equations as $\hat{G}(P, Q) = 0$. Because $\hat{G}$ is an approximation of the gradient, one gets successively closer to a solution by iteratively moving from one proposed solution P^t in iteration t to a better one $P^{t+1} = P^t + s_t \cdot \hat{G}(P^t, Q)$, provided the stepsize s_t is chosen sufficiently small and positive. After enough iterations that all the components of $\hat{G}(P^t, Q)$ are sufficiently small, one can adopt P^t as an approximation of the optimal price schedules.

The examples in Figure 12.2 are based on the linear-demand model described in Example 12.1. Units of measurement are normalized so that each diagonal coefficient is $b_{ii} = 1$ and we use the parameter $b \equiv -b_{12} = -b_{21}$ to indicate the magnitude of the off-diagonal coefficient representing substitution effects. The marginal cost of each product is assumed to be $c_i = 0$. Increasing the substitution parameter b raises the schedule of marginal prices, and decreasing the Ramsey number α bends the schedule down. The effect of increasing b is partly an artifact of the simple linear model since a high price for product 2 effectively augments the type parameter t_1 pertinent to type t's demand for product 1 without altering the slope of the demand function.

Caution is required in using the gradient procedure when the optimal price schedules have too steep or backward-bending segments of the sort depicted in Figure 4.4. Consider the case that the Ramsey number is $\alpha = 1$ and the substitution parameter is $b = 0.8$, which is quite large. Figure 12.3 shows five "solutions" obtained with the gradient procedure from different initial price schedules used to start the procedure. None of these is truly optimal since in fact the optimal schedule in this case has a gap. I have not undertaken to calculate exactly the optimal gap in the price schedule, but in the figure the arrow indicates approximately where it lies based on inference from the five schedules shown. The initial high-price segment presumably reflects the firm's strategy toward customers on the boundary. Consequently, if the customer who is indifferent across the gap is one whose purchase is on the boundary, then the slope of the price schedule across the gap should be the slope of that type's single-product demand function when the quantity of the other product is fixed at zero: this slope is $dq/dp = b^2 - 1 = -0.36$, as compared to the steeper slope -1 of the multiproduct demand function.[7]

Example 12.2: To illustrate further the role of substitution effects we consider an alternative linear-demand model derived from customers' benefit functions of the form

$$U(q,t) = \sum_{i=1}^{2} q_i \left[t_i - \frac{1}{2} \sum_{j=1}^{2} a_{ij} q_j \right]$$

7. Attempts to move the steeply declining segment further left or right lead to convergence to the right-most segment. The wavy portions around $q = 1$ apparently arise from the interaction between the two products when neither has an optimal gap; and the step up at $q \approx 1.2$ occurs where demand is exhausted for one type.

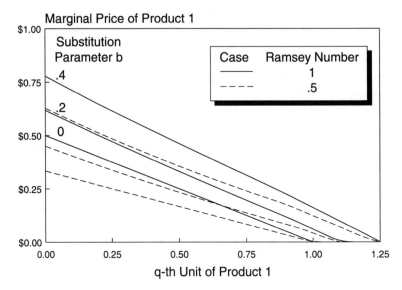

FIG. 12.2 Example 12.1: The marginal price schedule for one product, depending on the Ramsey number α and the substitution parameter b.

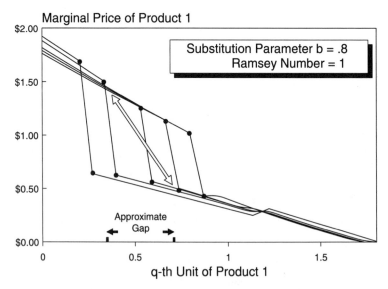

FIG. 12.3 Five solutions of the necessary condition for a solution when $b = 0.8$ and $\alpha = 1$. The arrow indicates the approximate location of the optimal gap in the price schedule, which has slope $-1/[1 - b^2]$ if the gap is associated with a customer on the boundary.

for type t. In this version, t_i represents type t's marginal valuation of an initial unit of product i. Normalizing units of measurement so that each $a_{ii} = 1$, we can use $a \equiv a_{12} = a_{21}$ as a measure of substitution between the products. Assume that t is distributed in the population according to a bivariate Normal distribution for which each t_i has mean $\bar{t}_i = 1$ and standard deviation 1; also, let r be the statistical correlation between t_1 and t_2. The demand profile is the bivariate Normal probability $N(p,q) = \Pr\{\xi \geq x(p,q) \mid \rho\}$, where the first components of ξ and $x(p,q)$ are

$$\xi_1 \equiv \frac{1}{\Delta}\{[t_1 - \bar{t}_1] - a[t_2 - \bar{t}_2]\} ,$$

$$x_1(p,q) \equiv \frac{1}{\Delta}\{[1 - a^2]q_1 + [p_1 - \bar{t}_1] - a[p_2 - \bar{t}_2]\} ,$$

using $\Delta \equiv \sqrt{1 + a^2 - 2ar}$, and symmetrically for the second components. The correlation between the random variables ξ_1 and ξ_2 is

$$\rho \equiv \frac{r[1 + a^2] - 2a}{[1 + a^2] - 2ar} .$$

The own-price and substitution effects are measured by the fluxes

$$L_1^* = \frac{\partial N}{\partial x_1}\frac{\partial x_1}{\partial p_1} \quad \text{and} \quad L_1 = \frac{\partial N}{\partial x_2}\frac{\partial x_2}{\partial p_1} ,$$

and symmetrically for product 2. To include bunching of customers on the boundary, we use the quadratic approximation

$$N_1^\circ(p_1,q_1;p_2(0)) \approx -L_2^*(p_1,p_2(0);q_1,0)p_2(0) - \frac{1}{2}\frac{\partial L_2^*}{\partial p_2}(p_1,p_2(0);q_1,0)p_2(0)^2 .$$

Figure 12.4 displays product 1's price schedule for two values $\alpha = 1$ and 0.5 of the Ramsey number and three values $a = 0, .2, .4$ of the substitution coefficient. Marginal costs are assumed nil and also the correlation between t_1 and t_2 is nil: $c_i = 0$ and $r = 0$. In this case the comparisons are more realistic: higher values of the substitution coefficient lower the price schedule. Figure 12.5 shows how changes in the correlation r affect the price schedules. Evidently, more correlation raises the price schedules. In both figures, high values of the substitution coefficient yield increasing segments in the price schedules, which need to be flattened using the ironing procedure described in §4.   ◇

Multipart tariffs

Applications of these results to the design of separable multipart tariffs require substantial amendments. First, even when the firm incurs no fixed cost serving a

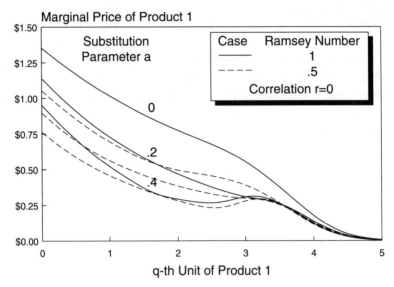

FIG. 12.4 Example 12.2: The marginal price schedule of one product depending on the Ramsey number α and the substitution coefficient a. Assumes $r = 0$ and each $c_i = 0$.

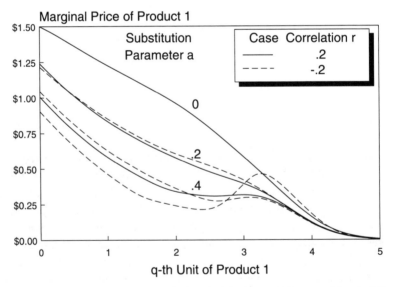

FIG. 12.5 Example 12.2: The marginal price schedules for correlations $r = 0.2$ and -0.2.

customer, a positive fixed fee is optimal and therefore customers' minimal purchase sizes are positive rather than zero, as elaborated in §6.4. Second, each price schedule is constant on intervals; indeed, from the viewpoint of customers, the total tariff for bundles of the two products is linear on rectangles. This produces substantial computational complications; viz., parameterized models predict that no customers will purchase bundles close to any boundary of any rectangle. Thus, a decrease in the marginal price of one product, say product 1, for one interval induces substitution by two segments of customers: (1) those for whom substitution leaves their purchased bundle still within the same rectangle—so they move locally, encountering no discrete change in the marginal price of either product; and (2) those who jump from one rectangle to an adjacent one. The second category includes: (2a) those who jump laterally to buy more of product 1 because of the own-price effect, so their marginal price of product 2 remains unchanged; and (2b) those who jump diagonally because of the substitution effect, and so they face different marginal prices for both products. An analysis of multiple multipart tariffs of this sort is complicated because the substitution terms included in the induced demand profiles should represent only the flux of those customers in category (2) who jump between rectangles. In particular, customers in (2) are included in the own-price flux L_1^* for product 1, and those in (2b) are included in the flux L_1 affecting the demand for increments of product 2.

An analysis of these features is omitted here because no computationally tractable formulation has been developed. By inference from the characterizations in §6.4 and §8.3, it seems likely that the optimality conditions for multipart tariffs can be represented as appropriate averages of the conditions applicable to fully nonlinear tariffs.

12.2   Monopolistic competition

In competitive markets, the demand for each firm's product depends on the terms offered by competing firms for their products. In the case of monopolistic competition between two firms, the demand profile for the first firm, say $N_1(p, q; P_2)$, depends on the second firm's tariff P_2 if the products are substitutes or complements. According to the Bertrand model, each firm chooses its tariff optimally in response to the other's tariff. The first firm, for instance, chooses its schedule $p_1(q_1)$ of marginal prices to maximize its profit contribution

$$N_1(p_1(q_1), q_1; P_2)[p_1(q_1) - c_1(q_1)]$$

from each incremental q_1-th unit. Similarly, the second firm has an optimal tariff in response to the first firm's tariff. Notice that each firm presumably pursues its own interest without taking account of the effect on the other firm or on their joint interests; that is, we assume the firms compete noncooperatively.

The outcome from this jostling for competitive advantage is a set of tariffs, one for each firm, such that each firm's tariff is the optimal response to the others' tariffs. This outcome is called an equilibrium of the game of tariff competition between the competing firms. Direct calculation of equilibrium tariffs is complicated by the interaction between the firms, but a simple procedure usually suffices: as in real life, repeatedly construct each firm's new optimal tariff in response to the other firms' current tariffs. This procedure usually converges quickly to the set of equilibrium tariffs. The only complication arises from the necessity of constructing the induced demand profile for each firm's product given the tariffs offered by the others.

There are two basic approaches to constructing a firm's demand profile. One is a practical wait-and-see approach: after other firms have adopted new tariffs, observe customers' demands and use that data directly to construct the demand profile; then calculate a new optimal tariff.

A second approach uses the multiproduct demand profile for all the firms' products. From this perspective, the number of customers purchasing a q_1-th unit of product 1 is the number purchasing this unit of product 1 and any amounts of other products. Thus with two firms, firm 1's induced demand profile is just

$$N_1(p_1, q_1; P_2) \equiv M(q_1, 0) = N(p_1, p_2(0); q_1, 0)$$
$$+ \int_0^\infty L_2(p_1, p_2(x_2); q_1, x_2) p_2'(x_2) \, dx_2 \,,$$

as defined previously for a multiproduct firm using separate tariffs for its two products. Consequently, the necessary condition that characterizes an optimal price schedule for product 1 is

$$N_1(p_1(q_1), q_1; P_2) + \frac{\partial N_1}{\partial p_1}(p_1(q_1), q_1; P_2) \cdot [p_1(q_1) - c_1(q_1)] = 0 \,,$$

in exact analogy to the single-product case—provided of course that the substitution effects are included in N_1 as above. Note that the right side is now zero because firm 1 does not temper its pricing strategy to ameliorate the effects on firm 2's profit contribution. A similar condition (with all subscripts reversed) characterizes the optimal price schedule for product 2 in response to firm 1's choice of its price schedule. The predicted equilibrium, therefore, is the pair of price schedules that satisfy these two conditions simultaneously. Equilibrium price schedules can be constructed by solving these two conditions using the methods described in Section 1 for the case of a single multiproduct firm.

For the linear-demand model in Example 12.1, Figure 12.6 shows the marginal price schedules for three values of the substitution parameter b, as described in Section 1. Compared to the schedules for a monopolist multiproduct firm in Figure 12.2, these are lower in the two cases that the substitution parameter is positive.

For the alternative linear-demand model in Example 12.2, Figure 12.7 shows the marginal price schedules for three values of the substitution parameter a in the case that the type parameters are distributed independently, namely the correlation is $r = 0$. Higher values of the substitution parameter lower the price schedule substantially. Because the schedule for $a = 0.4$ has an increasing segment, the ironing procedure described in §4 needs to be applied to flatten the schedule: a rough approximation, drawn freehand, is shown in the figure as the dashed horizontal line. The effect of altering the correlation between the type parameters is shown in Figure 12.8 for the two cases $r = 0.2$ and $r = -0.2$. In these cases the price schedule rises as the correlation increases but the reverse occurs when the substitution parameter is large, as shown in Figure 12.9 for the case $a = 0.8$.

12.3 Oligopoly

An oligopolistic market differs materially from monopolistic competition because the firms' products are perfect substitutes. Without some power to protect market share, price competition drives at least one firm's marginal prices down to marginal costs. The analysis hinges, therefore, on close examination of a firm's ability to maintain market share.

The Cournot model of this competitive process hypothesizes that firms maintain market shares by being prepared to cut prices as necessary, but also that they are unable to supply or unwilling to sell more than they planned in earlier stages of investment and production. Thus, each firm anticipates others' output levels and then prices monopolistically to meet residual demands unserved by other firms; moreover, it is committed (via earlier supply decisions) to serve these demands even if lower prices are required to dispose of its supplies. This is an extreme assumption: in practice, competitive responses are a mixture of price and supply adjustments, possibly via inventory accumulations or unused capacity, whereas the Cournot hypothesis supposes that firms' outputs are not adjusted.

Cournot models often have unique equilibria when firms use uniform prices, but nonlinear pricing introduces multiple equilibria depending on the formulation of their supply commitments and pricing policies. We describe the simplest of many versions.[8] These models allow asymmetries among firms, but we assume here that firms have identical technologies and costs.

According to the Cournot hypothesis in this model, each firm anticipates that others formulate their pricing policies in terms of market-share targets *in each volume band*. For example, an airline might plan to obtain specified market shares among those customers traveling occasionally (tourists), frequently (commercial),

---

8. Several other versions are described by Oren, Smith, and Wilson (1982b). The version here is Model I in their terminology: each firm commits to the market share it serves for each size of purchase. In another version, each firm commits to the market share it serves for each type of customer. This is more realistic for the airline industry, where firms focus on their market shares among tourists, business travelers, et cetera.

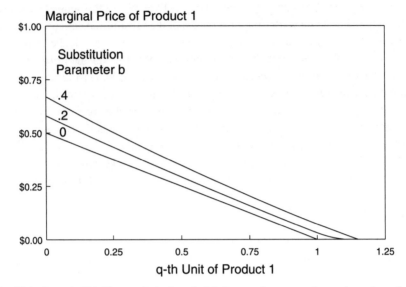

FIG. 12.6 Example 12.1: The marginal price schedule for one of two competing products, depending on the substitution parameter b.

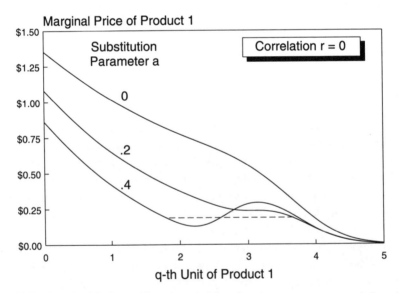

FIG. 12.7 Example 12.2: Competitive price schedules when the type parameters are independent ($r = 0$), for values $a = 0, .2, .4$ of the substitution parameter.

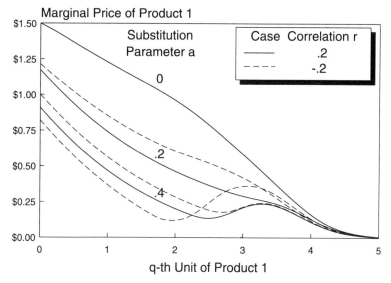

FIG. 12.8 Competitive price schedules for type correlations $r = 0.2$ and -0.2 and substitution parameters $a = 0,\ 0.2,\ 0.4$.

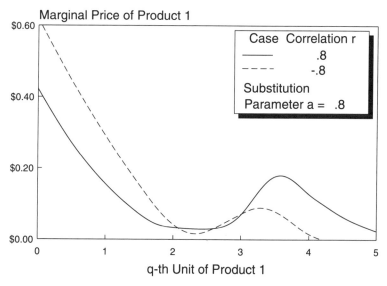

FIG. 12.9 Competitive price schedules for type correlations $r = 0.8$ and -0.8 and substitution parameter $a = 0.8$.

and constantly (professional business travelers, such as sales representatives and consultants). Airlines typically implement such plans by allocating quotas of seats available on each flight to each fare class, and by imposing various advance purchase requirements.

To represent such anticipations, suppose that each firm $i = 1, \ldots, n$ estimates that other firms will serve a number $m_i(q)$ of those customers whose purchase sizes are q; or equivalently, a number $M_i(q) \equiv \sum_{x \geq q} m_i(x)$ of those customers purchasing a q-th increment. If firm i believes that other firms will surely attain these targets (by cutting prices if necessary) and cannot supply more, then its optimization problem is quite similar to the one studied in §4 for a profit-maximizing monopolist. Using the aggregate demand profile $N(p, q)$, the objective is to maximize the profit contribution

$$[N(p_i(q), q) - M_i(q)][p_i(q) - c_i(q)]$$

from q-th increments by selecting its marginal price $p_i(q)$. This is equivalent to selecting its own target $N_i(q) \equiv N(p_i(q), q) - M_i(q)$ except that we use the price as the strategic variable in order to conform to the analysis in §4. That the price can be used equivalently can be seen by considering the market as an auction: the definition of the demand profile N says essentially that $p_i(q)$ is the price that the combined supply $N(p_i(q), q)$ of q-th increments brings in the auction. We apply a subscript i to firm i's price schedule only to indicate that it chooses this price in anticipation of others' supply commitments, but in fact the firms' products are perfect substitutes so eventually the firms must all obtain the same prices—and because they are symmetric, the same sales.

The optimal price for the i-th firm therefore satisfies the following necessary condition for an optimum:

$$[N(p_i(q), q) - M_i(q)] + \frac{\partial N}{\partial p}(p_i(q), q) \cdot [p_i(q) - c_i(q)] = 0.$$

At this point we invoke two considerations. First, the firms are identical with the same marginal cost $c_i(q) = c(q)$; and second, in an equilibrium each firm anticipates correctly the optimal choices of the others. Indeed, by symmetry each expects all firms to set the same targets. Thus, it must be that

$$M_i(q) = \frac{n-1}{n} N(p(q), q),$$

where $p(q)$ is the price that all firms charge for q-th increments. In sum, the equilibrium schedule of marginal prices is calculated from the condition that

$$\frac{1}{n} N(p(q), q) + \frac{\partial N}{\partial p}(p(q), q) \cdot [p(q) - c(q)] = 0.$$

According to this condition, Cournot competition among several identical firms drives marginal prices down, as compared to a monopoly, but it does not eliminate nonlinear pricing. Profit margins vanish only if the number of firms is very large, since the percentage profit margin is $1/n\eta(p(q), q)$.

This condition appeared previously in §5.1. The coefficient $1/n$ plays the role of the Ramsey number α in the optimality condition that applies when a regulated firm prices efficiently to meet a revenue requirement. We see here that α has the interpretation that the regulated firm prices as though it were one of $1/\alpha$ firms offering identical products and competing via a Cournot model.

Example 12.3: Suppose that each firm's marginal cost is the constant c and that the demand profile is

$$N(p, q) = 1 - \frac{q}{1-p} \qquad \text{if} \quad p < 1 - q.$$

Then the equilibrium schedule of marginal prices charged by each firm is

$$p(q) = 1 + mq - \sqrt{(mq)^2 + n[1 - c]q},$$

where $m = [n - 1]/2$. This price schedule is convex, starting at $p(0) = 1$ and declining until the largest increment purchased is $q = 1 - c$ at the marginal price $p(1 - c) = c$. Figure 12.10 shows the marginal price schedule $p(q)$ for various numbers of firms in the case that the marginal cost zero. As can be seen, the effect of competition is mild for small numbers of firms—and nil for the initial unit purchased.   ◇

Example 12.4: A different pattern emerges for the adaptation of Example 12.2 presented as Example 4.3. Figure 12.11 shows the marginal price schedule for $n = 1, 2, 4, 8$, and 16 firms in the case that the substitution parameter is $a = 0.4$, the correlation is $r = 0.4$, the price of an alternative commodity is $p^* = 0.5$, and the marginal cost is $c = 0$. In this case the price for an initial unit drops quickly but the schedules are the same for more than 5 units. In this case the actual optimal prices are obtained by flattening the schedules using the ironing procedure described in §4.2. Evidently the optimal schedules are uniform over most of their domain if the number of firms is large. Figure 12.12 shows the firms' and the industry profits per customer in the potential market and the market penetration for the price schedules depicted, without flattening via the ironing procedure. The potential market is defined here as the fraction 0.8086 of customers who would purchase an initial unit at a zero price; this is equivalent to normalizing so that $N(0, 0) = 1$.   ◇

In these examples, the price schedule decreases as the number n of firms increases. At the limit, the price of every unit equals marginal cost: $p(q) = c$ for

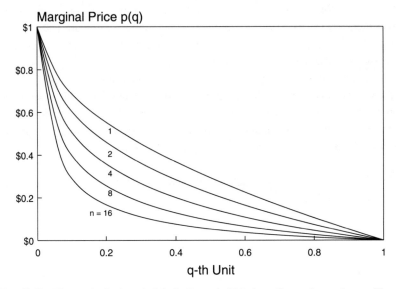

Fig. 12.10 The marginal price schedule for Example 12.3, depending on the number n of firms.

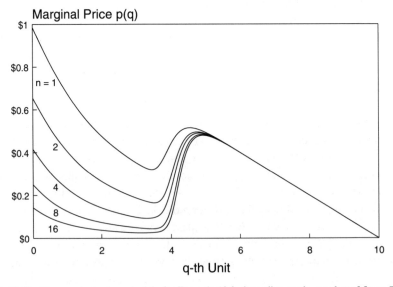

Fig. 12.11 The marginal price schedule for Example 12.3, depending on the number of firms. The parameters are $a = 0.4$, $r = 0.4$, $p^* = 0.5$, and $c = 0$.

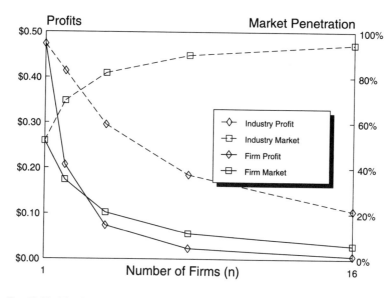

FIG. 12.12   The firms' and the industry profits and market penetration for Example 12.4.

every increment $q > 0$. This property is quite general. Moreover, it has a stronger form when marginal cost is an increasing function of the purchase size. At the limit, all units are offered at the uniform price $p = c(0)$. This is the marginal cost of the largest purchase made, which tends to zero. The price schedule cannot converge to the marginal cost schedule over its full range, since then the price schedule would also be increasing. Essentially, each customer splits his purchase among the firms and none pays more than the initial marginal cost. Similarly, if a firm's costs also depend on aggregate supply and this marginal cost is increasing then again all prices converge to the marginal cost of aggregate supply.

12.4   Nonlinear supply schedules

The previous sections consider competitive markets in which each firm offers a nonlinear tariff to each customer. An alternative view of competitive pricing envisions each firm using a pricing policy in which the average price depends on aggregate demand; that is, the entire schedule of prices, or perhaps a single uniform price, varies depending on the demand conditions that occur. This situation is represented by supposing that each firm selects a supply schedule consisting of a locus of combinations $(\bar{p}, Q)$, consisting of an average price and an aggregate quantity it is willing to supply at that price level. The point on this locus that is implemented depends on the demand that materializes. The motive for this kind of pricing strategy stems from an interaction between competitive factors and stochastic features of demand.

A prominent example is pricing by airlines. Each day, an airline offers several fares on hundreds of flights for the next hundred days. To manage this complex task it uses an established pricing policy implemented as computerized procedures that continually adjust the fare classes and prices and the numbers of seats offered at each price on each flight. The adjustment process is based on continually revised demand estimates, using the rates of early purchases as statistical indicators of the demands that will eventually materialize at the departure dates. By the time of departure, the average price of a seat and the number of booked seats on each flight are adapted closely to the actual demand conditions that materialize. One can interpret this dynamic process in terms of a static representation in which the pricing policy establishes a systematic relationship between average prices and aggregate quantity, as depicted by the locus described above.

Two factors explain this type of pricing policy. One factor is that demands for each flight are stochastic but practical necessity requires commitment to operational procedures before the uncertainty is resolved: customers require early price quotations, reservations, and bookings. This factor is insufficient in itself, however, since a monopolist could as well select prices based on average demands. The second factor is therefore competition, which in combination with stochastic demands leads firms to use supply schedules that are nonlinear. The reason can be seen by considering the special case of uniform prices and the two extreme modes of competition represented by the Bertrand and Cournot models. Bertrand competition supposes a particular kind of supply schedule in which the same price is associated with every magnitude of quantity demanded. Cournot competition supposes instead that the firm chooses the same quantity for every price. Both models suppose that the firm estimates the quantity or price that will materialize, but the supply schedule describes how the firm will respond to deviations from its estimate. These two types of schedules are evidently very limited in their ability to adapt to stochastic features of demand; in general, the optimal schedule is intermediate between these extremes, allowing some price increase to be associated with increases in demand. Such a policy evidently provides greater flexibility in adapting to variations in demand conditions.

We do not describe here the construction of optimal supply schedules, since it would depart from our main subject.[9] It is worth emphasizing, however, that some situations call for a nonlinear relationship between average prices and aggregate quantities. Based on the example of airline pricing, one can suppose that such a schedule is implemented by a dynamic procedure that adapts price and supply offers to evolving information about demand conditions. The market eventually clears at prices and quantities close to the objectives established by the overall pricing policy designed by the firm.

9. See Meyer and Klemperer (1989) for an exposition. Wilson (1979) develops the theory of nonlinear supply and demand schedules offered in competitive auctions affected by stochastic elements, including private information known by the bidders.

12.5 Summary

The substance of this chapter is the demonstration that nonlinear pricing is applicable also to multiproduct contexts. We study two extreme cases: in one a single firm offers separate tariffs for several products, and in the other each of several competing firms selects the tariff for its own product. In both cases an appropriate version of the multiproduct demand profile can be used to summarize demand data and to compute the optimal tariffs. The basic principles of nonlinear pricing are unaltered but the task of computing optimal tariffs is more complex when the effects of imperfect substitution and complementarity among the products must be included.

  A multiproduct firm designs its tariffs to maximize the total profit contribution obtained from all its products. Account can be taken of substitution and complementary among its products by separating total price effects into substitution and own-price effects representing the flux or rate at which customers alter their purchases by substituting one product for another in response to quantity discounts. When these effects are included, the construction of each product's price schedule is analogous to the single-product case except that:

- Each product's induced demand profile includes the substitution effects engendered by quantity discounts offered for the other product.
- The optimal profit margin on each product, say product 1, is raised sufficiently to account for the reduction in the profit contribution from product 2 that a low marginal price p_1 would cause by inducing customers to substitute product 1 for product 2 in the bundles purchased.

  In contrast, in a competitive industry each firm seeks to maximize its own profit contribution in response to the tariffs offered by other firms. Each firm's construction of an optimal tariff follows essentially the method in §4, but with the amendment that the induced demand profile depends on the price schedules or supply commitments adopted by other firms, since they are competing for the same customers.

- If the firms' products are imperfect substitutes or complements, and they compete entirely via prices according to the Bertrand model, then the separate demand profile for one firm given the others' tariffs can be constructed from the multiproduct demand profile for all their products. As for a single multiproduct firm, this is done by accounting for substitution effects: the total price effect is separated into its constituent substitution and own-price effects.
- If the firms' products are perfect substitutes, and they compete via supply or capacity commitments according to the Cournot model, then the demand profile for one firm is the residual after accounting for the anticipated market shares of other firms.

According to either model, the predicted outcome is an equilibrium in which each firm's tariff is an optimal response to the others' tariffs. In the Bertrand model, profit margins are significantly reduced if the products are close substitutes. The Cournot model considers competition among firms offering identical products that are perfect substitutes. Compared to a monopoly, the net result is to reduce profit margins but profits are not eliminated entirely because supply is limited by firms' prior commitments to capacity or production levels. In an industry with many firms, prices are close to marginal cost; consequently, the number of viable firms in an industry is limited whenever investment and fixed operating costs must be recovered from profits. Nonlinear pricing is then a predictable outcome if the conditions for feasibility enumerated in §1.3 are met, such as exclusion of resale markets.

The Cournot model also provides a useful interpretation of Ramsey pricing. Restricting a regulated firm's net revenue is essentially equivalent to a fictitious process of Cournot competition in which the firm is one of several offering identical products. In effect, the regulated firm is allowed to obtain monopoly profits only from a residual market share after the regulatory agency has claimed its share in the public interest.

Lastly, Section 4 indicates that nonlinear pricing can occur at another level of pricing strategy. In combination, stochastic demand and competitive pressures lead to a nonlinear relationship between average prices and aggregate supply.

13

MULTIPRODUCT PRICING

This chapter and the next describe the design of a tariff that specifies a total charge depending jointly on the quantities of several products purchased by a customer. For instance, a multiproduct tariff typically allows quantity discounts for each product separately and also for the combined bundle of purchases. The formulation in this chapter relies on an explicit model of customers' behaviors in which each customer is described by a list of type parameters, as in §6 for the case of a single product. The formulation in the next chapter relies on the multiproduct version of a demand profile estimated directly from aggregate demand data, as in §12. The analyses in §12 and §14 do not apply to some of the topics addressed in this chapter because those chapters assume that the demand profile induces a density function for purchased bundles. In this chapter we consider models in which the demand profile need not have an associated density—which is always the case when the number of products exceeds the number of type parameters.

Section 1 begins with some remarks about the special features of multiproduct tariffs. Section 2 specifies the ingredients of a fairly general formulation and then derives the conditions that characterize the optimal schedule of marginal prices. Section 3 uses these conditions to construct tariffs for priority service; this construction offers an alternative to the method developed in §10. Section 4 examines the simple case that customers are described by a single type parameter. Sections 5 and 6 study models with multiple type parameters. Multidimensional types are usually necessary for realistic modeling of practical problems but unlike the single product case, unfortunately, the combination of multiple products and multiple type dimensions introduces computational difficulties. Although the examples in Sections 5 and 6 are useful for studying some of the qualitative properties of multiproduct tariffs, in general the methods described in §14 are better for calculating a numerical approximation of an optimal tariff.

13.1   Special features of multiproduct tariffs

The basic principles involved in multiproduct pricing are unchanged from the single-product case. However, more data are required and calculations are more complicated. The greater data requirements are to be expected, since one must take account of substitution and complementarity effects among the products. The computational difficulties derive partly from the implicit restriction that customers cannot choose combinations of quantity and quality attributes freely; in the terminology of §9, this restriction appears geometrically as a constraint that purchase sets must be rectangular. The force of this constraint can be seen by supposing that a customer buys the bundle (q_1, q_2), where q_1 and q_2 are the quantity and quality of a single product. The multiproduct formulation implicitly assumes that the same quality q_2 applies uniformly to each of the q_1 units of the product: if this is not actually the case then a simpler formulation like the one in §9 can be used. It is often useful in a practical application, therefore, to relax this constraint by ensuring that customers are allowed the maximum feasible range of choice in assigning quality attributes. Several qualities of the same generic product might be analyzed better and easier via multidimensional pricing then via multiproduct pricing. One such case is priority pricing as studied in §10, where the analysis is simplified by treating different priorities as different magnitudes along a single quality dimension, rather than as different products. Similarly, peakload pricing might be better modeled via a quality dimension that represents the relative scarcity of capacity.

Multiproduct pricing is severely affected by the practical consideration that a complex tariff is costly to implement and difficult for customers to understand. To avoid undue complexity, firms often base multiproduct discounts on aggregate measures of the bundles purchased by customers. In §2 we noted that airlines offer frequent-flier rebates based on cumulative mileage, and *Time* and *Newsweek* base some of their discounts on the aggregate dollar value of advertising insertions; similarly, telephone tariffs for WATS lines aggregate calls to many different destinations. Aggregate measures can usually be designed to yield approximations of optimal tariffs. In important cases, moreover, the theory reveals an appropriate aggregate measure, as will be demonstrated in Section 5. Nevertheless, firms often prefer to constrain the tariff to a simple form. For instance, one might insist that the charge for a bundle can be computed by adding up charges for each component of the bundle; this is an additively separable tariff of the kind studied in §12. We caution that the formulation used in this chapter is not adapted to inclusion of such constraints.

Multiproduct pricing addresses the case that each customer selects a list $q = (q_1, \ldots, q_n)$ of quantities q_i of each of n products $i = 1, \ldots, n$, for which the tariff then specifies a total charge $P(q)$.[1] As in previous chapters, the analysis focuses

1. If the products differ only in terms of their embodied magnitudes of several quality attributes, then such a list is equivalent to an assignment-form description of the purchase set, as in the analysis

on determining the optimal schedule of marginal prices. Here, such a schedule specifies for each bundle q the marginal charge

$$p_i(q) = \frac{\partial P}{\partial q_i}(q)$$

imposed for an additional unit of the i-th product. We use $p(q) = (p_i(q))_{i=1,..,n}$ to indicate the list of marginal prices, one for each product. This list is an n-dimensional vector indicating the gradient of the tariff; that is, the magnitudes of marginal charges for increments of each of the products.

Characterizations of marginal prices are subject to an important restriction, called the integrability constraint. If the marginal price schedule is to be consistent with a tariff then it must have the property that for any two products i and j,

$$\frac{\partial p_i}{\partial q_j}(q) = \frac{\partial p_j}{\partial q_i}(q).$$

This property expresses the fact that if the tariff is twice differentiable, as we shall always assume, then the order in which partial derivatives (or finite differences in a discrete model) are taken is immaterial. Because the integrability constraint complicates the construction of multiproduct tariffs, the formulation in Section 2 takes an indirect approach.

The integrability constraint assures that the total charge is independent of which path is used to compute it from the marginal charges accumulated along the way. Recall that for a single product, the tariff's total charge can be found by accumulating the marginal prices charged for all the unit increments between 0 and q purchased by a customer. Similarly, for a multiproduct tariff, the total charge can be found by accumulating the marginal charges along any path from the null bundle 0 to the bundle q. In Figure 13.1, for instance, the total charge for the bundle $q = (q_1, q_2)$ of two products might be calculated by daily accumulation of the marginal charges as the customer makes successive incremental purchases along the solid curve to arrive at the bundle q at the end of the billing period. Alternatively, the marginal charges could be accumulated along either of the two other paths shown, in which first the purchase of one product is made and then the other. These three alternative methods of calculating the total charge must all arrive at the same total charge for the bundle.

of multidimensional pricing. However, if the firm's costs and customers' benefits do not satisfy the special assumptions invoked in §9, then it may still be necessary to use the multiproduct formulation. For example, peak and offpeak power can be considered different products, and this is the better formulation if customers' incentives to shift loads over time are not accurately represented by the additively separable benefit function used in §9.

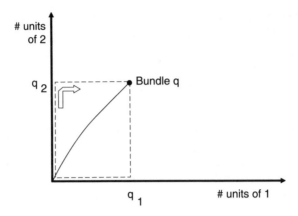

Fig. 13.1 Three alternative paths to accumulate marginal charges. The arrow indicates a path that first increases q_2, then q_1, to reach the bundle q.

In general, a path is described by a parameterization $q(\tau)$ for which $q(0) = 0$ and $q(1) = q$. The tariff's total charge is then

$$P(q) = P(0) + \int_0^1 \sum_i p_i(q(\tau))q_i'(\tau)\,d\tau \,,$$

where $P(0)$ is a fixed charge (if any, and which in principle might depend on the set of products purchased in positive amounts). In the figure, for instance, the parameter τ could indicate a measure of time within the billing period. An important special case is the rectilinear path that first increases the first quantity up to q_1, then the second up to q_2, et cetera. In this case the total charge imposed by the tariff is calculated as

$$P(q) = P(0) + \sum_{i=1}^{n} \int_0^{q_i} p_i(q^i, x_i, 0)\,dx_i \,,$$

where $(q^i, x_i, 0)$ is the bundle along the path for which the quantities of those products $j > i$ have not yet been increased. Thus, τ measures cumulative units of the various products $i = 1, \ldots, n$ in succession. The integrability constraint can also be interpreted as requiring that each of the rectilinear paths between any two bundles yields the same total charge for the difference between the two bundles.

In practice, tariffs are often specified directly in terms of the schedule of marginal prices, although usually simplified by assigning constant prices over ranges of bundles. Even so, the integrability constraint is necessary lest customers insist on calculating the total charge based on the most favorable least-cost path for accumulating marginal charges.

13.2 Formulation

This section describes an alternative formulation of Ramsey pricing that partially circumvents the integrability constraint when there are multiple products and multiple type parameters. This formulation interprets the problem as optimizing the allocation of bundles and net benefits among customers; thus, one obtains conditions that directly characterize this allocation. Account is taken of the integrability constraint only in a second stage when one constructs a schedule of marginal prices to induce customers to choose their allocated bundles—which is the hard part computationally.

The n products are indexed by $i = 1, \ldots, n$ and the vector $q = (q_i)$ is a list of n quantities describing a bundle purchased by some customer. Each customer is described by a vector $t = (t_j)$ consisting of m type parameters indexed by $j = 1, \ldots, m$ that suffice to specify demand behavior. The distribution of the type parameters in the population is given by a distribution function $F(t)$ that has a positive density $f(t)$ on a specified domain. We suppose this domain is rectangular, comprising those types for which $0 \leq t \leq T$. The value $F(t)$ of the distribution function at t indicates the fraction of potential customers with type parameters no greater than t in each component.

A customer of type t obtains the net benefit $U(q, t) - P(q)$ from the bundle q if the tariff imposes the total charge $P(q)$, or $U(0, t) = 0$ and $P(0) = 0$ if no purchase is made. Consequently, the customer's predicted net benefit is

$$W(t) = \max_{q \in Q} \{ U(q, t) - P(q) \}$$

if Q is the set of possible bundles that might be chosen. We assume that Q is the same for every customer, and it includes the null bundle 0 for which $P(0) = 0$. Thus, the model of demand behavior has two parts. One is the specification of how the gross benefit function U, or equivalently an associated multiproduct demand function $D(q, t)$, depends on the bundle q purchased and on the customer's type t. The second part is the distribution F of types in the population. Typically one builds such a model by estimating the dependence of demands on prices as well as various customer characteristics whose distribution is either observed directly in demand data or derived from measurable correlations.

As mentioned, §14 presents a method that computes the tariff directly from demand data, whereas here we first calculate an optimal allocation and then subsequently derive the tariff or marginal prices that implement this allocation. Thus, if the allocation indicates that type t should obtain the maximal net benefit $W(t)$ by purchasing the bundle $q(t)$ then we know that the tariff must charge

$$P(q(t)) = U(q(t), t) - W(t)$$

for the bundle $q(t)$. Further, because $q(t)$ is an optimal bundle it must satisfy the envelope property: for each type parameter j,

$$\frac{\partial W}{\partial t_j}(t) = \frac{\partial U}{\partial t_j}(q(t), t).$$

Hereafter we use $W'(t) \equiv (\partial W(t)/\partial t_j)$ to indicate the list of partial derivatives appearing on the left side, and $U_t(q, t) \equiv (\partial U/\partial t_j)$ to indicate those appearing on the right. Note that W' is the gradient vector of W but U_t reflects partial differentiation only with respect to the type parameter: the partial derivatives with respect to the bundle, which in turn depends on the customer's type, net to zero because the customer is presumed to optimize the bundle chosen.

In sum, posing the problem as allocating bundles $q(t)$ and net benefits $W(t)$ to each type t of customer, these two type-dependent quantities are connected by the constraint $W'(t) = U_t(q(t), t)$ to ensure that customers' choices are optimal. Also, the revenue obtained by the firm from each customer of type t is $U(q(t), t) - W(t)$.

The constraint $W'(t) = U_t(q(t), t)$ is only a necessary condition for the customer's choice to be optimal, but we assume here that it is sufficient as well.[2] To make this plausible we generally assume that U is bounded, increasing, and strictly concave in q, and both U and U_q are increasing in t. The feasible set of bundles is assumed to be $Q = \{q \mid q \geq 0\}$ and we adopt the normalization $U(0, t) = 0$ for each type t.

Recall now that Ramsey pricing is designed to maximize a measure of total surplus subject to a net revenue requirement for the firm—which can be the monopoly profit if the firm is an unregulated profit-maximizing enterprise. Suppose for simplicity only that the firm's costs are separable among customers; say, $C(q)$ is the cost of providing the bundle q to any customer. Allowing Lagrange multipliers for the constraints, the optimization problem is then to choose the allocation $\langle q(t), W(t) \rangle$ to maximize

$$\int_0^T \left\{ (w(t)W(t) + [1 + \lambda][U(q(t), t) - W(t) - C(q(t))]) f(t) \right.$$
$$\left. + [W'(t) - U_t(q(t), t)] \cdot \hat{\mu}(t) \right\} dt .$$

Here, the integral is taken over the entire domain of the type parameters, $w(t)$ is a nonnegative welfare weight assigned to type t's net benefit relative to a weight of 1

---

2. Assumptions that assure sufficiency are provided by Mirrlees (1976, 1986) and McAfee and McMillan (1988), among others. The customer's second-order necessary condition requires that the matrix of second-order derivatives of $U - P$ with respect to q is negative semi-definite, which can be rephrased as requiring that the matrix $W'' - U_{tt}$ of second-order derivatives with respect to t is positive semi-definite. For instance, if U is linear in t then W must be a convex function. In some applications where this constraint is binding, it is advantageous to impose this constraint directly.

for the firm's profit, λ is a nonnegative Lagrange multiplier on the firm's net revenue constraint, and $\hat{\mu}(t) = (\hat{\mu}_j(t))_{j=1,..,m}$ is a vector of Lagrange multipliers on type t's optimality constraints; also, the notation $x \cdot \hat{\mu}$ indicates the inner product $\sum_j x_j \hat{\mu}_j$. As usual, these Lagrange multipliers must be specified so that the corresponding constraints are satisfied; we have omitted specifying the amount of the revenue requirement. The integrand in curly brackets has three terms for each customer type t: the first is the customer's welfare-weighted net benefit to represent consumers' surplus; the second is the firm's profit, weighted by $1 + \lambda$ to include both the producer's surplus and the Lagrangian term arising from the revenue constraint; and the third is the Lagrangian term arising from the constraint representing the customer's optimization. The first and second terms are, of course, weighted also by the frequency $f(t)$ with which type t occurs in the population.

We have not explicitly included the feasibility constraint $q(t) \geq 0$ and the customer's participation constraint $W(t) \geq U(0,t) \equiv 0$, but it is intended that the maximization is subject to these further constraints.[3]

Because the gradient W' of W appears in this objective function, the problem must be addressed using the calculus of variations. The necessary conditions for an optimum include:[4]

$$[1 + \lambda][v(q(t), t) - c(q(t))]f(t) - v_t(q(t), t) \cdot \hat{\mu}(t) \leq 0,$$

$$[w(t) - (1 + \lambda)]f(t) - \sum_{j=1}^{m} \frac{\partial \hat{\mu}_j}{\partial t_j}(t) \leq 0.$$

Here, $v(q, t) \equiv U_q(q, t)$ is the list of type t's marginal benefit functions and as usual $c(q) \equiv C'(q)$ is the list of the firm's marginal costs: with multiple products each of these is a gradient vector with one component for each product. If aggregate costs depend also on aggregate supply then an additional term representing aggregate marginal costs can be added to c. The notation $v_t(q, t)$ indicates the two-dimensional array that is the Jacobian matrix $(\partial v_i / \partial t_j)$ of partial derivatives of the components of v with respect to the type parameters, and $v_t \cdot \hat{\mu}$ indicates the vector whose components are the inner products $\sum_j [\partial v_i / \partial t_j] \hat{\mu}_j$, one for each product i.

Hereafter we simplify by assuming that the customers' welfare weights are equal and the same as the firm's; thus, $w(t) = 1$, indicating that the objective is to

---

3. Although we do not do so here, in some cases it is useful also to take explicit account of the second-order necessary condition for the customer's optimization: the Hessian matrix $U_{qq}(q, t) - P''(q)$ evaluated at $q = q(t)$ should be negative semi-definite.

4. The Divergence Theorem implies that the second of these conditions cannot hold as an equality over the entire domain of type parameters; consequently, there must be some types who do not purchase and whose net benefit is nil.

maximize total surplus subject to the firm's revenue requirement. In this case we can let $\hat{\mu}(t) = \lambda\mu(t)$ and $\alpha = \lambda/[1 + \lambda]$ to express these conditions in the form:

$$v(q(t), t) - c(q(t)) - \alpha[v_t(q(t), t) \cdot \mu(t)]/f(t) \leq 0, \tag{1}$$

$$f(t) + \sum_{j=1}^{m} \frac{\partial \mu_j}{\partial t_j}(t) \geq 0. \tag{2}$$

We have written these conditions as inequalities, but in fact they are more complicated. The i-th component of the left side of (1) must equal zero if $q_i(t)$ is positive, and also (2) must be an equality if $W(t) > 0$. Thus, for a type t assigned positive amounts of all products, and therefore assigned a positive net benefit, both (1) and (2) must be equalities.

An alternative version of (1) is stated in terms of type t's multiproduct demand function $D(p, t)$, which satisfies the equation $q = D(v(q, t), t)$ by definition. For those products for which (1) is an equality, therefore,

$$D_p(p, t) \cdot [p - c] + \alpha[D_t(p, t) \cdot \mu(t)]/f(t) = 0 \tag{1'}$$

at marginal prices $p \equiv p(q(t))$ such that $q(t) = D(p, t)$. Note that D_p and D_t are Jacobian matrices of partial derivatives of demands with respect to prices and type parameters respectively.[5] This is an equivalent statement of (1) that parallels the single-product case in §6.5. In particular, suppose the tariff is represented as an assignment of a fixed fee $P_o(t)$ and a vector of marginal prices $p(t)$ to type t, so that the tariff payable for the assigned bundle $q(t) = D(p(t), t)$ is $P(t) = P_o(t) + p(t) \cdot q(t)$. In this case, incentive compatibility requires that $P'_o(t) + D(p(t), t) \cdot p'(t) = 0$ so that at his optimal purchase a customer's altered variable charges if he selects another nearby menu option are compensated by the altered fixed fee. If one specifies that $\mu(t)$ is the vector of Lagrange multipliers associated with this incentive compatibility constraint, then the formulation and derivation in §6.5 again yields the conditions (1') and (2) as the Euler conditions for optimal choices of $p(t)$ and $P_o(t)$.

In addition to these conditions there are further transversality conditions that apply to μ on the boundary of the domain of types. If $t_j = 0$ then $\mu_j(t) \geq 0$ and if also $W(t) > 0$ then $\mu_j(t) = 0$. Similarly, if $t_j = T_j$ then $\mu_j(t) \leq 0$ and if also $W(t) > 0$ then $\mu_j(t) = 0$. We summarize part of these conditions as

$$\mu_j(t) = 0 \quad \text{if} \quad t_j \in \{0, T_j\} \quad \text{and} \quad W(t) > 0; \tag{3}$$

in addition,

$$\mu_j(t) \geq 0 \quad \text{if} \quad t_j = 0, \quad \text{and} \quad \mu_j(t) \leq 0 \quad \text{if} \quad t_j = T_j.$$

5. The inner product $A \cdot x$ of a matrix $A = (a_{ij})$ and a (column) vector x is the vector with components $(\sum_j a_{ij}x_j)$, and the inner product $A \cdot B$ of two matrices is the matrix $(\sum_k a_{ik}b_{kj})$.

For example, if customers with small types get $W(t) = 0$ then the only requirement along the lower boundary of the domain is that $\mu(t) \geq 0$, but if large types get $W(t) > 0$ then the constraint $\mu(t) = 0$ is binding along the upper boundary of the domain of types. It is important to observe, however, that this constraint can also be binding along the lower boundary for types who obtain a positive net benefit, as we discuss in Section 5.

These conditions are familiar from the previous analysis in §6 for the case of one product and one type parameter. If there is a single type parameter ($m = 1$), even if there are many products ($n \geq 1$), then one solution to the differential equation specified by (2) is $\mu(t) = \bar{F}(t)$, where $\bar{F}(t) = 1 - F(t)$ is the right-cumulative distribution function, and the transversality condition (3) indicates this is the relevant solution when high types obtain positive net benefit. Then (1) merely expresses the optimality condition derived in §6.5 and §8.2.

The interpretation of conditions (1) and (2) derives from the fact that (1) is obtained by optimizing the bundle $q(t)$ assigned to type t, whereas (2) derives from optimizing the net benefit $W(t)$. Thus, (1) expresses the requirements for a (revenue constrained) efficient allocation of goods among the customers, whereas (2) chooses among these efficient allocations to select one that maximizes total surplus, or a weighted version of total surplus if the welfare weights $w(t)$ are unequal. Given the right choice of μ, the condition (1) usually determines fully the optimal assignment of quantities to customers.

As we shall see in Section 5, conditions (1)–(3) are discouraging when there are multiple products *and* multiple type parameters. For instance, when the numbers of products and type parameters are the same ($n = m$), the original problem of finding a tariff that is a single function of n quantity variables is converted by conditions (1)–(3) into the problem of finding the m functions μ_j of m type variables. Unless the structural features of the optimality conditions provide some useful information about the form of the solution, it is unlikely that this conversion represents practical progress.

Admittedly the Lagrange multipliers μ_j are difficult to interpret. Their primary role is to assure that customers' assigned bundles represent optimal choices in response to some tariff. A further insight into their role can be seen in the case that the marginal benefit function is linear in the type parameters, or equivalently v_t depends only on the bundle q, so that $v(q, t) = v_t(q) \cdot t + v(q, 0)$. In this case (1) takes the form $v(q(t), s(t)) = c(q(t))$, where $s(t) = t - \alpha\mu(t)/f(t)$. Thus, the fully efficient bundle $q^\circ(s)$ that is optimal for type s in the absence of any revenue requirement ($\alpha = 0$) is actually assigned to that higher type t for which $s = s(t)$ in order to raise the required revenue when $\alpha > 0$. The way this is done is to set the marginal prices above marginal costs by a margin

$$p(q(t)) - c(q(t)) = \alpha[v_t(q(t)) \cdot \mu(t)]/f(t)$$

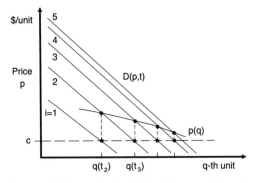

FIG. 13.2 Relation between efficient and assigned allocations: type t_3 is assigned the bundle $q(t_3)$ that is efficient for type t_2.

sufficient to restrain type t's purchases to the bundle $q(t) = q^\circ(s(t))$, which is less than the customer would purchase at prices equal to marginal costs. Although the bundle obtained is thereby smaller, the price increase more than offsets this decrease: by setting α appropriately the required revenue is obtained by the firm.

Marginal benefit functions that are linear in the type parameters have another consequence that is useful in applications. Generally the set $\{\,q(t) \mid 0 \le t \le T\,\}$ of bundles assigned to customers depends on α and the distribution function F, but type-linearity implies that it does *not* depend on these data. That is, each bundle $q(t)$ that is optimal for some type t given $\alpha > 0$ and some distribution function F, is also optimal for type $s(t)$ when $\alpha = 0$, independently of F. Thus, in this case the allocation problem involved in Ramsey pricing concerns only which type receives one of the optimal bundles, and not which bundles to supply.[6] More generally, if customers' benefit functions depend only on aggregate measures $A(q)$ and $B(q)$ in the form

$$U(q, t) = \hat{U}(A(q), t) + B(q),$$

then again the set of optimal assignments is independent of α and the distribution function F.

The general case is represented in Figure 13.2 for the case of a single product and a single type parameter. The figure shows the demand functions of five types t_i related by the property that $t_i = s(t_{i+1})$, where $s(t)$ is the type whose efficient bundle is allocated to t; that is,

$$v(q(t), t) - v_t(q(t), t)[\alpha\mu(t)/f(t)] = v(q(t), s(t)).$$

As shown in the figure, each type t_i obtains the bundle $q(t_i)$ that is efficient for type t_{i-1}, as indicated by the dashed line corresponding to pricing at the marginal cost c.

6. This argument fails if marginal costs depend on aggregate demand, since aggregate demand depends on α.

When the bundle q includes various quality attributes, this feature of the optimal assignment is sometimes interpreted as quality distortion. That is, customers obtain qualities that are lower than they would receive from the fully efficient assignment based on pricing at marginal cost. A substantial literature since the initial analysis by Mussa and Rosen (1978) addresses the welfare and policy considerations of this conclusion.[7]

The integrability constraints

When there are multiple products and multiple type parameters, conditions (1) and (2) are far from sufficient to determine a solution to the original optimization problem, as is evident from the fact that (2) specifies only a single differential equation that μ must satisfy, whereas μ is a vector comprising m different functions. The solution to this riddle is found by considering the task of implementing an assignment $q(t)$ of bundles to types of customers, which reveals the crucial role of the integrability constraints.

The tariff $P(q)$ must have the property that its associated schedule $p(q)$ of marginal prices satisfies the necessary condition

$$p(q(t)) \geq v(q(t), t),$$

for type t's personal optimization problem, where the i-th component inequality must be an equality if $q_i(t) > 0$. Indeed, taking this condition as an equality for the products purchased in positive quantities (for instance, all products), we can differentiate to obtain the further condition that

$$p'(q(t)) \cdot q'(t) = v_q(q(t), t) \cdot q'(t) + v_t(q(t), t).$$

In this condition, the Jacobian matrices p' and v_q must necessarily be symmetric because they are actually the Hessian matrices of second partial derivatives of P and U; hence, this condition imposes restrictions on what the Jacobian matrix $q'(t)$ can be. A simpler form of this condition recognizes that also the Hessian matrix $W''(t)$ of second partial derivatives of the net benefit assignment must be symmetric. Recall that its Jacobian is constrained to satisfy $W'(t) = U_t(q(t), t)$, so

$$W''(t) = v_t(q(t), t)^T \cdot q'(t) + U_{tt}(q(t), t),$$

where v_t^T indicates the transpose of the matrix v_t in which the roles of rows and columns are reversed. Now the Hessian matrix U_{tt} is also symmetric, so the relevant condition is that the matrix

$$v_t(q(t), t)^T \cdot q'(t) \qquad \text{is symmetric.} \tag{4}$$

7. See Besanko, Donnenfeld, and White (1987, 1988), Donnenfeld and White (1988, 1990), Spulber (1989), and Srinagesh and Bradburd (1989).

As we shall see in applications in Section 5, it is actually condition (4) in conjunction with (1)–(3) that determines what the vector $\mu(t)$ of Lagrangian functions must be. If $\mu(t)$ is chosen to assure that (4) is satisfied then the marginal price schedule can be integrated along any path to find the tariff; or alternatively, $W'(t)$ can be integrated along any path to find $W(t)$, from which the charge for the bundle $q(t)$ is obtained as $P(q(t)) = U(q(t), t) - W(t)$.

The complexity of this discussion of integrability conditions is a harbinger of the computational difficulties that ensue when actually computing an optimal multiproduct tariff.[8] As mentioned, these difficulties disappear if there is a single type parameter (or a single product, as shown in §8.4), so in Section 4 we consider multiproduct models that rely on a single type parameter. Applications with several type parameters are studied in Section 5.

Income effects

To be complete, we record the analogs of conditions (1) and (2) when customers' preferences include income effects. Suppose that type t's net benefit is $W(t) = \max_{q \in Q} U(q, P(q), t)$, where the utility function U is a decreasing function of the tariff P paid. In this case, $h(q, P, t) \equiv -U_P(q, P, t)$ is type t's marginal utility of income, and $v(q, P, t) = h(q, P, t)^{-1} U_q(q, P, t)$ is the vector of the customer's marginal rates of substitution between income and the products, expressed in \$/unit of each product. (When there are no income effects, $h = 1$, and therefore the marginal rates of substitution are given by $v = U_q$ as usual.) The analogs of (1) and (2) are then:

$$v(q(t), P(q(t)), t) - c(q(t)) - \alpha v_t(q(t), P(q(t)), t) \cdot [\mu(t)h]/f(t) \le 0,$$

$$[w(t)h/\lambda - 1/\alpha]f(t) - \sum_{j=1}^{m} \frac{\partial[\mu_j(t)h]}{\partial t_j} \le 0,$$

where h is evaluated at $(q(t), P(q(t)), t)$. The auxiliary condition

$$W(t) = U(q(t), P(q(t)), t)$$

determines the tariff $P(q(t))$ paid by type t. The key difference in these conditions is that the marginal utility of income need not be constant. As in §7, income effects can be minor or severe, depending on their exact specification.

8. Mirrlees (1976, p. 342; 1986, p. 1241) describes how (1) and (2) can be converted into a second-order partial differential equation for W when $m < n$, or a system of differential equations when $m \ge n$. Numerical methods for computing solutions when $m < n$ are given in Press *et al.* (1986, Chapter 17).

13.3   A reprise of priority service

In this section we apply the conditions derived in Section 2 to derive tariffs for priority service when only a limited number of service conditions is offered. Recall that §10 assumed that the entire spectrum of service reliabilities is offered by the firm, whereas here the firm offers n different service contracts indexed by $i = 1, \ldots, n$. Associated with each contract i is a service reliability r_i and a constant marginal cost c_i. Each contract represents a different product and therefore the aim is to construct an optimal multiproduct tariff.

The reliabilities are assumed to decrease as the index i increases, $r_1 > r_2 > \cdots > r_n$, indicating that lower numbered contracts have corresponding earlier positions in the service order for dispatch of available supplies. All units of demand under the same contract have the same service reliability r_i. The marginal cost c_i is interpreted unconditionally as an expectation: properly the marginal cost of a delivered unit under contract i is c_i/r_i whereas the expected marginal cost is $r_i[c_i/r_i] = c_i$. Assume further that the incremental cost of an increment in reliability i, defined as

$$\delta_i = \frac{c_i - c_{i+1}}{r_i - r_{i+1}},$$

is also decreasing in the index i. For notational convenience we adjoin an $n+1$-th contract with reliability $r_{n+1} = 0$ and marginal cost $c_{n+1} = 0$ that represents no service to the customer; thus, $\delta_n = c_n/r_n$.

As in Section 2, each customer is described by a type t and these types are distributed in the population according to a distribution function F. A customer of type t has a marginal valuation $u(x, t)$ for an x-th unit of service if actually delivered (and zero otherwise), assumed to be a decreasing function of x and an increasing function of t. Consequently, if the customer subscribes to q_i units of service under contract i, so that the bundle $q = (q_i)_{i=1,\ldots,n}$ is the total purchase, and the tariff charged is $P(q)$, then the net expected benefit is

$$U(q, t) - P(q) = \sum_{i=1}^{n} \int_0^{q_i} r_i u(Q_{i-1} + x, t) \, dx - P(q),$$

where $Q_i \equiv \sum_{j \leq i} q_j$. Note that the tariff is specified as an expected payment. This specification implies that

$$v_i(q, t) \equiv \frac{\partial U}{\partial q_i}(q, t) = \sum_{j=i}^{n} s_j u(Q_j, t),$$

where $s_i \equiv r_i - r_{i+1}$. Applying this specification in the efficiency condition (1) and then simplifying the resulting formulas yields the following conditions for each contract i:

$$u(Q_i, t) - \delta_i - \alpha[u_t(Q_i, t) \cdot \mu(t)]/f(t) = 0\,,$$

$$\frac{\partial P}{\partial Q_i}(Q) = s_i u(Q_i, t)\,.$$

In the second line we have expressed the tariff P as a function of the cumulates $Q = (Q_i)_{i=1,..,n}$ so that

$$\frac{\partial P}{\partial Q_i}(Q) = p_i(q) - p_{i+1}(q)\,.$$

The important feature of these reformulated conditions is that they can be solved for each contract separately as a function of the cumulative Q_i, thus eliminating the dependence across contracts. This is evident from the fact that $u(Q_i, t)$ has exactly the same role here as $v(q, t)$ does in (1). However, if there is a revenue requirement then α must still be the same for each contract.

The following example assumes that there is a single type parameter, in which case $\mu(t) = \bar{F}(t)$ as mentioned in Section 2. A further consequence of a single type parameter is that the i-th optimality condition can be solved to identify the type $t_i(Q_i)$ that the optimal tariff induces to purchase Q_i units from contracts $j \leq i$. The tariff is then specified by the formula

$$P(Q) = \sum_{i=1}^{n} s_i \int_0^{Q_i} u(x, t_i(x))\, dx\,.$$

Example 13.1: For this example assume that the marginal valuation function u is linear, and via appropriate choices of units let $u(x, t) = t - x$. Further, suppose t is uniformly distributed between zero and one, so that $\mu(t)/f(t) = 1 - t$. (This is the same example addressed in §10 for the case that the contracts provide a complete spectrum of reliabilities.) With these specifications, the optimality conditions indicate that the type induced to choose a Q_i-th cumulative unit under contract i is

$$t_i(Q_i) = [\alpha + \delta_i + Q_i]/[1 + \alpha]\,.$$

The optimal tariff is therefore

$$P(Q) = \sum_{i=1}^{n} s_i Q_i \left[\frac{\delta_i + \alpha}{1 + \alpha} - \frac{\alpha}{1 + \alpha}\frac{1}{2}Q_i\right]$$

$$= \frac{1}{1 + \alpha} \sum_{i=1}^{n} c_i q_i + \frac{\alpha}{1 + \alpha} \sum_{i=1}^{n} r_i q_i \{1 - \frac{1}{2}[Q_{i-1} + Q_i]\}\,.$$

The term in curly brackets indicates that for each contract i the quantity discount is based on the customer's cumulative purchases under contracts $j \leq i$. Customers' purchases have the following special structure, moreover. For each type t there is a contract $i(t)$ with the least index i for which the customer subscribes to a positive amount, and for this contract the customer's demand is

$$q_{i(t)}(t) = [1 + \alpha]t - \alpha - \delta_{i(t)},$$

or possibly the index t is so small that the customer makes no purchase ($i(t) = n + 1$). For each contract $i > i(t)$, however, the customer's demand is $q_i(t) = \delta_{i-1} - \delta_i$, which is independent of the customer's type. Thus, except for the highest priority contract to which a customer subscribes, all customers demand the same quantity of service under each contract.   ◇

13.4 Single type parameters

This section considers the special case that the population of potential customers is described by a single parameter t that varies among customers; thus, $m = 1$. As mentioned in Section 2, in this case the relevant solution of the optimality condition (2) and the transversality condition (3) is $\mu(t) = \bar{F}(t)$. The integrability condition (4) has no effect because the matrix in (4) has a single element and therefore symmetry is not a binding constraint. Assume that there are several products, namely $n > 1$.

In this case the assignment $q(t)$ of bundles to types of customers is a one-dimensional locus of points in the n-dimensional space of quantities of the products, as shown in Figure 13.3. That is, as the type index t varies from 0 to T, the assignment $q(t)$ traces out a curve that increases from $q(0)$ to $q(T)$.[9] Typically there is a greatest type t_* making no purchase, so $q(t) = 0$ for $t \leq t_*$, and for larger values of t one of more components of $q(t)$ is positive.

In principle, therefore, this curve describes an appropriate aggregation of the products from which one can construct a single-product tariff that depends only on the aggregate bundle. For example, if the curve is parameterized by the aggregate $x(q) = \sum_i q_i$, then it suffices to offer a tariff $\hat{P}(x)$ that depends only on this aggregate. The simplest parameterization uses the type index t itself, in which case the marginal price is

$$\hat{p}(t) = \sum_i p_i(q(t))q_i'(t)$$

9. Similarly, whenever $m < n$ the assignment describes an m-dimensional surface. In general, the number of product aggregates needed to model customers' behaviors is the minimum of m and n. Notice that whenever $m < n$ the marginal prices are well-determined only along the surface of assigned bundles. Consequently, there are many tariffs that implement the optimal allocation: they need to agree only in the schedule of marginal prices for assigned bundles.

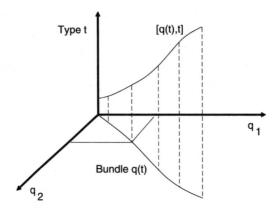

FIG. 13.3 The locus of the assignment of types to purchased bundles.

for the vector $(q'_i(t))$ of increments along the curve of optimal assignments. Recall that the marginal prices in this sum are obtained as $p_i(q(t)) = v_i(q(t), t)$ after one has solved (1) to find the optimal assignment: for each product $i = 1, \ldots, n$,

$$v_i(q(t), t) - \alpha v_{it}(q(t), t)\bar{F}(t)/f(t) = c_i(q(t)).$$

These n equations determine the n quantities $q_i(t)$ of the products assigned to type t, from which the marginal price schedule $\hat{p}(t)$ is constructed. More generally, for any aggregate $x(q)$ that is a differentiable function of the bundle q the tariff must satisfy $\hat{P}(x(q(t))) = P(q(t))$, so the marginal price schedule is characterized by the property

$$\hat{p}(x(q(t))) = \frac{\sum_i v_i(q(t), t)q'_i(t)}{\sum_i \frac{\partial x}{\partial q_i} q'_i(t)}.$$

One implication of this construction is that, as in the single-product case, the percentage profit margin included in the marginal price for increments of the aggregate is inversely proportional to the price elasticity of demand for such increments.

Example 13.2: For example, suppose the marginal benefit function is $v(q, t) = tA - B \cdot q$, the type parameter t is uniformly distributed between zero and one, and marginal costs are constant. Then

$$\hat{p}(t) = [c + \alpha(1 - t)A] \cdot \hat{q}'$$

is the marginal price schedule for increments[10]

$$\hat{q}' = [1 + \alpha] B^{-1} \cdot A .$$

That is, $\Delta \hat{p}(t)$ is charged for a small increment Δ in t that provides the incremental bundle $\Delta \hat{q}'$. Consequently,

$$\hat{P}(t) = t[c + \alpha(1 - \tfrac{1}{2}t)A] \cdot \hat{q}'$$

is the optimal tariff when t is used as the aggregate measure that parameterizes the locus of optimal assignments. Alternatively, if the aggregate used is $x(q) = \sum_i w_i q_i \equiv w \cdot q$, where w is a vector of weights or amounts of the products in the bundle, then

$$\hat{p}(x) = \gamma - \frac{\alpha}{1 + \alpha} \beta x ,$$

where

$$\beta = \delta^2 [A \cdot B^{-1} \cdot A] , \qquad \delta = [w \cdot B^{-1} \cdot A]^{-1} ,$$

$$\gamma = \delta[c \cdot B^{-1} \cdot A] + \frac{\alpha}{1 + \alpha} \beta [w \cdot B^{-1} \cdot [A - c]] .$$

◇

In practice, however, this approach is rarely used. A major reason is that a single parameter provides only an approximate description of customers' demand behaviors, so in fact many customers will not confine their purchases to the predicted locus. Temporal and stochastic variabilities in the environment produce additional deviations from the locus. A tariff defined solely for a fixed menu of bundles is therefore inadequate unless the firm, for administrative simplicity, chooses to ignore other variations in purchases.

Practical approaches typically use either an aggregate measure $x(q)$ as described above, or an additively separable tariff $P(q) = \sum_i P_i(q_i)$ that provides optimal pricing along the locus of optimal bundles, but also allows customers to choose other bundles. The simplest version of a separable tariff is constructed as follows. Given the assignments $q(t)$ let $t_i(x)$ be the type assigned x of the i-th product; that is, $q_i(t_i(x)) = x$. Optimal pricing along the locus of assigned bundles requires that the marginal price schedules satisfy

$$p_i(x) = v_i(q(t_i(x)), t_i(x)) ,$$

10. B^{-1} denotes the matrix that is inverse to B; thus $B \cdot B^{-1} = I$ where I is the matrix that has ones on the diagonal and zeros elsewhere. To ensure that U is a strictly concave function of q one assumes that B is a positive definite matrix, meaning that $q \cdot B \cdot q$ only if $q = 0$, and in this case B^{-1} surely exists. Customers' optimizing behavior requires that B is symmetric. Alternatively, type t's demand function is $D(p, t) = B^{-1} \cdot [tA - p]$ which provides B^{-1} directly.

so that customers will face the right marginal tradeoffs. Consequently, an optimal tariff has

$$P_i(q_i) = \int_0^{q_i} p_i(x)\, dx \,.$$

Example 13.3: Recall the formulation in the previous example. If a separable tariff is used then the marginal price schedule for the i-th product is

$$p_i(q_i) = c_i + a_i \left[\frac{\alpha}{1+\alpha} \right] \left[1 - \frac{\gamma_i + q_i}{b_i} \right],$$

where a_i, b_i, and γ_i are the i-th components of the vectors A, $B^{-1} \cdot A$, and $B^{-1} \cdot c$ respectively. The tariff for the i-th product is the corresponding quadratic function of q_i.   ◇

For instance, if each $a_i = 1$ and B is the matrix with diagonal elements 1 and off-diagonal elements b, then $1/b_i = 1 + [n-1]b$. Each product's marginal price schedule declines steeply if b is large or there are many products. This is because b measures the degree of substitutability among products: a firm with many competing, close-substitute products must offer significant quantity discounts to meet revenue requirements.

Demand profile formulations

The foregoing results can be replicated in terms of demand profiles of special kinds that take advantage of the supposition that demand data is explicable by a single type parameter.

Consider first a version in which demand data enable estimation of the number $N_i(p_i, q)$ of customers willing to pay the marginal price p_i for an incremental unit of the i-th product were they currently purchasing the bundle q. In terms of the previous notation,

$$N_i(p_i, q) \equiv \#\{t \mid v_i(q, t) \geq p_i\} = \bar{F}(t_i),$$

where t_i solves the equation $v_i(q, t_i) = p_i$. Considering only the profit-maximizing monopoly case ($\alpha = 1$), if the firm chooses the i-th product's marginal price schedule $p_i(q)$ to maximize the profit contribution $N_i(p_i, q) \cdot [p_i - c_i]$ then, as in §4, the optimal marginal price p_i at the bundle q satisfies

$$p_i = c_i - N_i(p_i, q) \div \frac{\partial N_i}{\partial p_i}(p_i, q),$$

$$= c_i + \frac{\bar{F}(t_i)}{f(t_i)} \frac{\partial v_i}{\partial t}(q, t_i).$$

Table 13.1 Coefficients of the Marginal Price Schedule

b_{ij}^*	$\frac{1}{2}a_i$	$\frac{1}{2}b_{ii}$	$\frac{1}{2}b_{ij}$
$-.1$	0.5556	0.5051	0.0505
$-.5$	1.0000	0.6667	0.3333
$-.9$	5.0000	2.6316	2.3684

Now when there is a single type parameter t and $q = q(t)$ then each $t_i = t$. Consequently, this condition for the optimal price is the same as (1). Caution is advised here, however, since the n demand profiles N_i estimated from the data must be consistent with the existence of a single type parameter for this approach to be exact.

Steeply declining marginal price schedules when products are close substitutes are evident here also. If type t's demand function is $D(p, t) = tA^* - B^* \cdot p$ then the marginal valuation function is $v(q, t) = tA - B \cdot q$ where $B = (B^*)^{-1}$ and $A = B \cdot A^*$, and if the types are uniformly distributed as in the above examples then the vector of marginal price schedules in the monopoly case ($\alpha = 1$) is $p(q) = \frac{1}{2}[c + A - B \cdot q]$.[11] The key feature is that the off-diagonal elements of B^*, which indicate substitutabilities among the products, need not be large in absolute value for the corresponding elements of B to be large. For instance, for two products if the elements of A^* and the diagonal elements of B^* are standardized to be 1 then the diagonal and off-diagonal elements of $\frac{1}{2}B$ are the values shown in Table 13.1 for three examples. As b_{12}^* increases in absolute value towards 1 (indicating perfect substitutability) the coefficients of B increase and become equal because in effect the firm is offering a single product in two equivalent forms. In all three examples only those types $t > 0.5$ purchase positive amounts of the products.

Example 13.4: A slightly different example with similar features supposes that the marginal valuations are $v(q, t) = A - [1/t] B \cdot q$, and again the type parameter t is uniformly distributed. Then the marginal price schedules are

$$p_i(q) = A_i - \sqrt{\beta_i(q)[A_i - c_i]},$$

where $\beta(q) = B \cdot q$.   ◇

A second version assumes customers and the firm anticipate that the purchased bundles lie on a one-dimensional locus. The single demand profile $N(p, q, q')$ specifies the number of customers willing to pay the marginal price p for the

---

11. The same marginal price schedule is optimal if $v(q, t) = t[A - B \cdot q]$.

incremental bundle q' in addition to the current bundle q. In terms of the previous notation, therefore,

$$N(p, q, q') \equiv \#\{t \mid v(q, t) \cdot q' \geq p\} = \bar{F}(t),$$

where t solves the equation $v(q, t) \cdot q' = p$. The firm can use the purchased quantity of one of the products, say product 1, to parameterize the marginal price $p(q_1)$ at the bundle $\hat{q}(q_1)$, where the first component necessarily satisfies $\hat{q}_1(q_1) = q_1$. Consequently, the total profit contribution is

$$\int_0^\infty N(p(q_1), \hat{q}(q_1), \hat{q}'(q_1)) \cdot [p(q_1) - c \cdot \hat{q}'(q_1)] \, dq_1 ,$$

which the firm maximizes by choosing the marginal price schedule $p(q_1)$ and the associated bundle $\hat{q}(q_1)$. This poses a problem in the calculus of variations whose necessary conditions for an optimum agree with the previously derived conditions when there is a single type parameter that explains the behavior represented by the demand profile N. In particular, the optimality condition for the marginal price schedule is familiar from §4 for the case of a single product:

$$N + \frac{\partial N}{\partial p} \cdot [p - c \cdot q'] = 0 ,$$

where arguments of functions are omitted for simplicity. This implies that the percentage profit margin included in $p(q_1)$ is inversely proportional to the price elasticity of the demand profile N.

13.5   Multiple type parameters

Designing multiproduct tariffs is more complicated when customers are described by several type parameters. First we provide a simple example from priority service to illustrate that multiple type parameters can be essential to construct an accurate model of customers' preferences for multiple products. Then we describe the technical complications that ensue. The next section sketches a numerical method that can be used to construct the tariff.

Motivation: priority service with multiple types

Suppose that a customer incurs a fixed shutdown cost c and a lost service value v per unit time of an interruption. Thus, the customer's cost of an interruption of duration d is $c + vd$. To take account of differences among customers in the magnitude of these two costs, the tariff should offer a menu of options (r_1, r_2) in which r_1 is the customer's service priority in interruption events, and when interrupted, r_2 is the customer's priority for resumption of service as the supply shortfall is recouped. Based on the utility's supply technology, each option $r = (r_1, r_2)$ is associated with a pair $q(r) = (q_1(r), q_2(r))$ of service quality characteristics in which, over the period of the contract, $q_1(r)$ is the expected number of interruptions and $q_2(r)$ is the expected cumulative duration of interruptions. Thus, if the tariff specifies a rebate or discount $\hat{P}(r)$ for accepting the option r, then a customer with the fixed cost c and service value v prefers to select the option for which the expected net cost $cq_1(r) + vq_2(r) - \hat{P}(r)$ is minimal among the several options offered. The design problem for the utility is then to specify an optimal rebate $\hat{P}(r)$ based on its knowledge of the supply technology and its estimate of the joint distribution of customers' fixed costs and service values in the population. This problem is essentially equivalent to specifying a rebate $P(q)$ that is a function of the vector q of qualities provided by each option, anticipating that a customer with type parameters (c, v) will select the one that minimizes the expected cost $cq_1 + vq_2 - P(q)$.

In terms of the notation in Section 2, each customer is described by a type vector $t = (t_1, t_2)$ in which, as above, $t_1 \equiv c$ is the fixed cost of an interruption and $t_2 \equiv v$ is the lost service value per unit time during an interruption. An option is similarly specified by a quality vector $q = (q_1, q_2)$ indicating the expected number and cumulative duration of interruptions. Thus, the customer of type t prefers the option that minimizes the expected net cost $t \cdot q - P(q)$.

Customers' purchasing behavior is typically described as in Figure 13.4. Types t in the cone emanating from $t(p, q)$ purchase more than q_i of each quality $i = 1, 2$. Those on the boundary purchase exactly q_i of the corresponding quality, and type $t(p, q)$ at the vertex purchases exactly the bundle q. The multiproduct demand profile used in §14 measures the number of customers whose types are in the cone; namely, the number demanding at least q at the price p. In the priority service example this cone is merely a translate of the positive orthant, but more generally its form differs and it can have curved boundaries.[12]

Explication of the integrability condition

As discussed in Sections 1 and 2, a difficulty in constructing multiproduct tariffs stems from the requirement that the solution to the optimality condition (2) and the transversality condition (3) must also satisfy the integrability condition (4). This condition is imposed to ensure that the marginal price schedules that induce efficient purchasing behavior by customers are also consistent with a well-defined tariff. Here we describe the technical connection between the integrability condition and the Lagrange multiplier functions $\mu_j(t)$ that appear in the efficiency conditions (1) and the surplus maximization condition (2).

---

12. The fact that the cone of types purchasing more than q differs geometrically from the orthant of bundles exceeding q is one way to represent the role of the integrability constraints.

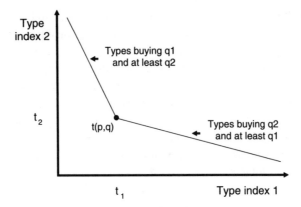

FIG. **13.4**   The types purchasing bundles exceeding q at price p lie in the wedge emanating from $t(p, q)$.

To illustrate the basic idea, consider a profit-maximizing monopoly offering two products with zero costs, and customers with two type parameters. Suppose that instead of formulating the customers' optimality conditions in terms of the constraint $W'(t) = U_t(q(t), t)$ having $\mu(t)$ as its Lagrange multiplier, we address the matter directly by including the integrability constraint (4) explicitly. This constraint requires that

$$\frac{\partial v_1}{\partial t_2}\frac{\partial q_1}{\partial t_1} + \frac{\partial v_2}{\partial t_2}\frac{\partial q_2}{\partial t_1} = \frac{\partial v_1}{\partial t_1}\frac{\partial q_1}{\partial t_2} + \frac{\partial v_2}{\partial t_1}\frac{\partial q_2}{\partial t_2}.$$

Subject to this constraint, the objective is to maximize the revenue $\int P(q(t))\,dF(t)$. Integrating by parts with respect to one of the types, say t_1, this revenue can be written (omitting constant terms) as

$$\int \bar{F}_1(t) \sum_i v_i(q(t), t)\frac{\partial q_i}{\partial t_1}\,dt_1 \cdots dt_m,$$

where

$$\bar{F}_1(t) \equiv \int_{t_1}^{\infty} f(t)\,dt_1,$$

and we have substituted v_i for $\partial P/\partial q_i$ to reflect the customer's optimality condition. Using this form of the objective function, and taking account of the integrability constraint with an associated Lagrange multiplier $m(t)$, the necessary condition from the calculus of variations for an optimal selection of $q_1(t)$ becomes, after cancellation of identical terms:

$$v_1(q(t), t) - [1/f(t)]\left\{\frac{\partial v_1}{\partial t_1}\left[\bar{F}_1(t) - \frac{\partial m}{\partial t_2}\right] + \frac{\partial v_1}{\partial t_2}\left[\frac{\partial m}{\partial t_1}\right]\right\} = 0.$$

This condition is essentially the same as the efficiency condition (1) in Section 2 provided

$$\mu_1(t) = \bar{F}_1(t) - \frac{\partial m}{\partial t_2}(t) \quad \text{and} \quad \mu_2(t) = \frac{\partial m}{\partial t_1}(t).$$

Moreover, using these to define $\mu(t)$, we obtain as a corollary that (2) must also be true:

$$f(t) + \frac{\partial \mu_1}{\partial t_1}(t) + \frac{\partial \mu_2}{\partial t_2}(t) = 0,$$

because

$$\frac{\partial^2 m}{\partial t_1 \partial t_2}(t) = \frac{\partial^2 m}{\partial t_2 \partial t_1}(t).$$

This analysis makes plain several general observations.

- The Lagrange multipliers $\mu(t)$ on the customers' optimality conditions are surrogates for Lagrange multipliers on the integrability constraints.
- The optimality condition (2) is itself an integrability constraint. In the case above, (2) expresses the fact that the Lagrange multiplier $m(t)$ can be recovered from $\mu(t)$.
- Making sure to check that the choice of $\mu(t)$ ensures integrability via the symmetry condition (4) is essential. It cannot be bypassed without invalidating the efficiency condition (1).

The role of the transversality conditions

The second complication in the construction of multipart tariffs is that the transversality conditions (3) impose severe constraints on the solution to (2) used in (1) to solve for the optimal assignment of bundles to customers. Here we use an example to illustrate the nature of the mathematical problem.[13] Later we provide an intuitive explanation in terms of the role of implicit bundling in determining the optimal assignment.

Consider the simplest example in which a monopolist firm offers two products with zero costs, and customers have two type parameters. A customer of type $t = (t_1, t_2)$ obtains the gross benefit $U(q, t) = \sum_{i=1}^{2}[t_i q_i - \frac{1}{2}q_i^2]$ from the bundle $q = (q_1, q_2)$, so the customer's marginal valuation functions are $v_i(q, t) = t_i - q_i$ for the two products $i = 1, 2$.[14] Suppose further that in the population the types are distributed uniformly on the unit square where $0 \le t_i \le 1$; in particular, the density is $f(t) = 1$ on this domain. These assumptions imply that the demand

13. I am indebted to Mark Armstrong and James Mirrlees for finding errors in a previous draft. See Mirrlees (1986, p. 1242) for an alternative statement of the problem that also emphasizes the key role of the transversality conditions.
14. Armstrong (1992) studies the equivalent formulation in which $v(t) = t$ and $c(q) = q$.

function for each product i depends only on the i-th type parameter, and there are no substitution effects between the two products; moreover, the two type parameters are statistically independent. Thus, in terms of the data of the problem there is no causal connection between the two products other than each customer's participation constraint $U(q(t), t) \geq 0$. We shall see that this seemingly tenuous thread has a dramatic effect on the design of the optimal tariff.

To see this, suppose that we were to ignore the connection and construct the optimal separable tariff that imposes charges for the two products independently. From this viewpoint, for each product i a customer's benefit function is $U_i(q_i, t_i) = t_i q_i - \frac{1}{2} q_i^2$ and the associated type parameter has the density function $f_i(t_i) = 1$ on the unit interval. Consequently, the i-th multiplier is $\mu_i(t_i) = 1 - t_i$, the optimal assignment of types to quantities is $q_i(t_i) = 2t_i - 1$, and the marginal price schedule is $p_i(q_i) = [1 - q_i]/2$. The flaw in this approach, however, is that it fails to satisfy the transversality condition (3) on the boundary wherever a customer purchases one product but not two. For instance, a customer with the type parameters $t = (t_1, 0)$ obtains a positive net benefit (from product 1) if $1/2 < t_1 \leq 1$ and in this case the transversality condition requires that $\mu_2(t) = 0$, whereas in fact the above construction supposes that $\mu_2(t) = 1$. The only remedy for this deficiency is a full analysis of conditions (2) and (4) that takes account explicitly of the transversality conditions (3) on the boundaries of the domain of type parameters.

Economic motivation.

Before developing this analysis it is useful to understand in economic terms why it is required. From the perspective of the firm, the separable tariff derived above is not fully optimal because it does not exploit the information derived from the customer's purchase of product 1. The observation that the customer purchased some of product 1 is an indication that a positive net benefit was obtained from that purchase. Consequently, the firm can infer that the customer's overall participation constraint is not binding; that is, the participation constraint regarding product 2 is relaxed, which invalidates the supposition of independence used for the derivation above. This indicates that the firm can profitably offer favorable terms to induce purchases of product 2. This conclusion does not apply exactly to a customer with $t_2 = 0$ but for one with $t_2 = \epsilon > 0$ it indicates that a small positive price for a small amount can induce purchase without encountering the participation constraint. Thus for optimality it is necessary that a marginal price for product 2 that is near the marginal cost of zero must be offered for small purchases of product 2 when they are bundled with purchases of product 1 that ensure a positive net benefit for the customer.

This economic analysis actually applies not just along the boundary of the type domain but also throughout the domain. Recall from §4.3 that nonlinear pricing can interpreted as an application of the principle of bundling. There we interpreted nonlinear pricing of a single product in terms of differentiated prices for successive units such that the tariff charged for a bundle of q units is less than the charge for q single units purchased separately. In the same fashion, the optimal nonlinear tariff for multiple products typically charges less for a bundle of several products than is charged for the same purchases of the products separately. Thus we can anticipate that even though the above example has statistically independent type parameters and independent demands for the two products, the optimal tariff will nevertheless involve bundling in some form in which discounts are offered for bundled purchases of the two products. Along the boundary of the type domain these discounts are reflected in favorable low marginal prices for small purchases of the unfavored product; in the interior of the domain the bundling is more generally of the form of a reduction in the marginal price of one product in some proportion to the quantity of the other product purchased.

Full solution of the example.

With this motivation we return to the analysis of the example and show how an exact analysis of conditions (2) and (4) in conjunction with the transversality condition (3) leads to a tariff design that includes aspects of bundling. For this example the Jacobian matrix $v_t(q, t)$ is the identity matrix, so the integrability condition (4) requires only that the Jacobian matrix of the assignment is symmetric. Because the assignment is $q(t) = t - \mu(t)$, symmetry requires that $\partial\mu_1(t)/\partial t_2 = \partial\mu_2(t)/\partial t_1$. Differentiating this condition with respect to t_2, and (2) with respect to t_1, and combining the results yields an equation that involves only the one multiplier μ_1:

$$\frac{\partial^2 \mu_1}{\partial t_1^2}(t) + \frac{\partial^2 \mu_1}{\partial t_2^2}(t) = 0 \, . \tag{2'}$$

A similar equation can be derived for μ_2. These equations implicitly include the integrability condition (4); consequently, one seeks solutions of these two equations that are linked by (2) and such that the transversality conditions (3) are satisfied on the portion of the boundary where (1) indicates that a customer of that type obtains a positive net benefit. Because these equations are second-order partial differential equations, they have many solutions, but essentially only one solution satisfies the specified constraints (cf. Armstrong (1992)).

The derived condition (2') can be applied as follows. One finds a family of solutions for μ_1 that satisfy the transversality condition $\mu_1(t) = 0$ on the boundaries where $t_1 = 0$ or $t_1 = 1$. For each member of this family one solves (2) as an ordinary differential equation for μ_2 and then selects that member of the family satisfying the transversality condition $\mu_2(t) = 0$ on the boundaries where $t_2 = 0$ or $t_2 = 1$. (An exception is that the solution is necessarily discontinuous at the origin.)

To apply this method we assume a solution of the form

$$\mu_1(t) = \sum_{k=1}^{K} a_k \sin(k\pi t_1) \cosh(k\pi[1-t_2]),$$

which satisfies (2′) and the requisite boundary conditions. Then (2) indicates that

$$\mu_2(t) = 1 - t_2 + \sum_{k=1}^{K} a_k \cos(k\pi t_1) \sinh(k\pi[1-t_2]),$$

which satisfies the boundary condition where $t_2 = 1$. Thus, it remains to determine the coefficients $b_k \equiv a_k \sinh(k\pi)$ so that

$$\sum_{k=1}^{K} b_k \cos(k\pi t_1) = -1$$

for each t_1 in the interval $0 < t_1 \leq 1$ to ensure that the remaining transversality condition is satisfied on the boundary where $t_2 = 0$. In fact, if one solves these linear equations for those K values $t_1 = 1/K, \ldots, 1$ equally spaced a distance $1/K$ apart then the solution is $b_k = 2$ except that $b_K = 1$. This solution indicates that an approximate solution of the problem is

$$\mu_1(t) \approx 2 \sum_{k=1}^{K-1} \sin(k\pi t_1) \cosh(k\pi[1-t_2])/\sinh(k\pi)$$
$$+ \sin(K\pi t_1) \cosh(K\pi[1-t_2])/\sinh(K\pi),$$

and analogously for μ_2. One uses these values of the multipliers in (1) to derive approximations of the optimal assignment and then the optimal marginal prices. For the results reported below I used $K = 40$, and checked the results using the numerical algorithm described in the next section.

Figure 13.5 describes the optimal assignment of customers' types to the bundles purchased. The figure shows only the quantity $q_1(t)$ of the first product as a function of the first type parameter t_1 for several values of t_2; the second quantity is $q_2(t_1, t_2) = q_1(t_2, t_1)$ due to the symmetry between the two products and types. Also shown for comparison is the assignment $q_1(t_1) = 2t_1 - 1$ for the case of a separable tariff. The key difference is that customers for whom t_1 is low nevertheless purchase positive quantities of product 1 if t_2 is high: they purchase a large quantity of product 2, which entitles them to a substantial discount in the purchase of product 1. This is illustrated in Figure 13.6, which shows that the marginal price of product 1 as a function of type parameter t_1 is lower if t_2 is higher. Figure 13.7

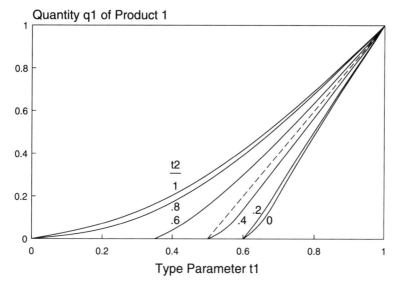

FIG. 13.5 The optimal assignment of types to bundles. For each $t_2 = 0(.2)1$, the assignment $q_1(t)$ is shown as a function of t_1. Also shown is the assignment $q_1(t_1) = 2t_1 - 1$ were it the case that only product 1 is offered.

shows the marginal price schedule $p_1(q)$ for the first product as a function of both quantities. The key feature is that the marginal price of product 1 is lower if a greater quantity of product 2 is purchased. In addition, one sees here the novel feature of multiproduct pricing that typically the optimal price schedule is initially *increasing* for small purchases, and therefore the tariff has an initial segment that is convex. The increasing segment is much steeper if the quantity of the second product is small, so steep in fact that the net effect resembles the effect of a fixed fee.

A striking feature of the optimal assignment is that it reflects pure bundling. That is, the tariff induces each customer to purchase positive quantities of both products or neither product, except those few customers for whom one of the type parameters is zero. The absence of "bunching" (in which substantial numbers of customers purchase only one product) on the boundary may be a characteristic feature of optimal multiproduct tariffs.

Additional examples with pure bundling

The key role of bundling in this example is illustrated in two variants of the formulation that allow explicit closed-form solutions.[15] In each case the optimal assignment reflects pure bundling, and the tariff depends only on an aggregate measure of the size of the purchase.

15. The method of solving these examples by exploiting radial symmetries is due to Mark Armstrong (1992).

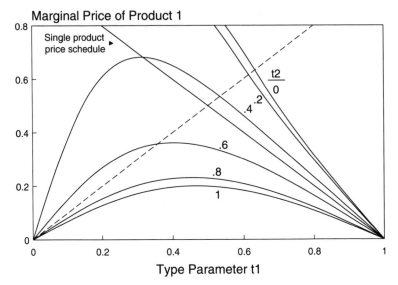

FIG. 13.6   The marginal price $p_1(q(t))$ for product 1. Only those prices below the dashed line pertain to positive quantities $q_1 > 0$. Also shown is the linear price schedule $p_1(q_1(t_1))$ were it the case that only product 1 is offered.

Example 13.5: For this variant we restrict the domain of the type parameters to the portion that lies within the unit circle. That is, the types are uniformly distributed with density 1 over the region for which $t_1 \geq 0$, $t_2 \geq 0$, and $t_1^2 + t_2^2 \leq 1$. In this case the transversality condition on the circular portion of the boundary is modified to require that $\sum_i t_i \mu_i(t) = 0$. This modification allows a solution in which the i-th multiplier is

$$\mu_i(t) = 2t_i[-1 + 1/T^2], \qquad \text{where} \qquad T^2 \equiv \sum_{i=1}^{2} t_i^2,$$

on the domain for which $2/3 < T^2 \leq 1$, which consists of those types making positive purchases. Consequently, the optimal assignment is

$$q_i(t) = t_i[3 - 2/T^2],$$

or in reverse, the type $t(q)$ purchasing the bundle q is

$$t_i(q) = q_i/[3 - 2/T(Q)^2],$$

where

$$T(Q) = Q/6 + \sqrt{[Q/6]^2 + 2/3}, \qquad \text{and} \qquad Q^2 \equiv \sum_{i=1}^{2} q_i^2.$$

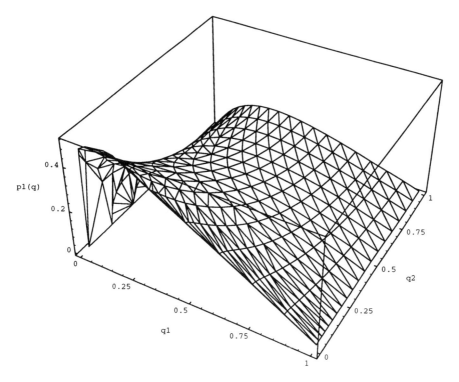

FIG. 13.7   The optimal multiproduct marginal price schedule $p_1(q)$.

The optimal marginal price schedule is therefore

$$p_i(q) = q_i \frac{2}{3} \left[\frac{1 - T(Q)^2}{T(Q)^2 - 2/3} \right].$$

This result implies that the tariff is a univariate function $P(Q)$ of the appropriate measure Q of the "size" of the bundle; namely,

$$P(Q) = Y(Q^2) + \ln(1 + Y(Q^2)) - \frac{1}{2}Q^2,$$

where $Y(x) \equiv \left[x + \sqrt{x^2 + 24x} \right] / 12$.   ◇

In sum, the firm uses $Q = \sqrt{q_1^2 + q_2^2}$ to measure the size of a bundle q, and charges a nonlinear tariff that depends only on this measure. The next example has the same property.

Example 13.6: For this example we modify the distribution of customers' type parameters so that the density is proportional to

$$f(t) = \exp\left[-\frac{1}{2}T^2\right], \qquad \text{where again} \qquad T^2 \equiv \sum_{i=1}^{2} t_i^2,$$

with a domain that is the entire positive orthant on which $t \geq 0$. That is, the type parameters have truncated independent Normal distributions with mean zero and variance 1. This case allows the multipliers $\mu_i(t) = t_i[1/T^2]f(t)$ and therefore the optimal assignments are

$$q_i(t) = t_i[1 - 1/T^2], \qquad \text{or} \qquad t_i(q) = q_i/[1 - 1/T(Q)^2],$$

where now

$$T(Q) \equiv Q/2 + \sqrt{[Q/2]^2 + 1},$$

and the types making positive purchases are those for whom $T^2 > 1$. Consequently, the optimal marginal prices are

$$p_i(q) = q_i/[T(Q)^2 - 1],$$

and again the tariff depends only on the bundle size Q:

$$P(Q) = \frac{1}{2}[Y(Q^2) + \ln(1 + Y(Q^2)) - Q^2],$$

where $Y(x) \equiv \left[x + \sqrt{x^2 + 4x}\right]/2.$

These conclusions apply equally to a formulation in which the numbers of products and type parameters are any integer n. In such a case one defines

$$T^2 \equiv \sum_{i=1}^{n} t_i^2, \qquad \text{and} \qquad Q^2 \equiv \sum_{i=1}^{n} q_i^2.$$

The tariff is again a function $P(Q)$ that depends only on the size Q of the bundle q. If n is an even number then to derive the assignments and the marginal prices one uses the multipliers

$$\mu_i(t) = t_i\left[\sum_{j=1}^{n/2} b_{nj}/T^{2j}\right] f(t).$$

Table 13.2 Coefficients for Example 13.6

n	a_n	b_{nj}				
1	1					
2		1				
3	1	1				
4		1	2			
5	3	1	3			
6		1	4	8		
7	15	1	5	15		
8		1	6	24	48	
9	105	1	7	35	105	
10		1	8	48	192	384
11	945	1	9	63	315	945
12		1	10	80	480	1920	3840

Similar formulas apply when n is odd but they involve the Normal distribution function:

$$\mu_i(t) = t_i \left[a_n [\bar{F}_N(T)/f_N(T)]/T^n + \sum_{j=1}^{[n/2]} b_{nj}/T^{2j} \right] f(t),$$

where $\bar{F}_N/f_N$ is the ratio of the standard Normal right-cumulative distribution function and its density. Table 13.2 shows the nonzero coefficients for the first twelve values of n.   ◇

These examples indicate two main points. First, bundling is an important feature of nonlinear pricing of multiple products. Second, when pure bundling is optimal it can be accomplished in some cases by a tariff that relies on an appropriately defined aggregate measure of the size of a customer's purchase. Tariffs that provide discounts based on aggregates are common in the transport, communications, and power industries. Typical examples are frequent-flyer plans, call charges that are discounted in rough proportion to the minutes used or the dollar amounts of monthly billings, and power charges based on monthly energy demands that aggregate peak and off-peak usages. One could wish for a theory of the optimal design of aggregate measures on which to base tariffs, but this topic has not been developed.

Summary

The analysis of this example indicates several important features that are peculiar to multiproduct pricing. From a technical perspective, the principal feature is that the integrability condition (4) and the transversality condition (3) are crucial to the accurate construction of the optimal tariff. The interplay between these conditions and the surplus maximization condition (2) accounts for the high degree of implicit bundling in the optimal tariff. Moreover, the construction of the optimal tariff is quite complex, largely because of the delicate calculations required to ensure that the outcome is pure bundling, with no bunching on the boundary. In general, the calculations require advanced mathematical methods that are beyond the scope of this monograph: Press *et al.* (1986, §17) describe some of the methods available.

From a practical perspective, the principal feature is that bundling is a dominant consideration in the selection of the tariff. The example provides evidence on this point since it illustrates a case in which the products and types would separate into two independent problems were it not for the key role of bundling. Further evidence is provided by the same example modified so that the type parameters have exponential distributions: in this case, separable tariffs would use uniform prices, but the optimal multiproduct price schedules have approximately the same shape as the one depicted in Figure 13.6, indicating that quantity discounts and bundling have important roles in this case also. These features suggest that observed multiproduct pricing practices, such as the use of "load factor discounts" by electric utilities discussed in §14, might be due to similar considerations.

13.6 . Construction of multiproduct prices

In this section we outline how a multiproduct tariff can be approximated using fairly simple numerical methods. A complete exposition is beyond the present scope so the calculations are illustrated only for the example analyzed in the previous section. This illustration conveys the main ideas but it omits some complications encountered in more complex problems. Our purpose is only to show that a numerical algorithm is feasible without undertaking to present its general form.

The numerical procedure

For the numerical procedure it is convenient to conduct the calculations in terms of the variables

$$a(t) = -\frac{\partial \mu_1}{\partial t_1}(t) \quad \text{and} \quad b(t) = -\frac{\partial \mu_1}{\partial t_2}(t).$$

In these terms the conditions (2) and (4) for the example require that

$$1 - a(t) = -\frac{\partial \mu_2}{\partial t_2}(t) \quad \text{and} \quad b(t) = -\frac{\partial \mu_2}{\partial t_1}(t).$$

Also, by definition and by (2') we require that

$$\frac{\partial a}{\partial t_2}(t) = \frac{\partial b}{\partial t_1}(t) \quad \text{and} \quad \frac{\partial a}{\partial t_1}(t) = -\frac{\partial b}{\partial t_2}(t).$$

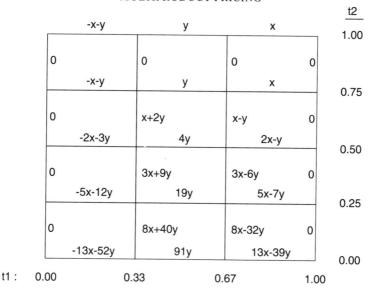

FIG. 13.8 A discrete grid of types and the values of $a(t)$ (on the horizontal segments) and $b(t)$ (on the vertical segments) as linear combinations of the unknown values $x = a(1, 1)\delta_1$ and $y = a(2/3, 1)\delta_1$ on the top boundary.

We also know from the transversality conditions (3) that

$$\mu_1(t) = 0 \quad \text{and} \quad b(t) = 0 \qquad \text{if } t_1 = 0,\ 1\,,$$

$$\mu_2(t) = 0 \quad \text{and} \quad b(t) = 0 \qquad \text{if } t_2 = 0,\ 1\,.$$

In the following we start from these conditions on the boundaries where t_1 or $t_2 = 1$ and then use the previous conditions to calculate values for $a(t)$ and $b(t)$ at a discrete grid of points spaced a distance δ apart. In doing so we take the values of $a(t)$ at points where $t_2 = 1$ as variables and calculate all subsequent values as linear combinations of these variables. The end result is a set of linear equations for the values of $\mu_2(t)$ on the bottom boundary where $t_2 = 0$ that can then be solved to find the values of $a(t)$ on the top boundary.

To convey how the algorithm works, Figure 13.8 shows a grid of combinations of the two type parameters for which $\delta_1 = 1/3$ for type 1 and $\delta_2 = 1/4$ for type 2. On the top boundary are shown the variables $x = a(1, 1)\delta_1$ and $y = a(2/3, 1)\delta_1$ that are to be determined. Note that $a(\delta_1, 1)\delta_1 = -x - y$ to ensure that $\mu_1(t) = 0$ on the left boundary; that is, one wants the rows to sum to zero so that there is no net change in $\mu_1(t)$ between the left and right boundaries. Those values shown on vertical segments for which $b(t)\delta_2 = 0$ are all implied by the transversality conditions. To fill in the other values one proceeds iteratively, starting from the upper right corner: one moves along successively lower diagonals, each going from upper left to lower right, until enough values have been determined on the bottom boundary to construct the set of linear equations that determine x and y. At each step one applies two rules:

1. If values have been assigned to three sides of a box then determine the fourth from the requirement that $\partial a(t)/\partial t_2 = \partial b(t)/\partial t_1$. That is,

$$a(t_1, t_2)\delta_1 = a(t_1, t_2 + \delta_2)\delta_1 + b(t_1 - \delta_1, t_2 + \delta_2)\delta_2 - b(t_1, t_2 + \delta_2)\delta_2 .$$

   In the figure one sees that the assigned values for each box satisfy the property that the sums of the top and left sides and the right and bottom sides are equal.

2. If three edges adjacent to a point have been assigned then determine the fourth from the requirement that $\partial a(t)/\partial t_1 = -\partial b(t)/\partial t_2$. That is,[16]

$$b(t_1, t_2)\delta_2 = b(t_1, t_2 + \delta_2)\delta_2 + a(t_1 + \delta_1, t_2)\delta_1 - a(t_1, t_2)\delta_1 .$$

   In the figure one sees that at each point the difference between the values assigned to the adjacent vertical edges equals the difference between the values assigned to the adjacent horizontal edges.

Proceeding according to these rules enables one to fill in all the values of $a(t)\delta_1$ on the horizontal edges and $b(t)\delta_2$ on the vertical edges, as shown in the figure. Finally, to determine the two values of x and y one uses the data constructed for the two rightmost columns of values of $a(t)\delta_1$ on horizontal edges. From condition (2) we know that $-\partial \mu_2(t)/\partial t_2 = 1 - a(t)$ and the transversality condition (3) requires that $\mu_2(t) = 0$ for $t_2 = 0$ or 1. For the discrete grid these imply that

$$\sum_{k=1}^{K} \{1 - [a(t_1, k\delta_2)\delta_1]/\delta_1\}\delta_2 = 0 ,$$

where $K = 1/\delta_2$, for each $t_1 = 1, \ldots, 2\delta_1$. The data in the figure, for instance, yield the equations

$$27x - 24y = 4 \qquad\qquad \text{for } t_1 = 1 ,$$
$$75y = 4 \qquad\qquad \text{for } t_1 = 2/3 ,$$

which imply that $x = 396/2025$ and $y = 4/75$, and therefore $a(1, 1) = 0.5867$ and $a(2/3, 1) = 0.16$. From these values the remainder of the values at points on the grid can be calculated.

---

16. A variant of this condition also ensures that in the analogous box for μ_2 the analog of rule 1 is satisfied.

To complete the calculation one computes the approximations

$$\mu_1(i\delta_1, j\delta_2) \approx \sum_{k=i+1}^{K} a(k\delta_1, j\delta_2)\delta_1 \,,$$

where $K = 1/\delta_1$, and similarly for μ_2; and then from (1)

$$q_1(t_1, t_2) = t_1 - \mu_1(t_1, t_2) \qquad \text{and} \qquad p_1(q(t)) = \mu_1(t) \,,$$

for those types for which $q_1(t) > 0$, and similarly for $q_2(t)$ and $p(q(t))$.

When this numerical procedure is used with a fine grid, say $\delta_1 = \delta_2 = 1/20$, it yields a price schedule that closely approximates the one derived in the previous section.[17] The calculation of the two marginal price schedules as functions $p_i(q)$ of the purchased bundle, rather than as functions $p_i(q(t))$ of the types t, is an arduous task, but fortunately the computer software *Mathematica* distributed by Wolfram Research (1991, Version 2.0) provides a package "Discrete Mathematics" with a program "Triangular Surface Plot" that accomplishes this task via the technique of Delaunay triangulation. Figure 13.7 depicts the result for the example studied in Section 5.

Representation of the tariff

The magnitudes $a(t)$ and $b(t)$ computed by this algorithm are directly useful in presenting the tariff. The tariff can be represented as

$$P(q) = p_1(q_1, 0) + p_2(0, q_2) + \int_{[q]} \pi(x)\, dx$$

where $[q]$ is the rectangle comprising all the small squares representing the increments purchased to obtain the bundle q. For this example one derives the price $\pi(q)$ of a small square as

$$\pi(q(t)) = -b(t)/|q'(t)| \qquad \text{where} \qquad |q'(t)| = [1 + a(t)][2 - a(t)] - b(t)^2 \,,$$

and the denominator is positive when $q(t) > 0$. Similarly,

$$p_1(q_1, 0) = \int_{t_1(q_1)}^{1} a(t)\, dt_1 \,,$$

17. One cannot use a finer grid unless special care is taken to control roundoff error. The coefficients in the linear equations are very large if the grid spacing is small, and these coefficients must be preserved as integers (not rounded off via floating point representations) to obtain the required accuracy.

where $(t_1(q_1), 0)$ is the type purchasing $(q_1, 0)$. The fact that $\pi(q)$ can be negative represents the effect of bundling via the discounts offered for each product depending on the quantity purchased of the other.

13.7 Summary

Many firms sell a variety of products to each customer. This is especially true of commercial and industrial customers who rely on a single vendor to provide a variety of related services or equipment, such as delivery services or data processing equipment. Among firms, multiple products are characteristic of the capital-intensive service industries such as airlines, communications, and power. Their services span multiple routes, times, reliabilities, and delivery conditions. Even governments use multiproduct tariffs in the form of fees, import duties, commodity taxes, and various taxes on income and capital gains.

The theory of multiproduct tariffs is not well developed, in part because it poses difficult computational problems. The practice is more advanced, however. Multiproduct tariffs are implicit in frequent-flier rebates used by airlines, wide-area discount plans used by telephone companies, and the patterns of peak and offpeak charges for communications and electric power, to name a few of many examples. In most cases these tariffs rely on simple aggregate measures that are easily appreciated by customers. One can surmise, moreover, that in many cases the additional gains from more elaborate multiproduct tariffs would be small compared to the costs of administration. As the example of taxation by governments illustrates, however, there are significant contexts in which a consistent overall tariff is important or necessary. More generally, it is often advisable to establish what an optimal comprehensive multiproduct tariff would be, if only to provide a standard against which to compare the effects of multiple single-product tariffs, or to provide a basis for negotiated charges for a combination of many products or services.

The elements of the theory presented in this chapter are fairly direct generalizations of the constructions introduced in earlier chapters for single products and products with multidimensional attributes. The main qualitative features persist, such as profit margins proportional to elasticities, and fortunately one example hints that reliance on aggregate measures is sufficient. The significant new feature is that bundling plays a major role in the design of the optimal tariff. On the other hand, this approach encounters practical difficulties regarding computation, and the theoretical analysis is limited by the complications introduced by the integrability and transversality conditions. In the next chapter, therefore, we return to a formulation in terms of the demand profile to obtain a characterization amenable to computation. The demand-profile approach does not take full account of customers' participation constraints, and therefore it does not capture the full effects of multiproduct bundling, such as the initially increasing price schedules evident in Figures 13.6 and 13.7. With this exception, however, it provides a simpler computational procedure than the scheme illustrated in Section 6.

One can hope that as more experience is gained with computing multiproduct tariffs for important practical examples the means and merits of joint pricing of several products or services will become clearer.

14

MULTIPRODUCT TARIFFS

This chapter describes a method of constructing multiproduct tariffs that is similar to those described in §4 and §12 for one or more single-product tariffs. As in §4, demand data is summarized by the multiproduct demand profile, but as in §12, total price effects are separated into portions representing own-price and substitution effects when there are multiple products.

Besides its computational simplicity, a practical advantage of this method stems from the possibility of estimating the demand profile directly from market data. The demand profile summarizes information about the distribution of customers' types in the population and it provides directly a measure of the total effect of changing the marginal price of each product. This reduces the modeling task to a specification of the separation of total price effects into portions representing own-price and substitution effects—although in some applications these portions too can be estimated from demand data. Because parameterized models of the sort used in §13 are often useful to explore issues and to develop qualitative characterizations, we also append a construction that relies directly on a specification of each type's demand function.

A further advantage of this method is that the optimality condition is expressed directly in terms of the demand profile and the tariff: unlike the characterization obtained in §13, there are no auxiliary Lagrange multipliers and the integrability constraint is included easily. The optimality condition can be solved numerically by standard techniques on a microcomputer.

On the other hand, this method has deficiencies that might be important in some applications. The computational procedure is based on an analysis that takes no account of customers' participation constraints. This differs from §13 where an explicit type-dependent representation of customers' benefit functions enables an exact characterization of customers' participation. The important consequence of participation constraints is the prevalence of pure bundling, implemented via marginal price schedules with increasing initial segments, as illustrated in Figures 13.6 and 13.7. In contrast, by omitting participation constraints the method in this chapter excludes pure bundling and the calculations do not provide the initially increasing segments of the price schedules—as can be seen in Figure 14.2. In applications where it is important to obtain the full effects of multiproduct bundling, it is necessary to rely on the analysis in §13.5.

The formulation is described in Section 1 for the case of two products ($n = 2$), which conveys the main ideas. The necessary condition that characterizes an optimal tariff is then derived in Section 2. We examine only the case of a profit-maximizing monopoly firm except when Ramsey pricing is introduced briefly in Section 2. Section 3 describes a simple computational procedure and provides some examples. Section 4 interprets load-factor discounts offered by some electric utilities as multiproduct tariffs. The analogous optimality condition based on explicitly specified demand functions is presented in Section 5.

The exposition assumes the demand profile represents a distribution function of purchased bundles that is described by an associated density function.[1] For models with explicit type parameters this requires that the number of type parameters is as large as the number of products, and that the distribution of type parameters has a density function. This is realistic, since an accurate model of customers' demands for several products typically requires at least as many parameters as products, but for analytical purposes it excludes simplified models such as those in §13.4 in which a few type parameters are used to capture salient aspects.

14.1 Formulation

The formulation is an elaboration of the one used in §12.1 for the special case of additively separable tariffs. The present context differs in that a single nonseparable tariff specifies the charge $P(q)$ for each bundle q. Because P is a multivariate function, the marginal price for an incremental unit of either product generally depends on the entire bundle. This feature motivates two extensions of the previous analysis: one addresses again the integrability condition, and the other specifies how own-price and substitution effects are included when both marginal prices vary as each quantity changes.

The price differential

One can envision a customer accumulating units of one or both products along a trajectory that moves from the origin to the final bundle q purchased in the current billing period. From the customer's perspective, each marginal price in the pair $p(x) = (p_1(x), p_2(x))$ charged at each stage $x \leq q$ along the trajectory depends on both components of the current bundle $x = (x_1, x_2)$. However, the total charge $P(q)$ depends only on the final bundle q, independently of which

1. This requires that customers purchases are not bunched on lower-dimensional subsets. That is, the distribution of purchase sizes represents a measure that is absolutely continuous with respect to the Lebesgue measure; cf. Guesnerie and Seade (1982) and Roberts (1979).

trajectory the customer follows. This property of path independence is equivalent to the integrability condition studied in §13.

In order for the accumulation of marginal charges to be the same along any path between the same two endpoints, it must be that the pair of marginal prices is the gradient of a single well-defined tariff: $p_i(q) \equiv \partial P(q)/\partial q_i$. In turn, this property requires that the function

$$\pi(q) \equiv \frac{\partial^2 P(q)}{\partial q_1 \partial q_2}$$

measures the same rate of change of each price with respect to the accumulated quantity of the other product:

$$\pi(q) = \frac{\partial p_1(q)}{\partial q_2} = \frac{\partial p_2(q)}{\partial q_1} .$$

Hereafter we refer to $\pi(q)$ as the *price differential*.

The role of the price differential is familiar from §9 where $\pi(q)$ was interpreted as the price assigned to a small square comprising an increment of each product. In that case the shape of a customer's purchase set was arbitrary, but in the present context one must contend with the implicit constraint that the purchase set corresponding to a bundle q must be a rectangle with sides of lengths q_1 and q_2.

To circumvent the problems posed by the integrability condition elaborated in §13, it suffices to take the price differential as the basic function from which the marginal prices and the tariff are constructed. The marginal prices and the tariff are obtained from the price differential by summing:

$$p_1(q) = \int_0^{q_2} \pi(q_1, x_2) \, dx_2 ,$$

and similarly for the marginal price $p_2(q)$ of product 2, and

$$P(q) = \int_0^{q_2} \int_0^{q_1} \pi(x) \, dx_1 dx_2 ,$$

is the resulting tariff for the bundle q. In general, the tariff can also include a fixed fee and additional marginal charges depending only on the quantities of single products: we focus initially on the construction of the price differential but later we sketch how a fixed fee and supplementary marginal charges are determined.

We shall cast the optimality condition, therefore, in a form that characterizes the optimal selection of the price differential $\pi(q)$. Similarly, computational procedures are based on finding numerical approximations of the optimal values of the price differential, from which the marginal prices and the tariff are then constructed.

The demand for increments

The second amendment required is to measure the demand for increments when both marginal prices vary with the quantity of each product. As in §12, let $N(p, q)$ be the multiproduct demand profile indicating the number of customers who at the uniform prices $p = (p_1, p_2)$ purchase bundles exceeding $q = (q_1, q_2)$; that is, they purchase bundles in the set $X(q) \equiv \{x \mid x_1 \geq q_1 \ \& \ x_2 \geq q_2\}$ of bundles that include q. Recall that for each product i the total price effect is separated as

$$\frac{\partial}{\partial p_i} N(p, q) = L_i^*(p, q) + L_i(p, q)$$

into two parts indicating the own-price effect L_i^* and the substitution effect L_i. As shown in Figure 12.1, the own-price effect L_1^* measures the flux of customers who respond to an increase in the price of product 1 by exiting $X(q)$ across its left boundary $X^1(q)$ where $x_1 = q_1$: they reduce their purchases of product 1 to quantities less than q_1. The substitution effect L_1 measures the flux of customers who enter $X(q)$ across its bottom boundary $X^2(q)$ where $x_2 = q_2$: they reduce their purchases of product 1 and substitute greater purchases of product 2, thereby entering $X(q)$.

Repetition of the method in §12 leads to the following formula for the number $M(q; P)$ of customers who purchase bundles exceeding q in response to the nonlinear tariff P:

$$M(q; P) = N(p(q), q) + \int_{q_1}^{\infty} [L_1 p_{11} + L_2^* p_{21}] \, dx_1 + \int_{q_2}^{\infty} [L_1^* p_{12} + L_2 p_{22}] \, dx_2 ,$$

where $p_{ij} \equiv \partial p_i / \partial q_j$. On the right side, arguments of functions are omitted, but in full the first integral is

$$\int_{q_1}^{\infty} [L_1(p(x_1, q_2); x_1, q_2) p_{11}(x_1, q_2) + L_2^*(p(x_1, q_2); x_1, q_2) p_{21}(x_1, q_2)] \, dx_1 .$$

This formula measures the number purchasing at least q as the sum of the number $N(p, q)$ purchasing at least q at the uniform prices $p = p(q)$, plus any changes due to leakage across the boundaries of $X(q)$ as customers respond to the actual schedule of marginal prices $p(x)$ for bundles $x > q$. The first integral, for instance, measures those who enter or depart $X(q)$ along its bottom boundary $X^2(q)$ due to the substitution effect L_1 as the marginal price p_1 of product 1 changes, plus those who enter or depart along this same boundary due to the own-price effect L_2^* as the marginal price p_2 of product 2 changes for successively larger purchases of product 1.

From this formula for the number of customers purchasing at least the bundle q, it follows that the density of customers purchasing exactly the bundle q is

$$\mu(q; P) = \frac{d^2 N(p(q), q)}{dq_1 \, dq_2} - \frac{d}{dq_2}[L_1 p_{11} + L_2^* p_{21}] - \frac{d}{dq_1}[L_1^* p_{12} + L_2 p_{22}].$$

Recall that this specification is related to formulations derived from parameterized models as described in §12.1. A parameterized model with two type parameters specifies the density $f(t)$ of each type t and its demand function $D(p, t)$. The density of customers purchasing exactly q in response to the uniform prices p is

$$\nu(q; p) \equiv \frac{\partial^2 N}{\partial q_1 \partial q_2}(p, q) = f(t) |D_t|^{-1},$$

at the type $t = t(p, q)$ purchasing q at the prices p. Moreover, the four leakage terms are identified from the properties

$$\frac{\partial L_1^*}{\partial q_2} = -\nu \frac{\partial D_1}{\partial p_1} \quad \text{and} \quad \frac{\partial L_1}{\partial q_1} = -\nu \frac{\partial D_2}{\partial p_1},$$

and symmetrically for L_2^* and L_2, together with the boundary conditions that, say, $L_1^* = 0$ at $q_2 = \infty$, and similarly for the others. Another fact derived in §12.1 is that

$$\frac{\partial L_2^*}{\partial p_1} - \frac{\partial L_1}{\partial p_2} = \frac{\partial L_1^*}{\partial p_2} - \frac{\partial L_2}{\partial p_1} = |D_p|^{-1},$$

which yielded an alternative formula for the density of purchasers at q:

$$\mu(q; P) = \nu(p(q), q) \left[1 - \sum_{i,j} D_{ij} p_{ji} + |D_p| \cdot |p'| \right],$$

where $D_{ij} \equiv \partial D_i / \partial p_j$ and $p' = (p_{ij})$. Each of these terms was computed explicitly in §12.1 for the linear-demand model specified in Example 12.1.

In the next section we use these specifications of the density and distribution functions of purchased bundles to derive the optimality condition that characterizes an optimal tariff.

14.2 The optimal multiproduct tariff

The optimal tariff can be constructed in several parts. In general, the tariff comprises a fixed fee P_o, a separate price schedule $\hat{p}_i(q_i)$ for increments of each of the two products, and a price differential $\pi(q)$ that pertains to purchases of joint increments of both products. If all these pieces are included, then the tariff has the general form

$$P(q) = P_\circ + \sum_i \int_0^{q_i} \hat{p}_i(x_i) dx_i + \int_0^{q_2} \int_0^{q_1} \pi(x)\, dx_1 dx_2 \,,$$

and the total marginal price of, say, product 1 is

$$p_1(q) = \hat{p}_1(q_1) + \int_0^{q_2} \pi(q_1, x_2)\, dx_2 \,.$$

The firm's cost function can be cast similarly in this form as

$$C(q) = C_\circ + \sum_i \int_0^{q_i} \hat{c}_i(x_i) dx_i + \int_0^{q_2} \int_0^{q_1} \gamma(x)\, dx_1 dx_2 \,,$$

for which the total marginal cost of product 1 is

$$c_1(q) = \hat{c}_1(q_1) + \int_0^{q_2} \gamma(q_1, x_2)\, dx_2 \,.$$

In this representation, $C_\circ$ represents a fixed cost, $\hat{c}_i(q_i)$ represents a separate marginal cost of supplying the q_i-th unit of product i, and the cost differential $\gamma(q)$ represents the cost of supplying an incremental small square comprising a unit increment of each product. One can also interpret the cost differential as the change in the marginal cost of supplying one product as the quantity of the other product increases; thus, it incorporates effects due to economies of scope or of substitution or complementarity in production.

Initially we address only the construction of the price differential π in the absence of any other components of the tariff or costs. Later we indicate how the analysis is extended to include separate marginal charges $\hat{p}_i$ for the two products. As mentioned initially, the following construction takes no account of customers' participation constraints.

The optimal price differential

Considering only price and cost differentials, a tariff P yields a profit contribution on the domain Q of positive bundles that can be represented as

$$\text{Pft} \equiv \int \int_Q [P(q) - C(q)] \cdot \mu(q; P) \, dq_1 \, dq_2 \,,$$

$$= \int \int_Q \{ N \cdot [\pi - \gamma] + [L_1 p_{11} + L_2^* p_{21}] \cdot [p_2 - c_2]$$

$$+ [L_1^* p_{12} + L_2 p_{22}] \cdot [p_1 - c_1] \} \, dq_1 \, dq_2 \,,$$

$$\equiv \int \int_Q \{ N \cdot [\pi - \gamma] + \lambda_1 \cdot [p_2 - c_2] + \lambda_2 \cdot [p_1 - c_1] \} \, dq_1 \, dq_2 \,.$$

As usual, the second line is obtained from the first using integration by parts.[2] The third line uses the abbreviations

$$\lambda_1 \equiv L_1 p_{11} + L_2^* p_{21} \qquad \text{and} \qquad \lambda_2 \equiv L_1^* p_{12} + L_2 p_{22} \,,$$

where $p_{12}(q) = p_{21}(q) = \pi(q)$. Thus, the profit contribution attributable to the incremental small square at q is

$$\text{Pft}(q) \equiv N(p(q), q) \cdot [\pi(q) - \gamma(q)] + \lambda_1 \cdot [p_2(q) - c_2(q)] + \lambda_2 \cdot [p_1(q) - c_1(q)] \,.$$

This representation of the profit has an intuitive rationale: the profit margin is $\pi(q) - \gamma(q)$ from each of the $N(p, q)$ customers purchasing the incremental small square at q at the uniform prices $p \equiv p(q)$, but then one subtracts the profit margins $p_i(q) - c_i(q)$ lost on those customers who leak across the i-th boundary of $X(q)$ due to own-price and substitution effects.

We do not display explicitly the Euler condition that characterizes an optimal tariff; instead, we present the form that results from integrating it over the domain $X(q)$. In this form it represents the condition for an optimal choice of the price differential $\pi(q)$:

$$M + L_1^* \cdot [p_1 - c_1] + L_2^* \cdot [p_2 - c_2] + \int_{q_2}^{\infty} I_1 \, dx_2 + \int_{q_1}^{\infty} I_2 \, dx_1 = 0 \,,$$

evaluated at $(p(q), q)$. In this condition, the two integrals represent own-price and substitution effects at bundles other than q: increasing the price differential at q alters the marginal prices at bundles with a larger amount of product 2 (but not 1)

---

2. The leakage terms require the form of integration by parts known as the Divergence Theorem.

or product 1 (but not 2). In the first integral, representing a sum along the boundary $X^1(q)$ where $x_1 = q_1$, the integrand is

$$
I_1 \equiv \frac{\partial}{\partial p_1} \{N[\pi - \gamma] + \lambda_1[p_2 - c_2] + \lambda_2[p_1 - c_1]\} - \frac{d}{dq_1} \{L_1[p_2 - c_2]\} ,
$$

$$
= L_1^*[\pi - \gamma] + \left[\frac{\partial L_1^*}{\partial p_1} \pi + \frac{\partial L_2}{\partial p_1} p_{22} \right] [p_1 - c_1] - \left[\frac{\partial L_1}{\partial q_1} \right.
$$

$$
- \left(\frac{\partial L_2^*}{\partial p_1} - \frac{\partial L_1}{\partial p_2} \right) \pi \left. \right] [p_2 - c_2] .
$$

A symmetric formula specifies the second integrand I_2 along the boundary $X^2(q)$ where x_1 varies.

This condition appears complicated but it has an intuitive rationale. A \$1 increase in the price differential $\pi(q)$ at q yields \$1 from each of the $M(q; P)$ customers who purchase bundles $x \geq q$ in $X(q)$. However, it also alters the number making such purchases, as follows. First, the increase in $\pi(q)$ also increases $p_1(q)$ and $p_2(q)$ by this same amount, and this loses customers according to the own-price effects L_1^* and L_2^*; thus the terms $L_1^*(p(q), q)[p_1(q) - c_1(q)]$ and $L_2^*(p(q), q)[p_2(q) - c_2(q)]$ measure the profit margins lost on those customers who decide not to purchase the q_1-th and q_2-th increments of products 1 and 2. Second, the increase in the price differential $\pi(q)$ also increases the marginal prices $p_1(x)$ at bundles $x \in X^1(q)$, and $p_2(x)$ at bundles $x \in X^2(q)$, and these effects are measured by the integrands I_1 and I_2 respectively. The first line of the formula for I_1 includes the direct effect $\partial Pft(x)/\partial p_1$ of increasing p_1 as the first term, offset in the second term by the profit recouped via the substitution effect from the increased purchases of product 2. The second version of the formula for the integrand I_1 is obtained by canceling like terms in the two parts of the first formula.

Ramsey pricing

A similar condition characterizes the optimal price differential when a Ramsey pricing formulation is used. On the domain of positive bundles the consumers' surplus can be represented as

$$
CS(P) = \int \int_Q \left\{ \int \int_{x \leq q} [u(x, t(q)) - \pi(x)] \, dx_1 dx_2 \right\} \mu(q; P) \, dq_1 dq_2 .
$$

For each of the $\mu(q; P)$ customers of type $t(q)$ purchasing the bundle q, this formula accumulates the difference between the customer's valuation $u \equiv \partial^2 U/\partial x_1 \partial x_2$ of the small square at each $x \leq q$ and the price differential $\pi(x)$ charged there. Consequently, a \$1 increment in the price differential at x reduces by \$1 the consumer's surplus obtained by each of the $M(x; P)$ customers purchasing bundles

$q \geq x$. As explained in §12.1, therefore, the net effect is to multiply the term M in the optimality condition by the Ramsey number α. This yields the modified optimality condition:

$$\alpha M + L_1^*[p_1 - c_1] + L_2^*[p_2 - c_2] + \int_{q_2}^{\infty} I_1 \, dx_2 + \int_{q_1}^{\infty} I_2 \, dx_1 = 0 \, .$$

Separate marginal charges on the boundaries

The preceding conditions characterize the optimal price differential even if additional separate marginal costs $\hat{c}_i(q_i)$ for the products are incurred and separate marginal charges $\hat{p}_i(q_i)$ are imposed. The only difference is that the marginal costs $c_i(q)$ and the marginal prices $p_i(q)$ used in the preceding formulas must include the separate components $\hat{c}_i(q_i)$ and $\hat{p}_i(q_i)$ as specified in the original definitions of the tariff $P(q)$ and the cost function $C(q)$.

To determine the separate marginal charges $\hat{p}_i(q_i)$ one proceeds as in §12.1. In total, the firm's profit can be written as

$$\text{Pft} = M(0; P)[P(0) - C(0)] + \int_0^{\infty} N_1[\hat{p}_1(q_1) - \hat{c}_1(q_1)] \, dq_1$$

$$+ \int_0^{\infty} N_2[\hat{p}_2(q_2) - \hat{c}_2(q_2)] \, dq_2 + \int \int_Q \text{Pft}(q) \, dq_1 \, dq_2 \, .$$

The last term on the right is the profit contribution from the price differential, as defined previously. The second and third terms are analogous to the representation of the profit contribution used in §12.1. In particular, the induced demand profile for product 1 along the boundary $X^2(0)$ where $q_2 = 0$ and q_1 varies is, in general,

$$N_1(p_1, q_1; P) \equiv N(p, q) + \int_0^{\infty} \lambda_2 \, dq_2 + \int_{q_1}^{\infty} \lambda_1 \, dx_1 \, .$$

As in §12.1, however, the flux across this boundary is $\lambda_1 = 0$ by definition (provided customers bunched along the boundary are included in N). In contrast to §12.1, on the other hand, the leakage term representing the flux of customers crossing the boundary $X^1(q_1, 0)$ is

$$\lambda_2(p(q), q) \equiv L_1^*(p(q), q)\pi(q) + L_2(p(q), q)\frac{\partial p_2}{\partial q_2}(q) \, ,$$

which is affected by the choice of the price differential. Thus, we see that the conditions for the optimal price differential must be solved in concert with the conditions for the optimal separate charges for the products.

Using the integrand I_1 defined previously, the optimality condition for the separate marginal charge $\hat{p}_1(q_1)$ imposed on product 1 can be expressed as

$$N(p(q), q) + \frac{\partial N}{\partial p_1}(p(q), q) \cdot [\hat{p}_1(q_1) - \hat{c}_1(q_1)] + \int_0^\infty [I_1 + \lambda_2]\, dq_2 = 0 \,,$$

where $p(q) = (p_1(q_1, 0), p_2(q_1, 0))$ at $q = (q_1, 0)$. The optimality condition for $\hat{p}_2$ is obtained symmetrically. Similarly, the modified formula for Ramsey pricing is obtained by multiplying the terms from N_1 by the Ramsey number α.

These conditions are generalized versions of the analogous conditions derived in §12.1 for separable tariffs. In applying this condition, it is important to include the separate components $\hat{p}_i$ and $\hat{c}_i$ in the construction of the marginal price schedules p_i and the marginal costs c_i in evaluating N, I_1, and λ_2. The optimal price differential and separate marginal charges are obtained by solving the previous optimality condition for the price differential in conjunction with these conditions for the separate marginal charges along the boundaries.

We omit the optimality condition for an optimal fixed fee. As in §4.4 and §6.7, it is based on consideration of the tradeoff between higher fixed fees (net of the fixed cost of service, if any) from those customers who elect service, and the resulting reduction in the market penetration.

14.3 Numerical examples

The optimality condition derived in Section 2 is amenable to numerical solution by a gradient procedure of the same design as the one in §12.1. We represent the optimality condition as the equality $G(\pi, \hat{p}; q) = 0$ for each bundle q in a discrete approximation of the set Q of positive bundles. Here, $\pi \equiv (\pi(q))_{q \in Q}$ represents the collection of price differentials assigned to bundles in Q, and similarly $\hat{p}$ represents the separate margin charges imposed on the boundaries. Also, in evaluating $G(\pi, \hat{p}; q)$ one uses discrete sums to approximate the integrals specified in the formulas. The combination $G(\pi, \hat{p}) \equiv (G(\pi, \hat{p}; q))_{q \in Q}$ represents the gradient of the firm's objective function with respect to the values of the price differential at points in Q, and on the boundaries, with respect to the values of the separate marginal charges for the products. Consequently, one can obtain a numerical approximation of the optimal price differential by calculating successive improvements that move in the direction indicated by the gradient. If π^t is the proposed price differential in iteration t, then a somewhat better approximation of the optimal price differential is

$$\pi(q)^{t+1} = \pi(q)^t + s_t G(\pi^t, \hat{p}; q) \qquad \text{for each } q \in Q \,,$$

and similarly for the separate marginal charges, provided the stepsize s_t is sufficiently small.

This technique was used to solve the following examples. Each example assumes that the Ramsey number corresponds to monopoly pricing ($\alpha = 1$), and that the cost function is nil ($C(q) \equiv 0$). The first example was solved using $\delta = 0.05$ for the spacing between points in Q, and the second, using $\delta = 0.20$. In each case, results are presented only for the price differentials and the marginal price schedules they generate: absent a fixed cost and separate marginal costs for each product, this is sufficient for an optimal tariff.

Example 14.1: We return to the linear-demand model used in Example 12.1. Recall that each customer is described by a pair $t = (t_1, t_2)$ of type parameters and the linear demand function

$$D_i(p, t) = t_i - \sum_j b_{ij} p_j \, ,$$

for the i-th product. Assume that the diagonal elements of the array B are $b_{ii} = 1$ and the off-diagonal elements are $b_{12} = b_{21} = -b$. The magnitude of the parameter b measures substitution effects. The type parameters are uniformly distributed in the population, so the demand profile is

$$N(p, q) = [1 - q_1 - b_{11}p_1 - b_{12}p_2][1 - q_2 - b_{21}p_1 - b_{22}p_2] \, .$$

For product 1, the total price effect is separated into the two terms

$$L_1(p, q) = -b_{21}[1 - q_1 - b_{11}p_1 - b_{12}p_2] \, ,$$
$$L_1^*(p, q) = -b_{11}[1 - q_2 - b_{21}p_1 - b_{22}p_2] \, ,$$

representing substitution and own-price effects.

We display results for two cases. In the first case the substitution parameter is $b = 0$, indicating that demands for the two products are independent. Figure 14.1 shows the price differential $\pi(q)$ as a function of q_1 for each of several values of q_2. Observe that the price differential is largest when both components of q are small, and it declines to zero as either component increases. Figure 14.2 shows the resulting marginal price schedule for product 1. Because no charges are imposed for increasing q_2 along the boundary, one interprets the customer as moving freely to a preferred quantity of product 2, and then moving along the corresponding locus (in the figure) of marginal prices for product 1 until his optimal bundle is obtained. If the selection of q_2 is large, then the marginal charges for initial units of product 1 are high too. Nevertheless, as shown in the previous figure, the rate at which they increase as q_2 increases is declining. Figure 14.3 and Figure 14.4 display similar results for the case that the substitution coefficient is $b = 0.2$. The main effect is to narrow the range of price differentials for small values of q_1, and to widen the range for large values.   ◇

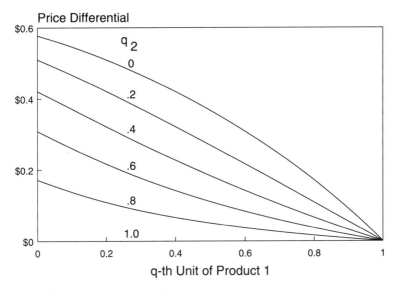

FIG. 14.1 Example 14.1: The price differential $\pi(q)$ when the products are independent ($b = 0$).

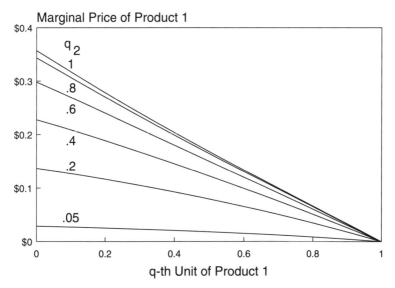

FIG. 14.2 Example 14.1: The marginal price schedule $p_1(q)$ when the products are independent ($b = 0$).

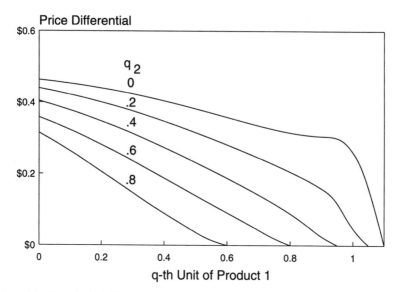

FIG. 14.3 Example 14.1: The price differential $\pi(q)$ when the substitution coefficient is $b = 0.2$.

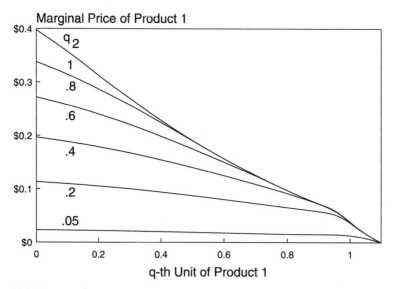

FIG. 14.4 Example 14.1: The marginal price schedule $p_1(q)$ when the substitution coefficient is $b = 0.2$.

Example 14.2: Next, we return to the alternative linear-demand model used in Example 12.2. The demand function of type t is

$$D_i(p, t) = \frac{1}{1 - a^2} \sum_j a^*_{ij}[t_j - p_j]$$

for product i, where $a^*_{ii} = 1$ and $a^*_{12} = a^*_{21} = -a$. In this version, the parameter t_i represents type t's marginal valuation of an initial unit of product i and the magnitude of the parameter a is a measure of substitutability between the products. The types are distributed in the population according to a bivariate Normal distribution for which each t_i has mean $\bar{t}_i = 1$ and standard deviation 1; also, r is the statistical correlation between t_1 and t_2. These data were used in §12.1 to construct the demand profile and the leakage functions.

We display results for several cases. In case I, both $a = 0$ and $r = 0$, so the products and the types are both independent. Figure 14.5 shows the price differentials and Figure 14.6 shows the resulting marginal price schedules for product 1, parameterized by several values of the quantity of product 2. In case II the substitution coefficient is raised to $a = 0.4$ while the correlation coefficient remains $r = 0$. Figure 14.7 shows the price differentials and Figure 14.8 shows the marginal price schedules. The main effect of raising the substitution coefficient is to lower the price differentials and therefore also the schedules of marginal prices. (Observe that in these and the subsequent figures the scale of the vertical axis is less because the prices are generally lower.) In case III the correlation coefficient is also raised to $r = 0.4$. Figure 14.9 and Figure 14.10 show the price differentials and the marginal price schedules, which rise and spread out due to the increase in the correlation. In case IV the substitution and correlation parameters are $a = 0.2$ and $r = -.2$. Figure 14.11 and Figure 14.12 show the price differentials and the marginal price schedules: the negative correlation shrinks the dispersion of the price differentials for large purchases, where it is nearly flat. More strongly negative correlations produce a valley in the price differential. ◇

14.4 Illustration: load-factor tariffs

Several electric utilities offer tariffs that provide discounts for customers with high load factors. To illustrate that multiproduct tariffs appear in various guises, we show how load-factor discounts can be interpreted in terms of the price differential for a multiproduct tariff. A stylized version of load-factor discounts conveys the essential features.

We consider a tariff that charges a uniform price p if the customer has a perfect load factor $\ell = 1$ and otherwise an average price $p + k[1 - \ell]$ if the load factor is imperfect, where k represents a premium charged for peaking capacity that is sometimes idle. Suppose the customer's demand at any time is $q = m + \xi s$ where

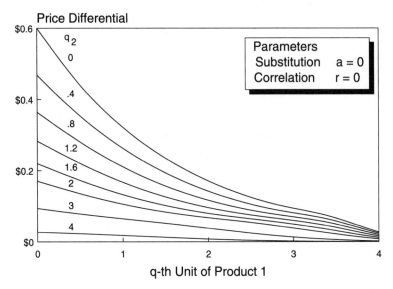

FIG. 14.5   Example 14.2: The price differential $\pi(q)$ in case I: $a = 0$ and $r = 0$.

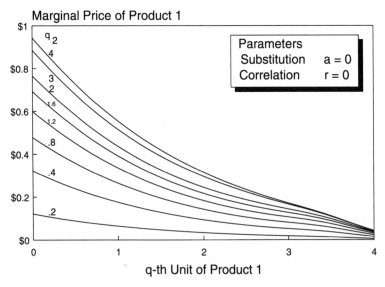

FIG. 14.6   Example 14.2: The marginal price schedule $p_1(q)$ in case I: $a = 0$ and $r = 0$.

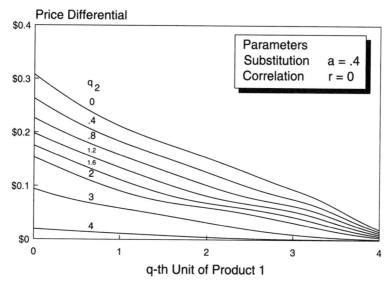

Fig. 14.7 Example 14.2: The price differential $\pi(q)$ in case II: $a = 0.4$ and $r = 0$.

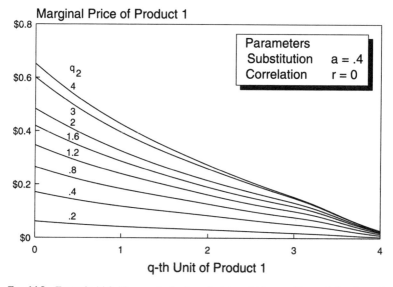

Fig. 14.8 Example 14.2: The marginal price schedule $p_1(q)$ in case II: $a = 0.4$ and $r = 0$.

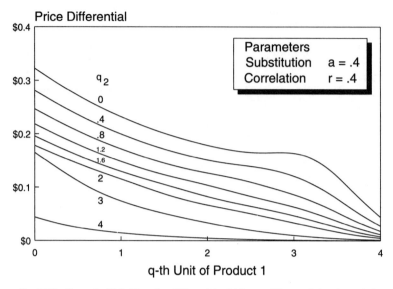

FIG. **14.9** Example 14.2: The price differential $\pi(q)$ in case III: $a = 0.4$ and $r = 0.4$.

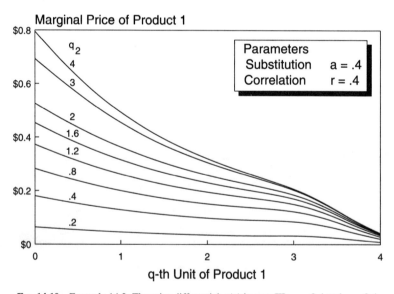

FIG. **14.10** Example 14.2: The price differential $\pi(q)$ in case III: $a = 0.4$ and $r = 0.4$.

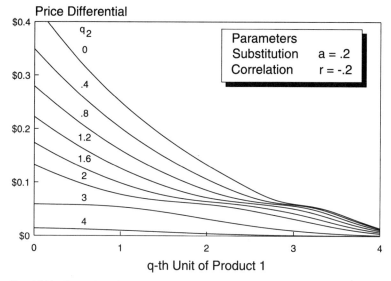

Fig. 14.11   Example 14.2: The price differential $\pi(q)$ in case IV: $a = 0.2$ and $r = -0.2$.

over the billing period the contingent factor ξ varies randomly or periodically between plus and minus one, with an average value of zero. Thus, the average demand is m, the base load is $m - s$, the peak load is $m + s$, and the load factor is $\ell = m/[m+s]$. The average hourly charge to the customer is therefore $P(m, s) = [p + ks/(m + s)]m$. Interpret the base load $m - s$ and the peaking capacity $2s$, or equivalently the mean demand m and the average idle capacity s, as two different

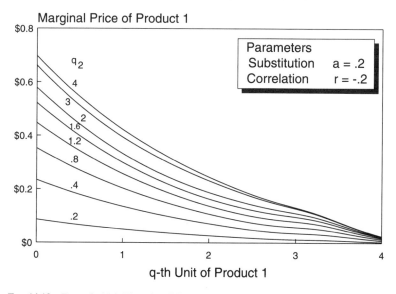

Fig. 14.12   Example 14.2: The price differential $\pi(q)$ in case IV: $a = 0.2$ and $r = -0.2$.

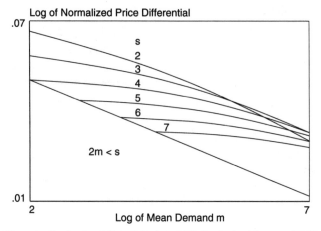

FIG. 14.13   The normalized price differential $\pi(m, s)/2k$ for the load-factor tariff $P(m, s)$ in the region $2m > s$ where it is decreasing. Both axes are scaled logarithmically.

products. Then the corresponding price differential is

$$\frac{\partial^2 P}{\partial m \partial s} \equiv \pi(m, s) = 2k \frac{ms}{[m + s]^3}.$$

Figure 14.13 shows this price differential for the values where the price differential is decreasing, which requires $2m > s$. A logarithmic scale is used for both m and the normalized price differential $\pi(m, s)/2k$, which is depicted for several values of s. Typically, the relevant portion is where s is a moderate fraction of m, neither very small nor very large relative to m. In this region the price differential is not unlike the ones displayed for the examples in Section 3, although for small values of m it is increasing and for large values the curves cross. Presumably an optimal load-factor tariff, designed according to the methods in Section 2, would exclude these anomalies.

14.5   An alternative formulation *

This section provides a formulation adapted to models with explicit demand functions parameterized by customers' types. The optimality condition for the price differential is derived from the optimality condition for the assignment of types to bundles presented in §13.2. The material in this section uses mathematical techniques from multivariate calculus.[3]

The optimality conditions (1) and (2) in §13.2 can be written as:

$$[v(q(t), t) - c(q(t))]f(t) - v_t(q(t), t) \cdot \phi(t) = 0, \tag{1}$$

3. A popular book on the Divergence Theorem used in this section is by Schey (1973).

$$\alpha f(t) + \sum_{j=1}^{m} \frac{\partial \phi_j(t)}{\partial t_j} = 0, \tag{2}$$

where $\alpha \equiv \lambda/[1 + \lambda]$ is the Ramsey number and $\phi(t)$ is a rescaled version of the Lagrange multiplier on type t's incentive compatibility constraint. Note that no account is taken in (1) and (2) of nonnegativity constraints. Recall that $v = U_q$ is the customer's marginal benefit function and $c = C_q$ is the firm's marginal cost function—each is a gradient vector with n components, one for each product.

Assume that the number m of type parameters is also n, so ϕ has n components too. Assume also that the Jacobian matrices v_t and q' of partial derivatives of v and q with respect to the type parameters are nonsingular matrices—as required when they are monotone functions. Let $T(q) = \{t \mid q(t) \geq q\}$ be the set of types purchasing at least the bundle q and assume that its boundary is the union of the sets $T^i(q) = \{t \in T(q) \mid q_i(t) = q_i\}$. That is, the i-th segment of the boundary of $T(q)$ is the locus of types purchasing exactly the quantity q_i of product i, for each product $i = 1, \ldots, n$.

Use (1) to obtain the Lagrange multiplier as $\phi = v_t^{-1}[v - c]f$ and substitute this result into (2); then the optimality condition becomes

$$\alpha f(t) + \sum_{j=1}^{m} \frac{\partial}{\partial t_j} \{v_t^{-1} \cdot [v - c]f\} = 0. \tag{3}$$

The Divergence Theorem of multivariate calculus can be applied to (3) to integrate over the domain $T(q)$. This yields the optimality condition in the form:[4]

$$\alpha M(q) + \sum_{i=1}^{n} \int_{T^i(q)} [dn^i] \cdot v_t^{-1} \cdot [v - c]f = 0, \tag{4}$$

which we now explain. First, $M(q) = \int_{T(q)} f(t)\, dt$ is the number of customers purchasing bundles exceeding q, namely the number purchasing bundles in $X(q)$, so this is the same $M(q)$ as used previously in Section 1. Second, the row vector dn^i is the differential in the direction of the outward unit normal to the boundary segment $T^i(q)$; that is, in the direction perpendicular to this boundary and pointing outward rather than inward. Apart from its length and sign, this normal vector is proportional to the gradient $q_i'(t)$ of the i-th component of $q(t)$.

The next step is to make the change of variable $x = q(t)$ in (4). This change yields the translation $p(x) = v(x, t(x))$, where $t(x)$ is the type assigned the bundle

---

4. Additional terms in the summation can also occur that reflect the transversality conditions on the outer boundary of $T(q)$.

x. Moreover, if $x = D(p, t)$ is the demand function of type t, then the translated differential $dt \equiv dt_1 \cdots dt_m$ is

$$dt = |t'(x)|\, dx = \left| D_t^{-1} - D_t^{-1} \cdot D_p \cdot p'(x) \right| dx \,,$$

where D_t and D_p are evaluated at $(p(x), t(x))$. The resulting density of purchases at x is

$$\mu(x) = f(t(x))\, |t'(x)| = \nu(p(x), x)\, |E(x)| \,,$$

as defined previously in Section 1, where $\nu(p, x) \equiv f(t(x))\, |D_t|^{-1}$ is the density of purchases at x with constant marginal prices, and $E(x) = I - D_p \cdot p'(x)$. These changes yield the following alternative form of the optimality condition:

$$\alpha M(q) + \sum_{i=1}^{n} \int_{X^i(q)} [E(x)^{-1}]^i \cdot D_p(x) \cdot [p(x) - c(x)]\mu(x)\, dx^i = 0 \,, \qquad (5)$$

where $[E(x)^{-1}]^i$ indicates the i-th row of the inverse of the matrix $E(x)$.

We now explain the translation from (4) to (5). First, the domain of the i-th integral translates from the boundary $T^i(q)$ to the i-th boundary $X^i(q)$ of $X(q)$ by definition. The density and differential $f(t)\, dt$ translates as $\mu(x)\, dx$, of which the portion applicable on the boundary $X^i(q)$ is $\mu(x)\, dx^i$ for $x^i \equiv (x_j)_{j \neq i}$. The factor $[v - c]$ translates directly as the profit margin $[p(x) - c(x)]$ on the bundle x, and the factor v_t^{-1} is the matrix $-D_t^{-1} \cdot D_p$. The outward normal to $T^i(q)$ translates to the outward normal to $X^i(q)$, where it points in the negative direction of x_i with unit length. Consequently, the translation of the matrix of such unit normals, $-q'(t)$, is $-t'(x)^{-1} = -E(x)^{-1} \cdot D_t$. When these translations are inserted in (4), the factors D_t and D_t^{-1} cancel and the result is (5).

Lastly, we write this condition in summary form as:

$$\alpha M(q) + \sum_{i=1}^{n} \int_{X^i(q)} K^i(p(x), p'(x), x) \cdot [p(x) - c(x)]\nu(p(x), x)\, dx^i = 0 \,, \qquad (6)$$

where

$$M(q) \equiv \int_{X(q)} \nu(p(x), x)\, |E(x)|\, dx \,, \qquad E(x) \equiv I - D_p(p(x), t(x)) \cdot p'(x) \,,$$
$$K(p, p', x) \equiv |E(x)|\, E(x)^{-1} \cdot D_p(p(x), t(x)) \,,$$

and K^i is the i-th row of K. The domains are

$$X(q) \equiv \{ x \mid x \geq q \} \qquad \text{and} \qquad X^i(q) \equiv \{ x \in X(q) \mid x_i = q_i \} \,.$$

This summary form represents the optimality condition for the price differential as in Section 2. The left side is therefore the gradient for making improving changes in the price differential. In principle, this provides the basis for an algorithm similar to the one used in Section 3. However, it is not clear how to extend this construction to include separate marginal charges along the boundaries. I have not computed examples by this method so I cannot vouch for its efficacy.

14.6 Summary

The aim of this chapter is to illustrate the feasibility of constructing an approximately optimal nonseparable multiproduct tariff from the same market data used for separable tariffs charged for multiple products. The conditions for an optimal tariff are based directly on the multiproduct demand profile. As in §12, total price effects must be divided into own-price and substitution effects. These two effects are estimated separately in most applications, often as own-price and cross-price elasticities. Moreover, they are explicit in most parameterized models. This aspect is therefore consistent with established practice.

The computational scheme is applied to optimality conditions that ignore customers' participation constraints. The results are therefore only approximate. In particular, the full effects of multiproduct bundling are not included, such as the initially increasing marginal price schedules that implement pure bundling for the examples in §13.5.

The computations are significantly more complex than the simple calculations required for a single product, as in §4, and slightly more complex than required for separable multiproduct tariffs, as in §12.1. They are feasible on a microcomputer, however, as the examples presented here illustrate. The simplicity of the gradient algorithm makes the procedure easy to apply. It is useful, moreover, that the gradient can be used as the direction in which improvements in the price differential can be made. In practice, it is often advantageous merely to know the direction and magnitude of possible improvements to an existing tariff, rather than to embark on construction of a supposedly optimal tariff that, in reality, must take account of practical considerations (such as regulatory policies and customer acceptance) that are not included in the mathematical formulation.

A basic issue raised by this chapter and §13 is to account for the scarcity of implementations of multiproduct tariffs. Multiproduct tariffs for peak and off-peak power (or telephone calls) appear feasible but in fact they are rarely used. A significant exception is the use of load-factor tariffs by some electric utilities, as illustrated in Section 4. Other applications, such as airline frequent-flier plans, conform more closely to the example in §13.5 in which a single aggregate measure of a customer's bundle of purchases suffices for the design of the tariff. We noted also in §2.1 that magazine publishers offer discounts based on total annual advertising billings. At the retail level, marketers of consumer products enclose coupons that enable a customer purchasing a unit of one product to obtain discounts on purchases of other products in the seller's product line. Because these coupons are nontransferable, are limited in use to one per purchase, and have negligible cash values (usually a hundredth of a cent), they have the same net effect as a multiproduct tariff.

Part V

SUPPLEMENT

15

OTHER APPLICATIONS OF NONLINEAR PRICING

Product pricing is one of several applications of the basic principles of nonlinear pricing. This chapter reviews briefly a few other applications, some of which reveal additional motivations for using nonlinear schedules. These applications have the common feature that the population is diverse, reflecting private information about preferences or technology. The tariff, price schedule, or other incentive scheme promotes efficiency partly by eliciting this information indirectly as revealed by the behavior it induces. The principles of Ramsey pricing provide a unifying framework to derive characterizations of efficient incentive schemes.

Section 1 summarizes additional contexts that use nonlinear pricing of products and quality-differentiated services. Section 2 describes three of many contexts in which nonlinear schedules are used to cope with incentive effects in insurance markets and other situations affected by private information. Section 3 reviews a portion of the literature on contracting, especially in labor markets where incentive effects are prominent. Section 4 describes applications to the design of taxation and regulatory policies. We omit technical details except for brief summaries in subsections indicated with an asterisk ($*$). Although terse, these formulations indicate how the principles of Ramsey pricing are applied to other contexts with incentive effects stemming from private information.

Good texts on the topics in this chapter are the two books and the survey article by Phlips (1983, 1988a, 1988b), and the four related surveys by Baron, Braeutigam, Varian, and Stiglitz in the *Handbook of Industrial Organization* (1989).

15.1   Product pricing applications

Previous chapters address mainly the case that a firm offers an explicit tariff to a large population of customers. In contrast, the tariff is often implicit in the applications in this section.

Product lines

A firm offering a product line usually organizes it along a one-dimensional scale representing the magnitude of a prominent attribute. In the simplest case the products are identical except for differing package sizes. The schedule of package prices is essentially a tariff; and, the price increments charged for size increments constitute the marginal price schedule. The same is true if the products differ along quality dimensions. If customers buy multiple units of various qualities, then joint pricing of quality and quantity is advantageous. The analysis in §10.2 of Ramsey pricing of priority service is an example.

In important cases, qualities are measured as output rates, and from a customer's viewpoint they are like quantities. For instance, a faster computer or copier is a substitute for several slower machines, and is therefore like a compact package. Nevertheless, product lines of this sort have other motivations. Design considerations may enable the firm to enhance the operating rate, durability, or maintenance costs of a machine with a less than proportionate increase in fabrication costs. For a customer, therefore, choices among machines involve tradeoffs between investment costs and operating costs. If a customer has a variable demand for usage, namely a peakload problem, then it may be preferable to purchase an expensive (large or fast) machine to serve baseloads, as well as a cheaper machine to serve peak loads. Discounts for multiple purchases from a product line are also used by some firms when customers incur costs of switching from one vendor to another; switching costs are potentially an important source of monopoly power.

Delivery conditions

Some quality dimensions occur pervasively: size, output rate, reliability, durability, speed, precision, ease of maintenance, operators' skill levels, et cetera. Indeed, several of these have small literatures applying principles of nonlinear pricing. Conditions of delivery are especially common and we mention two of the most important: place and time of delivery.

Spatial pricing

Firms use many different schemes to recoup delivery costs and to differentiate products via place or cost of delivery. As mentioned in §6.6, the two extreme forms are FOB pricing, in which the customer takes delivery at the firm's location or pays for shipment costs; and delivered pricing, in which the firm absorbs all delivery costs. An analysis based on nonlinear pricing generally indicates that an optimal scheme is intermediate between these two extremes. Suppose for instance that the populations of customers at different distances from the firm's plant are the same whereas the cost of serving customers increases with distance. Then generally it is optimal for the firm to absorb some delivery costs. Partial absorption of transport costs is implemented in many ways, including warehousing, basing points, and direct credits to customers.[1] When firms enjoy local monopolies, but compete near the boundaries of their service areas, this can produce strong effects; in particular, profit margins can be driven to zero at the boundaries.[2] In an oligopoly usually neither FOB pricing nor full absorption of delivery costs is a stable pattern (some firm has an incentive to switch to the other mode) but partial absorption is stable.

Temporal pricing

Nondurable products produced continually rarely offer significant opportunities for differentiation by time of delivery. Time is important for some durable products because unserved demand accumulates. An example is household goods, such as sheets and towels, which wear out steadily but can be replaced opportunistically by taking advantage of periodic sales. The deterioration of existing stocks and formation of new households produce a steady influx of potential demand, part of which is unserved until the backlog grows so large that the firm finds it advantageous to tap this market with a lower sale price. Stores selling such items typically use a recurring pattern in which periods of high prices are followed by sales at low prices. Customers with urgent needs buy immediately at whatever price prevails, whereas customers who can defer or store inexpensively prefer to wait until a sale. The price schedule over a cycle of price variation represents a form of nonlinear pricing in which the quality attribute is the time of delivery and customers differ in terms of their patience to wait for a sale or their valuations of the items.[3]

Even when demand is not recurring, the seller of a durable good generally prefers to differentiate prices according to the time of delivery. When there is no limitation on the supply and storage costs are positive or customers are impatient, this practice is an instance of inefficient quality distortion in the form of delayed delivery, of the sort described in §13, Figure 13.2. Typical examples are new books, films, and computer programs for which some customers are willing to pay more for earlier delivery. The prices of these products typically decline over time. For instance, hardcover editions of books are offered at higher prices initially than later soft cover editions; films in theaters are more expensive initially than later on videocassettes, and still later on television.

1. Although it is widely used elsewhere, basing-point pricing in oligopolistic markets violates antitrust laws in the United States.

2. See Anderson and Thisse (1988), Gabszewicz and Thisse (1990), and Spulber (1984) for more elaborate analyses of spatially differentiated pricing in this vein.

3. See Conlisk, Gerstner, and Sobel (1984) and Sobel (1991). In an oligopoly the timing of sales must be random, since each firm has an incentive to preempt the others. There is also a literature on firms' use of multiple prices at a single time, a practice called price dispersion, that we do not address here; cf. Stiglitz (1989) and Varian (1989). Such models require nonconvexities in their formulations and often imply randomization of prices. However, Charles Wilson (1988) shows that, for a monopolist firm using uniform prices, one or two prices are optimal if customers arrive randomly and buy at the lowest price for which supply remains, the aggregate demand curve is downward sloping, and marginal costs are increasing or supply is limited. Two prices are optimal when the optimal or limited supply occurs where the firm's marginal revenue curve is increasing.

The rate at which prices decline depends greatly on whether the firm can commit in advance to its price schedule. If the firm cannot commit then, after serving a high-valuation or impatient segment of the market, the firm perceives advantages from cutting its price beyond what it previously would have wanted. Indeed, anticipating this, the high-valuation customers are reluctant to pay as high a price initially because the advantage of waiting for the next, lower price is greater. An extreme form of this phenomenon is the Coase property: if the firm's marginal cost is constant and the firm can change its price rapidly, then the optimal price schedule is little more than marginal cost and most sales are made immediately.[4] A mild version of the Coase property is seen in the following example, where the initial price of $0.232 is less than half the monopoly price the firm would use in every period if it could commit to its price schedule. Further, if the firm changes its price weekly rather than monthly, then the initial price is $0.142 and all customers are served after nine weeks, rather than eight months.

Example 15.1: Suppose customers differ in their valuations of the product, but they are equally impatient. In particular, a customer whose valuation is v obtains the net benefit $[v - p_k]\delta^k$ if he purchases at the price p_k in month k, and zero if he never purchases. The firm's objective in choosing the sequence p_k of prices is to maximize the present value of its revenues, using the same discount factor δ. Table 15.1 shows the firm's optimal monthly price schedule for the case that there are ten types of customers, each comprising 10% of the population, whose valuations are $0.10, $0.20, ..., $1.00; the firm's marginal cost is zero, and the discount factor is $\delta = 0.95$. Anticipating this sequence of declining prices, each customer waits to purchase until the price is less than his valuation, and then waits further until he prefers to purchase immediately rather than wait for the next, lower price.[5]   ◇

Firms adopt various tactics to avoid the implications of the Coase property. The problem is severe in the case of durable capital equipment. The Coase property takes the form that the manufacturer is in effect selling items now with which its later output will compete via customers' opportunities to purchase in secondary resale or rental markets. This is another version of the requirement for fully optimal nonlinear pricing that resale markets must be excluded. To alleviate this problem the firm can reduce the durability of the product, which is usually inefficient, or

---

4. This property is described informally by Coase (1972) and proved in two versions by Gul, Sonnenschein, and Wilson (1986) and Gul and Sonnenschein (1988). Basic references on temporally differentiated pricing are Bulow (1982, 1986) and Stokey (1979, 1981).

5. The fraction of customers remaining (those who have not yet purchased) in some periods is not a multiple of 0.10 because the previous price made customers at the margin indifferent whether to purchase that month or wait until the next. The fraction predicted to accept is determined by customers' responses to deviant prices that might be offered by the firm. See Gul, Sonnenschein, and Wilson (1986) for details.

Table 15.1 Price Schedule for Example 15.1

Period k	Fraction of Customers Remaining	Price p_k	Fraction of those Remaining who Purchase
1	1.000	.232	.199
2	.801	.197	.182
3	.655	.170	.196
4	.527	.148	.221
5	.410	.129	.263
6	.303	.115	.339
7	.200	.105	.500
8	.100	.100	1.000

control the resale and rental markets by only leasing the product.[6] Alternative strategies are to restrain its production rate by commitments to limited capacity or a production technology that has increasing marginal costs.[7]

Temporal differentiation via nonlinear pricing applies also to the design of advance-purchase discounts. Most airlines offer such discounts: §2.6 describes the schedule offered by Delta Airlines. The diversity among customers that is important in designing such discounts concerns the expected cost of committing early to travel plans. In addition, firms schedule crews and equipment more efficiently when demand uncertainties are reduced in advance, so the firm's marginal cost is also affected. Gale (1992) shows that advance-purchase discounts can be an optimal way to induce those customers who can schedule their trips flexibly to avoid congested peak periods when capacity is scarce.

An illustrative formulation. *

We sketch a simplified formulation of the design of an airline's advance purchase fares adapted to the item-assignment model in §9.4. Customers' demands are interpreted as items requiring service in the form of trips requiring flights. Ticket purchases farther in advance of departure are interpreted as lower quality because there is a greater chance that intervening events will force cancellation.

Tickets are neither refundable nor transferable. To avoid complications, we make the extreme assumption that each customer buys tickets repeatedly until he is able to complete a single trip. That is, demand for a trip persists even if events force cancellation of a reservation. Moreover, a customer has ample time to reschedule

6. Bulow (1986) gives an example of optimal inefficient durability. Since IBM and Xerox were enjoined from leasing but refusing to sell, this practice has been construed as a violation of the United States' antitrust laws.
7. These strategies are analyzed by Stokey (1981) and Kahn (1986), respectively.

the trip: there are no time constraints on the next reservation. We assume the firm has a monopoly on the route and we ignore capacity constraints.[8]

Each customer is described by a pair (v, t) in which v is the value of a completed trip and t is a parameter affecting the probability $r(s, t)$ that he will be able to make the flight if he buys a ticket the duration s beforehand. That is, $1 - r(s, t)$ is the probability that some event in the intervening s days will force postponement of his travel plans. Usually one specifies that t is the mean arrival rate of events that would force cancellation of a reservation; that is, t tends to be higher for commercial travelers and therefore $r(s, t)$ is lower, and by definition $r(s, t)$ is lower if s is higher, so one assumes that r is a decreasing function of both parameters. If the price of a ticket purchased s days in advance is $p(s)$ then his expected net gain can be stated recursively as

$$V = \max_{s \geq 0} \left\{ r(s, t)v + [1 - r(s, t)]V - p(s) \right\} .$$

This says that if the present reservation is cancelled then the process repeats until the trip is completed. Equivalently, for the optimal choice of s, $V = v - p(s)/r(s, t)$, indicating that the expected sum of the prices paid for all the tickets purchased until the trip is completed is $p(s)/r(s, t)$. Only those customers for whom V is positive will purchase any ticket, but assuming a ticket is bought then the condition characterizing the optimal duration is

$$r_s(s, t)[v - V] - p'(s) = 0 ,$$

$$\text{or} \qquad r_s(s, t)/r(s, t) = p'(s)/p(s) ,$$

independently of v.

To complete the formulation, suppose that the density of those customers with parameter t and $v \geq P$ is $D(P, t)$. This is the demand function for *refundable* tickets at the price P among those customers with parameter t. This demand is the arrival rate of customers with newly acquired motives for an eventual trip. To apply these specifications to the present case, observe that if it is type $t(s)$ who purchases s days in advance, then the arrival rate of *new* customers for such tickets is $D(p(s)/r(s, t(s)), t(s)) \cdot |t'(s)|$ and to each such customer the firm sells on average $1/r(s, t(s))$ tickets at the price $p(s)$ before his trip is completed. (The absolute value is used because presumably $t(s)$ is a declining function.) The firm's

---

8. An oligopoly can be addressed using the methods in §12. The demand persistence assumption is used here to obtain the simplification that a customer's benefit from a completed trip has no effect on his choice of the optimal time to purchase a ticket.

expected profit contribution, also interpreted as an average rate per unit time, from a fare schedule p is therefore

$$\int_0^\infty [P(s) - c] \cdot D(P(s), t(s)) \, |t'(s)| \; ds \,,$$

where $P(s) = p(s)/r(s, t(s))$ is the average total revenue obtained from each customer purchasing at time s beforehand and c is the marginal cost of the single trip provided. Thus the two functions $P(s)$ and $t(s)$ are chosen to maximize this expected profit contribution subject to the customer's optimality constraint. This constraint can be restated in terms of P as:

$$P'(s) = P(s)q(s, t(s))t'(s) \,, \qquad \text{where} \qquad q(s, t) \equiv -r_t(s, t)/r(s, t) \,.$$

Having found $P(s)$ and $t(s)$, the fare schedule is obtained via $p(s) = P(s)r(s, t(s))$.

The optimal schedule can be characterized using the Euler condition from the calculus of variations in a fashion similar to the analysis of the item-assignment formulation in §9.4. For the practical applications, however, one considers only block-declining fare schedules that are piecewise constant, say differing fares for purchases within a few days, a week, two weeks, and a month of departure. Extensions to Ramsey pricing must include the costs imposed on customers; in particular, customers may incur substantial costs adhering to the original itinerary to avoid the high price of interrupting a roundtrip reservation midway in the trip.

Price discrimination and inefficient quality degradation

Some of the topics in this section are versions of price discrimination. The inefficiencies and distributional consequences they engender cast a shadow on the benefits of nonlinear pricing in other contexts where it enhances efficiency. As we emphasize in §5 and §10, careful application of nonlinear pricing can enhance efficiency without disadvantaging any customer. But versions of nonlinear pricing can also be used to exploit monopoly power inefficiently and with significant welfare consequences. Airlines' advance purchase discounts are possibly an example. These discounts are implemented by offering lower prices for tickets purchased in advance, but usually the quality is degraded by making the tickets nontransferable and partially or entirely nonrefundable; this is deemed necessary to make them unattractive to customers who highly value flexibility. The lower prices promote efficiency by enabling more customers to travel, but against this gain must be set the losses from quality degradation . Nontransferability produces empty seats when customers cancel trips, and nonrefundability causes costly consequences for travelers enroute who cannot change their itineraries by paying the actual cost imposed on the airline. The fact that firms with monopoly power often use inefficient quality degradation to implement nonlinear pricing of a product line of unbundled quality-differentiated services was noted by Dupuit (1844) in the first treatise addressing the subject.

The problem must always be studied with care. Even in the case of inefficient delays caused by temporal discrimination, there can be offsetting gains from customers who buy late at low prices, whereas at a single uniform price above marginal cost they would not be able to buy at all. In other contexts, differentiation of services and products by unbundling along one or more dimensions of quality generally improves efficiency, provided the differentiated products are priced appropriately. The case of priority service studied in §10 provides an example of quality differentiation in which a spectrum of lower and higher qualities is offered at prices that increase all customers' net benefits. A similar analysis of advance purchase discounts would determine the pricing policy and restrictions on itineraries that ensure that the net effect is to recover the firm's costs while extending service to customers with low valuations of service and low costs of restrictions on flexibility.

15.2   Incentives in markets with private information

We turn now to the role of nonlinear pricing in coping with incentive effects in markets affected by private information. Previous chapters deal with this topic only in the limited sense that the firm offers a single tariff to a diverse population of customers. The firm knows the distribution of customers' types in the population and the tariff is offered on equal terms to all; it is immaterial therefore whether the firm knows the types of individual customers. Of course this assumes that the firm's costs do not depend on the individual served. We consider first the alternative case that the firm is concerned about each individual's type, which materially affects the seller's costs and about which it is uncertain (although each individual knows his own type).

Insurance markets

The incentive problems resulting from private information are acute in insurance markets, so we use them to illustrate. Medical and property insurance are affected by private information in the form of a customer's superior information about the chances of incurring illnesses or damages for which claims would be payable by the firm. The firm is in effect buying a lottery about which the seller (the insured) has better knowledge. This situation is called adverse selection by actuaries since the firm anticipates that customers with greater chances of claims have greater incentives to purchase policies.

A typical device to mitigate adverse selection is a form of nonlinear pricing. The firm offers policies for which the premium is disproportionately higher if the coverage is greater or the deductible is lower.[9] The premium is more than proportionately greater for greater coverage because the firm (even a mutual company or beneficial society) anticipates that those customers purchasing greater coverage impose larger or more numerous claims. This has the inefficient consequence that low-risk customers are deterred from buying full coverage. Sometimes this is ameliorated by group policies that are affected less by adverse selection, or by preferred-risk policies that require the applicant to provide evidence of good health or a record of few claims. On the other hand, the firm collects sufficient premiums for each coverage to pay claims arising from those policies.[10]

An illustrative formulation. *

To illustrate details of a formulation of this problem, suppose that the firm is a profit maximizing monopolist. Assume that customers' types are described by their expected losses, so a customer of type t has expected losses equal to t, and the distribution function of these types in the population is $F(t)$. The firm then wants to maximize its expected profit

$$\int_T [P(q(t)) - tq(t)] \, dF(t) \, ,$$

where $q(t)$ is the coverage selected by type t, namely, the fraction of t's losses paid by the firm. The premium $P(q)$ charged for the coverage q is a tariff chosen in anticipation that type t will select the coverage that maximizes the expected utility

$$\int_Z U(qz - z - P(q)) \, dG(z; t) \, ,$$

where U is the customer's utility function describing his aversion to risk. Also, G is the distribution function of the customer's loss z conditional on his type being t; in particular, the mean of z is $\int_Z z \, dG(z; t) = t$ according to the definition of t. This formulation differs from §6.2 in that the customer is risk averse, so his choice process is more complicated, but the crucial feature is that the firm's marginal cost of coverage depends on (in fact, is) the customer's type t. It is this feature that characterizes adverse selection.

Using nonlinear pricing to assure that premiums match claims for each coverage assumes that cross-subsidization among risk classes is excluded. An alternative is a uniform price per unit of coverage, but this brings its own inefficiency: high-risk customers prefer to buy coverage exceeding their losses (if allowed) and in any case low-risk customers prefer to underinsure.

---

9. This produces a premium schedule that is an increasing and usually convex function of the coverage. A useful interpretation of the convexity of the schedule derives from the observation above that the firm can be interpreted as the buyer of a lottery rather than as the seller of a policy.
10. See Rothschild and Stiglitz (1976) and Stiglitz (1977).

Example 15.2: To illustrate, suppose that customers' losses are distributed independently and that type t's loss has a Normal distribution with mean t and variance σ^2. Further, suppose that all customers have the same utility function U, which is exponential with the risk aversion parameter r. In this case, type t's certainty equivalent for the net risk $qz - z - P(q)$ after purchasing coverage q is

$$u(q, t) = qt - t - P(q) - \frac{1}{2}r\sigma^2[1 - q]^2,$$

measured in dollars. Using this data, the condition that characterizes optimal Ramsey pricing, as in §5.1, is

$$\alpha \bar{F}(t) - f(t)r\sigma^2[1 - q(t)] = 0,$$

where α is the Ramsey number and $q(t)$ is the coverage selected by type t. The corresponding marginal price schedule that implements this allocation is

$$p(q) = t(q) + r\sigma^2[1 - q],$$

where $t(q)$ is the type purchasing coverage q. For example, if the types are uniformly distributed then $\bar{F}(t) = 1 - t$; therefore,

$$q(t) = 1 - \frac{\alpha}{r\sigma^2}[1 - t],$$

if $t \geq t_* \equiv \max\{0, 1 - r\sigma^2/\alpha\}$, and zero otherwise. The optimal price schedule is

$$p(q) = 1 - [(1/\alpha) - 1]r\sigma^2[1 - q],$$

provided $r\sigma^2 \leq \alpha/[1 - \alpha]$ so that $p(q) \geq 0$. Notice that with full monopoly power the price of coverage is uniform: if $\alpha = 1$ then $p = 1$ uniformly. Excluding a fixed fee, the firm's net revenue is

$$\text{Net Revenue} = \frac{1}{3}[1 + \alpha][1 - t_*]^3/[r\sigma^2/\alpha] - \frac{1}{2}[1 - t_*]^2.$$

This example shows some of the novel features that arise when the tariff design is affected by adverse selection. The price schedule is increasing, indicating that the tariff is convex. Also, the net revenue is negative if the Ramsey number is too small, indicating that some monopoly power is necessary to counter the effects of adverse selection.   ◇

Auctions and trading procedures

Auctions are another example of markets affected by private information. Indeed, auctions are allocative mechanisms designed mainly to elicit buyers' estimates of the values of the items offered for sale.[11] Familiar auctions in which each item is sold to the highest bidder are efficient in special cases; for example, when the buyers' valuations are statistically independent. However, if their valuations are dependent or their estimates are correlated, as in the usual case that they are all estimating a common value, then the seller can increase the expected sale price by using nonlinear pricing and allocation rules. The literature on designing auctions that are optimal for the seller is essentially a translation of the standard theory of a multiproduct monopolist using nonlinear pricing.[12] We describe briefly below its generalization to more general contexts in which the procedural rules for trading are designed to promote efficient outcomes.

An illustrative formulation. *

The theory of optimal trading procedures is based on models like the following. Consider a group of traders comprising several buyers and sellers. Each buyer i is willing to pay at most v_i for a single item, and his gain is $v_i - p$ if he obtains an item at the price p. Each seller j has a single item to sell and his gain is $p - c_j$ if he sells it at the price p. The sellers' items are identical and each has only one item to sell; also, the buyers have ample money and want only one item. Say that a subset K of the traders is feasible, in the sense that they can exchange items among themselves, if it has equal numbers of buyers and sellers (possibly zero), and let $\mathcal{K}$ be the collection of feasible subsets. Each individual trader k has a privately known type parameter t_k that is his valuation of an item: if $k = i$ for a buyer then $t_k = v_i$ and if $k = j$ for a seller then $t_k = -c_j$, and similarly their money transfers y_k when they trade are either the price $y_k = p$ for a buyer or its negative $y_k = -p$ for a seller. A general trading procedure, like an auction, allows each trader k to submit a bid $b_k(t_k)$ depending on his type and then based on these bids a feasible subset K is selected and the traders in K exchange items; also, trader k gets the money transfer $y_k^K(b)$ depending on the list $b = (b_k)$ of bids submitted. Let $x_K(b)$ be the probability that K is the selected feasible set when the list b is submitted. Feasibility requires that $\sum_{K \in \mathcal{K}} x_K(b) = 1$ for each list b and $\sum_k y_k^K(b) = 0$ for each $K \in \mathcal{K}$ and each list b. For the following derivation we assume that the traders' types are independently distributed: let $F_k(t_k)$ be the distribution function of k's type t_k as perceived by other traders, and let $f_k(t_k)$ be the corresponding density function. Assume that the hazard rate $f_k(t_k)/\bar{F}(t_k)$ is increasing, where $\bar{F}_k(t_k) = 1 - F_k(t_k)$.

We use the method in §8.2 to characterize the trading procedure that maximizes the traders' expected total surplus, calculated *ex ante* before they learn their types.

11. Surveys of the theory of auctions are in Wilson (1987, 1992a) and Wilson (1993) provides a general synthesis of the theory of mechanism design based on the methods in §8 and §13.
12. This is demonstrated by Bulow and Roberts (1989).

The bid $b_k(t_k)$ submitted by trader k must maximize his expected profit:

$$U_k(t_k) = \max_{b_k(t_k)} \mathcal{E}_k \left\{ \sum_{k \in K \in \mathcal{K}} x_K(b(t)) t_k - \sum_{K \in \mathcal{K}} x_K(b(t)) y_k^K(b(t)) \right\},$$

where in this case the expectation $\mathcal{E}_k$ is calculated over the possible types of all traders other than k. The envelope property therefore requires that

$$U_k'(t_k) = \mathcal{E}_k \left\{ \sum_{k \in K \in \mathcal{K}} x_K(b(t)) \right\},$$

which is just k's perceived probability that he gets to trade.[13] The individual rationality or participation constraint from §6.1 requires that $U_k(t_k) \geq 0$ so that k has a motive to participate in the procedure. Because the exchanges balance between the buyers and the sellers, feasibility implies that

$$\mathcal{E} \left\{ \sum_k U_k(t_k) \right\} = \mathcal{E} \left\{ \sum_{K \in \mathcal{K}} x_K(b(t)) \sum_{k \in K} t_k \right\}.$$

This appears to be a very weak constraint, requiring only that exchanges balance in expectation, but actually it is stronger in combination with the other constraints: the individual rationality constraint will ensure that the least type of each trader gets zero profit and then the envelope property determines the expected profit of each type. In sum, therefore, the design problem is to select a specification $\langle x, y \rangle$ of the procedure that maximizes the expected total surplus $\mathcal{E} \{\sum_k U_k(t_k)\}$ subject to the envelope property, the individual rationality constraints, and the balance constraint.

As in §8.2, this problem is addressed by maximizing an augmented objective that includes a Lagrange multiplier $\mu_k(t_k)$ for the envelope property and another multiplier $1+\lambda$ for the balance constraint. From this formulation one derives several necessary conditions, which are also sufficient due to the increasing hazard rate assumption. First, optimization of type t_k's profit $U_k(t_k)$ requires that $\mu_k(t_k) = \lambda \bar{F}_k(t_k)$ for those types large enough to obtain positive expected profit. Then, optimization of the probabilities $(x_K(b(t)))_{K \in \mathcal{K}}$ implies that it is sufficient to assign probability $x_K(b(t)) = 1$ for some feasible set $K \in \mathcal{K}$ for which the value of

$$\sum_{k \in K} \left[t_k - \alpha \frac{\bar{F}(t_k)}{f_k(t_k)} \right]$$

---

13. The trader's second-order necessary condition can be shown to require that $U''(t_k) \geq 0$; that is, higher types must have higher probabilities of trading, which is ultimately a consequence of the increasing hazard rate assumption.

is maximal, where $\alpha = \lambda/[1 + \lambda]$—including the value zero for the empty set of traders. This is the key result, since it identifies those types that get to trade. In effect, it says that the gains from trade are maximized with respect to "virtual" valuations that take account of buyers' incentives to submit bids below their true valuations and seller's incentives to submit offers above their true costs. The transfers and thereby the prices at which transactions are consummated can subsequently be inferred from these conditions. In fact, a large variety of transfer schemes will work, but in some implementations it suffices to select a single price that clears the market for the submitted bids and offers from the buyers and sellers, as we illustrate with an example.[14]

Example 15.3: Suppose there is a single buyer and a single seller whose valuations are uniformly distributed between zero and one. Thus, $F_k(t_k) = t_k$ if $k = 1$ and $t_1 = v$ is the buyer's valuation, and $F_k(t_k) = 1 + t_k$ if $k = 2$ and $t_2 = -c$ is the seller's cost. The preceding analysis implies that they should trade if and only if

$$[v - \alpha(1 - v)] - [c + \alpha c] \geq 0\,,$$

or $v - c \geq \beta \equiv \alpha/[1 + \alpha]$. Applying this characterization to the balance condition indicates that feasibility requires $\beta = 1/4$, corresponding to $\lambda = 1/2$ and $\alpha = 1/3$. An implementation that achieves this result stipulates that they trade if the buyer's bid $b(v)$ exceeds the seller's offer $a(c)$, in which case the price splits the difference: $p(a, b) = [1/2][a + b]$. The seller's optimal offer and the buyer's optimal bid are

$$a(c) = \max \{c, 1/4 + [2/3]c\} \quad \text{and} \quad b(v) = \min \{v, 1/12 + [2/3]v\}\,.$$

Caution is advised, however: this procedure allows other pairs of mutually optimal strategies that do not attain the efficient outcome.   ◇

This style of analysis can be applied to a great variety of optimal design problems, including ones involving many traders with elastic supplies and demands. Ramsey pricing as addressed in this book is merely the special case in which the purpose of the procedure is to identify an allocation of the firm's supply among customers that is efficient subject to the firm's revenue requirement. And, we focus on implementations that accomplish this allocation by having the firm offer a nonlinear tariff from which customers choose their preferred purchases based on private information about their types.

---

14. This example is due to Chatterjee and Samuelson (1983) and Myerson and Satterthwaite (1983).

Risk sharing

Partnerships and other joint ventures encounter different versions of adverse selection. Casualty insurance is sold to many customers with independent risks of
claims, and therefore total claims are largely predictable. In contrast, partners
share a common risk regarding the financial success of the enterprise. Efficient
risk sharing therefore depends sensitively on the nature of the uncertainty and
on each member's tolerance for risk. Private information can intrude in many
ways: each member's risk tolerance is private information, and each may have
privileged information about the prospects of the enterprise. This information can
be important both for risk sharing and for investment decisions. A few special
utility functions and probability distributions have the ideal property that linear
sharing rules are efficient for risk sharing and also provide sufficient incentives for
revelation of private information (Wilson (1984)). In general, however, nonlinear
sharing rules are required for efficient risk sharing, and they must be further modified (with some loss in efficiency) to encourage revelation of private information.
The formulation used for the preceding analysis of optimal trading procedures can
encompass the design of sharing rules in a partnership, as we illustrate briefly.

An illustrative formulation. *

We envision several members indexed by i who can choose among several risky
projects indexed by j. If chosen, the j-th project yields a net income $y_j(\theta)$ depending on the realization of a random variable $\theta = (t, \tau)$ that has a known distribution
function $F(\theta)$. The portion τ is never observed but $t = (t_i)$ is a list of parameters
known privately by the members; that is, member i knows t_i initially, and we
interpret t_i as the type of member i. A decision rule is a pair $\langle x, s \rangle$ in which
$x = (x_j)$ lists the probabilities that each project is chosen and $s = (s_{ij})$ lists the
members' shares of the income obtained. Naturally, $\sum_j x_j = 1$ and $\sum_i s_{ij} = y_j$.
The key feature is that each member i can submit a report $\hat{t}_i$ regarding his private
information; consequently, both $x_j(\hat{t})$ and $s_{ij}(y_j, \hat{t})$ can depend on the reports submitted, and of course the shares must depend on the income obtained. Incentive
compatibility is interpreted in this context as the requirement that each member
has an incentive to report truthfully if he expects others to do so. Thus, the decision
rule must be designed both to induce truthful reporting and to promote efficient
selection of the project. Assume that member i has a utility function u_{ij} that can
depend on the project j selected as well as his share and the outcome. Then his
expected utility is

$$U_i(t_i) = \max_{\hat{t}_i} \mathcal{E} \left\{ \sum_j x_j(\hat{t}) u_{ij}(s_{ij}(y_j, \hat{t}), \theta) \mid t_i \right\},$$

where the conditional expectation is calculated given t_i and the presumption that others report truthfully: $\hat{t}_k = t_k$ for members $k \neq i$. The envelope property requires in this case that

$$U_i'(t_i) = \mathcal{E}\left\{ \sum_j x_j(t)[u_{ij}\phi_i(\theta) + v_{ij}] \mid t_i \right\},$$

where if $f(t \mid \tau)$ and $f_i(t_i)$ are the conditional and marginal density functions then

$$\phi_i(\theta) = \frac{\partial f(t \mid \tau)/\partial t_i}{f(t \mid \tau)} - \frac{\partial f_i(t_i)/\partial t_i}{f_i(t_i)},$$
$$v_{ij}(s;\theta) = \partial u_{ij}(s;t,\tau)/\partial t_i.$$

The participation constraint is expressed by the requirement that $U_i(t_i) \geq U_i^\circ(t_i)$, where $U_i^\circ(t_i)$ represents a utility level that member i can obtain by severing his membership.[15] Finally, in view of the envelope property, one more constraint is needed to determine the absolute level of member i's expected utility: the identity

$$\mathcal{E}\left\{ U_i(t_i) - \sum_j x_j(t)u_{ij}(s_{ij}(y_j,t),\theta) \right\} = 0$$

suffices as this feasibility constraint. An efficient decision rule is therefore one that maximizes some weighted sum $\mathcal{E}\{\sum_i \lambda_i U_i(t_i)\}$ of the members' expected utilities subject to the restrictions represented by the envelope property, the participation constraint, and the feasibility constraint. The weights λ_i are intended to summarize a welfare criterion: they could also represent the outcome of a bargaining process among the members or in a market context the values of the resources they contribute, in which case each weight might depend on the member's type.

To apply the method of §8.2, a Lagrange multiplier $\mu_i(t_i)$ is associated with the envelope property, and another multiplier $\check{\lambda}_i$ is associated with the feasibility constraint. For simplicity we consider here only the case of one-dimensional types and presume sufficient monotonicity conditions so that $U_i(t_i)$ will be an increasing function of i's type. In this case, the necessary condition for an optimal choice of $U_i(t_i)$ indicates that $\mu_i(t_i) = [\check{\lambda}_i - \lambda_i]\bar{F}_i(t_i)$ if $U_i(t_i) > U_i^\circ(t_i)$. Consequently, we define the virtual utility

$$\check{u}_{ij}(s,\theta) = u_{ij}(s,\theta) - \alpha_i \frac{\bar{F}(t_i)}{f_i(t_i)}[u_{ij}(s,\theta)\phi_i(\theta) + v_{ij}(s,\theta)],$$

where $\alpha_i = [\check{\lambda}_i - \lambda_i]/\check{\lambda}_i$. Then the optimal shares assigned to each project j are selected to attain the aggregate benefit measure

$$\check{u}_j(y_j, t) = \max_{\sum_i s_{ij}=y_j} \mathcal{E}\left\{\sum_i \check{\lambda}_i \check{u}_{ij}(s_{ij}, \theta) \mid y_j, t\right\}.$$

Moreover, an optimal project is one that attains the maximal value of $\mathcal{E}\{\check{u}_j(y_j(\theta), t)$ $\mid t\}$. These calculations depend on the multipliers $\check{\lambda}_i$, but actually each can be determined from the feasibility condition, one form of which is

$$\mathcal{E}\left\{\sum_j x_j[\lambda_i u_{ij} - \check{\lambda}_i \check{u}_{ij}]\right\} = 0,$$

where arguments of functions are omitted for simplicity. If the members' utilities are linear in their shares then maximization of expected total surplus entails $\lambda_i = 1$ and $\check{\lambda}_i = \check{\lambda}$ independently of i; further, $\check{\lambda}$ is chosen so that

$$\mathcal{E}\left\{\sum_j x_j \sum_i \left[u_{ij} - \frac{\bar{F}_i}{f_i}[u_{ij}\phi_i + v_{ij}]\right]\right\} = 0$$

for the optimal decision rule.

A significant implication of this formulation is that private information useful for project selection affects efficient risk sharing. In effect, the members share risk according to their virtual utility functions rather than their actual ones. This provides incentives for truthful revelation of productive information, but it also hinders the more efficient risk sharing that would be possible if informational asymmetries did not intervene.

This formulation illustrates the variety of problems to which the methods of §8 can be applied. These methods were originally devised to study Ramsey pricing and optimal taxation. Recently, however, their applications have been extended to many other contexts in which incentive compatibility constraints derived from the participants' private information limit the outcomes that can be implemented. As seen here, the participants' risk aversion is not an impediment to the application of this mode of analysis.

15.3   Incentives in labor contracting

Many kinds of contracting invoke nonlinear pricing but it is especially significant in labor contracting. Its role stems from informational differences between the parties and the importance of risk sharing.[16] If labor inputs and outputs are verifiable by both parties then a linear compensation scheme such as a piece rate or a salary suffices; or failing this, if the employee is not risk averse, then the employer can as well sell the activity to the employee, since a worker bearing all the risk has ample incentive to expend effort and care in the task. More commonly, however, it is costly or impossible for the employer to observe some inputs or outputs, and the employee is unable or unwilling to bear the entire risk. In such cases it is efficient for the employer and the employee to share risk; moreover, the worker's share is an incentive to pursue the task vigorously. The worker's share, based on observable performance measures, is a form of nonlinear pricing of output.

We consider only the case that output is observed directly, and ignore team production in which an individual's contribution cannot be distinguished. Compensation that is a nonlinear function of measured output arises in this case when labor inputs by the worker are observed imperfectly by the employer. This input might be the worker's effort or care, or other factors that are costly for the worker to provide: we measure all outputs and inputs in money terms. It is important to realize that this case depends also on the presence of either private information or an exogenous source of uncertainty. Otherwise, from the output the input might be inferred. In the case of sharecropping, for instance, the size of the crop is observed but the effort required to produce that crop cannot be inferred: the worker may have information about fertility, pests and rainfall, but even given this information, output depends stochastically on other factors unobserved by either party. Although labor contracting usually has some aspects of bilateral monopoly, we assume here that the employer has all the bargaining power: the employer offers a compensation schedule and the worker either accepts or takes another job at the prevailing market wage.

Most labor contracting has important dynamic elements, since employment relationships often continue over time. Long term and repeated relationships differ greatly from short term ones, but these changes do not alter the role of nonlinear pricing, so we omit them here.[17]

Nonlinear compensation for output

The simplest case omits consideration of risk sharing. Suppose the worker knows a parameter t, interpreted as his type, but the employer is uncertain: a probability distribution $F(t)$ describes this uncertainty. The output q depends on both t and the worker's input x. Typically the type represents factors that reduce the effort

16. In the technical literature, contracting with these features is sometimes called a principle-agent problem, after the legal terminology referring to contracts affected by statutes and common law precedents regulating agency relationships: the worker's performance of a task as an agent for the principle allows discretionary choices by the worker.
17. A survey of contracting, including dynamic features, is by Hart and Holmström (1987).

required from the worker to produce a given output: in the sharecropping context these factors could include soil fertility, rainfall, and an absence of pests. This formulation can be stated alternatively by saying that the worker's net benefit is $P(q) - C(q, t)$ if he is paid $P(q)$ for the output q and he incurs the cost $x = C(q, t)$ to produce this output when the type parameter is t. Thus, the employer's objective is to maximize the expected value of output net of compensation, $q - P(q)$, anticipating that the worker will choose to produce the output $q(t)$ that maximizes his net benefit when he knows the type is t. Moreover, the employer must offer compensation sufficient to induce the worker to accept employment rather than to seek the alternative wage:

$$P(q(t)) - C(q(t), t) \geq w,$$

for each type t, assuming the alternative wage w is measured net of the worker's inputs.

This formulation is evidently the same as the formulation of the nonlinear pricing formulation in §6 except payments are reversed: the firm (employer) pays the customer (the worker). This is often true of pricing factor inputs: payments are reversed but otherwise the nonlinear pricing formulation remains intact. The reversed direction of payment does have the effect that typically the compensation function $P(q)$ is increasing and convex, rather than concave, as seen previously in the case of an insurance market.

Example 15.4: Suppose the worker's cost is $C(q, t) = [1 - t]q$, so that $1 - t$ represents directly the worker's cost per unit of output. If the type distribution has the special form $F(t) = t^a$ then the employer's optimal compensation function provides a fixed wage plus a constant price p per unit of output; for instance, $p = \$0.50$ if $a = 1$. But for most other distribution functions the schedule is nonlinear, as for the examples in §6.6.[18]   ◇

To illustrate an alternative interpretation, consider a negotiation between a homeowner and a construction contractor.[19] If the owner is uncertain about the contractor's costs, and prefers different designs depending on the prices charged, then a protracted negotiation might be avoided by a procedure in which the owner offers a schedule of prices and designs (say, size of the house) from which the contractor chooses. That is, the contractor selects from the menu of options based on private information about his costs. In general, the advantages of nonlinear pricing derive

18. The uniform price that splits profits equally with the worker is also the optimal maximin strategy for the employer over a wide class of possible cost functions for the worker. That is, rather than assessing the distribution function F the employer maximizes his minimum net profit, where the minimum is with respect to all the cost functions the worker might have. See Hurwicz and Shapiro (1978).
19. I am indebted to Gyu Wang for this illustration.

from offering a menu of options from which customers or contractors select based on private information. In the case of bilateral negotiations, a further advantage is that it can avoid costly delays in reaching an agreement.

Risk sharing

The employer's compensation design problem is more complicated when the worker is risk averse and there is exogenous uncertainty. Part of the complexity stems from the need to share risk efficiently; that is, the employer provides some insurance for the worker, but of course the worker cannot be insured entirely against output risks without eliminating his incentive to expend effort. We omit this aspect below and simply assume that the employer aims to minimize the expected cost of inducing the worker to expend a specified effort x°.

An illustrative formulation.*

It simplifies notation to assume that the worker chooses directly the probability distribution of output. Thus, more effort or care makes greater or better outputs more likely, and others, less likely. In particular, suppose there are n possible output levels $i = 1, \ldots, n$ and the net effect of the worker's effort is to choose the probabilities $x = (x_i)_{i=1,..,n}$ that each of these occurs, where of course $\sum_i x_i = 1$. Let $U(P(q) - C(x))$ be the worker's utility function defined on his net monetary gain after subtracting his cost $C(x)$ depending on the distribution x that he chooses. The utility function U is increasing, and strictly concave if the worker is risk averse. The employer's problem is to choose the utility level u_i that the worker obtains if the i-th output level q_i occurs. The expected cost of doing this when the worker is induced to choose the specified distribution x° is

$$\sum_{i=1}^{n} x_i^\circ P(q_i) = \sum_{i=1}^{n} x_i^\circ [V(u_i) + C(x^\circ)],$$

where V is the inverse of the utility function U. Namely $U(V(u)) = u$ for each possible value of u, so $V(u)$ is the net monetary amount that yields the utility u. Thus, the actual compensation if the output q_i occurs is $P(q_i) = V(u_i) + C(x^\circ)$. Note that V is increasing and convex if U is increasing and concave.

Inducing the worker to choose the specified distribution x° requires that these utility levels ensure that x° is the worker's optimal choice. This constraint requires that for each feasible choice x of the output distribution,

$$\sum_{i=1}^{n} x_i^\circ u_i \geq \sum_{i=1}^{n} x_i U(V(u_i) + C(x^\circ) - C(x)),$$

so that the worker's expected utility from choosing x° is no less than it is from any alternative choice. In addition, the feasibility constraint

$$\sum_{i=1}^{n} x_i^\circ u_i \geq U(w)\,,$$

is imposed to ensure that the worker is willing to accept the contract. These constraints are linear in the variables (u_i) if U is an exponential utility function. It is useful to note that if the worker also has some private information, then such constraints must be imposed for each possible state of the worker's information; that is, for each possible type t the worker must prefer to take the action $x^\circ(t)$ intended by the employer.

Taken together, these components of the employer's design problem define a nonlinear constrained maximization problem. From the perspective of nonlinear pricing, the key feature is that the net result is a compensation scheme that usually depends nonlinearly on output.[20]

Example 15.5: An alternative formulation supposes that the agent chooses an action that determines the probability distribution of output. Let $g(q \mid a)$ be the density function of the output q depending on the action a chosen by the agent. Suppose further that the agent's utility function has the additive form $U(P(q)) - C(a)$ in which the agent's cost $C(a)$ is measured in terms of utility. Assume that the range of possible outputs is independent of a. In this case, the condition that determines the optimal remuneration has the form

$$1/U'(P(q)) = \lambda - \mu \frac{g_a(q \mid a)}{g(q \mid a)}\,,$$

where the multiplier λ is chosen large enough to ensure the agent's participation, and the multiplier μ is chosen to ensure that the agent prefers the action selected by the principle. For instance, if the agent chooses the mean of the output distribution, which is either an exponential distribution or a Normal distribution, then g_a/g is a decreasing linear function of the output q. Consequently, if the utility function U is an exponential function then the remuneration $P(q)$ is proportional to the logarithm of a linear function of output. Or, if $U(P) = \sqrt{P}$ then $P(q)$ is a quadratic function of output.   ◇

---

20. One dynamic version of this formulation has the property that the worker's compensation depends only on aggregates constructed from the numbers of times that the various output levels occur; cf. Holmström and Milgrom (1987).

15.4   Taxation and regulatory policies

In this section we mention two applications in the public sector. The theory of Ramsey pricing was originally developed to provide a systematic framework to study commodity and income taxation. We mention here how the material in previous chapters can be interpreted in terms of income taxation; §16 provides a brief history of the subject. We then describe recent applications to the design of regulatory policies.

Taxation

In §6 we formulated Ramsey pricing as the design of a tariff that maximizes consumers' surplus subject to the constraint that the firm's net revenue is sufficient to cover its total costs. This formulation can be applied simplistically to the design of an income tax schedule by a reinterpretation. Interpreting the firm as the government, its objective is to maximize citizens' surplus subject to the requirement that it raise sufficient tax revenues to cover its expenditures for public goods. The tariff $P(q)$ is the tax assessed on the income q and in total the tax receipts must meet the government's revenue requirement. Citizens or households are diverse and the government is assumed to know the distribution of their types in the population. One of type t obtains the net benefit $U(q, t) - P(q)$ if its gross income is q and its net income is $q - P(q)$. The gross benefit $U(q, t)$ must be interpreted in this formulation as net of all nonmonetary expenditures of effort required to generate the income q given one's type t.

Practical applications address complications omitted in this formulation. One is that progressive taxation, in which the marginal tax rate is an increasing function of income, may be motivated by ethical considerations that in terms of the Ramsey formulation must be included by specifying individuals' welfare weights that are dependent on their incomes or their types, especially for types disadvantaged in producing income; or, it may reflect political realities, since votes are allocated equally. In addition, in some cases the tax schedule treats different classes of citizens differently, such as households with differing numbers of dependents; and incomes (and expenditures) from different sources are treated differently, such as the distinction between wage income and capital gains. A second is that the formulation must be considerably enriched to include risk aversion and other income effects as in §7; a variety of dynamic effects over time, such as individuals' investments in education and skills; and incentives to expend effort in work, especially when income derives from a concatenation of effort, luck, and inheritance—both financial and genetic. These complications are inadequately addressed by the simplistic interpretation above and explain why we omit a systematic presentation of the general theory of taxation even though it encompasses nonlinear pricing by firms as a special case.

Design of regulatory policies

In the United States many public services are provided by privately owned utilities whose operations are regulated by state commissions. A recent literature interprets the agency relationship between the regulator and the firm as a kind of contracting in which, via its policies regarding investments, products, and prices, the regulator provides incentives for the firm to provide services efficiently in the public interest. Ramsey pricing is an older approach to this topic, but the recent literature examines also the role of private information known by the firm regarding technology and costs. Some of the analyses along this line parallel the ones above: the regulator offers the firm a nonlinear schedule of allowed profits depending on observable magnitudes such as investments, outputs, and prices, and then the firm selects an option from this menu based on its more detailed knowledge of technology and costs.[21]

An illustrative formulation. *

A simple static formulation is the following. The regulatory commission is assumed to maximize a welfare measure that assigns weights 1 and $1 - \alpha$ to expected consumers' and producer's surplus, respectively.[22] Producer's surplus is uncertain because the firm's cost cannot be observed by the commission and it depends on a type parameter t known privately by the firm. The commission is therefore limited to specifying the revenue $P(q)$ that the firm is allowed, depending on a measure q of the output that it provides. In response to this incentive, the firm chooses an output level to maximize its profit:

$$R(t) = \max_{q} \left\{ P(q) - C(q,t) \right\} ,$$

where $C(q,t)$ is its cost function depending on output q and its type parameter t. The constraint $R(t) \geq 0$ expresses the requirement that the firm must break even. In addition, as in §8, the envelope property indicates that the firm optimizes its response to the incentive offered: $R'(t) = -C_t(q(t), t)$, where $q(t)$ is the optimal output level. Suppose that total surplus is the difference $W(q) - C(q, t)$ between a measure $W(q)$ of the social value of ouput and the firm's actual cost. Also, let $F(t)$

21. This is an overly simplified view of this subject, especially because regulation is affected importantly by a continuing relationship between the parties. See Baron and Myerson (1982) and Spulber (1988, 1989). An excellent survey is by Baron (1989).

22. One assumes $\alpha > 0$ to capture the political reality that regulatory commissions tend to favor consumers more than owners of regulated firms, perhaps because owners are not voters in the firm's service territory. An alternative view is that α reflects distortionary effects of taxation to provide transfers to the firm. Laffont and Tirole (1986) study an alternative formulation in which the firm's cost is observed by the regulator.

be the distribution function of the firm's type parameter. Then the commission's objective is to choose the function $P(q)$ to maximize the expectation

$$\int_0^\infty \{W(q(t)) - C(q(t), t) - \alpha R(t)\} \, dF(t)$$

of the welfare measure, subject to the constraints mentioned above. Assume that the cost function $C(q, t)$ and marginal cost function $c(q, t) \equiv C_q(q, t)$ are increasing functions of the output, and decreasing functions of the type parameter; in particular, $R(t)$ is increasing. Then the methods of §8 applied to this problem indicate that the optimal assignment of types to output levels is characterized by the condition that

$$W'(q) = c(q, t) + \alpha \frac{\bar{F}(t)}{f(t)} c_t(q, t)$$

at $q = q(t)$, provided this assignment is nondecreasing. Having identified the assignment $q(t)$ from this condition, the marginal revenue $p(q) \equiv P'(q)$ is inferred from the property that $p(q(t)) = c(q(t), t)$. In turn, the revenue function is $P(q) = P_\circ + \int_0^q p(x) \, dx$, where the fixed fee $P_\circ$ is chosen to satisfy minimally the requirement that the least type breaks even: $R(0) = 0$. In an application, one might assume that an inverse demand function $D^{-1}(q)$ specifies the market price at which the demand for output is q. Before cost is subtracted, total surplus is therefore the area under this demand function and the marginal gross benefit is $W'(q) = D^{-1}(q)$ if there are no income effects among consumers.

Example 15.6: Suppose that $C(q, t) = C_\circ + q/t$ and that the type parameter t is uniformly distributed on a positive interval $a \leq t \leq b$. Then the assignment satisfies the optimality condition

$$W'(q(t)) = 1/t + \alpha[b - t][-1/t^2].$$

Also, because $p(q(t)) = C_q = 1/t$ the marginal revenue allowed the firm satisfies the analogous condition,

$$W'(q) = [1 + \alpha]p(q) - \alpha b p(q)^2,$$

and therefore the optimal marginal revenue function is

$$p(q) = W'(q) \div \left\{ \beta + \sqrt{\beta^2 - \alpha b W'(q)} \right\},$$

where $\beta = [1 + \alpha]/2$, provided $W'(q) \leq \beta^2/\alpha b$, and otherwise $p(q) = W'(q)/\beta$. The key feature of this solution is that if $\alpha > 0$ then the marginal revenue allowed the firm exceeds the demand price $D^{-1}(q)$ for the same output: the difference is made up in expectation by the fixed fee P_o, which may be negative and therefore constitute a subsidy. The net result is that output is less than the perfectly efficient quantity, but in expectation output is more than the firm would provide if it were allowed to maximize its profit as an unregulated monopolist. Similarly, if $C(q, t) = C_o + qt$ and $D^{-1}(q) = 1 - q$ then $p(q) = 1 - q/[1 - \alpha]$, which again inflates marginal revenue and encourages the firm to expand output beyond the quantity an unregulated monopolist would provide.   ◇

15.5 Summary

The forms of nonlinear pricing studied in previous chapters are motivated by rate design in the communications, power, and transport industries. Firms in these industries specify tariffs to define service conditions for a large and stable, but diverse, population of customers with continuing demands. As in Ramsey pricing and its variants, increments in purchase size are differentiated to meet revenue requirements for cost recovery efficiently. The efficiency gains result primarily from taking account of the higher price elasticities of demands for increments to large purchase sizes. Via tactics such as Pareto-improving pricing, the firm can assure that no customer is disadvantaged compared to the uniform price that would raise the same revenue. The net effect is only to increase the supply provided by the firm.

Nonlinear pricing can also be used to exploit monopoly power. When it is applied inefficiently, without benefits for customers, it falls within the penumbra of price discrimination. An extreme example of price discrimination is temporally differentiated pricing in the case the firm disposes of an initial stock via a declining sequence of prices: the resulting delivery delays for customers are purely inefficient. In this and most other examples of the deleterious effects of price discrimination, the inefficiencies stem from quality degradation. That is, delivery time is a quality attribute and uniform pricing would result in the highest quality, namely immediate delivery. Regulatory agencies therefore examine proposals to ensure that inefficient quality degradation does not offset the gains from product differentiation, such as increased quantities supplied and a spectrum of qualities better adapted to customers' preferences.

The product pricing applications reviewed in Section 1 are only a sampling of the pervasive role of nonlinear pricing. They suffice nevertheless to indicate that the subject is richer than the coverage in this book. Among the broader topics are pricing and product design to meet customers' peakload requirements, the more general topic of bundling, and various forms of differentiation of delivery conditions. The latter in particular introduce complicating factors, such as the Coase property of temporal pricing.

The applications in Section 2 to markets with private information introduce a different motivation for nonlinear pricing. Adverse selection is important when one party to a transaction is affected by factors known only by the other. Nonlinear pricing can eliminate this problem by assuring that prices are sufficient to cover the costs imposed by those types selecting each option on the menu offered. Although this can impose inefficiencies, uniform prices are also inefficient in such situations.

Risk sharing among partners is a pure case of beneficial nonlinear pricing. Nonlinear sharing rules are generally essential to allocate risk efficiently, and also to promote revelation of private information useful for investment and production decisions.

The applications in Section 3 to labor contracting indicate, however, that the problem is complicated when risk sharing is further affected by the incentives it creates for expenditure of effort by workers. Absent risk sharing, optimal compensation schemes are direct applications of nonlinear pricing (with reversed payments). Related applications in Section 4 extend even to the design of regulatory policies in the context that the firm has private information about its technology or costs. But with risk sharing, designing an optimal compensation scheme requires solving a constrained optimization problem that is more complex than the ones studied in previous chapters. That the compensation function is designed in anticipation of the worker's selection of effort (in response to the incentives provided) is still the guiding principle, but the conditions required to induce selection of the actions preferred by the employer must usually be treated explicitly as auxiliary constraints. Previous chapters allow omission of such constraints because the customers' only actions are to select purchase sizes.

BIBLIOGRAPHY

Because few references are provided in the text, this chapter provides a bibliography of the literature on nonlinear pricing and a capsule summary of its theoretical development. No attempt is made to be exhaustive; rather, the main ideas are emphasized and references are given to the key technical articles on which the various chapters are based. This literature provides supplementary material on the topic of each chapter.

Stephen Brown and David Sibley (1986) provide a comprehensive exposition of nonlinear pricing that complements much of the material here. Bridger Mitchell and Ingo Vogelsang (1991) summarize the elements of the theory and review applications in the telecommunications industry. For expositions and bibliographies of a larger literature on related topics, see the texts by Louis Phlips (1983, 1988a, 1988b) and Jean Tirole (1988, Chapter 3) and the review articles by Ronald Braeutigam (1989) and Hal Varian (1989).

16.1   A short history

Although nonlinear pricing has long been used in practice, its theoretical development is recent. The principal achievement was also the first: the construction of a theory of optimal nonlinear taxation by James Mirrlees (1971). It is the basis for all the material in this book. This work is refined and exposited by Mirrlees (1976, 1986, 1990) and alternative formulations are developed by Kevin Roberts (1979) and Roger Guesnerie and Jesus Seade (1982). Tuomala (1990) reviews these contributions.

The root of this development is the theory of linear commodity taxation initiated by Frank Ramsey (1927), following a long tradition that goes back to Jules Dupuit's famous treatise "On the Measurement of the Utility of Public Works" (Paris, 1844). Its application to pricing by regulated utilities and public enterprises is initiated in seminal articles by Marcel Boiteux (1956, 1960); for an exposition see Jacques Drèze (1964) and modern versions by Egbert Dierker (1991) and Guesnerie (1980). A succinct presentation of the main ideas is by William Baumol and David Bradford

(1970). Eytan Sheshinski (1986) provides a survey and bibliography of recent developments in the theory of Ramsey pricing using uniform prices.

Mirrlees' work is cast in a general model that allows many complicating features, such as income effects and choice of production technology, and it focuses on the construction of welfare-maximizing tax policies. Its application to firms' pricing policies was not fully appreciated initially. Some contributions were made steadily (A. Gabor (1955) and M.M. Murphy (1977)), especially to the simpler theory of two-part tariffs; including Martin Feldstein (1972), Stephen Littlechild (1975), Walter Oi (1971), Yew Kwan Ng and M. Weissner (1974), and Richard Schmalansee (1981a). Three influential articles by George Akerlof (1970), Michael Spence (1973), and Michael Rothschild and Joseph Stiglitz (1976) emphasized the role of self-selection and implicitly the necessity of differentiated prices to achieve efficiency in markets with a heterogeneous population of customers. Development of the theory of nonlinear pricing as an integral part of the theory of the firm blossomed suddenly in the late 1970s. The initial flurry included articles by Gerald Faulhaber and John Panzar (1977), Michael Mussa and Sherwin Rosen (1978), Panzar (1977), Roberts (1979), Joel Sobel (1979), Spence (1976a, 1980), and Robert Willig (1978). An application to utility pricing is reported by Roger Koenker and Sibley (1979) and there have been several applications to related topics in general microeconomic theory; for instance, Stiglitz (1977). The articles by Willig (1978) and Janusz Ordover and Panzar (1980, 1982) emphasize the implications of nonlinear pricing for efficient regulatory policies.

Subsequent work (called "the articles" in Section 2) is represented by Barry Goldman, Hayne Leland, and Sibley (1984), Guesnerie and Jean-Jacques Laffont (1984), Guesnerie and Seade (1982), Michael Katz (1983, 1984a, 1984b), Laffont, Eric Maskin, and Jean-Charles Rochet (1987), Maskin and John Riley (1984a, 1984b), R. Preston McAfee and John McMillan (1988), Leonard Mirman and Sibley (1980), Sobel (1984), Daniel Spulber (1981), and Padmanabhan Srinagesh (1986). Part II of this book is based substantially on these and the prior contributions, which laid the foundations of the subject. The principal text is by Brown and Sibley (1986). Introductory expositions are included in the texts by Phlips (1983, 1988a, 1988b) and Tirole (1988, Chapter 3 and its Appendix) and the review article by Varian (1989, §2.3).

Some of the motives for nonlinear pricing in competitive markets are described by Marcel Boyer (1986), J. Crowther (1964), Robert Dolan (1987), Rajiv Lal and Richard Staelin (1984), J.P. Monahan (1984), and Sridhar Moorthy (1984). Applications to pricing of utility services are developed by Brown and Sibley (1986), Panzar and Sibley (1978), and Shmuel Oren, Stephen Smith, and Wilson (1982a, 1982b, 1985); for a survey see Braeutigam (1989). Pareto-improving tariffs are studied by Faulhaber and Panzar (1977), Ordover and Panzar (1980), and Willig (1978), and in detail by Brown and Sibley (1986). Hung-po Chao and Wilson (1987), N. Viswanathan and Edison Tse (1989), and Wilson (1989a, 1989b) study nonlinear pricing of service reliabilities when capacity limits the firm's supplies stochastically. Oren, Smith, and Wilson (1982b) extend nonlinear pricing to an oligopoly.

With few exceptions, much of the work on nonlinear pricing focuses on the special case of a monopolist vendor of a single product and/or a parameterized model of customers' benefits with a single type parameter. This book does the same in Part II to introduce the reader to the subject, but as we emphasize in §8, for a single product much of the analysis is unaffected by the restriction to a single type parameter. We also attempt to make the theory accessible and applicable by concentrating in Part I on the use of the demand profile to represent market data. This eliminates reliance on type parameters and it enables numerical calculation of multiproduct tariffs as in §14.

The recent work on nonlinear pricing developed in close relation to the more general theory of optimal auctions and other trading processes that account for incentive effects—such as customers' self-selection of their preferred purchases in the present context. The seminal articles are by Roger Myerson (1981), Myerson and Mark Satterthwaite (1983), and John Moore (1984). An application to regulatory policies developed by David Baron and Myerson (1982) initiated a literature that is surveyed by Baron (1989) and Spulber (1989b). The monograph by Laffont and Tirole (1992) develops a comprehensive theory of regulatory incentives as part of a general exposition of the principles involved in designing incentive provisions of procurement and agency contracts. An especially careful application to the design of incentives for an agent employed by a principal is by Guesnerie and Laffont (1984); as they illustrate, their construction also applies to a wider class of problems with a one-dimensional type parameter. Portions of this literature applicable to auctions and bargaining are surveyed by Wilson (1992) and John Kennan and Wilson (1992).

The literature on price discrimination

Price discrimination has had negative connotations at least since the indictment by Dupuit (1844) and subsequent analyses by Arthur C. Pigou (1920, 1932) and Joan Robinson (1933). A sampling of subsequent literature includes James Buchanan (1953), Ralph Cassady (1946a, 1946b), John Hartwick (1978), and Leland and R. Meyer (1976). The text by Phlips (1983) and the articles by Phlips (1988a) and Varian (1989) provide modern surveys and extensive bibliographies; the text by Frederick M. Scherer (1980, Chapter 11) provides a broad survey of related topics. Stiglitz (1989) elaborates various applications to topics motivated by the considerations in §15.

The association of nonlinear pricing with price discrimination stems from an inadequate and confusing categorization of pricing policies by Pigou. His analysis largely ignored customers' self-selection of preferred choices from a menu of options available equally to all customers: prices were implicitly assumed to be uniform and different prices were offered to different customers or market segments. The term first-degree price discrimination was coined by Pigou to describe pricing practices that exhaust all or most of consumers' surplus by charging each customer its reservation price, which was presumed known to the firm. Third-degree price discrimination referred to similar practices applied to separated market segments. Second-degree price discrimination referred to intermediate cases in which perfect price discrimination in a single market was limited by the seller's inability to distinguish among customers or an inability to prevent arbitrage by customers. Subsequent authors, such as Tirole (1988) and Varian (1989), include nonlinear pricing within the penumbra of second-degree price discrimination by interpreting it as an imperfect form limited by each customer's ability to select any one among the menu of the options offered. We have not used this terminology because it is hard to reconcile the pejorative interpretation of discrimination with the efficiency properties of nonlinear pricing derived from Ramsey pricing formulations.

The main strand of the recent literature on second-degree price discrimination uses nonlinear pricing of qualities as a paradigm, as in Mussa and Rosen (1978) and Maskin and Riley (1984a).[1] A main theme of this literature is that a monopolist's optimal prices lead each customer type to select a lesser quality and at a higher price than would result from efficient pricing at marginal cost—as shown in Figure 13.2—which is termed quality distortion by some authors. The literature on intertemporal pricing of durable goods dissents from this view by showing that quality distortion in the form of delayed purchases is small when the seller has limited powers of commitment. Called the Coase Conjecture (Coase, 1972), this proposition has been studied by Jeremy Bulow (1982, 1986), Faruk Gul (1987), Gul, Hugo Sonnenschein, and Wilson (1976), Gul and Sonnenschein (1988), Nancy Stokey (1979, 1981), and Peter Swan (1972). A different dissent is registered by Srinagesh and Ralph Bradburd (1989), who posit a plausible model in which quality is enhanced because customers with lower total benefit nevertheless have higher marginal valuations of quality increments.

In Pigou's lexicon, the term third-degree price discrimination described different (presumably uniform) prices offered to separate market segments. A typical example of third-degree price discrimination is a discount based on an observable attribute such as age (via discounts for senior citizens), location, or class, as in the usual distinction between residential, commercial, and industrial customers of regulated utilities. Subsequent interpretations of this category have included prices conditioned on other observable aspects, such as education, that are endogenously chosen signals of unobserved attributes, such as measures of ability in a labor market context; the seminal work by Spence (1973, 1974) initiated a

---

1. Subsequent extensions include articles by David Besanko, Shabtai Donnenfeld, and Lawrence White (1987, 1988), Russell Cooper (1984), Donnenfeld and White (1988, 1990), Jean Gabszewicz, Avner Shaked, John Sutton, and Jacques-François Thisse (1986), and Spulber (1989a).

large literature that in the product market context is described by Tirole (1988, §2.6.1.2). One strand of the literature on third-degree price discrimination empha-sizes market tests for unfavorable welfare consequences as compared to uniform pricing. Robinson (1933) established that charging different uniform prices in sep-arated markets with independent linear demand functions reduces total surplus. Schmalansee (1981b) shows more generally that an increase in aggregate output is a necessary condition for an increase in total surplus; Varian (1985) extends the analysis to cases with dependent demands and obtains general bounds on the change in welfare that allow, for instance, that differentiated prices are beneficial if they enable a market to be served that would not be otherwise.[2]

To counter negative connotations of second-degree price discrimination, we follow Brown and Sibley (1986) in emphasizing that nonlinear pricing is univer-sally beneficial compared to uniform pricing provided options, such as a Pareto-improving tariff, are offered to ensure that no customers are disadvantaged. This is consistent with an analysis by J. Stephen Henderson and Robert Burns (1989) that exempts nonlinear tariffs derived via Ramsey pricing from the undue price discrimination label used in statutory provisions of laws establishing standards for public utility regulation. However, little in this book addresses the potential problem of quality degradation described in §1 and §15, except the analysis of priority service in §10. Our analysis of this topic illustrates that differentiation of service qualities, in this case service reliabilities, can be accompanied by efficient pricing policies ensuring that all customers' net benefits are improved, without altering the firm's net revenue.

Summary

The methodology used to analyze nonlinear pricing stems from Mirrlees' adapta-tion of Ramsey's formulation of the problem of choosing prices to maximize an aggregate measure of total welfare subject to a revenue requirement. The optimal tariff (or tax schedule in Mirrlees' context) is generally nonlinear if the popula-tion of customers is diverse. Nonlinear pricing can be interpreted within Pigou's category of second-degree price discrimination by noting that customers with dif-ferent price elasticities of demand pay different average prices. Nevertheless, it is an efficient means of raising the required revenue: the nonuniformity of marginal prices is explained solely by the fact that the price elasticities of aggregate demand (as measured by the demand profile) are different for different increments. Thus, its main features derive from differentiated pricing of increments. As with linear pricing, each customer chooses a preferred selection from a menu of options, but the schedule of prices for successive increments is not restricted to be constant.

---

2. For related work, see DeGraba (1990), Edwards (1950), Finn (1974), Greenhut and Ohta (1976), Katz (1987), Nahata et al. (1990), and Schwarz (1990).

The technical literature developed since the late 1970s has brought nonlinear pricing within the standard economic theory of the firm, both in the analysis of quantity discounts and in the analysis of a product line comprising a spectrum of qualities. It has been applied to monopoly, oligopoly, and regulated contexts as well. This work relies substantially on models with convenient regularity properties, a single product, and a single type parameter to avoid technical problems. However, it can be extended to the more general contexts of multidimensional and multiproduct pricing addressed in Parts III and IV. The basic principle derived from this literature interprets nonlinear pricing as differentiated pricing of increments. The basic theory of bundling provides a unified methodology in which to conduct the analysis; in addition, the example in §13.5 suggests a wider role for bundling in multiproduct contexts. In the special context of quantity discounts, Mirrlees' formulation in terms of Ramsey pricing provides a framework that encompasses most of the applications to regulated industries, as well as many of the applications in §15 to markets affected by informational disparities. Extensions to multipart tariffs and other restricted forms follow modified versions of the same principles.

Nonlinear pricing is used by firms in many industries, although the forms of implementation vary substantially. Regulatory agencies increasingly condone offering a menu of optional tariffs provided old options are preserved to ensure that no customers are disadvantaged. This stems in part from acceptance of the basic conclusion that an efficient way to meet a regulated firm's revenue requirement is to exploit its monopoly power according to the principles of Ramsey pricing, possibly modified to meet distributional constraints. Even if nonlinear pricing has the onerous connotations of second-degree price discrimination, it is an efficient means of meeting the firm's revenue requirement. This conclusion about allocative efficiency is subject however to the important provisos that the firm's operations are productively efficient, and that the efficient spectrum of qualities of products or services is provided; in particular, the latter is always suspect because of the evidence that quality degradation can be used to facilitate price discrimination.

16.2 Chapter references

In this section we direct the reader's attention to portions of the literature pertaining to particular chapters.

Mathematical Techniques: The exposition in Parts I–III uses elementary methods of algebra and calculus except for occasional references to the Euler condition and the transversality conditions from the calculus of variations. These necessary conditions as well as various sufficiency conditions are presented in standard texts; I rely on Elsgolc (1961). Part IV depends on advanced methods of multivariate calculus but the exposition suppresses technical aspects in the formulations and derivations of optimality conditions. The formulations in §12 and §14 rely on the special form of multivariate integration by parts known variously as Green's Theorem, the Divergence Theorem, or in a generalized form, the fundamental theorem of multivariate calculus, sometimes called Stokes' Theorem; a popular reference is Schey (1973).

§1. **Introduction.** Some of the feasibility requirements for nonlinear pricing are mentioned by Scherer (1980, p. 315) who provides a long list of varieties of price discrimination, some of which can be interpreted as forms of nonlinear pricing.

§2. **Illustrations.** In addition to the illustrations in this chapter, several are presented in detail by Brown and Sibley (1986). Mitchell and Vogelsang (1991) provide a detailed description of applications to telecommunications. An application to pricing telephone services for customers with impaired hearing is described by Oren, Smith, and Wilson (1982a).

§3. **Models and Data Sources.** The material in this chapter is a composite of the articles cited above. Nearly all authors have made explicit assumptions that fit roughly within those cited in Section 4. Additional sufficiency conditions are presented in §8. The most general sufficiency assumptions are apparently those in Mirrlees (1976, 1986). In principle, the necessary and sufficient condition for the required monotonicity properties is based on the property of quasi-supermodularity developed by Milgrom and Shannon (1991).

§4. **Tariff Design.** The use of the demand profile to predict customers' responses to nonlinear tariffs is drawn from Oren, Smith, and Wilson (1982b). It has not been adopted by other authors except that Brown and Sibley (1986) and Goldman, Leland, and Sibley (1984) use a parallel formulation for one style of proof; see also Tirole (1986, §3.5.1.3). Mitchell and Vogelsang (1991) provide an exposition and critique of this formulation based on a previous version of this manuscript. Basic references on bundling are Adams and Yellan (1976), McAfee, McMillan, and Whinston (1989), and Schmalansee (1984).

§5. **Ramsey Pricing.** The interpretation of Ramsey pricing as an extension of monopoly pricing is standard in the literature, dating at least from Ramsey (1927) and more recently Mirrlees (1971, 1976). For a recent analysis more in the spirit of Boiteux's (1956) formulation, and with applications to regulatory policies, see Laffont and Tirole (1992). The initial work on Pareto-improving tariffs is by Faulhaber and Panzar (1977), Ordover and Panzar (1980), and Willig (1978). For an alternative analysis in a quality context based on regulation of minimum qualities or the imposition of a price cap, see Besanko, Donnenfeld, and White (1987). The material in this chapter is motivated by Brown and Sibley (1986, p. 83 ff.). The illustration in Section 3 on telephone tariffs is based on D. Heyman, J. Lazorchak, D. Sibley, and W. Taylor (1987). The application to a communication system for hearing-impaired customers is described in Oren, Smith, and Wilson (1982a). Train and Toyama (1989) describe an application to time-of-use tariffs for electricity used for pumping irrigation water by agricultural customers.

§**6. Single-Parameter Disaggregated Models.** The topics in this chapter are standard in the articles in the large journal literature on nonlinear pricing. Expositions of models with discrete types in which only the adjacent incentive compatibility constraints are binding include Cooper (1984) and Maskin and Riley (1984a); more general models are addressed by Guesnerie and Seade (1982) and Matthews and Moore (1987) and Moore (1984). The literature on two-part tariffs includes Feldstein (1972), Murphy (1977), Ng and Weissner (1974), Oi (1971), Panzar and Sibley (1989), Schmalansee (1981a), Sharkey and Sibley (1990), and Vohra (1990). Detailed analyses of two-part and multipart tariffs are included in the book by Brown and Sibley (1986, §4 and Appendix). Exposition of the theory of multipart and nonlinear tariffs in terms of customers' demand functions is not usual in the literature.

§**7. Income Effects.** Mirrlees (1976) and Guesnerie and Laffont (1984) include income effects in their formulations. The formulation in terms of the indirect utility function, introduced in §8, is used by Roberts (1979) to develop an alternative method of constructing tariffs when there are income effects of the type in the third example. His method has the advantage that it facilitates analysis of Ramsey pricing with variable welfare weights.

§**8. Technical Amendments.** This exposition relies on Goldman, Leland, and Sibley (1984), Guesnerie and Laffont (1984), and Mirrlees (1976). The formulation of nonlinear tariffs in terms of the indirect utility function is based on Roberts (1979). The extension to multidimensional types is developed by Srinagesh (1985, 1991a). Another version of the analysis of multidimensional types is by McAfee and McMillan (1988), who invoke an assumption somewhat weaker than type-linearity of the marginal benefit functions to reduce the problem to one with a single type parameter. Their exposition provides explicit sufficiency conditions. The analysis of multipart tariffs is analogous to results in Chao and Wilson (1987) and Wilson (1989a).

§**9. Multidimensional Pricing.** This chapter is based on Oren, Smith, and Wilson (1985), who provide sufficiency conditions. Section 4 on the item-assignment formulation is based on Wilson, Oren, and Smith (1980), who include a derivation of optimal fixed fees.

§**10. Priority Pricing.** In Section 1 on priority service, the analysis of supply uncertainty is based on Chao and Wilson (1987) and Wilson (1989a); and of demand uncertainty, on Harris and Raviv (1981). Spulber (1990ab) provides an alternative analysis, including the special case that customers' demands differ only by a multiplicative factor, for which equi-proportional curtailments are efficient. Section 2 on Ramsey pricing follows Wilson (1989b). The initial work on priority service is by Marchand (1974) and Tschirhart and Jen (1979); subsequent literature includes Chao, Oren, Smith, and Wilson (1986, 1989), Viswanathan and Tze (1989), and Woo (1990). Section 3 on priority queuing systems is based on Mendelson and Whang (1990). A different formulation applied to priority scheduling of airport landing and takeoff slots is developed by Pitbladdo (1990).

§11. **Capacity Pricing.** This chapter is based on Oren, Smith, and Wilson (1985) and Panzar and Sibley (1978). See Srinagesh (1990b) for further analysis of the Panzar and Sibley model.

§12. **Multiple Products and Competitive Tariffs.** Sections 1 and 2 are special cases of the construction in §14: see the cautionary comments below. Srinagesh (1991b) studies the topic of Sections 1 and 2 in the case that one product is priced linearly and another is priced nonlinearly. He finds, for instance, that when demands for the products are independent a multiproduct monopolist nevertheless sets a lower price for the first product than would a duopolist selling only that product: the motive is to increase customers' benefits that can then be extracted as profits via higher nonlinear prices for the other product. Section 3 regarding Cournot models is based on Oren, Smith, and Wilson (1982b), who also provide sufficiency conditions. The brief discussion in Section 4 is based on Meyer and Klemperer (1989) who provide detailed analysis of nonlinear pricing policies adapted ex post to realized demand conditions.

§13. **Multiproduct Pricing.** Sections 2 and 5 are based on Mirrlees (1976, 1986) and the analysis with one-dimensional type parameters in Section 4 is based on Mirman and Sibley (1980). Armstrong (1992) studies the example in Section 5, showing that a monopolist firm's optimal tariff always excludes some customers from purchasing, and that a multiproduct firm gains from using a nonseparable tariff. See Champsaur and Rochet (1989) for a study of Bertrand competition between duopolists offering a spectrum of qualities, of which each customer purchases a single unit, in the case that customers' type parameters are one-dimensional.

§14. **Multiproduct Tariffs.** This chapter is motivated by ideas presented in Wilson (1991). However, the formulas in that article are wrong (!) because own-price and substitution effects are not separated properly. Errors might remain in this revised version, which was not included in the manuscript reviewed by referees.

§15. **Other Applications of Nonlinear Pricing.** Introductory expositions of the topics in this chapter include Phlips (1983, 1988a, 1988b), Spulber (1989), and Tirole (1988). Guesnerie and Laffont (1984, §4,5) illustrate applications of nonlinear pricing to several of these topics. Baron, Braeutigam, Stiglitz, and Varian provide comprehensive surveys in *The Handbook of Industrial Organization* (1989, Chapters 24, 23, 13, and 10).

REFERENCES

Adams, W., and Janet Yellan (1976), "Commodity Bundling and the Burden of Monopoly," *Quarterly Journal of Economics* 90: 475-498.

Akerlof, George A. (1970), "The Market for 'Lemons': Qualitative Uncertainty and the Market Mechanism," *Quarterly Journal of Economics* 84: 488-500.

Anderson, Simon P., and Jacques-François Thisse (1988), "Price Discrimination in Spatial Competitive Markets," *European Economic Review* 32: 578-590.

Armstrong, Mark (1992), "Optimal Nonlinear Pricing by a Multiproduct Monopolist," Chap. 4, D. Phil. thesis, Institute of Economics and Statistics, Oxford University.

Armstrong, Mark, and John Vickers (1991), "Welfare Effects of Price Discrimination by a Regulated Monopolist," *RAND Journal of Economics* 22: 571-580.

Baron, David P. (1989), "Design of Regulatory Mechanisms and Institutions," in *The Handbook of Industrial Organization*, R. Schmalansee and R. Willig (eds.), Volume II, Chapter 24, 1347-1447. Amsterdam and New York: Elsevier Science Publishers B.V. (North-Holland).

Baron, David P., and Roger B. Myerson (1982), "Regulating a Monopolist with Unknown Costs," *Econometrica* 50: 911-930.

Battalio, Raymond C., and R.B. Ekelund Jr. (1972), "Output Change under Third-Degree Price Discrimination," *Southern Economic Journal* 39: 285-290.

Baumol, William J.(1987), "Ramsey Pricing," in: *The New Palgrave*, J. Eatwell, M. Milgate, and P. Newman (eds.), Vol. IV, 49-51. London: Macmillan Press, Ltd.

Baumol, William J., and David Bradford (1970), "Optimal Departures from Marginal Cost Pricing," *American Economic Review* 60: 265-283.

Baumol, William J., John C. Panzar, and Robert D. Willig (1982), *Contestable Markets and the Theory of Industrial Structure*. New York: Harcourt Brace Jovanovich.

Besanko, David, Shabtai Donnenfeld, and Lawrence J. White (1987), "Monopoly and Quality Distortion: Effects and Remedies," *Quarterly Journal of Economics* 102: 743-768.

Besanko, David, Shabtai Donnenfeld, and Lawrence J. White (1988), "The Multiproduct Firm, Quality Choice, and Regulation," *Journal of Industrial Economics* 36: 411-430.

Besanko, David, and David S. Sibley (1991), "Compensation and Transfer Pricing in a Principal-Agent Model," *International Economic Review* 32: 59-68.

Besanko, David, and Wayne L. Winston (1990), "Optimal Price Skimming by a Monopolist Facing Rational Consumers," *Management Science* 36: 555-567.

Boiteux, Marcel (1956), "Sur la gestion des monopolies publics astreint à l'équilibre budgétaire," *Econometrica* 24: 22-40. Translated as "On the Management of Public Monopolies Subject to Budgetary Constraints," *Journal of Economic Theory* 3: 219-240.

Boiteux, Marcel (1960), "Peak Load Pricing," *Journal of Business* 33: 157–179.

Boyer, Marcel (1986), "Intertemporal Nonlinear Pricing," *Canadian Journal of Economics* 19: 539–555.

Braden, David J., and Shmuel S. Oren (1988), "Nonlinear Pricing to Produce Information," Working Paper, University of Rochester and University of California at Berkeley.

Braeutigam, Ronald R. (1989), "Optimal Policies for Natural Monopolies," in *The Handbook of Industrial Organization*, R. Schmalansee and R. Willig (eds.), Volume II, Chapter 23, 1289–1246. Amsterdam and New York: Elsevier Science Publishers B.V. (North-Holland).

Brown, Donald J., and Geoffrey M. Heal (1980), "Two-Part Tariffs, Marginal Cost Pricing, and Increasing Returns in a General Equilibrium Framework," *Journal of Public Economics* 13: 25–49.

Brown, Lorenzo, Michael Einhorn, and Ingo Vogelsang (1991), "Toward Improved and Practical Incentive Regulation," *Journal of Regulatory Economics* 3: 323–338.

Brown, Stephen J., and David S. Sibley (1986), *The Theory of Public Utility Pricing*. Cambridge, UK: Cambridge University Press.

Buchanan, James M. (1953), "The Theory of Monopolistic Quantity Discounts," *Review of Economic Studies* 20: 199–208.

Bulow, Jeremy (1982), "Durable Goods Monopolists," *Journal of Political Economy* 90: 314–352.

Bulow, Jeremy (1986), "An Economic Theory of Planned Obsolescence," *Quarterly Journal of Economics* 101: 729–749.

Bulow, Jeremy, and John Roberts (1989), "The Simple Economics of Optimal Auctions," *Journal of Political Economy* 97: 1060–1090.

Caillaud, Bernard (1990), "Regulation, Competition, and Asymmetric Information," *Journal of Economic Theory* 52: 87–110.

Cain, Paul, and James M. Macdonald (1991), "Telephone Pricing Structures: The Effects on Universal Service," *Journal of Regulatory Economics* 3: 293–308.

Cassady, Ralph (1946a), "Some Economics of Price Discrimination under Non-perfect Market Conditions," *Journal of Marketing* 11: 7-20.

Cassady, Ralph (1946b), "Techniques and Purposes of Price Discrimination," *Journal of Marketing* 11: 135–150.

Champsaur, Paul, and Jean-Charles Rochet (1985), "Price Competition and Multiproduct Firms," Paper 8532, CORE, Université Catholique de Louvain.

Champsaur, Paul, and Jean-Charles Rochet (1986), "Existence of a Price Equilibrium in a Differentiated Industry," mimeo, INSEE, Paris.

Champsaur, Paul, and Jean-Charles Rochet (1989), "Multiproduct Duopolists," *Econometrica* 57: 533–557.

Chao, Hung-po (1990), "Priority Service and Optimal Rationing under Uncertainty," Electric Power Research Institute, Palo Alto, CA.

Chao, Hung-po, Shmuel S. Oren, Stephen A. Smith, and Robert B. Wilson (1986), "Multilevel Demand Subscription Pricing for Electric Power," *Energy Economics* 8: 199–217.

Chao, Hung-po, Shmuel S. Oren, Stephen A. Smith, and Robert B. Wilson (1989), "Priority Service: Market Structure and Competition," *Energy Journal* 9: 77–103.

Chao, Hung-po, and Robert Wilson (1987), "Priority Service: Pricing, Investment, and Market Organization," *American Economic Review* 77: 899–916.

Chatterjee, Kalyan, and William Samuelson (1983), "Bargaining under Incomplete Information," *Operations Research* 31: 835–851.

Clay, Karen B., David S. Sibley, and Padmanabhan Srinagesh (1992), "Ex Post vs. Ex Ante Pricing: Optional Calling Plans and Tapered Tariffs," *Journal of Regulatory Economics* 4:115–138.

Coase, Ronald (1972), "Durability and Monopoly," *Journal of Law and Economics* 15: 143–149.

Conlisk, John, E. Gerstner, and Joel Sobel (1984), "Cyclic Pricing by a Durable Goods Monopolist," *Quarterly Journal of Economics* 99: 489–505.

Cooper, Russell (1984), "On Allocative Distortions in Problems of Self-Selection," *RAND Journal of Economics* 15: 568–577.

Cournot, Augustin (1838), *Researches into the Mathematical Principles of the Theory of Wealth*, translation from the French, 1927. New York: Macmillan Publishing Co.

Crew, Michael A., and Paul R. Kleindorfer (1978), "Reliability and Public Utility Pricing," *American Economic Review* 68: 31–40.

Crowther, J. (1964), "Rationale for Quantity Discounts," *Harvard Business Review*, March, 121–127.

De Fontenay, Alain, Mary Shugard, and David Sibley (1990), *Telecommunications Demand Modelling*. Amsterdam: North-Holland.

DeGraba, Patrick (1990), "Input Market Price Discrimination and the Choice of Technology," *American Economic Review* 80: 1246–1253.

Dierker, Egbert (1991), "The Optimality of Boiteux-Ramsey Pricing," *Econometrica* 59: 99–121.

Dixit, Avinash, and Joseph Stiglitz (1979), "Quality and Quantity Competition," *Review of Economic Studies* 46: 587–599.

Dolan, Robert (1987), "Quantity Discounts: Managerial Issues and Research Opportunities," *Marketing Science* 6: 1–22.

Donnenfeld, Shabtai (1988), "Commercial Policy and Imperfect Discrimination by a Foreign Monopolist," *International Economic Review* 29: 607–620.

Donnenfeld, Shabtai, and Lawrence J. White (1988), "Product Variety and the Inefficiency of Monopoly," *Economica* 55: 393–401.

Donnenfeld, Shabtai, and Lawrence J. White (1990), "Quality Distortion by a Discriminating Monopolist: Comment," *American Economic Review* 80: 941–945.

Drèze, Jacques (1964), "Some Postwar Contributions of French Economists to Theory and Public Policy," *American Economic Review* 54 (Supplement): 1–64.

Dupuit, Jules (1844), "On the Measurement of the Utility of Public Works," translation by R.H. Barbak (1952), *International Economic Papers* 2.

Ebert, Uwe (1988), "The Optimal Income Tax Problem: On the Case of Two-dimensional Populations," Economics Department Discussion Paper A-169, University of Bonn, Germany.

Edwards, E.O. (1950), "The Analysis of Output under Discrimination," *Econometrica* 18: 163–172.

Ekelund, R.B. (1970), "Price Discrimination and Product Differentiation in Economic Theory: An Early Analysis," *Quarterly Journal of Economics* 84: 268–278.

Elsgolc, L. E. (1961), *Calculus of Variations*. International Series of Monographs on Pure and Applied Mathematics, Volume 19. London, UK: Pergamon Press Ltd.; and Reading, MA: Addison-Wesley Publishing Company.

Faulhaber, Gerald (1975), "Cross Subsidization: Pricing in Public Enterprises," *American Economic Review* 65: 966–977.

Faulhaber, Gerald (1979), "Cross Subsidization in Public Enterprise Pricing," Chapter 4 in John T. Wenders (ed.), *Pricing in Regulated Industries: Theory and Application II*, 76–121. Denver, CO: Mountain States Telephone and Telegraph Company.

Faulhaber, Gerald, and John Panzar (1977), "Optimal Two Part Tariffs with Self-Selection," Discussion Paper 74. Morristown, NJ: Bell Laboratories.

Feldstein, Martin (1972), "Equity and Efficiency in Public Sector Pricing: The Optimal Two-Part Tariff," *Quarterly Journal of Economics* 86: 175–187.

Finn, T.J. (1974), "The Quantity of Output in Simple Monopoly and Discriminating Monopoly," *Southern Economic Journal* 41: 239–243.

Fudenberg, Drew, and Jean Tirole (1991), *Game Theory*, Chapter 7. Cambridge, MA: MIT Press.

Gabor, A. (1955), "A Note on Block Tariffs," *Review of Economic Studies* 23: 32–41.

Gabszewicz, Jean Jaskold, Avner Shaked, John Sutton, and Jacques-François Thisse (1986), "Segmenting the Market: The Monopolist's Optimal Product Mix," *Journal of Economic Theory* 39: 273–289.

Gabszewicz, Jean Jaskold, and Jacques-François Thisse (1992), "Spatial Competition and the Location of Firms," Chapter 9 in *The Handbook of Game Theory*, R. Aumann and S. Hart (eds.). Amsterdam and New York: Elsevier Science Publishers B.V. (North-Holland).

Gale, Ian (1992), "Advance-Purchase Discounts and Monopoly Allocation of Capacity," *American Economic Review* 82: to appear.

Goldman, M. Barry, Hayne E. Leland, and David S. Sibley (1984), "Optimal Nonuniform Pricing," *Review of Economic Studies* 51: 305–319.

Greenhut, Melvin L., and Hiroshi Ohta (1976), "Joan Robinson's Criterion for Deciding Whether Market Discrimination Reduces Output," *Economic Journal* 86: 96–97.

Greenwood, Jeremy, and R. Preston McAfee (1991), "Externalities and Asymmetric Information," *Quarterly Journal of Economics* 106: 103–122.

Griffin, James M., and Thomas H. Mayor (1987), "The Welfare Gain from Efficient Pricing of Local Telephone Services," *Journal of Law and Economics* 30: 465–487.

Guesnerie, Roger (1980), "Second-Best Pricing Rules in the Boiteux Tradition: Derivation, Review, and Discussion," *Journal of Public Economics* 13: 51–80.

Guesnerie, Roger, and Jean-Jacques Laffont (1984), "A Complete Solution to a Class of Principal-Agent Problems with an Application to the Control of a Self-Managed Firm," *Journal of Public Economics* 25: 329–369.

Guesnerie, Roger, and Jesus Seade (1982), "Nonlinear Pricing in a Finite Economy," *Journal of Public Economics* 17: 157–179.

Gul, Faruk (1987), "Noncooperative Collusion in Durable Goods Oligopoly," *RAND Journal of Economics* 18: 248–254.

Gul, Faruk, and Hugo Sonnenschein (1988), "On Delay in Bargaining with One-Sided Uncertainty," *Econometrica* 56: 601–612.

Gul, Faruk, Hugo Sonnenschein, and Robert Wilson (1986), "Foundations of Dynamic Monopoly and the Coase Conjecture," *Journal of Economic Theory* 39: 155–190.

Hagen, Kåre P. (1979), "Optimal Pricing in Public Firms in an Imperfect Market Economy," *Scandinavian Journal of Economics* 81: 475–493.

Hansen, Ward, and R. Kipp Martin (1990), "Optimal Bundle Pricing," *Management Science* 36: 155–174.

Harris, Milton, and Artur Raviv (1981), "A Theory of Monopoly Pricing Schemes with Demand Uncertainty," *American Economic Review* 71: 347–365.

Hart, Oliver, and Bengt Holmström (1987), "The Theory of Contracts," Chapter 3 in *Advances in Economic Theory*, T. Bewley (ed.), 71-155. Cambridge, UK: Cambridge University Press.

Hartwick, John (1978), "Optimal Price Discrimination," *Journal of Public Economics* 31: 83–89.

Hausman, Jerry A., and Jeffrey K. MacKie-Mason (1988), "Price Discrimination and Patent Policy," *RAND Journal of Economics* 19: 253–265.

Henderson, J. Stephen, and Robert E. Burns (1989), "An Economic and Legal Analysis of Undue Price Discrimination," NRRI Report 89-12. Columbus, OH: National Regulatory Research Institute.

Heyman, D., J. Lazorchak, D. Sibley, and W. Taylor (1987), "An Analysis of Tapered Access Charges for End Users." Murray Hill, NJ: Bell Communications Research Inc. Published in Harry Trebing (ed.), *Proceedings of the Eighteenth Annual Williamsburg Conference on Regulation*, East Lansing, MI: Michigan State University Press.

Hillman, Jordan Jay, and Ronald Braeutigam (1989), *Price Level Regulation for Diversified Public Utilities: An Assessment*. Dordrecht, NL: Kluwer Academic Publishers.

Holmström, Bengt R., and Paul Milgrom (1987), "Aggregation and Linearity in the Provision of Intertemporal Incentives," *Econometrica* 55: 303–328.

Hurwicz, Leonid, and Leonard Shapiro (1978), "Incentive Structures Maximizing Residual Gain under Incomplete Information," *Bell Journal of Economics* 9: 180–191.

Itoh, M. (1983), "Monopoly, Product Differentiation, and Economic Welfare," *Journal of Economic Theory* 31: 88–104.

Joskow, Paul, and Richard Schmalansee (1983), *Markets for Power*. Cambridge, MA: MIT Press.

Jucker, James V., and Meir Rosenblatt (1985), "Single-Period Inventory Models with Demand Uncertainty and Quantity Discounts: Behavioral Implications and a New Solution Procedure," *Naval Research Logistics Quarterly* 32: 537–550.

Kahn, Charles (1986), "The Durable Goods Monopolist and Consistency with Increasing Cost," *Econometrica* 54: 275–294.

Katz, Michael L. (1982), "Nonuniform Pricing and Rate-of-Return Regulation," Woodrow Wilson School, Report 27, Princeton University.

Katz, Michael L. (1983), "Non-Uniform Pricing, Output and Welfare Under Monopoly," *Review of Economic Studies* 50: 37–56.

Katz, Michael L. (1984a), "Nonuniform Pricing with Unobservable Numbers of Purchases," *Review of Economic Studies* 51: 461–470.

Katz, Michael L. (1984b), "Price Discrimination and Monopolistic Competition," *Econometrica* 52: 1453–1472.

Katz, Michael L. (1987), "The Welfare Effects of Third-Degree Price Discrimination in Intermediate Good Markets," *American Economic Review* 77: 154–167.

Kennan, John F., and Robert B. Wilson (1992), "Bargaining with Private Information," *Journal of Economic Literature* 30: to appear.

Koenker, Roger W., and David S. Sibley (1979), "Nonuniform Pricing Structures in Electricity," Chapter 2 in *Public Utility Ratemaking in an Energy-Conscious Environment*, Werner Sichel (ed.), 23–39. Boulder CO: Westview Press.

Kohli, Rajeev, and Heungsoo Park (1989), "A Cooperative Game Theory Model of Quantity Discounts," *Management Science* 35: 693–707.

Laffont, Jean-Jacques, Eric Maskin, and Jean-Charles Rochet (1987), "Optimal Nonlinear Pricing with Two-Dimensional Characteristics" in T. Groves, R. Radner, and S. Reiter (eds.), *Information, Incentives, and Economic Mechanisms*, 256–266. Minneapolis, MN: University of Minnesota Press.

Laffont, Jean-Jacques, and Jean Tirole (1986), "Using Cost Observation to Regulate Firms," *Journal of Political Economy* 94: 614–41.

Laffont, Jean-Jacques, and Jean Tirole (1990a), "The Regulation of Multiproduct Firms," *Journal of Public Economics* 43: 1–66.

Laffont, Jean-Jacques, and Jean Tirole (1990b), "Optimal Bypass and Cream Skimming," *American Economic Review* 80: 1042–1061

Laffont, Jean-Jacques, and Jean Tirole (1992), *A Theory of Incentives in Regulation and Procurement*. Cambridge, MA: MIT Press.

Lal, Rajiv, and Richard Staelin (1984), "An Approach for Developing an Optimal Quantity Discount Policy," *Management Science* 30: 1524–1539.

Lancaster, Kelvin (1990), "The Economics of Product Variety: A Survey," *Marketing Science* 9: 189–206.

Lee, Hau L., and Meir J. Rosenblatt (1986), "A Generalized Quantity Discount Pricing Model to Increase Supplier's Profits," *Management Science* 32: 1177–1185.

Leland, Hayne E., and R.A. Meyer (1976), "Monopoly Pricing Structures with Imperfect Information," *Bell Journal of Economics* 7: 449–462.

Littlechild, Stephen C. (1975), "Two Part Tariffs and Consumption Externalities," *Bell Journal of Economics* 6: 661–670.

Ma, Ching-to Albert (1991), "Adverse Selection in Dynamic Moral Hazard," *Quarterly Journal of Economics* 106: 255–276.

Marchand, M. G. (1974), "Pricing Power Supplied on an Interruptible Basis," *European Economic Review* 5: 263–274.

Maskin, Eric, and John Riley (1984a), "Monopoly with Incomplete Information," *The RAND Journal of Economics* 15: 171–196.

Maskin, Eric, and John Riley (1984b), "Optimal Auctions with Risk Averse Buyers," *Econometrica* 52: 1473–1518.

Maskin, Eric, and Jean Tirole (1988), "A Theory of Dynamic Oligopoly," Parts I and II, *Econometrica* 56: 549–99.

Matthews, Steven, and John Moore (1987), "Monopoly Provision of Quality and Warranties: An Exploration in the Theory of Multidimensional Screening," *Econometrica* 55: 441–468.

Matzkin, Rosa L. (1991), "Axioms of Revealed Preference for Nonlinear Choice Sets," *Econometrica* 59: 1779–1786.

McAfee, R. Preston (1991), "Efficient Allocation with Continuous Quantities," *Journal of Economic Theory* 53: 51–74.

McAfee, R. Preston, and John McMillan (1988), "Multidimensional Incentive Compatibility and Mechanism Design," *Journal of Economic Theory* 46: 335–354.

McAfee, R. Preston, John McMillan, and Michael D. Whinston (1989), "Multiproduct Monopoly, Commodity Bundling, and Correlation of Values," *Quarterly Journal of Economics* 103: 371–383.

McFadden, Daniel L., and Kenneth E. Train (1991), "The Value of Service Reliability: Statistical Inference in a Dynamic Stochastic Control Process with Discrete Decision Variables," Department of Economics, University of California at Berkeley.

Mendelson, Haim, and Seungjin Whang (1990), "Optimal Incentive-Compatible Priority Pricing for the M/M/1 Queue," *Operations Research* 38: 870–883.

Meyer, Margaret A., and Paul D. Klemperer (1989), "Supply Function Equilibria in Oligopoly Under Uncertainty," *Econometrica* 57:1243–1277.

Milgrom, Paul R., and Christina Shannon (1991), "Monotone Comparative Statics," Stanford Institute for Theoretical Economics, Technical Report 11.

Mirman, Leonard J., and David S. Sibley (1980), "Optimal Nonlinear Prices for Multiproduct Monopolies," *The Bell Journal of Economics* 11: 659–670.

Mirrlees, James A. (1971), "An Exploration in the Theory of Optimal Taxation," *Review of Economic Studies* 38: 175–208.

Mirrlees, James A. (1976), "Optimal Tax Theory: A Synthesis," *Journal of Public Economics* 6: 327–358.

Mirrlees, James A. (1986), "The Theory of Optimal Taxation," Chapter 24 in K.J. Arrow and M.D. Intriligator (eds.), *Handbook of Mathematical Economics*, Volume III, 1197–1249. Amsterdam and New York: Elsevier Science Publishers B.V. (North-Holland).

Mirrlees, James A. (1990), "Taxing Uncertain Incomes," *Oxford Economic Papers* 42: 34–45.

Mitchell, Bridger M. (1979a), "Optimal Pricing of Local Telephone Service," *American Economic Review* 68: 517–536.

Mitchell, Bridger M. (1979b), "Telephone Call Pricing in Europe: Localizing the Pulse," Chapter 2 in John T. Wenders (ed.), *Pricing in Regulated Industries: Theory and Application II*, 19–50. Denver, CO: Mountain States Telephone and Telegraph Company.

Mitchell, Bridger M., and Ingo Vogelsang (1991), *Telecommunications Pricing: Theory and Practice*. Cambridge, UK: Cambridge University Press.

Monahan, J.P. (1984), "A Quantity Discount Pricing Model to Increase Vendor Profits," *Management Science* 30: 720–726.

Moore, John (1984), "Global Incentive Constraints in Auction Design," *Econometrica* 52: 1523–1535.

Moorthy, K. Sridhar (1984), "Marketing Segmentation, Self-Selection, and Product Line Design," *Marketing Science* 3: 288–307.

Murphy, M.M. (1977), "Price Discrimination, Market Separation, and the Multi-Part Tariff," *Economic Inquiry* 15: 587–599.

Mussa, Michael, and Sherwin Rosen (1978), "Monopoly and Product Quality," *Journal of Economic Theory* 18: 301–317.

Myerson, Roger B. (1981), "Optimal Auction Design," *Mathematics of Operations Research* 6: 58–63.

Myerson, Roger B., and Mark A. Satterthwaite (1983), "Efficient Mechanisms for Bilateral Trading," *Journal of Economic Theory* 28: 265–281.

Nahata, Babu, Krzysztof Ostaszewski, and P.K. Sahoo (1990), "Direction of Price Changes in Third-Degree Price Discrimination and Some Welfare Implications," *American Economic Review* 80: 1254–1258.

Ng, Yew Kwan, and M. Weissner (1974), "Optimal Pricing with a Budget Constraint: The Case of the Two-Part Tariff," *Review of Economic Studies* 41.

Oi, Walter J. (1971), "A Disneyland Dilemma: Two-Part Tariffs for a Mickey Mouse Monopoly," *Quarterly Journal of Economics* 85: 77–96.

Ordover, Janusz A., and John C. Panzar (1980), "On the Nonexistence of Pareto Superior Outlay Schedules," *The Bell Journal of Economics* 11: 351–354.

Ordover, Janusz A., and John C. Panzar (1982), "On the Nonlinear Pricing of Inputs," *International Economic Review* 23: 659–676.

Oren, Shmuel S., and Stephen A. Smith (1981), "Critical Mass and Tariff Structure in Electronic Communications Markets," *The Bell Journal of Economics* 12:467–487.

Oren, Shmuel S., Stephen A. Smith, and Robert B. Wilson (1982a), "Nonlinear Pricing in Markets with Interdependent Demand," *Marketing Science* 1: 287–313.

Oren, Shmuel S., Stephen A. Smith, and Robert B. Wilson (1982b), "Competitive Nonlinear Tariffs," *Journal of Economic Theory* 29: 49–71.

Oren, Shmuel S., Stephen A. Smith, and Robert B. Wilson (1982c), "Linear Tariffs with Quality Discrimination," *The Bell Journal of Economics* 13: 455–471.

Oren, Shmuel S., Stephen A. Smith, and Robert B. Wilson (1985), "Capacity Pricing," *Econometrica* 53: 545–566.

Panzar, John C. (1977), "The Pareto Dominance of Usage Sensitive Pricing," in H. Dorick (ed.), *Proceedings of the Sixth Annual Telecommunications Policy Research Conference*. Lexington, MA: Lexington Books.

Panzar, John C., and Andrew Postlewaite (1982), "Sustainable Outlay Schedules," Discussion Paper 626S, Northwestern University.

Panzar, John C., and David S. Sibley (1978), "Public Utility Pricing under Risk: The Case of Self-Rationing," *American Economic Review* 68: 888–895.

Panzar, John C., and David S. Sibley (1989), "Optimal Two-Part Tariffs for Inputs," *Journal of Public Economics* 40: 237–249.

Pavarini, Carl (1979), "The Effect of Flat-to-Measured Rate Conversions on Local Telephone Usage," Chapter 3 in John T. Wenders (ed.), *Pricing in Regulated Industries: Theory and Application II*, 51–75. Denver, CO: Mountain States Telephone and Telegraph Company.

Phlips, Louis (1983), *The Economics of Price Discrimination*. Cambridge, UK: Cambridge University Press.

Phlips, Louis (1988a), "Price Discrimination: A Survey of the Theory," *Journal of Economic Surveys* 2: 135–167.

Phlips, Louis (1988b), *The Economics of Imperfect Information*. Cambridge, UK: Cambridge University Press.

Pigou, Arthur Cecil (1920), *The Economics of Welfare*. London: Macmillan Press, Ltd. Fourth edition, 1932.

Pitbladdo, Richard (1990), "Decentralized Airline Scheduling via Priority Runway Pricing," Graduate School of Management, University of Rochester.

Press, William H., Brian P. Flannery, Saul A. Teukolsky, and William T. Vetterling, *Numerical Recipes*. Cambridge, UK: Cambridge University Press, 1986.

Ramsey, Frank P. (1927), "A Contribution to the Theory of Taxation," *Economic Journal* 37: 47–61.

Roberts, Kevin W.S. (1979), "Welfare Considerations of Nonlinear Pricing," *Economic Journal* 89: 66–83.

Robinson, Joan (1933), *The Economics of Imperfect Competition*. London: Macmillan Press Ltd.

Rochet, Jean-Charles (1985), "The Taxation Principle and Multi-Time Hamilton-Jacobi Equations," *Journal of Mathematical Economics* 14:113–128.

Rochet, Jean-Charles (1987), "Monopoly Regulation with Two Dimensional Uncertainty," mimeo, Ecole Polytechnique, Paris.

Rosenblatt, Meir J., and Hau L. Lee (1985), "Improving Profitability with Quantity Discounts under Fixed Demand," *IIE Transactions* 17: 388–395.

Rothschild, Michael, and Joseph Stiglitz (1976), "Equilibrium in Competitive Insurance Markets," *Quarterly Journal of Economics* 90: 629–649.

Salant, Stephen W. (1989), "When is Inducing Self-Selection Optimal for a Monopolist?," *Quarterly Journal of Economics* 103: 391–397.

Salop, Steven (1979), "Monopolistic Competition with Outside Goods," *Bell Journal of Economics* 10: 141–156.

Sappington, David E.M., and David S. Sibley (1989), "Strategic Nonlinear Pricing under Price Cap Regulation." Morristown, NJ: Bell Communications Research.

Scherer, Frederic M. (1980), *Industrial Market Structure and Economic Performance*, Second Edition. Chicago: Rand McNally Publishing Co.

Schey, H. M. (1973), *Div, Grad, Curl, and All That*. New York: W. W. Norton Company.

Schmalansee, Richard (1981a), "Monopolistic Two-Part Pricing Arrangements," *Bell Journal of Economics* 8: 445–467.

Schmalansee, Richard (1981b), "Output and Welfare Implications of Monopolistic 3rd Degree Price Discrimination," *American Economic Review* 71: 242–247.

Schmalansee, Richard (1984), "Gaussian Demand and Commodity Bundling," *Journal of Business* 57 (Supplement): S211–S235.

Schwartz, Marius (1990), "Third-Degree Price Discrimination and Output: Generalizing a Welfare Result," *American Economic Review* 80: 1259–1262.

Shaked, Avner, and John Sutton (1982), "Relaxing Price Competition Through Product Differentiation," *Review of Economic Studies* 44: 3–13.

Sharkey, William W., and David Sibley (1990), "Regulatory Preference over Customer Types: The Case of Optional Two-Part Tariffs." Morristown, NJ: Bell Communications Research.

Shepard, Andrea (1991), "Price Discrimination and Retail Configuration," *Journal of Political Economy* 99: 30–53.

Sheshinski, Eytan (1986), "Positive Second Best Theory: A Brief Survey of the Theory of Ramsey Pricing," Chapter 25 in K.J. Arrow and M.D. Intriligator (eds.), *Handbook of Mathematical Economics*, Volume III, 1251–1280. Amsterdam and New York: Elsevier Science Publishers B.V. (North-Holland).

Sibley, David (1989), "Asymmetric Information, Incentives, and Price-Cap Regulation," *RAND Journal of Economics* 20: 392–404.

Sibley, David, and Padmanabhan Srinagesh (1992), "Multiproduct Nonlinear Pricing and Bundling," Technical Report, Economics Department, University of Texas, Austin.

Smith, Stephen A. (1989), "Efficient Menu Structures for Pricing Interruptible Electric Power Service," *Journal of Regulatory Economics* 1: 203–223.

Sobel, Joel (1979), "Optimal Non-Linear Prices," University of California, San Diego.

Sobel, Joel (1984), "Nonlinear Prices and Price-Taking Behavior," *Journal of Economic Behavior and Organization* 5: 387–396.

Sobel, Joel (1991), "Durable Goods Monopoly with Entry of New Consumers," *Econometrica* 59: 1455–1485.

Spence, A. Michael (1973), "Job Market Signaling," *Quarterly Journal of Economics* 87: 355–374.

Spence, A. Michael (1974), *Market Signaling: Information Transfer in Hiring and Related Processes*. Cambridge, MA: Harvard University Press.

Spence, A. Michael (1976a), "Nonlinear Prices and Welfare," *Journal of Public Economics* 8: 1–18.

Spence, A. Michael (1976b), "Product Selection, Fixed Costs, and Monopolistic Competition," *Review of Economic Studies* 43: 217–235.

Spence, A. Michael (1980), "Multi-Product Quantity-Dependent Prices and Profitability Constraints," *Review of Economic Studies* 47: 821–841.

Spulber, Daniel (1981), "Spatial Nonlinear Pricing," *American Economic Review* 71: 923–933.

Spulber, Daniel (1984), "Competition and Multiplant Monopoly with Spatial Nonlinear Pricing," *International Economic Review* 25: 425–439.

Spulber, Daniel (1988), "Bargaining and Regulation with Asymmetric Information about Demand and Supply," *Journal of Economic Theory* 44: 251–268.

Spulber, Daniel (1989a), "Product Variety and Competitive Discounts," *Journal of Economic Theory* 48: 510–525.

Spulber, Daniel (1989b), *Regulation and Markets*. Cambridge, MA: MIT Press.

Spulber, Daniel (1992a), "Optimal Nonlinear Pricing and Contingent Contracts," *International Economic Review* 33:to appear.

Spulber, Daniel (1992b), "Capacity-Contingent Nonlinear Pricing by Regulated Firms," *Journal of Regulatory Economics* 4:to appear.

Spulber, Daniel F. (1992c), "Monopoly Pricing Strategies," *Journal of Economic Theory* 52:to appear.

Srinagesh, Padmanabhan (1985), "Nonlinear Prices with Heterogeneous Consumers and Uncertain Demand," *Indian Economic Review* 20(2): 299–315.

Srinagesh, Padmanabhan (1986), "Nonlinear Prices and the Regulated Firm," *Quarterly Journal of Economics* 101: 51–68.

Srinagesh, Padmanabhan (1990a), "Why Marginal Prices are Below Marginal Cost: Mixed Linear-Nonlinear Pricing." Livingston, NJ: Bell Communications Research.

Srinagesh, Padmanabhan (1990b), "Self-Rationing and Nonlinear Prices." Livingston, NJ: Bell Communications Research.

Srinagesh, Padmanabhan (1991a), "Nonlinear Prices with Multidimensional Consumers." Livingston, NJ: Bell Communications Research.

Srinagesh, Padmanabhan (1991b), "Mixed Linear-Nonlinear Pricing with Bundling," *Journal of Regulatory Economics* 3: 251–263.

Srinagesh, Padmanabhan, and Ralph M. Bradburd (1989), "Quality Distortion by a Discriminating Monopolist," *American Economic Review* 78: 96–105.

Stiglitz, Joseph E. (1977), "Monopoly, Nonlinear Pricing, and Imperfect Information: The Insurance Market," *Review of Economic Studies* 44: 407–430.

Stiglitz, Joseph E. (1989), "Imperfect Information in the Product Market," Chapter 13 in R. Schmalansee and R. Willig (eds.), *The Handbook of Industrial Organization*, Volume I, 769–847. Amsterdam and New York: Elsevier Science Publishers B.V. (North-Holland).

Stokey, Nancy (1979), "Intertemporal Price Discrimination," *Quarterly Journal of Economics* 93: 355–371.

Stokey, Nancy (1981), "Rational Expectations and Durable Goods Pricing," *Bell Journal of Economics* 12: 112–128.

Swan, Peter L. (1972), "Optimum Durability, Second-Hand Markets, and Planned Obsolescence," *Journal of Political Economy* 80: 575–585.

Taylor, Lester D. (1975), "The Demand for Electricity: A Survey," *Bell Journal of Economics* 6: 74–110.

Tirole, Jean (1988), *The Theory of Industrial Organization*. Cambridge, MA: MIT Press.

Train, Kenneth E., Moshe Ben-Akiva, and Terry Atherton (1989), "Consumption Patterns and Self-Selecting Tariffs," *Review of Economics and Statistics* 71: 62–73.

Train, Kenneth E., Daniel L. McFadden, and Moshe Ben-Akiva (1987), "The Demand for Local Telephone Service: A Fully Discrete Model of Residential Calling Patterns and Service Choices," *RAND Journal of Economics* 18: 109–123.

Train, Kenneth E., Daniel L. McFadden, and Andrew A. Goett (1987), "Consumer Attitudes and Voluntary Rate Schedules for Public Utilities," *Review of Economics and Statistics* 69: 383–391.

Train, Kenneth E., and Gil Mehrez (1992), "Optimal Time-of-Use Prices for Electricity: Economic Analysis of Tariff Choice and Time-of-Use Demand," University-wide Energy Research Group, University of California, Berkeley, mimeo.

Train, Kenneth E., and N. Toyama (1989), "Pareto Dominance Through Self-Selecting Tariffs: The Case of TOU Electricity Rates for Agricultural Customers," *Energy Journal* 10: 91–109.

Tschirhart, J., and F. Jen (1979), "Behavior of a Monopoly Offering Interruptible Service," *Bell Journal of Economics* 10: 244–258.

Tuomala, Matti (1990), *Optimal Income Tax and Redistribution*. Oxford UK: Clarendon Press.

Varian, Hal (1985), "Price Discrimination and Social Welfare," *American Economic Review* 75: 870–875.

Varian, Hal (1989), "Price Discrimination," Chapter 10 in R. Schmalansee and R. Willig (eds.), *The Handbook of Industrial Organization*, Volume I, 597–654. Amsterdam and New York: Elsevier Science Publishers B.V. (North-Holland).

Viswanathan, N., and Edison T.S. Tse (1989), "Monopolistic Provision of Congested Service with Incentive-Based Allocation of Priorities," *International Economic Review* 30: 153–174.

Vohra, Rajiv (1990), "On the Inefficiency of Two-Part Tariffs," *Review of Economic Studies* 57: 415–438.

Whinston, Michael D. (1990), "Tying, Foreclosure, and Exclusion," *American Economic Review* 80: 837–859.

Willig, Robert D. (1978), "Pareto-Superior Nonlinear Outlay Schedules," *The Bell Journal of Economics* 9: 56–69.

Willig, Robert D., and Elizabeth Bailey (1977), "Ramsey-Optimal Pricing of Long Distance Services," Chapter 4 in John T. Wenders (ed.), *Pricing in Regulated Industries: Theory and Application I*, 68–97. Denver CO: Mountain States Telephone and Telegraph Company.

Wilson, Charles (1988), "On the Optimal Pricing Policy of a Monopolist," *Journal of Political Economy* 96: 164–176.

Wilson, Robert B. (1979), "Auctions of Shares," *Quarterly Journal of Economics* 93: 675–689.

Wilson, Robert B. (1984), "A Note on Revelation of Information for Joint Production", *Social Choice and Welfare* 1: 69–73.

Wilson, Robert B. (1987), "Bidding" and "Exchange," entries in J. Eatwell, M. Milgate, and P. Newman (eds.), *The New Palgrave: A Dictionary of Economics*, Volume I, 238–242, and Volume II, 202–207. London: The Macmillan Press Ltd.

Wilson, Robert B. (1988), "Credentials and Wage Discrimination," *Scandinavian Journal of Economics* 90: 549–562.

Wilson, Robert B. (1989a), "Efficient and Competitive Rationing," *Econometrica* 57: 1–40.

Wilson, Robert B. (1989b), "Ramsey Pricing of Priority Service," *Journal of Regulatory Economics* 1: 189–202.

Wilson, Robert B. (1991), "Multiproduct Tariffs," *Journal of Regulatory Economics* 3: 5–26; and "Erratum," *Ibid*, 3: 211–212.

Wilson, Robert B. (1992a), "Strategic Analysis of Auctions," Chapter 8 in R. Aumann and S. Hart (eds.), *The Handbook of Game Theory*, Volume I. Amsterdam and New York: Elsevier Science Publishers B.V. (North-Holland).

Wilson, Robert B. (1992b), "Entry Deterrence," Chapter 10 in R. Aumann and S. Hart (eds.), *The Handbook of Game Theory*, Volume I. Amsterdam and New York: Elsevier Science Publishers B.V. (North-Holland).

Wilson, Robert B. (1993), "Design of Efficient Trading Procedures," in D. Friedman et al., *The Double Auction Market*, Chapter 5. Reading, MA: Addison-Wesley Publishing Co.

Wilson, Robert B., Shmuel Oren, and Stephen A. Smith (1980), "Optimal Nonlinear Tariffs for Quantity and Quality," ARG Technical Report 80-17. Palo Alto CA: Xerox Palo Alto Research Center.

Woo, Chi-Keung (1990), "Efficient Electricity Pricing with Self-Rationing," *Journal of Regulatory Economics* 2: 69–81.

Yamey, Basil (1974), "Monopolistic Price Discrimination and Economic Welfare," *Journal of Law and Economics* 17: 377–380.

INDEX

McAfee, R. Preston, 318, 402, 407, 408
McGuire, Timothy, 28
McMillan, John, 318, 402, 407, 408
Marchand, M. G., 408
Marginal benefit, 48, 127, 134, 221, 244
Marginal charge, 315
Marginal cost, 127, 134
  of reliability, 245, 247
  pricing, 103
Marginal price
  of purchase set, 221
  of reliability, 238
  schedule, 48
Marginal rate of substitution, 165, 324
Marginal subscriber, 137
Marginal utility, 135; of income, 324
Marginal valuation, 70, 133
Market penetration, 69, 137, 139, 240
Market segment, 76; segmentation, 15
Markets, imperfectly competitive, 10
Maskin, Eric, 98, 402, 404, 408
Master profile, 205
Mathematical notation, 48
Matthews, Steven, 128, 408
Maximum power level, 267
Measured Toll Service, 40
Mechanism design, 385
Mendelson, Haim, 257, 409
Menu, of options, 6, 141
Merit order, 15, 220
Meyer, Margaret, 310, 403, 409
Milgrom, Paul, 394, 407
Minimal charge, 160, 203–06.
Minimal purchase, 89, 160, 166, 203–06.
Mirman, Leonard, 402, 409
Mirrlees, James, 318, 324, 335, 401, 407, 408, 409
Mitchell, Bridger, 4, 6, 40, 41, 69, 401, 407
Models
  disaggregated, 125
  discrete types, 126
  implicit types, 54
  multiproduct, parameterized, 288
  one-dimensional types, 132
  parameterized, 125
Monahan, J. P., 402
Monetary measure of net benefits, 165
Monitoring, 12
Monopolistic competition, 281, 301
Monopoly power, 10
Monopoly pricing, 103
Monotonicity properties, 136, 207
Moore, John, 128, 403, 408
Moorthy, Sridhar, 402

Multidimensional products, 212
Multiple products, 281–301, 313–71
Multiple solutions, 85, 178
Multiproduct
  demand function, 317, 320
  demand profile, 283, 285, 289, 302
  monopolist, 385
  tariff, 281, 313, 314, 350, 355, 368
Murphy, M. M., 402, 408
Mussa, Michael, 323, 402, 404
Myerson, Roger, 387, 396, 403

Nahata, Babu, 405
Necessary condition
  alternative multiproduct form, 370
  assignment of types to prices, 151, 152
  as average, 140, 161
  Bertrand competition, 302
  capacity pricing, 270
  continuum of types, 129
  Cournot model, 306
  customer's second-order, 136
  in terms of demand functions, 131
  direct derivation, 83
  discrete types, 127–29
  equivalent forms, 136
  income effects, 165
  insufficiency of, 177
  intuitive rationale, 357
  item-assignment form, 230
  minimal charge, 205
  minimal purchase, 160
  multipart tariff, 144
  multiple capacities, 275
  multiple products, 319–20
  multiple solutions, 178, 179
  multiproduct demand function, 320
  multiproduct marginal charge, 359
  multiproduct price differential, 356
  multiproduct Ramsey pricing, 294, 358
  multiproduct tariff, separable, 292
  nonlinear price schedule, 79
  priority service, 243, 246
  purchase set, 222
  Ramsey pricing, 102
  second-order, 179, 318
  sufficiency, 84
  in terms of surrogate type, 182
  two-part tariff, 138
Negotiation, 392
Net benefit, 133, 137, 142, 164, 222, 229, 238, 268, 317
Network externality, 121, 203
New England Telephone, 120